Jeremiah 48 as Christian Scripture

Princeton Theological Monograph Series

K. C. Hanson, Charles M. Collier, D. Christopher Spinks,
and Robin Parry, Series Editors

Recent volumes in the series:

William A. Tooman
*Transforming Visions: Transformations of Text, Tradition,
and Theology in Ezekiel*

Donald E. Gowan
The Bible on Forgiveness

Myk Habets
The Anointed Son: A Trinitarian Spirit Christology

David H. Nikkel
Radical Embodiment

Jeff B. Pool
*God's Wounds: Hermeneutic of the Christian Symbol
of Divine Suffering, Volume Two: Evil and Divine Suffering*

Poul F. Guttesen
*Leaning Into the Future: The Kingdom of God in the Theology
of Jürgen Moltmann and the Book of Revelation*

Christopher W. Skinner
*John and Thomas—Gospels in Conflict?: Johannine Characterization
and the Thomas Question*

David Paul Parris
Reception Theory and Biblical Hermeneutics

Randall W. Reed
*A Clash of Ideologies: Marxism, Liberation Theology,
and Apocalypticism in New Testament Studies*

Jeremiah 48 as Christian Scripture

JULIE IRENE WOODS

With a foreword by Walter Moberly

☙PICKWICK *Publications* · Eugene, Oregon

JEREMIAH 48 AS CHRISTIAN SCRIPTURE
Princeton Theological Monograph Series 149

Copyright © 2011 Julie Irene Woods. All rights reserved. Except for brief quotations in critical publications or reviews, no part of this book may be reproduced in any manner without prior written permission from the publisher. Write: Permissions, Wipf and Stock Publishers, 199 W. 8th Ave., Suite 3, Eugene, OR 97401.

Some Scripture quotations contained herein are from The New Revised Standard Version of the Bible, Anglicized Edition, copyright © 1989, 1995 by the Division of Christian Education of the National Council of the Churches of Christ in the United States of America, and are used by permission. All rights reserved.

Quotations marked NETS are taken from A New English Translation of the Septuagint, © 2007 by the International Organization for Septuagint and Cognate Studies, Inc. Used by permission of Oxford University Press. All rights reserved.

Pickwick Publications
An Imprint of Wipf and Stock Publishers
199 W. 8th Ave., Suite 3
Eugene, OR 97401

www.wipfandstock.com

ISBN 13: 978-1-60899-842-5

Cataloging-in-Publication data:

Woods, Julie Irene.

    Jeremiah 48 as Christian Scripture / Julie Irene Woods, with a foreword by Walter Moberly.

    Princeton Theological Monograph Series 149

    xvi + 356 p.; 23 cm. Includes bibliographical references and indexes.

    ISBN 13: 978-1-60899-842-5

    1. Bible. O.T. Jeremiah—Criticism, interpretation, etc. 2. Moab (Kingdom)—Antiquities. I. Moberly, R. W. L. II. Title. III. Series.

BS1525.52 W38 2011

Manufactured in the U.S.A.

Dedicated to my parents,
Ken and Elizabeth Woods

"I thank my God in all my remembrance of you" (Phil 1:3)

Contents

List of Tables • *viii*

Foreword—Walter Moberly • *ix*

Acknowledgments • *xi*

Abbreviations • *xii*

Introduction • *xv*

1. An Overview of the Field of Jeremiah's Oracles Against the Nations • 1
2. A Comparison of Jeremiah's Oracle Concerning Moab in MT (ch. 48) and LXX (ch. 31) • 23
3. Jeremiah 48 in the Light of Isaiah 15–16 • 67
4. An Analysis of Fretheim's, Miller's, and Brueggemann's Readings of Jeremiah 48 • 99
5. An Analysis of Jones' and Clements's Readings of Jeremiah 48 • 150
6. The Curious Curse in Jeremiah 48:10 • 188
7. A Christian Reading of Jeremiah 48 • 217

Coda 1: Literary Storyboard of the Film of Jeremiah 48 (6th century context) • 282

Coda 2: Literary Storyboard of the Film of Jeremiah 48 (with a Christian Frame of Reference) • 289

Conclusion • 297

Bibliography • 303

Scripture Index • 323

General Index • 337

Tables

Table 1: Jeremiah's oracle concerning Moab in MT (48) and LXX (31) • 25

Table 2: Order of nations in Jeremiah's OANs in MT and LXX • 39

Table 3: Emphasis on Babylon in MT's Jeremiah 25:1–14 compared to LXX's • 40

Table 4: Parallels between Jeremiah 48 and other OT texts • 67

Table 5: Commentators' breakdown of Jeremiah 48 into sections • 218

Table 6: Number of times a country is named in Jeremiah's OANs • 226

Table 7: Nations' Sins in the OANs other than those against Israel/Judah • 236

Table 8: Nations' sins against Israel/Judah in the OANs • 240

Table 9: Reasons for Moab's judgment in Jeremiah 48 found elsewhere in OANs • 243

Foreword

THE ORACLES AGAINST NATIONS OTHER THAN ISRAEL OCCUPY A SUBstantial part of the prophetic books of the Old Testament. But they are arguably the least congenial and most perplexing portions of those books. As a matter of ancient history it is unclear what the nature and purpose of these texts was; and in terms of enduring significance as Scripture for Jews and Christians it is unclear what believers should do with them.

Julie Woods tackles Jeremiah 48 as a representative oracle against the nations, in this case addressed specifically to Israel's neighbour Moab. Although she is attentive to the text as an ancient text, in both its Hebrew and Greek forms, her primary concern is with the constructive question of what, if anything, contemporary Christian faith might make of it. Can it be more than simply part of Christianity's pre-Christian history, perhaps best regarded somewhat as a box stored in a far corner of the attic, occasionally retrieved to see if there is something of interest inside, but then returned to its far corner?

In addition to a discussion of standard scholarly issues relating to the interpretation of Jeremiah's oracle against Moab, there are perhaps three areas in which Woods breaks fresh ground. First, she looks at eminent Christian scholars who have written commentaries on Jeremiah in recent years, and analyses their hermeneutical strategies in their handling of Jeremiah 48. Part of the interest here lies in seeing how the emphases they draw out of the text as enduringly significant relate to characteristic emphases in their writings elsewhere. Secondly, she proposes a fresh interpretation of arguably the most famous and most used verse of the chapter, "Accursed is the one who is slack in doing the work of the LORD; and accursed is the one who keeps back the sword from bloodshed" (48:10). Thirdly, she imaginatively re-envisages the text by casting it into movie mode, and offers two complementary renderings, one portraying the text in a pre-Christian frame of reference, and the other portraying it in a Christian frame of reference.

Jeremiah 48 remains a text that is unlikely to feature in most people's shortlist of preferred passages within the Old Testament. Nonetheless, Julie Woods suggestively shows how the study of a hard text can be surprisingly fruitful.

Walter Moberly,
Abbey House,
Palace Green,
Durham, UK

Acknowledgments

THIS WORK IS THE PUBLISHED FORM OF MY PHD DISSERTATION, SO FIRST and foremost I would like to thank my supervisor, Walter Moberly, for his guidance throughout the doctorate process. Secondly, I would like to thank my editor, Robin Parry, my typesetters, Patrick Harrison and Heather Carraher, and others at Wipf and Stock for their help in the subsequent stages.

There are too many others amongst my family and friends to thank individually, but whose love, friendship, and encouragement I have valued immensely. Their expressions of care have ranged from giving me a check and taking me out for meals, through aiding me with my German translations, proof-reading, and printing, to confidence-boosts and good laughs. Nevertheless, I would particularly like to thank Mo Sharratt, Paul Brush, and Christina Dreher for having regularly supported me financially throughout my PhD years. Above all, however, I would like to thank Frederick Jowett and my parents, Ken and Beth Woods, about whom most of the above could be said, and it is my parents to whom I dedicate this monograph.

Few are so fortunate to be able to genuinely thank God for every remembrance of their parents, yet this privilege is mine. Their love and care have been constant and their support for my life choices unswerving. Furthermore, they have taught me by their examples what it means to be a Christian. I can also truly say that my first memory of wanting to teach Old Testament was as a child hearing my mother bring down the walls of Jericho and the two older Sunday school classes. I also remember my father encouraging me to read the New Testament story about the fish with the coin in its mouth. Sorry for going Old Testament, Dad—I guess she was more persuasive!

Abbreviations

Reference Works

ABD	*The Anchor Bible Dictionary.* 6 vols. Edited by David Noel Freedman. New York: Doubleday, 1992.
BDB	Francis Brown, S. R. Driver, and Charles A. Briggs. *Hebrew and English Lexicon of the Old Testament.* Oxford: Clarendon, 1907.
IDBSup	*The Interpreter's Dictionary of the Bible. Supplementary Volume.* Edited by Keith Crim. Nashville: Abingdon, 1976.
NIDOTTE	*New International Dictionary of Old Testament Theology and Exegesis.* 5 vols. Edited by Willem A. VanGemeren. Carlisle: Paternoster, 1997.
TDOT	*Theological Dictionary of the Old Testament.* 14 vols. Edited by G. Johannes Botterweck and Helmer Ringgren. Translated by Geoffrey W. Bromiley et al. Grand Rapids: Eerdmans, 1974–2004.

Other Abbreviations

AB	Anchor Bible
ANE	Ancient Near East
BETL	Bibliotheca Ephemeridum Theologicarum Lovaniensium
BHS	Biblia Hebraica Stuttgartensia
CBQ	Catholic Biblical Quarterly
ESV	English Standard Version
FNO(s)	Foe from the north oracle(s)

ICC	International Critical Commentary
IOSCS	The International Organization for Septuagint and Cognate Studies
JPS	Jewish Publication Society
JBL	*Journal of Biblical Literature*
JSOT	*Journal for the Study of the Old Testament*
JSOTSup	Journal for the Study of the Old Testament Supplement Series
KJV	King James Version
LXX	Septuagint
MT	Masoretic Text
NASB	New American Standard Bible
NEB	New English Bible
NET	New English Translation
NETS	(The) New English Translation of the Septuagint
NIV	New International Version
NLT	New Living Translation
NRSV	New Revised Standard Version
OAN(s)	Oracle(s) against the nations
OTL	Old Testament Library
PTMS	Princeton Theological Monograph Series
REB	Revised English Bible
RSV	Revised Standard Version
SBL	Society of Biblical Literature
VT	*Vetus Testamentum*
VTSup	Supplements to Vetus Testamentum
WBC	Word Biblical Commentary
ZAW	*Zeitschrift für die alttestamentliche Wissenschaft*

Introduction

JEREMIAH 48 IS AN ORACLE CONCERNING MOAB. IT BELONGS TO THE genre of oracles against the nations (hereafter OANs), in which YHWH[1] condemns non-Israelite nations, and it occurs in the middle of the OAN collection in Jeremiah (46–51). Clements writes that the OANs are, "amongst the most obscure and difficult passages of the entire prophetic corpus of the Old Testament to understand."[2] For example, were the oracles intended for the nations' hearing or not? Either way, what purpose do they have? Were the OANs written in the context of holy war? What purpose might they have for Christians?

Jeremiah 48 is one of the strangest texts in some ways. Apart from the oracle concerning Babylon in chapters 50–51, which is often treated as a special case, Jeremiah's oracle concerning Moab is the longest OAN in Jeremiah (and longer than most of the OANs in other books, too). Yet it does not sit in first or last position in the collection (even if the Babylon oracle is excluded). However, perhaps the most distinct element in this oracle is the strong note of lament that sounds almost constantly from beginning to end and even includes YHWH's tears and wailing.

The aim of this monograph is to investigate Jeremiah 48 as Christian Scripture. Chapter 1 will begin by giving an overview of the field of OAN studies with attention given to significant contributions, especially those relating to Jeremiah's OANs. Then, before I engage with the main concerns of the book, I will address two preliminary issues about which something needs to be said. Chapter 2 will deal with the first: an examination of the differences between MT and LXX. This analysis is particularly pertinent, since there is more disparity between Jeremiah's OANs than is usual between MT and LXX—in the OT generally as well as Jeremiah specifically. The second is a comparative study between Isaiah 15–16 and Jeremiah 48, since these two oracles concerning Moab are remarkably similar. Chapter 3 will cover this, giving at-

1. I use YHWH even when the Tetragrammaton is vocalized.
2. Clements, *Isaiah 1–39*, 130.

tention to the distinct nuances of each in order to build up a picture of their individual characteristics and emphases.

The next two chapters will then analyze how recent Christian theologians have interpreted Jeremiah. Chapter 4 will examine the three U.S. interpreters—Terence Fretheim, Patrick Miller, and Walter Brueggemann—and chapter 5 will add two UK scholars—Douglas Jones and Ronald Clements—in order to give a slightly more comprehensive scope. As well, having representatives from both the U.S. and UK might highlight any obvious differences in the approaches of the two nations, though this is not a main aim of this study. In the course of analyzing these interpreters' approaches to the chapter, it will also become clear what the key themes and major questions relating to Jeremiah 48 are.

Chapter 6 will deal with Jeremiah 48:10, a curious curse that sits awkwardly in its context. The chapter will tentatively suggest a plausible account of the verse so that its place and role in Jeremiah 48 as a whole becomes clearer. Finally, chapter 7 attempts to propose ways in which Jeremiah 48 may be read as Christian Scripture, paying particular attention to the reasons given for Moab's punishment, as well as the pervading tone of lament. The reading utilizes figural interpretation in addition to making value judgments within a Christian frame of reference. It concludes with two film-like imaginative readings that explore the possible continuities and differences between Jeremiah 48 in its ancient and Christian contexts.

My understanding of Jeremiah's oracle concerning Moab in chapter 48 has developed through studying the works of others, especially Fretheim, Miller, Brueggemann, Jones, and Clements, and their words have sometimes sparked ideas of my own. Therefore, if I may utilize the words of Jones, "If there is anything fresh here, it is only because a dwarf has been able to sit on the shoulders of giants! Some of the giants are listed in the bibliography."[3] In this case Jones himself is one of the giants.

---

3. Jones, *Haggai*, 13.

1

An Overview of the Field of Jeremiah's Oracles Against the Nations

Prolegomenon: A Lack of Interest

THE MOST NOTABLE ASPECT IN THE FIELD OF OAN STUDIES IS THE lack of attention that has traditionally been given to the OANs. This state of affairs is commonly lamented by scholars of the OANs (either Jeremiah's or the OANs more generally). For instance, Christensen begins his 1971 dissertation, *Transformations of the War Oracle in Old Testament Prophecy,* with the comment, "The oracles against the nations (OAN) in Old Testament prophecy have received relatively little attention in biblical research of the past century."[1] Another example is Davies who in 1989 observes in *The Book of Isaiah,* "There is very little in the standard textbooks on prophecy about the oracles against foreign nations and related material, despite their evident theological interest, and even detailed studies in this area are rather rare, except perhaps for the protracted discussion over whether it is proper to regard Deutero-Isaiah as a universalist."[2]

One of the reasons attributed to the lack of interest in the OANs is because they have often been considered later additions and therefore of secondary importance. Indeed, Holladay writes in 1960 in his essay on "Style, Irony, and Authenticity in Jeremiah" that, "One of the chief goals of critics of the book of Jeremiah has always been to isolate the *ipsissima verba* of the prophet and thereby to enter more understandingly into his message."[3] This is reflected in Eissfeldt's *The Old Testament:*

---

1. Christensen, *Transformations*, 1.
2. Davies, "Destiny," 93. See also Geyer, *Mythology and Lament*, 6.
3. Holladay, "Style," 44.

An Introduction where he speaks only of the authenticity and authorship of Jeremiah's OANs, plus their placement in relation to chapter 25.[4] As well, Frank North's essay on the Ammonites in Jeremiah 49:1–6 is solely concerned with glosses and corruptions in order to reconstruct the text.[5]

Christensen also argues that in the nineteenth century the main aim of prophecy was seen as concerned with universal monotheism and moral values, and thus "the narrow nationalism of the foreign-nation oracles appeared to have little relevance for anyone. The OAN tradition constituted the dregs of the prophetic movement."[6] Another reason is given by Bellis in 1999 who remarks (though it is not her view) in "Poetic Structure and Intertextual Logic in Jeremiah 50": "The literary genre of the oracles in Jeremiah 50 is that of prophecies against the nations. In the whole Hebrew Bible this genre has perhaps been paid the least attention. The reason is understandable. The hatred and bloodthirst displayed in these oracles is an embarrassment to the more humane sensibilities of modern believers, both Christian and Jewish."[7] However, some have tackled the subject and as a starting point we will take the surveys provided by Christensen, Reimer, and Kessler.

Brief Overview of History of Scholarship

Christensen divides the history of OAN scholarship into three periods of increasing refinement of methodology: nineteenth century German literary criticism; German form criticism; and the proliferation of extra-biblical materials, which meant that ancient Israelite prophecy could be studied religio-historically. In general, he argues, the early literary critics (for example, Schwally, Volz) relegated the OANs to exilic or post-exilic times, whereas form critics (for example, Gressmann, Bardtke) reversed the picture and saw them as among the earliest forms of prophetic speech.

Reimer laments twentieth-century disregard of Jer 50–51 "after the interest shown by the nineteenth century writers" and claims, as Christensen similarly does, that when these chapters were not ignored,

---

4. Eissfeldt, *OT*, 362–64.
5. North, "Oracle against Ammonites," 37–43.
6. Christensen, *Transformations*, 1.
7. Bellis, "Poetic Structure," 180.

their study was dominated by two questions: authenticity; and structural problems.[8] Reimer's own dissertation is itself a structural analysis of Jer 50–51.

Kessler argues that Bardtke's 1936 paper, "Jeremia der Fremdvölkerprophet," in which he proposed that Jeremiah prophesied to the nations in his youth (Jer 1:5), marked the end of the older literary criticism in some ways and that following it, "some sort of a passive consensus emerged, in large part because these oracles have failed to attract much attention."[9] Kessler supports his assertion by drawing attention to the commentaries. John Bright's Anchor Bible commentary was the main work between 1965 and 1986, and in 1968 Rudolph's classic commentary was published. Though Rudolph's 1968 commentary was more nuanced, Kessler observes, neither Bright nor Rudolph differed much from the general consensus regarding the OANs being an early genre but largely inauthentic.[10]

The change came in the 1980s with Holladay's and Carroll's commentaries, and the first volume of McKane's. Holladay was interested in the literary and historical questions and considered much of Jer 50–51 to be authentic. Carroll denied that the book of Jeremiah gives much access to the historical Jeremiah. McKane's commentary was concerned with the history of the text and in his first volume McKane introduced the idea of the rolling corpus. However, in Kessler's view it is Brueggemann's 1998 commentary that is the most useful, particularly for a wider public, with its attention to historical, literary, and theological concerns.[11]

Characteristic Emphases and Notable Contributions

Although the above surveys mainly cite works on Jer 50–51, their emphases are characteristic of the study of Jeremiah's OANs in general in that issues of authenticity and authorship are common ones within a historical-critical paradigm. However, by no means have all historical-

---

8. Reimer, *Oracles*, 1–6.

9. Bardtke, "Jeremia," part 1, 209–39; Bardtke, "Jeremia," part 2, 240–62; Kessler, *Battle*, 19.

10. Kessler, *Battle*, 21. Rudolph, *Jeremiah*, 266, attributes much of chs. 46–49 to Jeremiah, but not ch. 48.

11. Kessler, *Battle*, 7–31.

critical studies dealt exclusively with these two questions and other points of interest have emerged. The *Sitz im Leben* of the OANs is a case in point, as is the comparative analysis of the OANs with other ANE cultures. All these topics will now be addressed, along with notable contributions to the field, namely McKane's "rolling corpus." These areas of interest are not discrete units within scholarship and there is significant overlap between them. This is particularly so in the field of comparative studies, which has sometimes formed the basis for furthering the understanding of the OAN's *Sitz im Leben*.

Authorship and Date

There are three scholars who stand out as major contributors in the development of OAN studies: Eichhorn, Budde, and Gottwald. The first of these, Eichhorn (1752–1827),[12] is notable not for any discovery in the OAN field, but because he influenced the methodology, or, to put it another way, changed the nature of study. Eichhorn stands at the beginning of modern biblical studies and set the trend for much of the nineteenth and twentieth centuries, for he was a key person in introducing in the late eighteenth/early nineteenth century the new approach to modern biblical scholarship in which concerns about authorship and dating were paramount. He concluded in *Die hebräischen Propheten* that Jer 50–51 was not authentic, dating the chapters between 535 and 160 BCE since the Persians (who conquered Babylon in about 535 BCE according to Eichhorn) had not emerged as a threat before then.[13]

Budde, a colleague of Wellhausen, continued the historical-critical approach and in 1878 published his article on 50–51, "Ueber die Capitel 50 und 51 des Buches Jeremia." Budde's detailed study was, in Kessler's words, "One of the most thorough studies ever undertaken of Jeremiah 50–51"[14] (it is seventy seven pages in length) and proved to be influential. His essay was a piece of literary criticism in which he was greatly concerned with issues of authenticity. Here he argued that the prose and poetic passages should be treated separately, a stance that most of the subsequent commentaries (for example, Weiser's) later accepted. Due to his study of the vocabulary, Budde also thought that the editor of

12. Kessler, *Battle*, 13.
13. Eichhorn, *Die hebräischen Propheten*, 255, 257.
14. Kessler, *Battle*, 15.

50–51 was dependent on the late exilic, anti-Babylonian oracles of Isa 13 as well as Deutero-Isaiah, and Ezekiel, though he retained the prose narratives as authentic.[15]

Gottwald is the third of the scholars noted here. He utilized the work of three Israeli scholars (Diman-Haran, Kaufmann, and Seeligman) and concluded in 1964 in *All the Kingdoms of the Earth* that the OANs were one of the earliest, if not the earliest, forms of Hebrew poetry and that they incorporated non-Israelite motifs and styles.[16] Furthermore, as the title of his book suggests, his work is a detailed examination of the relationship between Israel and her neighbors in the different OT prophetic periods. Though Gottwald did not take the same approach as von Rad,[17] the latter also argued in his definitive study, *Holy War in Ancient Israel* in 1958, and then again in *Old Testament Theology* in 1960, that the war oracles are one of the oldest in prophetic tradition and that the OANs are one form of the war oracle.[18]

There have been others who have changed the face of Jeremiah studies, such as Duhm, who introduced in his commentary the idea of three major sources to Jeremiah. However, since his theories are largely irrelevant to the OANs (he followed the school of thought that considered them inauthentic) he has not been selected for representation here.

Writing in 1971 (though his dissertation was not published until 1975), Christensen claimed that the authenticity debate was ongoing.[19] In fact the debate continues still as can be seen from the work of Geyer, whose 2009 response to Hagedorn is the latest publication on the OANs.[20] Issues of dating and textual analysis also form a major component of Geyer's earlier works.[21]

---

15. Budde, "Kapitel 50 und 51," 428–70, 529–62.
16. Gottwald, *All the Kingdoms*, 49.
17. Gottwald, "Holy War," 942.
18. Von Rad, *OT Theology*, 199.
19. Christensen, *Transformations*, 1–15.
20. Geyer, "Another Look," 80–87.
21. Geyer, "Mythology and Culture," 129–45.

Sitz im Leben, Form, and Function

One of the characteristic emphases within the historical-critical paradigm has been to provide a *Sitz im Leben* for the OANs and these have ranged from war, through covenant festivals, ascension rituals, and lamentation rituals, to the royal court.[22] The *Sitz im Leben* often determines what form the OANs are seen to be. They have been designated as war oracles, prophetic judgment speeches, curses, part of cult liturgy, treaty curses, political speeches, and early apocalyptic literature. Sometimes the boundaries merge or it is thought that the OAN developed over time, moving from one category through to another.

Von Rad's analysis (more than Gottwald's) had a significant impact on the understanding of the OANs and found wide acceptance, at least in part, and continues to do so. His influence is apparent in Christensen's attempt in *Transformations of the War Oracle* to plot the evolution of the war oracle. He argued that the OANs stemmed from the war oracle and underwent two main transformations: First, the war oracle as a military strategy became a literary mode of prophetic judgment speech (that is, OAN) in the tenth to eighth centuries BCE, around the time of Amos. Secondly, it moved from the world of international politics to the historical realm of early apocalyptic literature in the opening decades of the sixth century BCE in Jeremiah's time. That is, it moved from judgment on YHWH's national foes to the preservation of the Divine Warrior's people in exile until they returned to Zion.[23] Christensen divided Jeremiah's OANs into three categories: Jeremianic oracles; "archaic" (that is, pre-Jeremianic) oracles; and exilic oracles against Babylon. The oracle against Moab is one of the archaic kind,[24] which means it stemmed from the period of political expansion under Josiah and was subsequently reused and expanded. Thus it was more developed and complex than the Jeremianic OANs.[25]

Where Christensen found three categories within Jeremiah's OANs, Geyer argued in *Mythology and Lament* that there were two basic forms of OANs. The first relates to Amos 1–2 and Ezek 25, which are characterized by a strong note of indictment but a lack of mythological

22. Christensen, *Transformations*, 1–15.
23. Ibid.
24. Ibid., 208.
25. Ibid., 248.

language. The second form encompasses the rest of the major bodies of OANs: Isa 13–23; Jer 46–51; and Ezek 25–32 and belongs to the realm of mythology.[26] Geyer's classifications have not been adopted by other scholars and the OANs are not generally seen in terms of mythology. Nevertheless, Geyer's book is a rare work in that one chapter deals specifically with the oracles against Moab in Isa 15–16 and Jer 48. He argues that the language is largely liturgical, the themes mythological and the core is lament. According to Geyer, Jeremiah's oracle concerning Moab describes the struggle between chaos and cosmos.[27] Again, most commentators do not see Jer 48 in cosmic terms, no doubt because the language is not cosmic; in fact the OANs rarely use cosmic language.

More recently, Smelik concluded that the OANs had both a military-political level and an ideological one.[28] Brueggemann, too, is interested in the ideological and rhetorical function of the OANs. In "At the Mercy of Babylon" he surmised that when Israel spoke of the mercy of God it first talked of the mercy of Babylon, daring rhetoric that "asserted that no savage power in the world could separate Israel from God's mercy."[29]

In Hayes' work on international treaties, "The Usage of Oracles against Foreign Nations in Ancient Israel," he suggests that the OANs mean salvation for Israel because in the lamentation, ritual judgment on the nation denotes salvation for Israel.[30] The idea that the OANs function as salvation oracles to Judah still endures, for instance Diamond's introductory chapter in *Troubling Jeremiah* and Carroll's on chapter 25.[31] Another example is Holt, whose interesting slant is that the "foe from the North" oracles are OANs directed against *YHWH's own people*.[32] That the OANs are not always equated with salvation for Israel will be discussed in due course.

---

26. Geyer, *Mythology and Lament*, 9–20.
27. Ibid., 151–72.
28. Smelik, "Approach to Jeremiah," 1–11.
29. Brueggemann, "Mercy (2004)," 129–30.
30. Hayes, "Usage of OANs," 81–92.
31. Carroll, "Halfway," 82, 85; Diamond, "Introduction," 22. Interestingly, in 2002 Barstad ("Prophecy," 93) phrased it the other way round—promises of salvation to foreigners were words of doom against YHWH's own people.
32. Holt, "Meaning of an Inclusio," 185.

In contrast to the above scholars, Hill, in "The Construction of Time in Jeremiah 25," sees the OANs as demonstrating, as in Amos, that judgment is the same for both Israel/Judah and the nations.[33] Amesz makes similar observations and argues that Jer 50–51 displays YHWH's vengeance and sovereignty.[34] The idea that the OANs function as a declaration of YHWH's sovereignty is a common one and Bellis is representative of many when she claims that Jer 50 "expresses the conviction that there is one Lord of history, who is just and powerful and who will punish those who do evil and vindicate those whose cause is just."[35]

Comparative Studies

Interest in extrabiblical materials increased after the Second World War and in 1968 there were two main works published that studied the OANs in relation to other ANE contexts. The first was Hayes' paper, mentioned above, in which he looked at Sumerian curses.[36] The second was van Dijk's monograph on Ezekiel's prophecy to Tyre, in which the OANs are examined in the light of comparative Canaanite and Semitic studies in terms of linguistic parallels in Ugaritic and other North Western Semitic dialects. Van Dijk optimistically judged such philological and syntactical comparisons as being the way forward in clearing up some of the problematic aspects of the text, which had previously been treated by either emending the text or excising parts in order to "meet the poetical and metrical requirements favoured by the commentators themselves."[37] Boadt too, in 1980 in *Ezekiel's Oracles Against Egypt*, conducted a comparative analysis, concentrating on the grammar and usage of Ugaritic and Phoenician texts. This included examination of ANE OANs outside of the OT. He himself acknowledged that in some ways his work continued that of van Dijk's and, indeed, both these comparative studies were written for the *Biblica et Orientalia* series.

Despite van Dijk's expectation, and although knowledge of ANE languages has aided translation and interpretation of words and phrases, the main contribution of comparative studies in relation to the

---

33. Hill, "Construction of Time," 149, 155.
34. Amesz, "God of Vengeance?" 99–116.
35. Bellis, "Poetic Structure," 199.
36. Hayes, "Usage of OANs," 81–92.
37. Van Dijk, *Ezekiel's Prophecy*, vii.

OANs has still been in regard to their possible original *Sitz im Leben*. Hagedorn's 2007 paper, "Looking at Foreigners in Biblical and Greek Prophecy" is one such recent example and here he argues, from comparisons with Greek prophecy (in Homer and Herodotus), that the context was one of war (real or imagined). In his view, OANs were one means of reaffirming one's own identity and tended to imply salvation for the nation pronouncing them.[38]

Geyer also is concerned with comparative extra-biblical texts, for example, the Sumerian laments and Ugaritic texts. In his recent response to Hagedorn, he asserts that Hagedorn's comparison is invalid, not least because the Greek OANs were uttered by individuals on particular occasions whereas, as he argues elsewhere, the OT OANs were part of cultic liturgy when the Day of Atonement became linked with the Jubilee.[39] He also disagrees that the OANs were salvation oracles for the nation that uttered them. Geyer bases his comments on an assumption of the *Sitz im Leben* of the OANs, which he addresses in an earlier paper. That is, as discussed above, a cosmic battle between the gods in the sphere of mythology.

Rolling Corpus

Perhaps the most significant development in the field of Jeremiah studies has been the concept of McKane's rolling corpus. Put simply, McKane looks at MT Jeremiah in relation to the shorter LXX Jeremiah and accounts for the difference by means of two separate *Vorlagen*. The MT version developed piecemeal over time via authors and redactors adding short commentary notes on previous verses. McKane comes to this conclusion by investigating places in MT that are very similar to LXX and noticing that where there are divergences, they are usually in the form of explanatory notes present in MT but absent in LXX. Having perceived the method of redaction in MT, he notices other places where this appears to have occurred (even though there are no clues in LXX).[40] McKane develops his theory over chapters 1–25 in the first volume of his commentary, but although he does not seem to use the term "rolling corpus" in relation to chapters 26–52, he sees the same process at work.

---

38. Hagedorn, "Looking at Foreigners," 432–48.
39. Geyer, "Blood," 1; Geyer, "Another Look," 80–187.
40. McKane, *Jeremiah, vol. 1*, l–lxxxiii.

This is interesting, because it brings Jeremiah's OANs into the same purview as the rest of the book in this respect and, in fact, McKane does not deem the OANs to have been a separate corpus added later to MT and LXX, but considers that they originally existed in MT after 25:13 (where they are in LXX).[41] McKane's rolling corpus thesis is now widely accepted, though Diamond deems all of the papers in *Troubling Jeremiah* to provide counter-texts to the idea, at least in "overcoming some of the inconcinnity McKane has sensed afflicting the tradition."[42]

Work Specifically on Jeremiah's OANs

There are two main distinctive elements in the work on Jeremiah's OANs as opposed to OAN studies in general. First, there is the issue of the order and placement of the OANs being different in LXX and in MT. Secondly, there is the question of the role of Babylon and the significance of the oracle concerning Babylon being last in the collection. The significance arises because Babylon is the specific tool in the rest of the book of Jeremiah that YHWH uses to punish the nations. There is no such equivalent in the other prophetic books.[43]

LXX

Much of the discussion on MT's versus LXX's ordering and placement of the OANs has centered around which came first, with the consensus historically tending to rest on LXX as the more original.[44] Now, however, with the discovery of Qumran fragments witnessing to both traditions, it is generally thought that the two had separate *Vorlagen* and distinct re-

41. McKane, *Jeremiah*, vol. 2, clxiv.
42. Diamond, "Introduction," 24.
43. See also McConville, *Judgment and Promise*, 137.
44. Those who consider LXX's placing of the oracles to be original are: Allen, *Jeremiah*, 458; Clements, *Jeremiah*, 246; Fretheim, *Jeremiah*, 577; Holladay, *Jeremiah*, vol. 2, 313, 315; Lundbom, *Jeremiah 37–52*, 181; McKane, *Jeremiah*, vol. 2, 1109; Miller, "Jeremiah," 878 (tentatively); Rudolph, *Jeremiah*, 265; Smothers in Keown et al., *Jeremiah 26–52*, 276; Volz, *Der Prophet Jeremia*, 381. Jones (*Jeremiah*, 484) is one of few who consider MT's placing to be original. Those who consider LXX's sequence to be more original are: Carroll, *Jeremiah*, 497, 759; Duhm, *Jeremiah*, 337; Jones, *Jeremiah*, 484–85; Smothers in Keown et al., *Jeremiah 26–52*, 276. Those who consider MT's sequence to be original are: Holladay, *Jeremiah*, vol. 2, 313; Lundbom, *Jeremiah 37–52*, 181; McKane, *Jeremiah*, vol. 2, 1110; Rudolph, *Jeremiah*, 265; Volz, *Der Prophet Jeremia*, 382.

dactional histories.⁴⁵ Nevertheless, the debate still continues. In his 1992 article, "Text and Redaction in Jeremiah's Oracles Against the Nations," Watts is almost solely concerned with the differences between MT and LXX and seeks to demonstrate that one author was responsible for most of them.⁴⁶ Yet, in his final paragraph he asserts that the response to his results should be that the OANs are no longer "dismissed as a secondary scribal addition" and that ultimately they should "be integrated into interpretations of the message of the book as a whole and given the attention which their prominent positions in both the LXX and MT suggest they deserve."⁴⁷

Carolyn Sharp's 1997 article, "'Take Another Scroll and Write'" is a detailed textual analysis of the differences between MT and LXX. In this paper, like McKane, she tentatively concludes that the textual state of the oracles seem to support the idea that there were two different *Vorlagen* underlying MT and LXX.⁴⁸ Also in 1997 Lundbom wrote a book on ancient Hebrew rhetoric in Jeremiah in which he concluded similarly, even speculating that Baruch was the custodian of LXX's *Vorlage* and Seraiah that of MT.⁴⁹

Babylon

Most of the books and papers on Jeremiah's OANs published in the twenty-first century have focused mainly on Babylon. That is, van Hecke's "Metaphorical Shifts in the Oracles against Babylon (Jer 50–51)," Kessler's *Battle of the Gods*, and Holt's "The Meaning of an Inclusio," all in 2003, and Smelik's, Amesz's, and Brueggemann's essays in *Reading the Book of Jeremiah* in 2004.⁵⁰ Previously, discussions concentrated on the

---

45. Sharp, "Take Another Scroll," 509; see also Allen, *Jeremiah*, 458; Carroll, *Jeremiah*, 51–55, 757; Clements, *Jeremiah*, 246; Craigie et al., *Jeremiah 1–25*, xlii–xlv; Feinberg, *Jeremiah*, 16; Fretheim, *Jeremiah*, 25; Holladay, *Jeremiah, vol. 2*, 313, 467; Jones, *Jeremiah*, 49–50; Kreuzer, "Old Greek," 226–27; Lundbom, *Jeremiah 37–52*, xiv; McKane, *Jeremiah, vol. 1*, 1-li; *Jeremiah, vol. 2*, clxxii–clxxiii, clxxiv; Miller, "Jeremiah," 567–68; Stulman, *Jeremiah*, 8; Thompson, *Jeremiah*, 29, 119, 686; Watts, "Text and Redaction," 446.

46. Watts, "Text and Redaction," 446–47.

47. Ibid., 447.

48. Sharp, "Take Another Scroll," 487–516.

49. Lundbom, *Jeremiah Rhetoric*, 40.

50. Some of these essays have been published previously, e.g., Brueggemann's essay was first published in 1991 in *JBL*.

putative turnaround in Jeremiah's views regarding Babylon in that up until chapters 50–51 Jeremiah has insisted that Judah must submit to Babylon as YHWH's tool of punishment, but in these two chapters he castigates Babylon. However, recent works, such as Brueggemann's, have tended to move away from this debate to more ideological questions. In Brueggemann's case these relate to Babylon's political power. However, since the focus on Babylon concerns only Jer 50–51 and has little bearing on Jer 48, or the OANs in general, no more will be said here on the issue. Nevertheless, the increased interest in the oracle concerning Babylon (the longest oracle concerning the biggest player on the ANE field in the sixth century) highlights the fact that there has not been an equivalent rise in attention given to the oracle concerning Moab.

Significance of Literary / Synchronic Readings

Shift in Focus

By the beginning of the twenty-first century, scholars were beginning to talk of some aspects of historical-critical study in the past tense. For instance, Holt writes "Gone are the questions of former times concerning Jeremiah's biography or the historical circumstances behind the poetry and prose of the Book of Jeremiah."[51] Kessler talks in 2003 about "bygone historicism" when he gives the aim of his own work:

> Since the goal of this work is "to hear" the text (to discover what it "says"), concerns with the shape, form, and sound of the text are high on the agenda. However, literary artistry is never viewed as an appropriate goal in itself. Such a goal stops prematurely, neglecting serious interpretation which should flow from a thoughtful preoccupation with the text. It is assumed that our preoccupation demands a positive, sympathetic perspective on the text. There may be a connection between the fact that 19th century writers were often quite negative in their comments on the text and the fact that they often failed to grasp its proclamatory aspect: what the text is trying to say. More often than not, they spent virtually all their energy on what might lie behind the text (historical criticism), with the unhappy result that they ran out of steam when they should have engaged in constructive exegesis. Such is the heritage of bygone historicism.[52]

---

51. Holt, "Meaning of an Inclusio," 184.
52. Kessler, *Battle*, 9.

In his essay in *Troubling Jeremiah* Kessler writes, "Reading numerous commentaries and their judgments about what is 'authentic' and what is not, or what could be Jeremiah speaking, and what could not possibly be him, becomes not only tiresome, it provides no help in understanding the text."[53] Kessler tries to move beyond the limits of literary and form criticism in his own work and give a literary reading of the text by introducing rhetorical criticism as a methodological tool.[54]

Kessler also takes issue with those who see no coherence in Jeremiah: "Jeremiah has enjoyed an honoured place in the canon, having been cherished by the faith communities of both synagogue and church as a respected part of the 'holy book.' It therefore falls to the responsible exegete to elucidate the text for the benefit of its readers: what are the words, the form, the structure, seen in their context—in their totality and unity—saying? What is its rhetorical function of the text [sic], but more crucially, what is its kerygma?"[55] For Kessler, then, the move away from purely historical-critical questions is a welcome one.

Perdue's chapter ("The Book of Jeremiah in Old Testament Theology") in *Troubling Jeremiah* also acknowledges that, at the time of compiling *A Prophet to the Nations*, the key issues had been "largely historical in nature" but that there were now new methods of interpretations and fresh questions.[56] Certainly, the essays in *Troubling Jeremiah* regarding the OANs tend to de-emphasize the historical questions. Perdue, in contrast to Kessler, however, has reservations about this move:

> The most pressing question for me nowadays, however, is whether these more recent methods may be adapted to and incorporated within previous historical-critical work, or whether they represent what some of our colleagues call a "paradigm shift" that, for the most part, tends to dismiss the past in order to make room for the new . . . Today the cacophony of competing attempts to be heard has become a din of dissonance and a Tower of Babel in modern scholarship. This fragmentation (I prefer not to use the term "crisis") is centered in epistemology, for in these times we have many ways of knowing, issuing

---

53. Kessler, "Function," 72.
54. Kessler, *Battle*, 7–31.
55. Ibid., 10.
56. Perdue, "Jeremiah in OT Theology," 321–22.

from different genders, sexual orientations, ethnic groups, and cultures.[57]

Brueggemann takes the in-between position in his chapter on the future of Jeremiah studies when he states that "It is not news any longer that scholarship has moved decisively from *diachronic* to *synchronic* ways of reading. And while some scholars may be polemical about the matter, most are inclined to adopt something of a both/and approach."[58] At the same time he points out that "It is clear that *synchronic reading* and *canonical interpretation* are not to be equated. Nonetheless, an important convergence may be seen in these approaches."[59] Brueggemann sees the shift from diachronic to synchronic as marked by a move from historical analysis to rhetorical study.[60]

This is probably best reflected in the commentaries. The earlier German commentaries (Duhm, Volz, Weiser, Rudolph) were primarily concerned with textual variants and emendations, authenticity and redaction, and literary style. More recent commentaries (for example, Brueggemann's, Miller's, and Fretheim's) speak of power struggles, the nature of YHWH's involvement with other nations, and the wider implications of such texts. Carroll's 1986 commentary, with its ideological focus, was probably the first to depart from the mainstream in this way. Obviously, there have still been recent historical-critical commentaries published on Jeremiah, for example, Holladay's Hermeneia volumes (1986 and 1998), and McKane's ICC volumes (1986 and 1996). Lundbom's three volume Anchor Bible commentary (1999, 2004, and 2004) is also primarily in this mould, despite having other concerns as well.

The tide has changed even in relation to the OANs for there has been increased interest in the last decade or two, particularly in relation to Jer 50–51. Just four years after Bellis was lamenting the dearth of literature relating to the OANs[61] Kessler was able to write in *Battle of the Gods*:

---

57. Ibid., 322.
58. Brueggemann, *Covenanted Self*, 405.
59. Ibid., 408.
60. Ibid., 409.
61. Quoted earlier as referenced by footnote 7.

> In our survey of scholarship on the Jeremian oracles against Babylon, we have witnessed a growing interest in these oracles after many years of neglect. At one time, compared to the rest of the book, Jer 50–51 resembled a quiet pool, removed from the tumult of the main stream of scholarship, which habitually shunted aside (or just plain ignored!) the OAN, but above all the oracles against Babylon. Clearly, an enormous change has taken place in Jeremiah studies generally.[62]

This change is most easily demonstrated by glancing at collections of essays on Jeremiah. When *A Prophet to the Nations* was published in 1984, none of the twenty three papers comprising the book was dedicated to chapters 46–51. This is perhaps particularly surprising given the title of the collection. In the introductory chapter to *Prophet to the Nations*, Perdue writes that the history of biblical criticism "is clearly mirrored in Jeremiah studies."[63] Whether this is the reason that the OANs are not represented in any of the essays in the book is not discussed. However, he does list the issues that draw most attention and the OANs are not among them: date of Jeremiah's call; Jeremiah's view of and / or relation to the Deuteronomic reform; the identity of the enemy from the North; textual differences between MT and LXX; and the composition and development of the book. "Undergirding and stimulating most Jeremianic research since the inception of modern criticism is the concern to discover the Jeremiah of history."[64] Perdue himself attributes the OANs to later redactors.[65]

By the time *Troubling Jeremiah* was published in 1999 there were two essays out of twenty-five that related to the OANs; both of these papers dealt in different ways with Jeremiah's oracle concerning Babylon in chapters 50–51. This interest in Babylon did not abate, so that when *Reading the Book of Jeremiah* was published in 2004, out of fourteen essays the three concerning the OANs all related to Babylon, though only one of these was solely concerned with chapters 50–51.

It seems that the situation was a little better in Isaianic studies, for in 1989 four of thirty essays in *The Book of Isaiah* were dedicated to the nations: one concerned the destiny of the nations; another cen-

---

62. Kessler, *Battle*, 28.
63. Perdue, "Jeremiah in Modern Research," 1.
64. Ibid.
65. Ibid., 7.

tered on Babylon; the third addressed the OANs in chapters 13–23 as a whole; and the fourth concerned the oracle against Babylon and Assyria in 14:22–27. Interestingly, studies of the book of Amos tend to give more attention to the OANs found within it than do studies on other prophetic books. In fact, in the 1974 collection of essays, *Studies on Prophecy* there is one essay (amongst twelve) on Amos's OANs (the only essay on either the OANs or Amos). How much of this is due to the fact that Amos opens with the OANs (they come in the middle of Isaiah and at the end of MT Jeremiah) is impossible to judge, but their position at the start of the book means that they are hard to ignore.

Nevertheless, overall, there has been increased interest in the OANs and this shift has taken place since the inception of Brevard Childs' canonical approach. This is unlikely to be purely coincidental, for privileging the final form of the text raises the profile of later textual additions (if such they be). At the same time, one does not necessarily lead to the other for even a canonical approach allows for a view of "a canon within a canon" and the OANs are not normally seen as the most central texts of the OT. I would venture to suggest that one factor in the renewed interest may be (Western) cultural climate changes. First, the world has become a "global village" and international issues are high on the agenda at many levels. Secondly, in Western "post-modern" society, traditional social norms and expectations are challenged and hard questions are asked. This may in part account for what seems to be a greater fascination in scholarship than previously with the "hard texts of the Bible," though such is still a minority interest. As well, in "post-Christian" UK, at least, as the general populace has moved away from regarding the Bible as "inspired Scripture," such a focus may also have arisen from a need to justify the Bible/OT. In addition, new hermeneutical perspectives have also enabled the hard texts of the Bible to be readdressed and perhaps reclaimed; one thinks immediately of Phyllis Trible's feminist readings in *Texts of Terror*.

The interest in Babylon in the twenty-first century may be because of the prominent role of Babylon elsewhere in Jeremiah, because Babylon is the epitome of a "wicked" foreign nation, or because in a contemporary world with arguably only one major superpower (the U.S.), which dominates much of the rest, Babylon is the nation that resonates the clearest. As will become apparent throughout the book, Brueggemann is an example of a scholar who draws links between the

U.S. and Babylon. Nevertheless, whilst Babylon has become the focus of some studies and more has been written on the OANs in general, the oracles concerning other nations still appear to be under-represented in Jeremiah scholarship.

The OANs in Their Literary Context

The mix of interests, some with a purely historical-critical focus and others concerned with the final form, is indicative of the state of current scholarship in Biblical Studies. That is, the work of historical criticism continues (as Hagedorn's and Geyer's latest papers demonstrate), whilst those privileging the final form of the text work in parallel with this older method, if not in tandem with it. Sometimes the research is similar though the aims take diverging paths, for instance intricate textual studies are undertaken as a means of building up a literary image rather than a historical one. Steinmann's 1992 paper on the order of Amos's OANs is one such example of a literary study. Here he seeks to demonstrate that there is coherence in the order of Amos's OANs and, convinced that he does so successfully, calls on those who view some OANs as later additions to prove their case. Acknowledging Paul's work on catchphrases twenty-one years previously, he surmises that the order is determined by the type of nation (for example, city state, nation, or special nation) plus its geographical location.[66]

The work of Shalom M. Paul cited by Steinmann is his 1971 paper on Amos's OANs. In this, Paul is concerned with discovering a pattern in the ordering of the OANs rather than in their historic setting. This he achieves by noting that the nation oracles are linked to each other by means of catchwords or phrases.[67] Paul's literary contribution came some time before such studies became common in the field of biblical studies. This may be due at least in part to his background of midrashic teaching where the text in its final form was read imaginatively. That is, a literary approach would have been more congenial to a Jewish mind such as Paul's than it would to a Protestant historical-critical scholar standing against the backdrop of the Reformation and Enlightenment.[68]

---

66. Steinmann, "Order," 683–89.

67. Paul, "Amos 1:3–2:3," 397–403.

68. For a further discussion on Jewish thinking and historical criticism see Levenson, *Death*, 33–61, 82–105.

Another example of textual work undertaken in order to understand the literary form is by another Jewish scholar, Adele Berlin in her 1995 article on Zephaniah's OANs and Israelite Cultural Myth in *Fortunate the Eyes that See*. Here she accounts in a literary rather than historical manner for the selection and omission of nations.[69] Van Hecke, too, looks at the coherence of the oracle and its position within the final form by means of its metaphors, specifically the pastoral ones.[70]

Kessler's *Battle of the Gods* is also largely a literary study, though in chapter 7 he looks at the canonical context of the oracle in ever widening contexts (Jeremiah's OANs, the rest of the book of Jeremiah, Isaiah's OANs), and chapter 8 is a historical discussion. In fact, he states that, "Whilst the approach is literary, its ultimate orientation is biblical-theological."[71] He concludes that Babylon's sins were: doing her task of subduing nations too enthusiastically; hubris; and idolatry (idolatry among the nations will be discussed in chapter 7).[72] As might be expected from the title of his book, he considers that YHWH defeats Marduk. He observes that there are not only contrasts but analogies between Judah and Babylon and sees the OANs against Babylon as the only ones that are not salvation oracles for Judah (but are rather judgment on Babylon).[73]

Stulman's 2005 commentary on Jeremiah is, perhaps, a little disappointing in its treatment of Jer 48, for whilst the structure indicates that it will give a sequential reading of the chapter, Stulman does little more than retell Jer 48 in prosaic form. On the other hand, Allen's Jeremiah commentary published in 2008 yields one or two nuggets that are new. For instance, he argues that some of the OANs have a lexical link to the ones immediately preceding and following it, in terms of shared vocabulary or ideas.[74] Though Paul did similarly regarding the OANs in Amos (see above), nothing comparable appears to have been attempted in Jeremiah. It is the link with the vocabulary of chapter 47 (weeping, falling silent, sword, etc.) that persuades Allen that Jer 48 has been placed where it now stands in MT, a suggestion

---

69. Berlin, "Zephaniah," 175–84.
70. Van Hecke, "Metaphorical Shifts," 68–88.
71. Kessler, *Battle*, 12.
72. Ibid., 209.
73. Ibid., 211–13, 222.
74. Allen, *Jeremiah*, 460.

that has not previously been offered.⁷⁵ Also unique to Allen is the dividing of Jeremiah 48 into two roughly symmetrical parts: 1a*b*–27 and 28–44 with 45–47 an addition. Apart from this, however, his main commentary proceeds verse by verse through the chapter and the comments run along conventional lines.

Paul Raabe

Paul Raabe's 1995 article, "Why Prophetic Oracles against the Nations?" published in *Fortunate the Eyes that See*, explicitly addresses the purpose of the OANs and, in my opinion, his paper stands as a beacon in the field of OANs in terms of perspicacity in handling the text in its final form. Raabe begins by pointing out that the OANs are a significant part of prophecy. He then takes Isa 13–23 as his test case and lists all the reasons for judgment that are given in the texts themselves, grouping them in categories.

His paper has clear headings, including one clarifying his title question, which he argues needs to be split into two: 1) the ultimate goal of the future *act* of divine judgment; and 2) the rhetorical purpose of the *speech*. Also, he breaks down the purpose of the OANs according to Israel and the nations, arguing that the nations were an implicit audience, even if they did not actually hear the speech. Some of these purposes overlap and it is arguable whether they are all distinct from each other, but nevertheless Raabe organizes the material lucidly.

Also unique to Raabe are the three models of OANs he proposes based on the relationship of woe and weal. These are: the Jonah model (divine repentance view), in which judgment is pronounced in an unconditional form, though if a nation repents, YHWH will relent; the Amos model (sequential view) in which judgment is irrevocable but the nation can still have a future bound up in Israel's; and the Obadiah model (eschatological view) in which a nation is accused and summoned to change its ways before the inevitable, universal-eschatological day of YHWH. Jer 48 falls under his second model, for judgment is inevitable and inescapable but restoration follows.

Finally, Raabe looks at the rhetorical purpose of the oracles, again according to hearer, that is, all hearers (nations cannot escape by relying on their own resources), Israelite hearers (promises of rescue, warning

---

75. Ibid., 478.

against foreign alliances, warnings against desiring other nations' gods, and a background for accusations against Israel—to show that they are no better than the goyim) and non-Israelite hearers. The purpose for non-Israelite hearers correlates with the three OAN models: that if a nation repents then YHWH might relent; that judgment is inevitable; that the accusations are designed to change a nation's ways. The weakest section of his paper is that in which he argues that the non-Israelite hearers might actually have heard the OANs. For while the oracles might have been addressed to the nations and there are no logistical reasons why a nation could not have heard them (for example, a prophet or representative could have travelled or uttered their words to a foreign personage in Judah), he argues that texts like Jer 18:7–8 imply that a nation must have heard the message since there is a possibility of repentance. Other commentators do not draw out this logic in 18:7–8, which may well be because the context of Jer 18:7–8 is Judah and not the nations. Nevertheless, whether or not nations heard the oracles, they are an implied audience and Raabe addresses this.

Antecedents for Reading as Christian Scripture

Raabe concludes his paper by asserting that "Indeed, one can say that from the prophetic point of view when the God of Israel intervenes in history, the whole world ultimately benefits."[76] This final sentence of Raabe's is understated in terms of a Christian reading (in fact there is nothing specifically Christian about it), but is typical of the kind of comments that scholars tend to make when addressing wider questions about God and the world (often in their final paragraph). For, generally, modern biblical scholarship has not directly engaged with faith questions. However, this has changed in recent years and along with a move towards literary and synchronic readings, there has been a greater interest in the interpreter's role and context. Therefore, questions of reading texts as Christian Scripture have come more explicitly to the fore. Brueggemann formulates this effectively when he writes:

> We read the texts where we are. We read the text, as we are bound to read it, on the horizon of China's Tiananmen Square and Berlin's wall, of Panama's canal and South Africa's changing situation, of Kuwait's lure of oil. Or among us, when we are dar-

---

76. Raabe, "Why Prophetic Oracles?" 254.

ing, we may read the text in relation to the politics of publication, the play of power in promotion and tenure, the ambiguities of acquiring grants, and the seductions of institutional funding. We inevitably read the text where we sit. What happens in the act of theological interpretation is not an "application" of the text, nor an argument about contemporary policy, but an opening of a rhetorical field in which an urgent voice other than our own is set in the midst of imperial self-sufficiency and "colonial" despair. We continue to listen while the voice of this text has its say against other voices that claim counterauthority.[77]

Whilst the above quotation is not specifically Christian in focus, Brueggemann's wider framework is and this sits within it.

Conclusion

So, then, in the last century, the questions brought to the book of Jeremiah and chapters 46–51 particularly have ranged from authorship and identity of the *ipsissima verba*, through the *Sitz im Leben* and historical setting, to the rhetorical function and ideological intentions. That the OANs were deemed not relevant to discussions on the *ipsissima verba* of Jeremiah is probably one reason why they were under-represented in scholarship. Therefore, one of the major milestones on the journey has been a shift to literary and synchronic approaches. Others have been McKane's rolling corpus, scholars asking what purpose the OANs had, and Carroll, and Brueggemann, *et al.* bringing contemporary perspectives and situations to the text.

Though the move has generally been from a diachronic to a synchronic approach, historical questions are still addressed. Furthermore, whilst historical-critical commentaries tend not to ask what the text might mean in a context other than that of the original, such as a Christian (or Jewish) frame of reference, they are nevertheless hospitable to these other questions. Likewise, few works interested in literary and canonical issues ignore historical-critical observations. Nevertheless, the type of investigation that Jeremiah's OANs have undergone has changed over time. That is, to paint with a broad brush, whereas once almost every piece of work was of a historical-critical nature, many competing perspectives are now also brought to bear upon the texts

---

77. Brueggemann, "Mercy (2004)," 133–34.

(or vice versa), for example, ideological, rhetorical, etc. As well, there has been a fresh move to take into account the interpreter's context, including that of faith, and to read texts as Christian Scripture within a contemporary context. Fretheim, Miller, Brueggemann, Jones, and Clements all operate within a Christian framework and draw out different aspects of the text. Since these commentators explicitly read Jeremiah as Christian Scripture, they will be analyzed in due course. Before that, however, there are two pieces of analysis that need to be undertaken: a comparison of Jeremiah's oracle concerning Moab in MT with, first, LXX and, secondly, Isaiah's parallel oracle. Thus the investigation will now turn to MT Jer 48 in the light of LXX Jer 31.

2

A Comparison of Jeremiah's Oracle Concerning Moab in MT (ch. 48) and LXX (ch. 31)

Introduction

THE BOOKS OF JEREMIAH VARY MORE BETWEEN EACH OTHER IN MT and LXX than is usual, not least because LXX is substantially shorter (by about one eighth of the length of MT),[1] but also, as discussed, because there is particular variance in the handling of the OAN chapters. First, the order of the nations differs within each OAN collection and, secondly, Jeremiah's collection of OANs is placed at the end of the book in MT, but in the middle in LXX. This chapter compares Jeremiah's oracle concerning Moab in MT (chapter 48) with that of LXX (chapter 31) in order to seek out possible variances in nuance, even perhaps divergences in their theologies. The ultimate purpose is that the study might help the quest of interpreting Jer 48 (MT). This task is facilitated by The New English Translation of the Septuagint (NETS), a project by The International Organization for Septuagint and Cognate Studies (IOSCS) that was completed in 2007.

There are no commentaries on LXX Jeremiah, but McKane, as is widely recognized, dedicates a considerable amount of space to the text and its development and makes use of LXX (and other versions). No other commentator does anything comparable in terms of thoroughness. Therefore, McKane's ICC commentary is the prime work consulted in this evaluation with regard to the text of LXX and its translation.

The discussion will open with the most striking and obvious difference: the canonical positioning of the oracle. The examination will then focus on what is arguably the next most noticeable disparity

1. Carroll, *Jeremiah*, 50.

between the two texts: material that is in MT but absent in LXX. That is, the last three verses in MT (48:45–47), as well as verses 40b and 41b. There is little in the way of material found in LXX but not MT, so the next section of the chapter will deal with significant differences between the two. By "significant" I exclude translational ambiguities that have little impact on the meaning, particularly those relating to place names. Although I have not commented where the *qere* of MT and LXX are in accord, I will include the instance (verse 20) where LXX and the *ketib* of MT cohere. The concluding section to this chapter will summarise the insights gained and determine whether the theologies of MT and LXX are distinct from each other and, if so, how this might impact an interpretation of Jer 48 (MT).

Since the verse ordering within the chapter is the same in both MT and LXX, I will not always specify whether a verse number refers to MT Jer 48, LXX Jer 31, or both, for the context will determine this. Both MT and LXX use masculine and feminine pronouns for Moab, but for the sake of consistency I will use the feminine throughout.

To clarify: Table 1 is a parallel presentation of the texts of MT and LXX, together with standard English translations (NRSV for MT and NETS for LXX). Divergences between the two texts have been emphasised. I have used the Göttingen critical edition of LXX by Ziegler as recommended by IOSCS.[2] It is worth pointing out that occasionally the English versions may indicate that there are differences even though there is none in the original versions. For example, זְרֹעַ and ἐπίχειρον may both be translated "arm" (see NRSV verse 25), although here it is clearly a metaphor for "strength" (also a legitimate translation of זְרֹעַ), which is closer to the sense of Pietersma's (NETS) "effort."

---

2. IOSCS, "'Critical Editions,'" Online.

TABLE 1: Jeremiah's Oracle Concerning Moab in MT (48) and LXX (31)

NRSV	Jer 48 MT	Jer 31 LXX	NETS
Concerning Moab. Thus says the LORD <u>of hosts, the God of Israel</u>: Alas for Nebo, it is laid waste! Kiriathaim <u>is put to shame</u>, it is taken; <u>the fortress is put to shame and broken down</u>;	¹ לְמוֹאָב כֹּה־אָמַר יְהוָה צְבָאוֹת אֱלֹהֵי יִשְׂרָאֵל הוֹי אֶל־נְבוֹ כִּי שֻׁדָּדָה הֹבִישָׁה נִלְכְּדָה קִרְיָתָיִם הֹבִישָׁה הַמִּשְׂגָּב וָחָתָּה:	¹ Τῇ Μωαβ. Οὕτως εἶπε κύριος Οὐαὶ ἐπὶ Ναβαυ, ὅτι ὤλετο· ἐλήμφθη Καριαθαιμ, ᾐσχύνθη <u>Αμασαγαβ</u> καὶ Αταθ.	For Moab. Thus did the Lord say: Woe for Nabau, because he perished! Kariathaim was taken; <u>Hamasagab</u> was put to shame, and <u>Hatath</u>.
the <u>renown</u> of Moab is no more. In Heshbon they planned evil against her: "<u>Come</u>, let us cut her off from being a nation!" <u>You also, O Madmen, shall be brought to silence</u>; the sword shall pursue you.	² אֵין עוֹד תְּהִלַּת מוֹאָב בְּחֶשְׁבּוֹן חָשְׁבוּ עָלֶיהָ רָעָה לְכוּ וְנַכְרִיתֶנָּה מִגּוֹי גַּם־מַדְמֵן תִּדֹּמִּי אַחֲרַיִךְ תֵּלֶךְ חָרֶב:	² οὐκ ἔστιν ἔτι <u>ἰατρεία</u> Μωαβ· ἐν Εσεβων ἐλογίσαντο ἐπ' αὐτὴν κακά· ἐκόψαμεν αὐτὴν ἀπὸ ἔθνους, <u>καὶ παῦσιν παύσεται</u>, ὄπισθέν σου βαδιεῖται μάχαιρα.	<u>Healing</u> of Moab is no more; in Hesebon they planned evil against her: "We cut her off from being a nation!" <u>She shall stop with a stop</u>; a dagger shall go after you,
Hark! a cry from Horonaim, "Desolation and great destruction!"	³ קוֹל צְעָקָה מֵחֹרוֹנָיִם שֹׁד וָשֶׁבֶר גָּדוֹל:	³ ὅτι φωνὴν κεκραγότων ἐξ Ωρωναιμ, ὄλεθρον καὶ σύντριμμα μέγα	because a voice of people that cry from Horonaim, "Desolation and a great fracture!"
"Moab is destroyed!" <u>her little ones cry out</u>.³	⁴ נִשְׁבְּרָה מוֹאָב הִשְׁמִיעוּ זְּעָקָה [כ = צְעוֹרֶיהָ] [ק = צְעִירֶיהָ]:	⁴ Συνετρίβη Μωαβ, ἀναγγείλατε εἰς <u>Ζογορα</u>.	"Moab was crushed!" announce to <u>Zogora</u>.

3. NRSV has taken השמיעו זעקה together as "cry out."

NRSV	Jer 48 MT	Jer 31 LXX	NETS
For <u>at the ascent</u> of Luhith they <u>go up</u> weeping <u>bitterly</u>; for <u>at the descent</u> of Horonaim they have heard the distressing cry of anguish.	⁵ כִּי מַעֲלֵה [כ =] הַלֻּחוֹת [ק =] הַלּוּחִית*[⁴ בִּבְכִי יַעֲלֶה־בֶּכִי כִּי בְּמוֹרַד חוֹרֹנַיִם צָרֵי צַעֲקַת־שֶׁבֶר שָׁמֵעוּ׃	⁵ ὅτι <u>ἐπλήσθη</u> Αλαωθ ἐν <u>κλαυθμῷ</u>, ἀναβήσεται κλαίων <u>ἐν ὁδῷ</u> Ωρωναιμ, κραυγὴν συντρίμματος ἠκού<u>σατε</u>	Because Halaoth <u>was filled</u> by weeping, he will go up <u>weeping by way</u> of Horonaim; a cry of fracture <u>you</u> have heard.
Flee! Save yourselves! Be like <u>a wild ass</u>⁵ in the desert!	⁶ נֻסוּ מַלְּטוּ נַפְשְׁכֶם וְתִהְיֶינָה כַּעֲרוֹעֵר בַּמִּדְבָּר׃	⁶ Φεύγετε καὶ σώσατε τὰς ψυχὰς ὑμῶν καὶ ἔσεσθε ὥσπερ <u>ὄνος ἄγριος</u> ἐν ἐρήμῳ.	Flee, and save your souls, and you shall be like <u>a wild ass</u> in a wilderness!
Surely, because you trusted in your <u>strongholds</u>⁶ and <u>your treasures</u>, you also shall be taken; Chemosh shall go out into exile, with his priests and his attendants.	⁷ כִּי יַעַן בִּטְחֵךְ בְּמַעֲשַׂיִךְ וּבְאוֹצְרוֹתַיִךְ גַּם־אַתְּ תִּלָּכֵדִי וְיָצָא [כ =] כְּמִישׁ [ק =] כְּמוֹשׁ בַּגּוֹלָה כֹּהֲנָיו וְשָׂרָיו [כ =] יַחַד [ק =] יַחְדָּיו׃	⁷ ἐπειδὴ ἐπεποίθεις ἐν <u>ὀχυρώμασί</u> σου, καὶ σὺ συλλημφθήσῃ· καὶ ἐξελεύσεται Χαμως ἐν ἀποικίᾳ, οἱ ἱερεῖς αὐτοῦ καὶ οἱ ἄρχοντες αὐτοῦ ἅμα.	Seeing that you trusted in your <u>strongholds</u>, you also shall be seized. And Chamos shall go out in exile, his priests and his rulers together.
The destroyer shall come upon every town, <u>and no town</u> shall escape; the valley shall perish, and the plain shall be destroyed, as the LORD has spoken.	⁸ וְיָבֹא שֹׁדֵד אֶל־כָּל־עִיר וְעִיר לֹא תִמָּלֵט וְאָבַד הָעֵמֶק וְנִשְׁמַד הַמִּישֹׁר אֲשֶׁר אָמַר יְהוָה׃	⁸ καὶ ἥξει ὄλεθρος ἐπὶ πᾶσαν πόλιν, <u>οὐ μὴ σωθῇ</u>, καὶ ἀπολεῖται ὁ αὐλών, καὶ ἐξολεθρευθήσεται ἡ πεδινή, καθὼς εἶπε κύριος.	And destruction shall come upon every city; <u>it</u> shall <u>not</u> be saved. And the valley shall perish, and the plain shall be destroyed utterly, as the Lord has said.

4. * Corrections of the BHS marked with asterisk—typographical errors, corrected towards Leningrad Codex (that is, Jer 48:5).

5. MT "juniper," but NRSV has read כערוד with LXX.

6. MT "works" but NRSV has accepted LXX's reading here.

NRSV	Jer 48 MT	Jer 31 LXX	NETS
Set aside salt[7] for Moab, for she will surely fall[8]; her towns shall become a desolation, with no inhabitant in them.	9 תְּנוּ־צִיץ לְמוֹאָב כִּי נָצֹא תֵּצֵא וְעָרֶיהָ לְשַׁמָּה תִהְיֶינָה מֵאֵין יוֹשֵׁב בָּהֵן:	9 δότε σημεῖα τῇ Μωαβ, ὅτι ἀφῇ ἀναφθήσεται, καὶ πᾶσαι αἱ πόλεις αὐτῆς εἰς ἄβατον ἔσονται· πόθεν ἔνοικος αὐτῇ;	Give signs to Moab, because she will be kindled with kindling, and all her cities shall become untrodden; from where will she get an inhabitant?
Accursed is the one who is slack in doing the work of the LORD; and accursed is the one who keeps back the sword from bloodshed.	10 אָרוּר עֹשֶׂה מְלֶאכֶת יְהוָה רְמִיָּה וְאָרוּר מֹנֵעַ חַרְבּוֹ מִדָּם:	10 ἐπικατάρατος ὁ ποιῶν τὰ ἔργα κυρίου ἀμελῶς ἐξαίρων μάχαιραν αὐτοῦ ἀφ᾽ αἵματος.	Accursed is the one who is doing the work of the Lord carelessly by keeping back his dagger from bloodshed.
Moab has been at ease from his youth, settled like wine on its dregs; he has not been emptied from vessel to vessel, nor has he gone into exile; therefore his flavor has remained and his aroma is unspoiled.	11 שַׁאֲנַן מוֹאָב מִנְּעוּרָיו וְשֹׁקֵט הוּא אֶל־שְׁמָרָיו וְלֹא־הוּרַק מִכְּלִי אֶל־כֶּלִי וּבַגּוֹלָה לֹא הָלָךְ עַל־כֵּן עָמַד טַעְמוֹ בּוֹ וְרֵיחוֹ לֹא נָמָר:	11 ἀνεπαύσατο Μωαβ ἐκ παιδαρίου καὶ πεποιθὼς ἦν ἐπὶ τῇ δόξῃ αὐτοῦ, οὐκ ἐνέχεεν ἐξ ἀγγείου εἰς ἀγγεῖον καὶ εἰς ἀποικισμὸν οὐκ ᾤχετο· διὰ τοῦτο ἔστη γεῦμα αὐτοῦ ἐν αὐτῷ, καὶ ὀσμὴ αὐτοῦ οὐκ ἐξέλιπε.	Moab was at rest from childhood and trusted in his glory; he did not pour from vessel to vessel, and he was not going into exile; therefore his flavor remained in him, and his aroma did not leave.

7. NRSV reads ציץ as "salt" after a Ugaritic gloss (see section "Wings, signs, salt" and footnote 59).

8. Better "fly away" (see section "Wings, signs, salt").

NRSV	Jer 48 MT	Jer 31 LXX	NETS
Therefore, the time is surely coming, says the LORD, when I shall send to him decanters to decant him, and empty his vessels, and break his[9] jars in pieces.	12 לָכֵן הִנֵּה־יָמִים בָּאִים נְאֻם־יְהוָה וְשִׁלַּחְתִּי־לוֹ צֹעִים וְצֵעֻהוּ וְכֵלָיו יָרִיקוּ וְנִבְלֵיהֶם יְנַפֵּצוּ׃	12 διὰ τοῦτο ἰδοὺ ἡμέραι ἔρχονται, φησὶ κύριος, καὶ ἀποστελῶ αὐτῷ κλίνοντας, καὶ κλινοῦσιν αὐτὸν καὶ τὰ σκεύη αὐτοῦ λεπτυνοῦσι καὶ τὰ κεράσματα αὐτοῦ συγκόψουσι.	Therefore behold, days are coming, quoth the Lord, and I shall send to him people that deviate, and they will make him deviate, and they shall pulverize his vessels and break up his mixtures.
Then Moab shall be ashamed of Chemosh, as the house of Israel was ashamed of Bethel, their confidence.	13 וּבֹשׁ מוֹאָב מִכְּמוֹשׁ כַּאֲשֶׁר־בֹּשׁוּ בֵּית יִשְׂרָאֵל מִבֵּית אֵל מִבְטֶחָם׃	13 καὶ καταισχυνθήσεται Μωαβ ἀπὸ Χαμως, ὥσπερ κατῃσχύνθη οἶκος Ισραηλ ἀπὸ Βαιθηλ πεποιθότες ἐπ' αὐτοῖς.	And Moab shall be ashamed of Chamos, as the house of Israel was ashamed of Baithel, when they had confidence in them.
How can you say, "We are heroes and mighty warriors"?	14 אֵיךְ תֹּאמְרוּ גִּבּוֹרִים אֲנָחְנוּ וְאַנְשֵׁי־חַיִל לַמִּלְחָמָה׃	14 πῶς ἐρεῖτε Ἰσχυροί ἐσμεν καὶ ἄνθρωπος ἰσχύων εἰς τὰ πολεμικά;	How will you say, "We are strong and a strong person in warfare"?
The destroyer of Moab[10] and his towns has come up, and the choicest of his young men have gone down to slaughter, says the King, whose name is the LORD of hosts.	15 שֻׁדַּד מוֹאָב וְעָרֶיהָ עָלָה[11] וּמִבְחַר בַּחוּרָיו יָרְדוּ לַטָּבַח נְאֻם־הַמֶּלֶךְ יְהוָה צְבָאוֹת שְׁמוֹ׃	15 ὤλετο Μωαβ πόλις αὐτοῦ, καὶ ἐκλεκτοὶ νεανίσκοι αὐτοῦ κατέβησαν εἰς σφαγήν·	Moab perished; his city and his choice young men went down to slaughter.

9. MT "their" but NRSV reads with Aquila וּנְבָלָיו.

10. Literally "Moab has been destroyed."

11. This is a singular construction where one would expect a plural in order to agree with ועריה "and her towns."

NRSV	Jer 48 MT	Jer 31 LXX	NETS
The calamity of Moab is near at hand and his <u>doom</u> approaches swiftly.	¹⁶קָר֤וֹב אֵיד־מוֹאָב֙ לָב֔וֹא וְרָ֣עָת֔וֹ מִהֲרָ֖ה מְאֹֽד׃	¹⁶ἐγγὺς ἡμέρα Μωαβ ἐλθεῖν, καὶ <u>πονηρία</u> αὐτοῦ ταχεῖα σφόδρα.	Moab's day is near to come, and his <u>wickedness</u>, very swiftly.
<u>Mourn</u> over him, all you his neighbors, and all who know his name; say, "How the mighty scepter is broken, the glorious staff!"	¹⁷נֻ֤דוּ לוֹ֙ כָּל־סְבִיבָ֔יו וְכֹ֖ל יֹדְעֵ֣י שְׁמ֑וֹ אִמְר֗וּ אֵיכָ֤ה נִשְׁבַּר֙ מַטֵּה־עֹ֔ז מַקֵּ֖ל תִּפְאָרָֽה׃	¹⁷<u>κινήσατε</u> αὐτῷ, πάντες κυκλόθεν αὐτοῦ, πάντες εἰδότες ὄνομα αὐτοῦ· εἴπατε Πῶς συνετρίβη βακτηρία εὐκλεής, ῥάβδος μεγαλώματος.	<u>Stir</u> for him, all you round about him and all who know his name; say, "How has the renowned staff broken to pieces, a rod of magnificence!"
Come down from glory, and sit on the <u>parched</u> ground, enthroned daughter Dibon! For the destroyer of Moab has come up against you; he has destroyed your <u>strongholds</u>.	¹⁸רְדִ֣י מִכָּב֗וֹד [כ = וּשְׁבִי] [ק = וּשְׁבִ֣י] בַצָּמָ֔א יֹשֶׁ֖בֶת בַּת־דִּיב֑וֹן כִּֽי־שֹׁדֵ֤ד מוֹאָב֙ עָ֣לָה בָ֔ךְ שִׁחֵ֖ת מִבְצָרָֽיִךְ׃	¹⁸κατάβηθι ἀπὸ δόξης καὶ κάθισον ἐν <u>ὑγρασίᾳ</u>, καθημένη <u>ἐκτρίβεται</u>, ὅτι ὤλετο Μωαβ, ἀνέβη εἰς σὲ λυμαινόμενος <u>ὀχύρωμά</u> σου.	Come down from glory, and sit on <u>moist</u> ground; seated <u>she is being destroyed</u>, because Moab has perished; he that ruins your <u>stronghold</u> came up against you.
Stand by the road and watch, you inhabitant of Aroer! Ask the man fleeing and the <u>woman escaping</u>; say, "What has happened?"	¹⁹אֶל־דֶּ֤רֶךְ עִמְדִי֙ וְצַפִּ֔י יוֹשֶׁ֖בֶת עֲרוֹעֵ֑ר שַׁאֲלִי־נָ֣ס וְנִמְלָ֔טָה אִמְרִ֖י מַה־נִּהְיָֽתָה׃	¹⁹ἐφ' ὁδοῦ στῆθι καὶ ἔπιδε, καθημένη ἐν Αροηρ, καὶ ἐρώτησον φεύγοντα καὶ <u>σῳζόμενον</u> καὶ εἰπόν Τί ἐγένετο;	Stand by the road, and watch, you that sit in Aroer! And ask him that flees and <u>escapes</u>, and say, "What has happened?"

NRSV	Jer 48 MT	Jer 31 LXX	NETS
Moab is put to shame, for it is broken down; wail and cry! Tell it by the Arnon, that Moab is laid waste.	20 הֹבִישׁ מוֹאָב כִּי־חַתָּה [כ = הֵילִילִי] [ק = הֵילִילוּ] [כ = וּזְעָקִי] [ק = וּזְעָקוּ] הַגִּידוּ בְאַרְנוֹן כִּי שֻׁדַּד מוֹאָב׃	20 κατῃσχύνθη Μωαβ, ὅτι συνετρίβη· ὀλόλυξον καὶ κέκραξον,[12] ἀνάγγειλον ἐν Αρνων ὅτι ὤλετο Μωαβ.	Moab was put to shame, because he was broken to pieces; wail, and cry! Tell it in Arnon that Moab has perished.
Judgment has come upon the <u>tableland</u>, upon Holon, and <u>Jahzah</u>, and Mephaath,	21 וּמִשְׁפָּט בָּא אֶל־אֶרֶץ הַמִּישֹׁר אֶל־חֹלוֹן וְאֶל־יַהְצָה וְעַל־[כ = מוֹפָעַת] [ק = מֵיפָעַת]׃	21 καὶ κρίσις ἔρχεται εἰς γῆν τοῦ <u>Μισωρ</u> ἐπὶ Χελων καὶ ἐπὶ <u>Ρεφας</u> καὶ ἐπὶ Μωφααθ	And judgment is coming to the land of <u>Misor</u>, upon Chelon and upon <u>Rephas</u> and upon Mophaath
and Dibon, and Nebo, and <u>Beth</u>-diblathaim,	22 וְעַל־דִּיבוֹן וְעַל־נְבוֹ וְעַל־בֵּית דִּבְלָתָיִם׃	22 καὶ ἐπὶ Δαιβων καὶ ἐπὶ Ναβαυ καὶ ἐπ' <u>οἶκον</u> Δεβλαθαιμ	and upon Daibon and upon Nabau and upon the <u>house</u> of Deblathaim
and Kiriathaim, and <u>Beth</u>-gamul, and <u>Beth</u>-meon,	23 וְעַל־קִרְיָתַיִם וְעַל־בֵּית גָּמוּל וְעַל־בֵּית מְעוֹן׃	23 καὶ ἐπὶ Καριαθαιμ καὶ ἐπ' <u>οἶκον</u> Γαμωλ καὶ ἐπ' <u>οἶκον</u> Μαων	and upon Kariathaim and upon the <u>house</u> of Gamol and upon the <u>house</u> of Maon
and Kerioth, and Bozrah, and all the towns of <u>the land of</u> Moab, far and near.	24 וְעַל־קְרִיּוֹת וְעַל־בָּצְרָה וְעַל כָּל־עָרֵי אֶרֶץ מוֹאָב הָרְחֹקוֹת וְהַקְּרֹבוֹת׃	24 καὶ ἐπὶ Καριωθ καὶ ἐπὶ Βοσορ καὶ ἐπὶ πάσας τὰς πόλεις Μωαβ τὰς πόρρω καὶ τὰς ἐγγύς.	and upon Karioth and upon Bosor and upon all the cities of Moab, those far and those near.
The horn of Moab is cut off, and his arm is broken, <u>says the LORD</u>.	25 נִגְדְּעָה קֶרֶן מוֹאָב וּזְרֹעוֹ נִשְׁבָּרָה נְאֻם יְהוָה׃	25 κατεάχθη κέρας Μωαβ, καὶ τὸ ἐπίχειρον αὐτοῦ συνετρίβη.	Moab's horn was cut off, and his effort was crushed.

12. LXX is in agreement with MT's *ketib* in using the singular form of the imperatives. LXX also reads הגידו (plural) as הגידי (singular) when it has ἀνάγγειλον.

A Comparison of Jeremiah's Oracle Concerning Moab in MT and LXX

NRSV	Jer 48 MT	Jer 31 LXX	NETS
Make him drunk, because he magnified himself against the LORD; let[13] Moab wallow in his <u>vomit</u>; he too shall become a laughingstock.	26 הַשְׁכִּירֻהוּ כִּי עַל־יְהוָה הִגְדִּיל וְסָפַק מוֹאָב בְּקִיאוֹ וְהָיָה לִשְׂחֹק גַּם־הוּא:	26 μεθύσατε αὐτόν, ὅτι ἐπὶ κύριον ἐμεγαλύνθη· καὶ ἐπικρούσει Μωαβ ἐν χειρὶ αὐτοῦ καὶ ἔσται εἰς γέλωτα καὶ αὐτός.	Make him drunk, because he was magnified against the Lord, and Moab shall clap with his <u>hand</u>, and he too shall become a laughingstock.
Israel was a laughingstock for you, though he was not caught among thieves; <u>but whenever you spoke of him you shook your head!</u>	27 וְאִם לוֹא הַשְּׂחֹק הָיָה לְךָ יִשְׂרָאֵל אִם־בְּגַנָּבִים [כ = נִמְצָאָה] [ק = נִמְצָא] כִּי־מִדֵּי דְבָרֶיךָ בּוֹ תִּתְנוֹדָד:	27 καὶ εἰ μὴ εἰς γελοιασμὸν ἦν σοι Ισραηλ; εἰ ἐν κλοπαῖς σου εὑρέθη, ὅτι ἐπολέμεις αὐτόν;	And if not, was Israel a jest for you? If he was found among your thefts, <u>is it because you kept fighting him?</u>
<u>Leave</u> the towns, and live on the rock, O inhabitants of Moab! Be like the dove that nests <u>on the sides</u> of the mouth of a gorge.	28 עִזְבוּ עָרִים וְשִׁכְנוּ בַּסֶּלַע יֹשְׁבֵי מוֹאָב וִהְיוּ כְיוֹנָה תְּקַנֵּן בְּעֶבְרֵי פִי־פָחַת:	28 κατέλιπον τὰς πόλεις καὶ ᾤκησαν ἐν πέτραις οἱ κατοικοῦντες Μωαβ, ἐγενήθησαν ὡς περιστεραὶ νοσσεύουσαι <u>ἐν πέτραις</u> στόματι βοθύνου.	The inhabitants of Moab <u>left</u> the cities and lived among rocks; they became like doves that nest <u>among rocks</u> at the mouth of a gorge.
<u>We</u> have heard of the pride of Moab—he is very proud—of <u>his loftiness, his pride, and his arrogance</u>, and the haughtiness of his heart.	29 שָׁמַעְנוּ גְאוֹן־מוֹאָב גֵּאֶה מְאֹד גָּבְהוֹ וּגְאוֹנוֹ וְגַאֲוָתוֹ וְרֻם לִבּוֹ:	29 ἤκουσα ὕβριν Μωαβ, ὕβρισε λίαν ὕβριν αὐτοῦ καὶ ὑπερηφανίαν αὐτοῦ, καὶ ὑψώθη ἡ καρδία αὐτοῦ.	<u>I</u> heard of Moab's insolence; he was very insolent in <u>his insolence and his arrogance</u>. And his heart was lifted up.

13. NRSV has translated וספק as an imperative, which fits with the first half of the verse, though the form is actually a third person masculine *waw* consecutive perfect.

NRSV	Jer 48 MT	Jer 31 LXX	NETS
I myself know his insolence, says the LORD; his boasts are false, his deeds are false.	30 אֲנִי יָדַעְתִּי נְאֻם־יְהוָה עֶבְרָתוֹ וְלֹא־כֵן בַּדָּיו לֹא־כֵן עָשׂוּ׃	30 ἐγὼ δὲ ἔγνων ἔργα αὐτοῦ· οὐχὶ τὸ ἱκανὸν αὐτοῦ, οὐχ οὕτως ἐποίησε.	But I knew his works. It was not enough for him; he did not do thus.
Therefore I wail for Moab; I cry out for all Moab; for the people of Kir-heres I mourn.[14]	31 עַל־כֵּן עַל־מוֹאָב אֲיֵלִיל וּלְמוֹאָב כֻּלֹּה אֶזְעָק אֶל־אַנְשֵׁי קִיר־חֶרֶשׂ יֶהְגֶּה׃	31 διὰ τοῦτο ἐπὶ Μωαβ ὀλολύζετε πάντοθεν, βοήσατε ἐπ' ἄνδρας Κιρ Αδας αὐχμοῦ.	Therefore wail for Moab on all sides; shout to the men of Kir Hadas, of drought.
More than for Jazer I weep for you, O vine of Sibmah! Your branches crossed over the sea, reached as far as Jazer;[15] upon your summer fruits and your vintage the destroyer has fallen.	32 מִבְּכִי יַעְזֵר אֶבְכֶּה־לָּךְ הַגֶּפֶן שִׂבְמָה נְטִישֹׁתַיִךְ עָבְרוּ יָם עַד יָם יַעְזֵר נָגָעוּ עַל־קֵיצֵךְ וְעַל־בְּצִירֵךְ שֹׁדֵד נָפָל׃	32 ὡς κλαυθμὸν Ιαζηρ ἀποκλαύσομαί σοι, ἄμπελος Σεβημα· κλήματά σου διῆλθε θάλασσαν, πόλεις Ιαζηρ ἥψαντο· ἐπὶ ὀπώραν σου, ἐπὶ τρυγηταῖς σου ὄλεθρος ἐπέπεσε.	As with the weeping for Iazer I will weep for you, O vine of Sebema! Your branches crossed over the sea; cities reached Iazer; upon your summer fruit, upon your grape gatherers destruction has fallen.
Gladness and joy have been taken away from the fruitful land of Moab; I have stopped the wine from the wine presses; no one treads them with shouts of joy; the shouting is not the shout of joy.	33 וְנֶאֶסְפָה שִׂמְחָה וָגִיל מִכַּרְמֶל וּמֵאֶרֶץ מוֹאָב וְיַיִן מִיקָבִים הִשְׁבַּתִּי לֹא־יִדְרֹךְ הֵידָד הֵידָד לֹא הֵידָד׃	33 συνεψήσθη χαρμοσύνη καὶ εὐφροσύνη ἐκ γῆς Μωαβίτιδος, καὶ οἶνος ἦν ἐπὶ ληνοῖς σου· πρωὶ οὐκ ἐπάτησαν· αιδεδ αιδεδ, οὐκ [ἐποίησαν] αιδεδ.	Joy and gladness were swept away from the land of Moabitis, and wine was in your vats; they did not tread in the early morning; "aided" "aided," [they did] not "aided"

14. Whilst NRSV translates יהגה as "I mourn," MT actually has the third person; NRSV is following a variant reading here as proposed by Rudolph in BHS. Furthermore, "moan" would probably be a better translation (e.g., NASB).

15. NRSV has followed the oriental manuscripts and Isa 16:8, but MT has "the sea of Jazer" here.

A Comparison of Jeremiah's Oracle Concerning Moab in MT and LXX

NRSV	Jer 48 MT	Jer 31 LXX	NETS
Heshbon and Elealeh cry out; <u>as far as Jahaz</u> they utter their voice, from Zoar to Horonaim and Eglath-shelishiyah. For even the waters of Nimrim have become <u>desolate</u>.	³⁴ מִזַּעֲקַת חֶשְׁבּוֹן עַד־אֶלְעָלֵה <u>עַד־יַהַץ</u> נָתְנוּ קוֹלָם מִצֹּעַר עַד־חֹרֹנַיִם עֶגְלַת שְׁלִשִׁיָּה כִּי גַּם־מֵי נִמְרִים <u>לִמְשַׁמּוֹת</u> יִהְיוּ׃	³⁴ ἀπὸ κραυγῆς Εσεβων ἕως Ελεαλη <u>αἱ πόλεις αὐτῶν</u> ἔδωκαν φωνὴν αὐτῶν, ἀπὸ Ζογορ ἕως Ωρωναιμ καὶ Αγελα Σαλασια, ὅτι καὶ τὸ ὕδωρ Νεβριμ εἰς <u>κατάκαυμα</u> ἔσται.	From a cry of Hesebon as far as Eleale, <u>their cities</u> gave forth their voice, from Zogor as far as Horonaim and Agela Salasia, because even the water of Nebrim shall become something <u>burnt</u>.
And I will bring to an end in Moab, says the LORD, those who offer sacrifice at a high place and make offerings to their gods.	³⁵ וְהִשְׁבַּתִּי לְמוֹאָב נְאֻם־יְהוָה מַעֲלֶה בָמָה וּמַקְטִיר לֵאלֹהָיו׃	³⁵ καὶ ἀπολῶ τὸν Μωαβ, φησὶ κύριος, ἀναβαίνοντα <u>ἐπὶ</u> βωμὸν καὶ θυμιῶντα θεοῖς αὐτοῦ.	And I will destroy Moab, quoth the Lord, since he ascends <u>upon</u> an altar and offers incense to his gods.
Therefore my heart moans for Moab like a flute, and my heart moans like a flute for the people of Kir-heres; for the <u>riches</u> <u>they</u> gained have perished.	³⁶ עַל־כֵּן לִבִּי לְמוֹאָב כַּחֲלִילִים יֶהֱמֶה וְלִבִּי אֶל־אַנְשֵׁי קִיר־חֶרֶשׂ כַּחֲלִילִים יֶהֱמֶה עַל־כֵּן <u>יִתְרַת עָשָׂה</u> אָבָדוּ׃	³⁶ διὰ τοῦτο καρδία μου τοῦ Μωαβ ὥσπερ αὐλοὶ βομβήσουσι, καρδία μου ἐπ' ἀνθρώπους Κιρ Αδας ὥσπερ αὐλὸς βομβήσει· διὰ τοῦτο ἃ περιεποιήσατο, <u>ἀπώλετο</u> [ἀπὸ ἀνθρώπου].	Therefore my heart will rumble for Moab as pipes will rumble; my heart will rumble like a pipe for the people of Kir Hadas. Therefore, what one gained perished [from a person].

NRSV	Jer 48 MT	Jer 31 LXX	NETS
For every head is shaved and every beard cut off; <u>on all the hands there are gashes</u>, and on the loins sackcloth.	³⁷ כִּי כָל־רֹאשׁ קָרְחָה וְכָל־זָקָן גְּרֻעָה עַל כָּל־יָדַיִם גְּדֻדֹת וְעַל־מָתְנַיִם שָׂק׃	³⁷ πᾶσαν κεφαλὴν <u>ἐν παντὶ τόπῳ</u> ξυρηθήσονται, καὶ πᾶς πώγων ξυρηθήσεται, καὶ πᾶσαι χεῖρες κόψονται, καὶ ἐπὶ πάσης ὀσφύος σάκκος.	They will have every head <u>in every place</u> shaved, and every beard shall be shaved, and all hands shall beat,[16] and sackcloth on every loin,
On all the housetops of Moab and in the squares there is <u>nothing but lamentation</u>; for I have broken <u>Moab</u> like a vessel that no one wants, <u>says the LORD.</u>	³⁸ עַל כָּל־גַּגּוֹת מוֹאָב וּבִרְחֹבֹתֶיהָ כֻּלֹּה מִסְפֵּד כִּי־שָׁבַרְתִּי אֶת־מוֹאָב כִּכְלִי אֵין־חֵפֶץ בּוֹ נְאֻם־יְהוָה׃	³⁸ <u>καὶ</u> ἐπὶ πάντων τῶν δωμάτων Μωαβ καὶ ἐπὶ πλατείαις αὐτῆς, ὅτι συνέτριψα, φησὶ κύριος, ὡς ἀγγεῖον, οὗ οὐκ ἔστι χρεία αὐτοῦ.	<u>even</u> on all the housetops of Moab and in her squares, because I have crushed her, quoth the Lord, like a container for which no one has any use.
How it is <u>broken</u>! How they wail! How Moab has turned his back in shame! So Moab has become a derision and a horror to all his neighbors.	³⁹ אֵיךְ חַתָּה הֵילִילוּ אֵיךְ הִפְנָה־עֹרֶף מוֹאָב בּוֹשׁ וְהָיָה מוֹאָב לִשְׂחֹק וְלִמְחִתָּה לְכָל־סְבִיבָיו׃	³⁹ πῶς Ατατ ἠλάλαξε· πῶς ἔστρεψε νῶτον Μωαβ. ᾐσχύνθη καὶ ἐγένετο Μωαβ εἰς γέλωτα καὶ ἐγκότημα πᾶσι τοῖς κύκλῳ αὐτῆς.	How <u>Hatat</u> shouted! How Moab turned her back! Moab was ashamed and became a laughingstock and an object of indignation to all those about her—
For thus says the LORD: <u>Look, he shall swoop down like an eagle, and spread his wings against Moab;</u>	⁴⁰ כִּי־כֹה אָמַר יְהוָה הִנֵּה כַנֶּשֶׁר יִדְאֶה וּפָרַשׂ כְּנָפָיו אֶל־מוֹאָב׃	⁴⁰ ὅτι οὕτως εἶπε κύριος	because thus did the Lord say:

---

16. Pietersma translates κόψονται as "shall beat," but McKane (*Jeremiah*, vol. 2, 1190) deems "κόψονται to correctly understand גדדת as a reference to 'gashes' on the hands associated with mourning, which is the sense given by Rashi and Kimchi."

NRSV	Jer 48 MT	Jer 31 LXX	NETS
the towns shall be taken and the strongholds seized. The hearts of the warriors of Moab, on that day, shall be like the heart of a woman in labor.	⁴¹ נִלְכְּדָה הַקְּרִיּוֹת וְהַמְּצָדוֹת נִתְפָּשָׂה וְהָיָה לֵב גִּבּוֹרֵי מוֹאָב בַּיּוֹם הַהוּא כְּלֵב אִשָּׁה מְצֵרָה׃	⁴¹ Ἐλήμφθη Ακκαριωθ, καὶ τὰ ὀχυρώματα συνελήμφθη·	Hakkarioth was seized, and the strongholds were also seized.
Moab shall be destroyed as a people, because he magnified himself against the LORD.	⁴² וְנִשְׁמַד מוֹאָב מֵעָם כִּי עַל־יְהוָה הִגְדִּיל׃	⁴² καὶ ἀπολεῖται Μωαβ ἀπὸ ὄχλου, ὅτι ἐπὶ κύριον ἐμεγαλύνθη.	And Moab shall be destroyed from being a crowd, because he was magnified against the Lord.
Terror, pit, and trap are before you, O inhabitants of Moab! says the LORD.	⁴³ פַּחַד וָפַחַת וָפָח עָלֶיךָ יוֹשֵׁב מוֹאָב נְאֻם־יְהוָה׃	⁴³ παγὶς καὶ φόβος καὶ βόθυνος ἐπὶ σοί, καθήμενος Μωαβ·	Trap and fear and pit are upon you, you seated one of Moab!
Everyone who flees from the terror shall fall into the pit, and everyone who climbs out of the pit shall be caught in the trap. For I will bring these things upon Moab in the year of their punishment, says the LORD.	⁴⁴ [כ = הַנִּיס] [ק = הַנָּס] מִפְּנֵי הַפַּחַד יִפֹּל אֶל־הַפַּחַת וְהָעֹלֶה מִן־הַפַּחַת יִלָּכֵד בַּפָּח כִּי־אָבִיא אֵלֶיהָ אֶל־מוֹאָב שְׁנַת פְּקֻדָּתָם נְאֻם־יְהוָה׃	⁴⁴ ὁ φεύγων ἀπὸ προσώπου τοῦ φόβου ἐμπεσεῖται εἰς τὸν βόθυνον, καὶ ὁ ἀναβαίνων ἐκ τοῦ βοθύνου συλλημφθήσεται ἐν τῇ παγίδι, ὅτι ἐπάξω ταῦτα ἐπὶ Μωαβ ἐν ἐνιαυτῷ ἐπισκέψεως αὐτῶν.	He who flees from before fear shall fall into the pit, and he who climbs out of the pit shall be caught in the trap, because I will bring these things upon Moab in the year of their visiting.

NRSV	Jer 48 MT	Jer 31 LXX	NETS
In the shadow of Heshbon fugitives stop exhausted; for a fire has gone out from Heshbon, a flame from the house of Sihon; it has destroyed the forehead of Moab, the scalp of the people of tumult.	⁴⁵בְּצֵ֥ל חֶשְׁבּ֖וֹן עָמְד֣וּ מִכֹּ֣חַ נָסִ֑ים כִּי־אֵ֞שׁ יָצָ֣א מֵחֶשְׁבּ֗וֹן וְלֶֽהָבָה֙ מִבֵּ֣ין סִיח֔וֹן וַתֹּ֨אכַל֙ פְּאַ֣ת מוֹאָ֔ב וְקָדְקֹ֖ד בְּנֵ֥י שָׁאֽוֹן׃		
Woe to you, O Moab! The people of Chemosh have perished, for your sons have been taken captive, and your daughters into captivity.	⁴⁶אֽוֹי־לְךָ֣ מוֹאָ֔ב אָבַ֖ד עַם־כְּמ֑וֹשׁ כִּֽי־לֻקְּח֤וּ בָנֶ֙יךָ֙ בַּשֶּׁ֔בִי וּבְנֹתֶ֖יךָ בַּשִּׁבְיָֽה׃		
Yet I will restore the fortunes of Moab in the latter days, says the LORD. Thus far is the judgment on Moab.	⁴⁷וְשַׁבְתִּ֧י שְׁבוּת־ מוֹאָ֛ב בְּאַחֲרִ֥ית הַיָּמִ֖ים נְאֻם־יְהוָ֑ה עַד־הֵ֖נָּה מִשְׁפַּ֥ט מוֹאָֽב׃		

A list of minor divergences that will not be addressed is as follows:

- instances where LXX renders בית as οἶκον where in MT בית appears to be part of the place name itself (see verses 22–23).
- the reverse of the above; where המישר is a place name in LXX, although it naturally translates as "tableland" (see NRSV's translation of 48:21); see also LXX's Αμασαγαβ compared to MT's הַמִּשְׂגָּב "stronghold" (v. 1), Ατατ for חַתָּה "he / it is shattered" (v. 39) and Ακκαριωθ for הַקְּרִיּוֹת "Kerioth / the towns" (v. 41).
- cases where there appear to be differences in tense between past and present / future.
- variation in singular and plural verbs and nouns, for example, MT's plural מבצריך "your fortified towns" compared to LXX's singular ὀχύρωμά σου "your stronghold" in verse 18.
- slight variations in word order, probably the most major being verse 43 where MT has פחד ופחת ופח "terror and pit and trap" and LXX has παγὶς καὶ φόβος καὶ βόθυνος "trap and fear and pit."
- MT's declaration in verse 2 that Moab's praise (תהלה) is no more, whereas it is her healing (ἰατρεία) that no longer exists in LXX.
- the inclusion of MT's reference to Madmen (מדמן) in verse 2.
- LXX's translation of כערור "wild ass" in verse 6 (ὄνος ἄγριος) as opposed to MT's כערוער "juniper" (see footnote 5).
- the land described as בצמא "thirsty / parched" in verse 18 of MT but ὑγρασίᾳ "moist" in LXX (perhaps from a *Vorlage* of בגבא "in a pool" or בצאה "in filth").[17]
- MT's use of a masculine participle in MT (נס), followed by a feminine one (נמלטה) in verse 19, as opposed to two masculine participles in LXX (φεύγοντα and σῳζόμενον)
- a difference of place names in verse 21 (יהצה in MT and Ρεφας in LXX)
- the strange phrase בעברי פי־פחת "on the other side of the mouth of the pit" in MT's verse 28 compared to LXX's ἐν πέτραις στόματι

---

17. McKane, *Jeremiah*, vol. 2, 1175.

βοθύνου "among rocks at the mouth of a gorge" (perhaps from the *Vorlage* בצורי)[18]

- expanded descriptions of YHWH, where MT gives a fuller designation of YHWH than just his name: יהוה צבאות אלהי ישראל (v. 1) and המלך יהוה צבאות שמו (v. 15) (LXX does not have any instances where YHWH is described by anything other than κύριος)

- simple textual corruptions, such as ר/ד confusion. These include: verse 31 where LXX renders הדש, not חרש, as Αδας; verse 32 where LXX's πόλεις "cities" represents ערים rather than עד ים "as far as (the) sea";[19] and verse 34, where MT's עד־יהץ "as far as Jahaz" is rendered by αἱ πόλεις αὐτῶν "their cities" cry out, which Ziegler puts down to a *Vorlage* of עריהם (the צ and מ also differ here). Verse 30 where MT has עברתו "his insolence" and LXX ἔργα αὐτοῦ "his works" from עבדתו will be discussed briefly.[20]

Differing Sequence and Canonical Position

In LXX, Jeremiah's OANs come between what is 25:13 and 25:15 in MT (there is no equivalent of MT's 25:14 in LXX), whereas they almost conclude the book in MT (and probably once did, since chapter 52, very similar to 2 Kgs 24–25, is usually considered to be a later addendum).[21] The order of nations within their respected collections is shown in Table 2.

---

18. Ibid., 1182.
19. Cornhill cited in McKane, *Jeremiah*, vol. 2, 1185.
20. McKane, *Jeremiah*, vol. 2, 1183.
21. Allen, *Jeremiah*, 536–37; Clements, *Jeremiah*, 245; Fretheim, *Jeremiah*, 651; Holladay, *Jeremiah*, vol. 2, 23–24; Lundbom, *Jeremiah 37–52*, 510, 512; McKane, *Jeremiah*, vol. 2, clxxi–ii; Miller, "Jeremiah", 925; Thompson, *Jeremiah*, 30; and implied by Carroll, *Jeremiah*, 757, 858.

TABLE 2: Order of Nations in Jeremiah's OANs in MT and LXX

MT	LXX
Egypt	Elam
Philistia	Egypt
Moab	Babylon
Ammon	Philistia
Edom	Edom
Damascus	Ammon
Kedar [22]	Kedar
Elam	Damascus
Babylon	Moab

As discussed in chapter 1, it is now generally accepted that the two had separate redactional histories. The question here is what difference the final form makes to the overall reading of Jeremiah in general and, in particular, the collection of OANs. Given that beginnings and endings are often significant, it is unlikely that the nuances of MT and LXX remain unaffected, since the two versions depart from each other in the way they end the book and also in the nations that open and close their OAN collections (chapters 46–51 in MT and 25:14–31:44 in LXX). We shall look at the ordering first.

Order of Nations

Perhaps the most striking aspect of the two collections is that Babylon ends MT's collection, whereas it sits third in LXX's (Moab's case is the reverse; it is third in MT, but last in LXX). Babylon's position in MT is more intuitively explainable than Moab's in LXX, for the hammer that smashed all the other nations, the major threat at the time in the literary world of Jeremiah, is herself finally broken. Babylon does not only have a pre-eminence in MT Jeremiah's collection of OANs, but Babylon also

---

22. Where MT also includes the kingdoms of Hazor in the oracle concerning Kedar, LXX does not and instead of חצור has αὐλή "court."

has a greater prominence in chapter 25 of MT.[23] The relevant references to Babylon (in verses 1, 9, 11, 12) have been emphasized in Table 3.

TABLE 3: Emphasis on Babylon in MT's Jer 25:1–14 compared to LXX's

NRSV	Jer 25:1–14 MT	Jer 25:1–13 LXX	NETS
The word that came to Jeremiah concerning all the people of Judah, in the fourth year of King Jehoiakim son of Josiah of Judah (that was the first year of King Nebuchadrezzar of Babylon),	¹ הַדָּבָר אֲשֶׁר־הָיָה עַל־יִרְמְיָהוּ עַל־כָּל־עַם יְהוּדָה בַּשָּׁנָה הָרְבִעִית לִיהוֹיָקִים בֶּן־יֹאשִׁיָּהוּ מֶלֶךְ יְהוּדָה הִיא הַשָּׁנָה הָרִאשֹׁנִית לִנְבוּכַדְרֶאצַּר מֶלֶךְ בָּבֶל:	¹Ὁ λόγος ὁ γενόμενος πρὸς Ιερεμίαν ἐπὶ πάντα τὸν λαὸν Ιουδα ἐν τῷ ἔτει τῷ τετάρτῳ τοῦ Ιωακιμ υἱοῦ Ιωσία βασιλέως Ιουδα,	The word that came to Ieremias regarding all the people of Iouda, in the fourth year of King Ioakim son of Iosias of Iouda,
which the prophet Jeremiah spoke to all the people of Judah and all the inhabitants of Jerusalem:	² אֲשֶׁר דִּבֶּר יִרְמְיָהוּ הַנָּבִיא עַל־כָּל־עַם יְהוּדָה וְאֶל כָּל־יֹשְׁבֵי יְרוּשָׁלִַם לֵאמֹר:	² ὃν ἐλάλησε πρὸς πάντα τὸν λαὸν Ιουδα καὶ πρὸς τοὺς κατοικοῦντας Ιερουσαλημ λέγων	which he spoke to all the people of Iouda and to the inhabitants of Ierousalem, saying:
For twenty-three years, from the thirteenth year of King Josiah son of Amon of Judah, to this day, the word of the LORD has come to me, and I have spoken persistently to you, but you have not listened.	³ מִן־שְׁלֹשׁ עֶשְׂרֵה שָׁנָה לְיֹאשִׁיָּהוּ בֶן־אָמוֹן מֶלֶךְ יְהוּדָה וְעַד הַיּוֹם הַזֶּה זֶה שָׁלֹשׁ וְעֶשְׂרִים שָׁנָה הָיָה דְבַר־יְהוָה אֵלָי וָאֲדַבֵּר אֲלֵיכֶם אַשְׁכֵּים וְדַבֵּר וְלֹא שְׁמַעְתֶּם:	³Ἐν τρισκαιδεκάτῳ ἔτει τοῦ Ιωσία υἱοῦ Αμως βασιλέως Ιουδα καὶ ἕως τῆς ἡμέρας ταύτης εἴκοσι καὶ τρία ἔτη καὶ ἐλάλησα πρὸς ὑμᾶς ὀρθρίζων καὶ λέγων	In the thirteenth year of King Iosias son of Amos of Iouda, and until this day for twenty-three years, and I spoke to you, being early and speaking,

23. See also Holt, "Meaning of an Inclusio," 198–99; Watts, "Text and Redaction," 443.

NRSV	Jer 25:1–14 MT	Jer 25:1–13 LXX	NETS
And though the LORD persistently sent you all his servants the prophets, you have neither listened nor inclined your ears to hear	⁴וְשָׁלַח יְהוָה אֲלֵיכֶם אֶת־כָּל־עֲבָדָיו הַנְּבִאִים הַשְׁכֵּם וְשָׁלֹחַ וְלֹא שְׁמַעְתֶּם וְלֹא־הִטִּיתֶם אֶת־אָזְנְכֶם לִשְׁמֹעַ׃	⁴καὶ ἀπέστελλον πρὸς ὑμᾶς τοὺς δούλους μου τοὺς προφήτας ὄρθρου ἀποστέλλων, καὶ οὐκ εἰσηκούσατε καὶ οὐ προσέσχετε τοῖς ὠσὶν ὑμῶν,	and I would send to you my slaves the prophets, sending them at dawn, but you have not listened and have not paid heed to your ears
when they said, "Turn now, everyone of you, from your evil way and wicked doings, and you will remain upon the land that the LORD has given to you and your ancestors from of old and forever;	⁵לֵאמֹר שׁוּבוּ־נָא אִישׁ מִדַּרְכּוֹ הָרָעָה וּמֵרֹעַ מַעַלְלֵיכֶם וּשְׁבוּ עַל־הָאֲדָמָה אֲשֶׁר נָתַן יְהוָה לָכֶם וְלַאֲבוֹתֵיכֶם לְמִן־עוֹלָם וְעַד־עוֹלָם׃	⁵λέγων Ἀποστράφητε ἕκαστος ἀπὸ τῆς ὁδοῦ αὐτοῦ τῆς πονηρᾶς καὶ ἀπὸ τῶν πονηρῶν ἐπιτηδευμάτων ὑμῶν, καὶ κατοικήσετε ἐπὶ τῆς γῆς, ἧς ἔδωκα ὑμῖν καὶ τοῖς πατράσιν ὑμῶν ἀπ' αἰῶνος καὶ ἕως αἰῶνος·	when I was saying, "Do turn, everyone from his evil way and from your evil doings, and dwell upon the land that I have given to you and your fathers from of old and forever;
do not go after other gods to serve and worship them, and do not provoke me to anger with the work of your hands. Then I will do you no harm."	⁶וְאַל־תֵּלְכוּ אַחֲרֵי אֱלֹהִים אֲחֵרִים לְעָבְדָם וּלְהִשְׁתַּחֲוֹת לָהֶם וְלֹא־תַכְעִיסוּ אוֹתִי בְּמַעֲשֵׂה יְדֵיכֶם וְלֹא אָרַע לָכֶם׃	⁶μὴ πορεύεσθε ὀπίσω θεῶν ἀλλοτρίων τοῦ δουλεύειν αὐτοῖς καὶ τοῦ προσκυνεῖν αὐτοῖς, ὅπως μὴ παροργίζητέ με ἐν τοῖς ἔργοις τῶν χειρῶν ὑμῶν τοῦ κακῶσαι ὑμᾶς.	do not go after foreign gods to be slaves to them and to do obeisance to them in order that you may not provoke me to anger with the works of your hands so as to do you harm."

NRSV	Jer 25:1–14 MT	Jer 25:1–13 LXX	NETS
Yet you did not listen to me, says the LORD, and so you have provoked me to anger with the work of your hands to your own harm.	‏וְלֹא־שְׁמַעְתֶּם אֵלַי נְאֻם־יְהוָה לְמַעַן [כ = הִכְעִסוּנִי] [ק = הַכְעִיסֵנִי] בְּמַעֲשֵׂה יְדֵיכֶם לְרַע לָכֶם׃	⁷καὶ οὐκ ἠκούσατέ μου.	And you did not hear me.
Therefore thus says the LORD of hosts: Because you have not obeyed my words,	⁸לָכֵן כֹּה אָמַר יְהוָה צְבָאוֹת יַעַן אֲשֶׁר לֹא־שְׁמַעְתֶּם אֶת־דְּבָרָי׃	⁸διὰ τοῦτο τάδε λέγει κύριος Ἐπειδὴ οὐκ ἐπιστεύσατε τοῖς λόγοις μου,	Therefore this is what the Lord says: Because you have not believed my words,
I am going to send for all the tribes of the north, says the LORD, even for King Nebuchadrezzar of Babylon, my servant, and I will bring them against this land and its inhabitants, and against all these nations around; I will utterly destroy them, and make them an object of horror and of hissing, and an everlasting disgrace.	⁹הִנְנִי שֹׁלֵחַ וְלָקַחְתִּי אֶת־כָּל־מִשְׁפְּחוֹת צָפוֹן נְאֻם־יְהוָה וְאֶל־נְבוּכַדְרֶאצַּר מֶלֶךְ־בָּבֶל עַבְדִּי וַהֲבִאֹתִים עַל־הָאָרֶץ הַזֹּאת וְעַל־יֹשְׁבֶיהָ וְעַל כָּל־הַגּוֹיִם הָאֵלֶּה סָבִיב וְהַחֲרַמְתִּים וְשַׂמְתִּים לְשַׁמָּה וְלִשְׁרֵקָה וּלְחָרְבוֹת עוֹלָם׃	⁹ἰδοὺ ἐγὼ ἀποστέλλω καὶ λήμψομαι πατριὰν ἀπὸ βορρᾶ καὶ ἄξω αὐτοὺς ἐπὶ τὴν γῆν ταύτην καὶ ἐπὶ τοὺς κατοικοῦντας αὐτὴν καὶ ἐπὶ πάντα τὰ ἔθνη τὰ κύκλῳ αὐτῆς καὶ ἐξερημώσω αὐτοὺς καὶ δώσω αὐτοὺς εἰς ἀφανισμὸν καὶ εἰς συριγμὸν καὶ εἰς ὀνειδισμὸν αἰώνιον·	behold, I am sending for you and I will take a paternal family from the north, and I will bring them against this land and against its inhabitants and against all nations around it, and I will utterly devastate them and render them into an annihilation and into a hissing and into an everlasting disgrace.

NRSV	Jer 25:1–14 MT	Jer 25:1–13 LXX	NETS
And I will banish from them the sound of mirth and the sound of gladness, the voice of the bridegroom and the voice of the bride, the sound of the millstones and the light of the lamp.	10 וְהַאֲבַדְתִּי מֵהֶם קוֹל שָׂשׂוֹן וְקוֹל שִׂמְחָה קוֹל חָתָן וְקוֹל כַּלָּה קוֹל רֵחַיִם וְאוֹר נֵר:	10 καὶ ἀπολῶ ἀπ' αὐτῶν φωνὴν χαρᾶς καὶ φωνὴν εὐφροσύνης, φωνὴν νυμφίου καὶ φωνὴν νύμφης, ὀσμὴν μύρου καὶ φῶς λύχνου.	And I will banish them from a sound of mirth and a sound of gladness, a voice of bridegroom and a voice of bride, a fragrance of perfume and light of a lamp.
This whole land shall become a ruin and a waste, and these nations shall serve <u>the king of Babylon</u> seventy years.	11 וְהָיְתָה כָּל־הָאָרֶץ הַזֹּאת לְחָרְבָּה לְשַׁמָּה וְעָבְדוּ הַגּוֹיִם הָאֵלֶּה אֶת־מֶלֶךְ בָּבֶל שִׁבְעִים שָׁנָה:	11 καὶ ἔσται πᾶσα ἡ γῆ εἰς ἀφανισμόν, καὶ δουλεύσουσιν ἐν <u>τοῖς ἔθνεσιν</u> ἑβδομήκοντα ἔτη.	And the whole land shall become an annihilation, and they shall be slaves amongst <u>the nations</u> seventy years.
Then after seventy years are completed, I will punish <u>the king of Babylon and</u> that nation, <u>the land of the Chaldeans, for their iniquity</u>, says the LORD, making the land an everlasting waste.	12 וְהָיָה כִמְלֹאת שִׁבְעִים שָׁנָה אֶפְקֹד עַל־מֶלֶךְ־בָּבֶל וְעַל־הַגּוֹי הַהוּא נְאֻם־יְהוָה אֶת־עֲוֹנָם וְעַל־אֶרֶץ כַּשְׂדִּים וְשַׂמְתִּי אֹתוֹ לְשִׁמְמוֹת עוֹלָם:	12 καὶ ἐν τῷ πληρωθῆναι ἑβδομήκοντα ἔτη ἐκδικήσω τὸ ἔθνος ἐκεῖνο καὶ θήσομαι αὐτοὺς εἰς ἀφανισμὸν αἰώνιον·	And when seventy years are completed, I will punish that nation, and I will make them an everlasting waste.
I will bring upon that land all the words that I have uttered against it, everything written in this book, which Jeremiah prophesied against all the nations.	13 [כ = וְהֵבֵאיתִי] [ק = וְהֵבֵאתִי] עַל־הָאָרֶץ הַהִיא אֶת־כָּל־דְּבָרַי אֲשֶׁר־דִּבַּרְתִּי עָלֶיהָ אֵת כָּל־הַכָּתוּב בַּסֵּפֶר הַזֶּה אֲשֶׁר־נִבָּא יִרְמְיָהוּ עַל־כָּל־הַגּוֹיִם:	13 καὶ ἐπάξω ἐπὶ τὴν γῆν ἐκείνην πάντας τοὺς λόγους μου, οὓς ἐλάλησα κατ' αὐτῆς, πάντα τὰ γεγραμμένα ἐν τῷ βιβλίῳ τούτῳ.	And I will bring upon that land all my words that I have spoken against it, everything written in this book.

NRSV	Jer 25:1–14 MT	Jer 25:1–13 LXX	NETS
For many nations and great kings shall make slaves of them also; and I will repay them according to their deeds and the work of their hands.	¹⁴ כִּי עָבְדוּ־בָם גַּם־הֵמָּה גּוֹיִם רַבִּים וּמְלָכִים גְּדוֹלִים וְשִׁלַּמְתִּי לָהֶם כְּפָעֳלָם וּכְמַעֲשֵׂה יְדֵיהֶם׃		

MT 25:18–26 provides an extensive list of those YHWH would punish, making the point that after these had drunk from his cup of wrath, Babylon would have to drink. Thus chapters 46–51 loosely parallel chapter 25 in their structure (as well as the order in which the nations are listed) in that chapters 50–51 show that YHWH's punishment has been exhaustive. This unique status of Babylon's role has led commentators to regard MT's collection as being comprised of two parts: 46–49 and 50–51.²⁴ If one does separate out Babylon, then Elam becomes the last of the collection in 46–49 and thus assumes significance akin to that given by its first position in LXX.

Rudolph and Weiser deem LXX to understand Elam as Persia and therefore that the list begins with three great empires: Persia, Egypt and Babylon.²⁵ Conversely, Holladay (following Rietzschel) dismisses this idea since LXX distinguishes between Elam and Persia.²⁶ Others suggest that LXX's oracles are arranged chronologically (Duhm),²⁷ though the same suggestion, along with geographical arrangement, has been made for MT's order (Holladay, McKane, Rudolph).²⁸ However, Elam's significance could perhaps be explained thus: Elam was a distant empire to the East of Judah and thus if YHWH's judgment had reached Elam, it might signify that he had satisfied the limits of כל־הגוים האלה סביב "all

---

24. Brueggemann, *Jeremiah*, 421; Carroll, *Jeremiah*, 753–54; Clements, *Jeremiah*, 247; Fretheim, *Jeremiah*, 577; Holladay, *Jeremiah*, vol. 2, 313; Jones, *Jeremiah*, 520; Lundbom, *Jeremiah 37–52*, 182; Miller, "Jeremiah", 911 (implied). Cf. Volz (*Der Prophet Jeremia*, 389) who assigns 46–51 to one author.

25. Rudolph, *Jeremiah*, 266; Weiser, *Der Prophet Jeremia*, 389.

26. Holladay, *Jeremiah*, vol. 2, 314.

27. Duhm, *Jeremia*, 336.

28. Holladay, *Jeremiah*, vol. 2, 313; McKane, *Jeremiah*, vol. 2, 1110; Rudolph, *Jeremiah*, 265; Volz, *Der Prophet Jeremia*, 382.

these nations around" (25:9), πάντα τὰ ἔθνη τὰ κύκλῳ αὐτῆς in LXX. The oracle concerning Babylon then naturally follows in MT.

If Elam does represent the borders of YHWH's punishment, then LXX's order of OANs becomes a little more understandable, for the list starts by demonstrating that YHWH's judgment is complete. The next two nations in the list (Egypt and Babylon respectively) then almost act as demonstration of this in that it becomes clear that Israel's first enemy has received YHWH's word against her, as has Israel's last oppressor. After these nations, which perhaps represent the boundaries and completeness of YHWH's punishment, come the rest. Thus both MT's and LXX's arrangements of nations in Jeremiah's OANs pay tribute to the fact that YHWH's punishment has been exhaustive.

Nevertheless, it is easier to recognize why Egypt should top the list in MT than Elam in LXX; after all, Egypt was the first "superpower" to oppress Israel (as opposed to Babylon, the last). Unsurprising as well, if central positions are also important, is that Edom comes middle of the list in both traditions. For Edom was another age-old enemy, which, unlike Egypt, had loose blood-ties to Israel. In addition the oracles concerning Edom in MT and LXX are relatively long ones, which is in accord with their significant positions in the list. Other than Babylon, of the nations listed some are to be expected, for example, the old enemies, Egypt, Philistia, Moab, Ammon, and Edom (found in the first half of MT's collection), whilst others perhaps are not so, for example, Damascus, Kedar, and Elam (found in the second half).

It is a little harder to explain the length of the oracle concerning Moab in MT's Jeremiah given that it does not have a significant location in the list. In contrast, its position at the end of LXX's arrangement is in keeping with its length, though a new question arises; why should the oracle against Moab close LXX's collection? The question is not why the oracle against Babylon is not last (and its third place position can be explained), but rather, why that concerning Moab and not one of the other nations stands last.

Again, it is possible to provide a plausible explanation for Moab's final position in LXX. Apart from the oracle against Babylon (whose position has already been accounted for) the oracle concerning Moab is the only one that explicitly has the image of drunkenness, (whilst the oracle concerning Edom mentions drinking from the cup in 30:6, it does not speak of drunkenness). Thus, from a literary perspective, this oracle most naturally leads into chapter 32 with its motif of the cup of wrath from which the nations are to drink until they vomit. Interestingly, though, unlike MT, LXX's oracle concerning Moab does not refer to Moab vomiting (48:26 cf. 30:26). Nevertheless, the extraordinary length of the oracle might suggest that it is especially important and that its position at the end of the list is for impact and not merely because it shares subject matter with the next chapter. At this point we turn in more detail to the canonical position of Jeremiah's OANs in MT and LXX to see if this throws any light on the matter.

Canonical Position

In LXX Jeremiah, with the exception of chapters 37–38 (MT 30–31), the poetic, oracular portions tend to be in the first half of the book (1–32), whilst the second half is mainly narrative (there are also narrative portions in the first half).[29] Thus, in LXX's arrangement, the last chapter (52), which is seemingly out of place in MT, more smoothly follows the other narrative passages. Again, then, it may have been a literary or stylistic choice that drove the LXX redactors to organize the material as they did (whether or not it was the original arrangement or a subsequent alteration). However, in LXX's arrangement, Judah receives her oracles, then the oracles concerning the nations are uttered and only after that is the new covenant promised—a few chapters later in 37–38. Therefore, as LXX stands, there is a logical movement in the first part of the book from punishment (Judah's then the nations) to promises of restoration of Judah in chapters 37–38.

In contrast, the promise of Judah's bright future in MT (30–31) comes after most of the poetic oracles of judgment against her, but before those against the nations. As well, the large narrative sections, which also proclaim judgment on Judah, precede the OANs. Thus, loosely, from the structure of the two books, whilst LXX proclaims judgment upon

---

29. It is sometimes thought that LXX Jeremiah had two translators; one for chapters 1–28 and one for 29–52, though Tov (*Septuagint*, 1, 6) deems there to have been one translator and then an editor for 29–52. It is interesting that the OANs fall across both parts of this traditional divide and this fact might call into question either the division marker of the book or the usual understanding that the OANs form one collection. At any rate, I use the term "first half" rather more loosely, based on what appears to be literary style, i.e., poetry versus prose.

all before it signals Judah's restoration, after which come the narrative sections,[30] MT deals with Judah in entirety (judgment and restoration) and the narrative sections (mainly relating to Judah) before it turns to the nations.[31]

Therefore, their place at the end of Jeremiah in MT gives the nations a prominence that they do not have in LXX, a stance that is supported by the fact that Babylon has a greater profile in chapter 25 of MT, as has been seen. The status of the nations is also heightened by the fact that near the beginning of the book, the prophet Jeremiah is commissioned as a נביא לגוים "prophet to the nations" (1:5–10), though it must be noted that LXX is identical here. Thus in MT, at the beginning of the book, the middle (ch. 25) and the end, the focus is on the nations, with increasing intensity and greater specificity each time: 1:5–10 briefly sets the scene and reveals that the nations *en masse* are involved; chapter 25 lists many countries by name and provides a short overview of how the story will play out and then chapters 46–51 give the detailed oracles for some of the lands mentioned in chapter 25. To a lesser extent the same could be said of the first half of LXX, though the balanced structure of beginning, middle and end is not there across the whole book.

Holt says similarly when she considers that the "foe from the north" oracles (FNOs) are OANs directed against YHWH's own nation and therefore that the FNOs near the beginning of MT's book of Jeremiah and the OANs towards its close "function as each other's intertexts" and give the book a circular composition.[32] At the epicenter is the prophecy of punishment for Israel/Judah and the nations, particularly Babylon.[33]

Therefore, the OANs can be seen as the final act of YHWH's judgment on the ANE world at that time as described in chapter 25; once Babylon has drunk from the cup, this particular story is over. Carroll, too, comments that "MT ends on a dramatic note; G is much more mod-

---

30. See also Fretheim, *Jeremiah*, 578.

31. Gosse ("Masoretic Redaction," 78–79) argues that chapter 36 (MT) largely determined the organization of LXX whereas the "new perspective of chs. 30–31" caused the MT redactors to reposition the OANs. In this new perspective, the wounds of Jerusalem are healed by transferring the malediction from Jerusalem to Babylon.

32. Holt, "Meaning of an Inclusio," 197, 200, 204.

33. Ibid., 200.

est."[34] That a new story will begin is adumbrated by the promise of restoration that is given to Moab in MT 48:47. This verse is absent in LXX, along with the equivalent of 48:45–46 (the song in Num 21:28–29), for LXX's oracle stops three verses before MT's.

Material Absent from LXX

Promise of Restoration (MT 48:47)

LXX's ending to Jeremiah's oracle concerning Moab (31:44) is a natural conclusion; ὅτι ἐπάξω ταῦτα ἐπὶ Μωαβ ἐν ἐνιαυτῷ ἐπισκέψεως αὐτῶν "because I will bring these things upon Moab in the year of their visiting." MT, on the other hand, ends with ושבתי שבות־מואב באחרית הימים נאם־יהוה עד־הנה משפט מואב "Yet I will restore the fortunes of Moab in the latter days, says the LORD. Thus far is the judgment on Moab" (48:47).

Promises of restoration are relatively rare in MT's OANs, but they are even scarcer in LXX where, usually, they either do not appear at all or the wording is slightly different from MT's. In fact, whereas Egypt, Moab, Ammon and Elam are all offered restoration in MT Jeremiah, only Elam in LXX receives an offer.[35] Thus, whilst MT seems more concerned than LXX to give prominence to the nations and their punishment in Jeremiah (by placing the OANs at the end of the book), it also has a greater emphasis on their restoration, although such an emphasis should not be overstated. MT therefore tends to have a slightly more nuanced perspective on the nations than LXX in that it portrays more facets of YHWH's involvement with them. Furthermore, that not all nations are offered restoration indicates that YHWH's dealings with them are not uniform. For although the OT usually makes a sharp distinction between Israel and "the others," a closer look at "the others" in MT

---

34. Carroll, *Jeremiah*, 757; see also McConville, *Judgment and Promise*, 148.

35. Outside of Jeremiah, LXX has Egypt's promise of restoration in Ezek 29:14, but it does not have Isaiah's blessing on Egypt in MT (19:25). The dubious promise to Tyre and Sidon in Isa 23:17–18 occurs in both MT and LXX. McConville (*Judgment and Promise*, 145) points out that the inclusion of Elam's restoration in LXX Jeremiah weakens the argument that MT Jeremiah's verses of restoration in the OANs were later additions.

shows that each one is treated on an individual basis. This diversity is less obvious in LXX.

As discussed, in LXX the chapters that promise a prosperous future for Israel follow both the poetic oracles against Judah and those against the nations. Having the OANs before chapters 37–38 means that they do not detract from this hope. Similarly, the lack of hope for the nations in Jeremiah's OANs in LXX means that Judah stands in clearer contrast to the state of the nations than perhaps she does in MT. This is particularly so in the case of Moab, for if the oracle against Moab included a final verse of restoration, then the whole corpus of Jeremiah OANs in LXX would end on this note of promise for the nations. As the last verse it would carry greater significance and perhaps even signal hope for the nations as a whole.

In the structure of MT's Jeremiah, on the other hand, the promises to the nations add literary balance to the book. For as Judah is threatened with punishment and later given a glorious promise, the nations are also threatened with punishment and, although they do not receive anything on the scale of chapters 31–32, there are slight hints scattered throughout the OANs that suggest that they, too, might see a brighter future. Having looked at the last verse of restoration in MT, it is time to look at the two previous verses (45–46), which are also absent in LXX.

The Taunt Song of Num 21:28–29 (MT 48:45–46)

Milgrom helpfully summarizes the three theories of the origin of the taunt song in Num 21:28–29.[36] Whatever its origins, however, it appears that in Num 21 only the northern part of Moab had been conquered, whereas in Jer 48 the southern part is affected as well.[37] Lundbom argues that one is not to suppose that in Jer 48 the fugitives came from the south to Heshbon (the enemy was coming from the north), but rather that this is the beginning of the invasion and the fugitives are

---

36. Milgrom, *Numbers*, 462–63; see also Ashley, *Numbers*, 424; Gray, *Numbers*, 303; Budd, *Numbers*, 245, 247; Levine, *Numbers 21–36*, 103–4. Levine also observes that Moab is referred to as עַם־כְּמוֹשׁ in this taunt song (in both Num 21 and Jer 48), but that no other nation (other than Israel) is depicted as the people of their gods (pp. 106–7).

37. Rudolph, *Jeremiah*, 284–88; van Zyl, *Moabites*, 55–56.

from around Heshbon.[38] At any rate, Jer 48:45–46 reemphasizes what the previous three verses have predicted—that Moab will be destroyed as a people—for if the inhabitants escape from one calamity they will be caught by the next until they are all destroyed (48:42–44). Or, as Fretheim puts it, "They will flee, but soon fall exhausted, hardly beyond the shadow of the city from which they flee."[39]

Why the taunt song is quoted in Jer 48 is not clear (and commentators do not tend to ask the question). However, these penultimate two verses of chapter 48 could be understood as an implicit declaration that history repeats itself for Moab. That is, what they said then about Moab they now say again. That could be the case regardless of the tone in which it is sung (though sad irony would fit the overall tone of the chapter).[40] If MT's oracle of judgment finished with these verses, it would be even bleaker than LXX's ending. However, the final verse of restoration completes the cycle and turns the situation around. In the same way that Moab recovered as a nation from Sihon's (and then Israel's) conquests in Num 21 (and countless times since), she will once again stand as a nation on this occasion too. The cycle of destruction followed by restoration seems set to continue, at least for Moab.

Such a cycle is absent in LXX Jer 31 for two reasons. First, since it does not quote the taunt song, there is no link to Moab's repeated history and secondly because it does not address Moab's restoration, there is no sense that Moab has come full circle by the end of the chapter. In this way, then, LXX seems to have a slightly narrower focus in that it concentrates on the offences of Moab and their consequences (in terms of YHWH's judgment) at one particular point in time without reference to Moab's wider story. However, Moab's story in Jer 48 is not "just history," for it is YHWH who restores Moab's fortunes in 48:47, just as it is YHWH who brings punishment upon her (48:44).

---

38. Lundbom, *Jeremiah 37–52*, 309; see also Allen, *Jeremiah*, 487; Duhm, *Jeremia*, 352; Freedman, *Jeremiah*, 312–13; McKeating, *Jeremiah*, 208; McKane, *Jeremiah*, vol. 2, 1197; Rudolph, *Jeremiah*, 283; Weiser, *Der Prophet Jeremia*, 410.

39. Fretheim, *Jeremiah*, 603.

40. Most commentators do not suggest the words are those of mockery, although Lundbom (*Jeremiah 37–52*, 308, 311) points out the text reuses an original mocking song. Rather they implicitly seem to accept the words at face value, even if they do not attribute "genuine grief" to them as Clements (*Jeremiah*, 255) does.

YHWH's involvement is also perhaps drawn out from an extrapolation of Ashley's observation that grammatically "he made" in Num 21:29 refers to Chemosh, not Sihon.⁴¹ That is:

אוי־לך מואב	Woe to you, O Moab!
אבדת עם־כמוש	You are undone, O people of Chemosh!
נתן בניו פליטם	He has made his sons fugitives,
ובנתיו בשבית	and his daughters captives,
למלך אמרי סיחון	to an Amorite king, Sihon. (NRSV)

Though the first half of Jer 48:46 is identical to Num 21:29, the second half diverges, and there is no ambiguous reference to Chemosh as the source behind Moab's predicament.

אוי־לך מואב	Woe to you, O Moab!
אבד עם־כמוש	The people of Chemosh have perished,
כי־לקחו בניך בשבי	for your sons have been taken captive,
ובנתיך בשביה	and your daughters into captivity. (NRSV)

It is obviously impossible to know whether a scribe of Jer 48 had in front of him a text equivalent to MT's Num 21:29 and whether he deliberately altered it (Jer 48:45–46 also does not include the reference to rebuilding Sihon's city in Num 21:27). Nevertheless, in the final form of the text, there is only one hand behind Moab's exile and that is YHWH's.

Jer 48 might even act as a commentary on Num 21 in that it makes explicit at least three factors that are absent in Num 21, the first being YHWH's involvement. Secondly, Jer 48 recognizes that Moab's destruction is not arbitrary, but the result of her sin. Thirdly, Jer 48 adds the new idea that Moab's restoration is also from YHWH, which means that the cycle is more precisely one of sin–punishment–restoration. In fact, the first two ideas seem to emerge with more clarity each time the taunt song is sung over Moab. For there is no indication that Moab's defeat was the result of her wrongdoing when Sihon seized the land and the taunt song was first sung, but by the time the Israelites reused the song,

---

41. Ashley, *Numbers*, 426.

the implication is that Moab was defeated because she did not allow them to pass through her land. Similarly, YHWH's involvement is not apparent when Sihon first conquers the land, but it is implied when the Israelites seize Moab from Sihon. However, when the taunt song is reused in Jer 48 the link between Moab's offences and YHWH's punishment is perspicuous.

Also interesting is that whereas MT concludes verse 44 with an unambiguous נאם־יהוה, there is no equivalent in LXX, despite this verse concluding the oracle. This is not the only instance where MT explicitly attributes words to YHWH where LXX does not; there are five occasions where MT has נאם־יהוה (or, in the case of 48:15 a fuller version) where LXX does not: 48:15, 25, 30, 43, and 44.[42] There is no apparent reason for the difference, either in terms of LXX omitting or MT expanding, and it might simply be a stylistic difference (see the discussion in chapter 3), but the contrast highlights YHWH's high profile in MT Jer 48.

The Eagle and the Laboring Woman (MT 48:40–41)

For thus says the LORD: <u>Look, he shall swoop down like an eagle, and spread his wings against Moab;</u>	⁴⁰ כִּי־כֹה אָמַר יְהוָה הִנֵּה כַנֶּשֶׁר יִדְאֶה וּפָרַשׂ כְּנָפָיו אֶל־מוֹאָב׃	⁴⁰ ὅτι οὕτως εἶπε κύριος	because thus did the Lord say:
<u>the towns</u> shall be taken and the strongholds seized. <u>The hearts of the warriors of Moab, on that day, shall be like the heart of a woman in labor.</u>	⁴¹ נִלְכְּדָה הַקְּרִיּוֹת וְהַמְּצָדוֹת נִתְפָּשָׂה וְהָיָה לֵב גִּבּוֹרֵי מוֹאָב בַּיּוֹם הַהוּא כְּלֵב אִשָּׁה מְצֵרָה׃	⁴¹ Ἐλήμφθη Ακκαριωθ, καὶ τὰ ὀχυρώματα συνελήμφθη·	<u>Hakkarioth</u> was seized, and the strongholds were also seized.

The final major text that is not present in LXX is found across the last half of verses 40 and 41. Together these two half verses are almost identical to MT Jer 49:22 (see Table 4). As with 48:45–46, then, the material that is missing from LXX in 31:40–41 is that which is shared with

---

42. Jeremiah 48:47 also has the term, but since LXX has no equivalent at all to this verse, it is not counted here.

other texts. In fact, the same could be said of 48:47. This may indicate that these verses in MT were quotations that were subsequently inserted, especially as the shared material is interleaved with 48:40–41. For it is perhaps more likely that an MT redactor would weave new material into an original text than an LXX author would remove "quoted" parts from two verses, but leave the "unquoted" elements.[43]

The metaphors mean that MT's version is more poetic (a topic to which we will return). As well, the force is slightly stronger in MT with its depiction of the strength of the destroyer[44] (an eagle) compared to the weakness of Moab's strongest men (women in labor). This adds to the weighty conclusion of MT's oracle, which I argued is given by the quotation of the taunt song found in Numbers. That is, 40–41 and 45–46 reiterate the desperate and weak predicament of Moab and the inevitability of her destruction in a way that LXX does not at this point. Against such verses, the final verse of restoration stands in stark contrast.

Having looked at the main phrases present in MT but not LXX, we now turn to the differences between the two texts, including single words found only in MT. These are often only small variations and whether they have an impact on the nature of the two oracles is the matter now under investigation.

Differing Material

Rather than discuss each individual variation in turn, I have grouped them according to subject matter, in line with issues that, as will become clear throughout the rest of the work, are key ones in MT Jer 48.

---

43. Indeed, those who deem these verses to be an addition in MT are: Duhm, *Jeremia*, 351; Holladay, *Jeremiah, vol. 2*, 353; McKane, *Jeremiah, vol. 2*, clxvii, 1194; Rudolph, *Jeremiah*, 283; Volz, *Studien*, 314. However, Thompson (*Jeremiah*, 713) and Weiser (*Der Prophet Jeremia*, 409) consider that LXX removed the verses, since they are repeated material.

44. E.g., McKane, *Jeremiah, vol. 2*, 1194.

Lament

For every head is shaved and every beard cut off; on all the hands there are gashes, and on the loins sackcloth.	³⁷ כִּי כָל־רֹאשׁ קָרְחָה וְכָל־זָקָן גְּרֻעָה עַל כָּל־יָדַיִם גְּדֻדֹת וְעַל־מָתְנַיִם שָׂק:	³⁷ πᾶσαν κεφαλὴν ἐν παντὶ τόπῳ ξυρηθήσονται, καὶ πᾶς πώγων ξυρηθήσεται, καὶ πᾶσαι χεῖρες κόψονται, καὶ ἐπὶ πάσης ὀσφύος σάκκος.	They will have every head <u>in every place</u> shaved, and every beard shall be shaved, and all hands shall beat, and sackcloth on every loin,
On all the house-tops of Moab and in the squares there is <u>nothing but lamentation</u>; for I have broken <u>Moab</u> like a vessel that no one wants, <u>says the LORD</u>.	³⁸ עַל כָּל־גַּגּוֹת מוֹאָב וּבִרְחֹבֹתֶיהָ כֻּלֹּה מִסְפֵּד כִּי־שָׁבַרְתִּי אֶת־מוֹאָב כִּכְלִי אֵין־חֵפֶץ בּוֹ נְאֻם־יְהוָה:	³⁸ <u>καὶ</u> ἐπὶ πάντων τῶν δωμάτων Μωαβ καὶ ἐπὶ πλατείαις αὐτῆς, ὅτι συνέτριψα, φησὶ κύριος, ὡς ἀγγεῖον, οὗ οὐκ ἔστι χρεία αὐτοῦ.	<u>even</u> on all the housetops of Moab and in her squares, because I have crushed her, quoth the Lord, like a container for which no one has any use.

There is a slightly greater emphasis on lament in MT than in LXX.⁴⁵ Perhaps the most striking example is in verse 38 of MT, which has a phrase that is not in LXX; כלה מספד "[in] all of her [there is] a wailing." Furthermore, LXX begins the verse with a conjunction (καὶ) that links it with the previous verse. These two minor differences mean that in LXX, the first half of verse 38 expands what verse 37 means by the mourning rituals happening ἐν παντὶ τόπῳ "in every place" (a phrase that is not in MT), by explicitly stating that it takes place on all the housetops and in the squares. MT, on the other hand, notes, like LXX, that all heads and beards are shaved but then adds as a separate "sentence" that on all the housetops and in the squares there is wailing. There is little difference between them, but MT reiterates the act of mourning, rather than em-phasizing the extent of it as LXX does. Similarly, the reference to זעקה "cry" in verse 4 is absent in LXX.

---

45. I will argue in chapter 7 that the lament in MT Jer 48 and MT Isa 15–16 should not be taken as mockery but should be read as genuine. I do not repeat the arguments here since they stand for LXX too and there is nothing significantly different in LXX in this respect.

For <u>at the ascent</u> of Luhith they <u>go up</u> weeping <u>bitterly</u>; for <u>at the descent</u> of Horonaim <u>they</u> have heard the distressing cry of anguish.	= כ] מַעֲלֵה כִּי [5 = ק] הַלֻּחוֹת [46*הַלּוּחִית בִּבְכִי יַעֲלֶה־בֶּכִי כִּי בְמוֹרַד חוֹרֹנַיִם צָרֵי צַעֲקַת־ שֶׁבֶר שָׁמֵעוּ׃	5 ὅτι <u>ἐπλήσθη</u> Αλαωθ ἐν <u>κλαυθμῷ</u>, ἀναβήσεται κλαίων ἐν ὁδῷ Ωρωναιμ, κραυγὴν συντρίμματος ἠκούσ<u>ατε</u>	Because Halaoth <u>was filled</u> by weeping, he will go up weeping <u>by way</u> of Horonaim; a cry of fracture <u>you</u> have heard.

Verse 5 in MT reads בבכי יעלה־בכי "they go up weeping bitterly," but LXX's version is rephrased in a way that appears to incorporate both בבכי and בכי.[47] Thus neither LXX nor MT have a greater emphasis than the other on the aspect of lament at this point; in MT the weeping is more intense but it only occurs once, whereas in LXX the weeping is not as intense, but there are two mentions of it. The first "they" in MT would naturally denote the little ones in the previous verse and presumably the "he" in LXX refers to Halaoth, there being no reference to the little ones in verse 4. The second "they" and "you," respectively, refer to the Moabites and even if it is not clear exactly which party of Moabites are in focus, in both cases the bitter weeping is intensified through hearing the cries of others' anguish elsewhere.

In verse 17, Moab's neighbors are instructed to mourn over her in NRSV and to "stir for him" in NETS. נוד can take a variety of meanings and κινέω is an appropriate Greek translation of it, although κινέω does not carry a sense of grief as נוד does. Therefore, since the context suggests that נוד means "to show grief," the element of lament is somewhat removed from LXX at this point.

Therefore <u>I</u> wail for Moab; <u>I</u> cry out for all <u>Moab</u>; for the people of Kir-<u>heres</u> <u>I mourn</u>.	עַל־כֵּן עַל־מוֹאָב 31 אֲיֵלִיל וּלְמוֹאָב כֻּלֹּה אֶזְעָק אֶל־אַנְשֵׁי קִיר־חֶרֶשׂ יֶהְגֶּה׃	31 διὰ τοῦτο ἐπὶ Μωαβ ὀλολύ<u>ζετε</u> πάντοθεν, βοήσ<u>ατε</u> ἐπ' ἄνδρας Κιρ Αδας αὐχμοῦ.	Therefore wail for Moab on all sides; shout to the men of Kir <u>Hadas, of drought</u>.

46. See footnote 4.
47. See also McKane, *Jeremiah*, vol. 2, 1159.

The intensity of lament is also heightened in MT in verse 31. The structure of the verse is somewhat different in LXX and MT, but there are two main points to note. First, the final word is יהגה "he mourns" in MT (see footnote 14 for NRSV's translation "I mourn"), whereas it is αὐχμοῦ "of drought" in LXX.[48] Secondly, LXX summons others to wail and cry for Moab (imperative verbs), whereas in MT, YHWH himself wails and cries (first person verbs).

| More than for Jazer I weep for you, O vine of Sibmah! Your branches crossed over the sea, reached as far as Jazer; upon your summer fruits and your vintage the destroyer has fallen. | ³²מִבְּכִי יַעְזֵר אֶבְכֶּה־לָּךְ הַגֶּפֶן שִׂבְמָה נְטִישֹׁתַיִךְ עָבְרוּ יָם עַד יָם יַעְזֵר נָגָעוּ עַל־קֵיצֵךְ וְעַל־בְּצִירֵךְ שֹׁדֵד נָפָל: | ³² ὡς κλαυθμὸν Ιαζηρ ἀποκλαύσομαί σοι, ἄμπελος Σεβημα· κλήματά σου διῆλθε θάλασσαν, πόλεις Ιαζηρ ἥψαντο· ἐπὶ ὀπώραν σου, ἐπὶ τρυγηταῖς σου ὄλεθρος ἐπέπεσε. | As with the weeping for Iazer I will weep for you, O vine of Sebema! Your branches crossed over the sea; cities reached Iazer; upon your summer fruit, upon your grape gatherers destruction has fallen. |

Also in MT, YHWH weeps over the vine of Sibmah (verse 32) "more" (מן) than he does over Jazer, whereas in LXX there is no comparative; simply ὡς "as."[49] Since the variations later in the verse concerning ים appear to have little impact on the meaning of the text, they will not be discussed here.

There are other slight variations in these verses of lament (verses 31–38), which are seemingly insignificant, but which are included here for completeness (except for the ד/ר confusion in verses 32 and 34, which are mentioned in the introduction). In verse 33, LXX has the additional πρωὶ "in the morning" but no equivalent of כרמל "fruitful land" and in verse 37 there is no equivalent in LXX of the preposition על "on" in (על כל־ידים גדדת "on all the hands there are gashes").

Overall, however, the weeping is more bitter and widespread in MT than LXX. Furthermore, YHWH's wailing in the first person in verse 31 in MT, as opposed to LXX's call to mourn, raises the issue of

---

48. McKane (*Jeremiah, vol. 2*, 1184) deems LXX's translation to be "obscure" here.
49. See discussion in McKane, *Jeremiah, vol. 2*, 1184–85.

whether MT and LXX present YHWH's involvement with Moab any differently to each other.

Divine Involvement

| Gladness and joy have been taken away from the <u>fruitful</u> land of Moab; <u>I have stopped</u> the wine from the wine presses; no one treads them with shouts of joy; the shouting is not the shout of joy. | ³³וְנֶאֶסְפָה שִׂמְחָה וָגִיל מִכַּרְמֶל וּמֵאֶרֶץ מוֹאָב וְיַיִן מִיקָבִים הִשְׁבַּתִּי לֹא־יִדְרֹךְ הֵידָד הֵידָד לֹא הֵידָד: | ³³ συνεψήσθη χαρμοσύνη καὶ εὐφροσύνη ἐκ γῆς Μωαβίτιδος, καὶ οἶνος ἦν ἐπὶ ληνοῖς σου· <u>πρωὶ οὐκ ἐπάτησαν</u>· αιδεδ αιδεδ, οὐκ [ἐποίησαν] αιδεδ. | Joy and gladness were swept away from the land of Moabitis, and wine was in your vats; they did not tread <u>in the early morning</u>; "aided" "aided," [they did] not "aided" |

Verse 33 in LXX is hardly comprehensible, which perhaps indicates that the Greek translator has been unable to make sense of the underlying text and, in fact, gives up completely at the end. This raises the question of whether he had a damaged text. Nevertheless, this verse is the one occasion other than verse 31 where YHWH speaks in the first person in MT but not in LXX. For MT has השבתי "I have put an end to," a word that finds no counterpart in LXX. Thus in MT YHWH is explicitly responsible for Moab's state and therefore, like the lament in verse 31, Moab's predicament is given stronger weight by YHWH's admission.

| <u>We</u> have heard of the pride of Moab—he is very proud—of <u>his loftiness, his pride, and his arrogance</u>, and the haughtiness of his heart. | ²⁹שָׁמַעְנוּ גְאוֹן־מוֹאָב גֵּאֶה מְאֹד גָּבְהוֹ וּגְאוֹנוֹ וְגַאֲוָתוֹ וְרֻם לִבּוֹ: | ²⁹ <u>ἤκουσα</u> ὕβριν Μωαβ, ὕβρισε λίαν <u>ὕβριν αὐτοῦ καὶ ὑπερηφανίαν αὐτοῦ</u>, καὶ ὑψώθη ἡ καρδία αὐτοῦ. | <u>I</u> heard of Moab's insolence; he was very insolent in <u>his insolence and his arrogance</u>. And his heart was lifted up. |

There is one instance where LXX uses the first person singular where MT does not; instead of the ambiguous "we" (שמענו) in 48:29, LXX has "I" (ἤκουσα). However, there seems to be little significance in this as far as divine involvement is concerned, for here YHWH is not engaged in some action over or against Moab (for example, weeping or judging); rather, he simply hears of Moab's insolence.

Of more import is the reference to בת־דיבון in verse 18 of MT, for which LXX has no equivalent (except Sept.^(AQ*)).[50] If בת־דיבון is a relational term ("daughter Dibon") rather than merely denoting a certain people ("daughter of Dibon")[51] then this is an aspect that is missing in LXX, even if the term is used in mockery in MT. Such a connection between YHWH and Moab may also be implicit in the reference to זעקה צעיריה (qere) "cry of her little ones" in verse 4.[52] LXX seems, instead, to have had as its *Vorlage* צעורה (Ζογορα "Zogora / Zoar"), a reading attested to by four Hebrew manuscripts as well.[53]

In the second half of verse 38, MT specifies that YHWH has broken את־מואב, whereas Moab is not explicitly named in Ziegler's edition of LXX. MT's naming of Moab a second time in a section in which YHWH's lament and his punishment are intermingled stresses the fact that this whole exchange is between these two parties alone and that YHWH's purview extends only to Moab at this point. Again, then, when all these small differences are placed together it can be argued that MT presents YHWH as being slightly more involved with Moab than he is in LXX.

Moab's Offences

We have heard of the pride of Moab—he is very proud—of his loftiness, his pride, and his arrogance, and the haughtiness of his heart.	²⁹ שָׁמַעְנוּ גְאוֹן־מוֹאָב גֵּאֶה מְאֹד גָּבְהוֹ וּגְאוֹנוֹ וְגַאֲוָתוֹ וָרֻם לִבּוֹ:	²⁹ ἤκουσα ὕβριν Μωαβ, ὕβρισε λίαν ὕβριν αὐτοῦ καὶ ὑπερηφανίαν αὐτοῦ, καὶ ὑψώθη ἡ καρδία αὐτοῦ.	I heard of Moab's insolence; he was very insolent in his insolence and his arrogance. And his heart was lifted up.

---

50. McKane, *Jeremiah*, vol. 2, 1174.

51. See chapter 4 for a short discussion on this.

52. זעקה is an absolute noun and therefore ungrammatical in connection with צעיריה.

53. McKane, *Jeremiah*, vol. 2, 1159.

I myself know his <u>insolence</u>, <u>says the LORD</u>; his <u>boasts</u> are false, his deeds are false.	30 אֲנִ֤י יָדַ֨עְתִּי֙ נְאֻם־יְהוָ֔ה עֶבְרָת֖וֹ וְלֹא־כֵ֑ן בַּדָּ֖יו לֹא־כֵ֥ן עָשֽׂוּ׃	30 ἐγὼ δὲ ἔγνων ἔργα αὐτοῦ· οὐχὶ τὸ <u>ἱκανὸν αὐτοῦ</u>, οὐχ οὕτως ἐποίησε.	But I knew his <u>works</u>. It was not <u>enough for him</u>; he did not do thus.

    MT is also more expansive than LXX in describing Moab's offences in verses 29–30. Both MT and LXX begin verse 29 by stating that Moab is very proud and end with her haughtiness of heart. In between, however, MT describes her pride in three ways (גבהו וגאונו וגאותו "his haughtiness and his pride and his arrogance"), whereas LXX uses only two (ὕβριν αὐτοῦ καὶ ὑπερηφανίαν αὐτοῦ "his insolence and his arrogance"). In addition, the ר/ד confusion in verse 30 means that in MT, YHWH specifically knows of עברתו "his insolence" whereas in LXX he knows more generally about ἔργα αὐτοῦ "his works." Furthermore, whereas MT has בדיו "his boasts / idle chatter" in verse 30, LXX seems to have a *Vorlage* of דַּיּוֹ "his sufficiency."[54] The result is that Moab's pride is more forcefully presented in MT than in LXX in these two verses. Similarly, in verse 7, MT accuses Moab of trusting both במעשיך ובאוצרותיך "in your deeds and in your treasures," whereas LXX only maligns her for trusting ἐν ὀχυρώμασί σου "in your strongholds."

    The reverse is the case in verse 11, however, for in LXX Moab is accused because πεποιθὼς ἦν ἐπὶ τῇ δόξῃ αὐτοῦ "he trusted in his glory," whereas in MT, Moab has simply been ושקט הוא אל־שמריו "(and) settled like wine on its dregs." Moab's wickedness is also emphasized in LXX in verse 16, where (apparently) the ambiguous רעה has been translated as πονηρία "wickedness." In MT, the sense of רעה appears to be one of misery or distress, for which LXX could have used either τὰ κακά (for example, Jer 25:17; 28:60, 64), which has a broader meaning more akin to רעה, or it could even have employed κάκωσις "cruel suffering, oppression" (for example, Jer 28:2).

    Another interesting textual point worth noting is Rösel's observation that LXX often uses εἰδώλοί rather than θεοί to denote foreign gods (for example, Moab's εἰδώλοί in Num 25:2). However, in Jer 31:35, Moab's gods are referred to as θεοί, which might imply (if Rösel is correct) that the oracle is not as polemical as it might be and even that idolatry is not the main focus of 31:35.

54. Ibid., 1183.

There are other minor differences between MT and LXX in the verses relating to Moab's offences, but they seemingly bear little weight on a reading of the texts. These are: the accusation in MT's verse 7 that Moab trusted במעשיך "in your deeds" as opposed to LXX's ὀχυρώμασί "in your strongholds"; the absence of the first כי in LXX's verse 30; and LXX's preposition ἐπὶ in verse 35 (ἀναβαίνοντα ἐπὶ βωμὸν "when he ascends upon an altar"), in contrast to MT's lack of preposition, leading to the awkward reading מעלה במה. As well, the end of verse 27 in MT has כי־מדי דבריך בו תתנודד "but whenever you spoke of him you shook your head," whereas LXX has ὅτι ἐπολέμεις αὐτόν; "is it because you kept fighting him?" Though in MT the sense seems to be one of mockery whereas LXX implies violent action, the idea in both is that Moab mistreated Israel in some way. On balance, then, it seems that neither LXX nor MT focus more on Moab's offences than the other. Whether the same can be said for the punishment YHWH inflicts on Moab is the matter now at hand.

Moab's Punishment

Concerning Moab. Thus says the LORD <u>of hosts, the God of Israel</u>: Alas for Nebo, it is laid waste! Kiriathaim <u>is put to shame</u>, it is taken; <u>the fortress is put to shame and broken down</u>;	¹ לְמוֹאָב כֹּה־אָמַר יְהוָה צְבָאוֹת אֱלֹהֵי יִשְׂרָאֵל הוֹי אֶל־נְבוֹ כִּי שֻׁדָּדָה הֹבִישָׁה נִלְכְּדָה קִרְיָתָיִם הֹבִישָׁה הַמִּשְׂגָּב וָחָתָּה:	¹ Τῇ Μωαβ. Οὕτως εἶπε κύριος Οὐαὶ ἐπὶ Ναβαυ, ὅτι ὤλετο· ἐλήμφθη Καριαθαιμ, ᾐσχύνθη <u>Αμασαγαβ</u> καὶ <u>Αταθ</u>.	For Moab. Thus did the Lord say: Woe for Nabau, because he perished! Kariathaim was taken; <u>Hamasagab</u> was put to shame, and <u>Hatath</u>.
The destroyer shall come upon every town, <u>and no town shall escape</u>; the valley shall perish, and the plain shall be destroyed, as the LORD has spoken.	⁸ וְיָבֹא שֹׁדֵד אֶל־כָּל־עִיר וְעִיר לֹא תִמָּלֵט וְאָבַד הָעֵמֶק וְנִשְׁמַד הַמִּישֹׁר אֲשֶׁר אָמַר יְהוָה:	⁸ καὶ ἥξει ὄλεθρος ἐπὶ πᾶσαν πόλιν, <u>οὐ μὴ σωθῇ</u>, καὶ ἀπολεῖται ὁ αὐλών, καὶ ἐξολεθρευθήσεται ἡ πεδινή, καθὼς εἶπε κύριος.	And destruction shall come upon every city; <u>it shall not be saved</u>. And the valley shall perish, and the plain shall be destroyed utterly, as the Lord has said.

In verse 1 MT asserts that Kiriathaim is put to shame (הבישׁה) as well as taken, whereas LXX does not have an equivalent to this first instance of הבישׁה. In verse 8, too, MT reiterates the fact that ועיר לא "no city" will escape, whereas LXX does not repeat the subject. Whilst these do not make any significant difference to the sense, MT gives a slightly fuller and therefore arguably more emphatic, account of Moab's punishment than LXX.

Verse 26 in MT informs us that וספק מואב בקיאו. This literally reads "and Moab shall clap in his vomit," which most English translations render something akin to "and Moab will wallow / splash in his vomit."[55] In contrast, LXX has καὶ ἐπικρούσει Μωαβ ἐν χειρὶ αὐτοῦ "and Moab shall clap with his hand." The final result is that MT paints a more graphic (and abhorrent) picture of Moab's punishment than LXX at this point.

On the other hand, it could be argued that LXX's descriptions of Moab's judgment are sometimes more striking than MT's, for in two instances Moab falls to waste in MT but is burnt in LXX (verses 9 and 34).[56] As well, in MT verse 32, the destroyer (שׁדד) falls upon Moab's vineyards (בציר), but in LXX, destruction (ὄλεθρος) falls on her grape-gatherers (τρυγηταὶ). Therefore, whilst in MT the destroyer is personified, it is only the vintage that is affected, whereas in LXX the people themselves are attacked.

Again, there are slight variations that have little impact on the oracle. First, MT silences (תדמי) whereas LXX brings to a stop (καὶ παῦσιν παύσεται) in verse 2. Secondly, as opposed to MT, which has ונבליהם "their jars" in verse 12, LXX has τὰ κεράσματα αὐτοῦ "his mix-

---

55. Brueggemann, *Jeremiah*, 447; Carroll, *Jeremiah*, 786–87; Duhm, *Jeremia*, 349 ("hinklatschen wird Moab in sein Gespei"); Feinberg, *Jeremiah*, 304; Freedman, *Jeremiah*, 308; Jones, *Jeremiah*, 505; Lundbom, *Jeremiah 37–52*, 283; McKane, *Jeremiah*, vol. 2, 1178, 1180; Miller, "Jeremiah", 888, 891; Stulman, *Jeremiah*, 364. Allen (*Jeremiah*, 475) has "empty its stomach with its vomit"; Holladay (*Jeremiah*, vol. 2, 343, 360) has "overflow" as does Thompson (*Jeremiah*, 707), whilst Smothers (in Keown et al., *Jeremiah 26–52*, 304) has "dash his hand in his vomit," and Volz (*Der Prophet Jeremia*, 413) has "über seinem Gespei speien" ("vomit over his vomit"—see also *Studien*, 310–11). Calvin (*Jeremiah*, 27, 28, 29) has "he clapped / struck his hands together" ("complodo") though he suggests the text should be translated to mean that Moab would roll in its own vomit ("involvit").

56. The idea of water being burnt is strange in v. 34.

tures" (possibly a scribal error for τὰ κέραμα αὐτοῦ "his horn-shaped bowls").[57] Thirdly, in LXX verse 36, what (ἃ) Moab has made has perished (ἀπώλετο), whereas MT specifies that the riches she made (יתרת עשׂה) have perished (אבדו).[58] Fourthly, in verses 21–24 MT has a reference to ערי ארץ מואב "cities of the land of Moab" (verse 24), whereas LXX just has πόλεις Μωαβ "cities of Moab."

In summary, then, the variations between MT and LXX with regard to Moab's punishment demonstrate that sometimes MT has the more vivid portrayal, but on other occasions LXX does. On balance, however, taking into account the material that is additional to MT (40–41, 45–46), YHWH's punishment is more forceful in MT than LXX.

Wings, Signs, Salt (v. 9)

| Set aside <u>salt</u> for Moab, for she will <u>surely fall</u>; her towns shall become a <u>desolation</u>, with no inhabitant in them. | ⁹ תְּנוּ־צִיץ לְמוֹאָב כִּי נָצֹא תֵּצֵא וְעָרֶיהָ לְשַׁמָּה תִהְיֶינָה מֵאֵין יוֹשֵׁב בָּהֵן׃ | ⁹ δότε <u>σημεῖα</u> τῇ Μωαβ, ὅτι <u>ἀφῇ ἀναφθήσεται</u>, καὶ πᾶσαι αἱ πόλεις αὐτῆς εἰς <u>ἄβατον</u> ἔσονται· <u>πόθεν</u> ἔνοικος αὐτῇ; | Give <u>signs</u> to Moab, because she will <u>be kindled with kindling</u>, and all her cities shall become <u>untrodden</u>; <u>from where</u> will she get an inhabitant? |

In 48:6 the speaker of the oracle turns to Moab and urges her to flee, whilst in verse 9 he compels others to give wings / salt (MT) or signs (LXX) to her so that she may fly away (MT) or be kindled (LXX). There are textual difficulties with the first half of the verse in MT, partly because it appears that נצא תצא stem from two different roots, and partly because of the difficulty in translating the *hapax legomenon*, ציץ. Space precludes a proper discussion here, but a brief summary is as follows. Traditionally, ציץ has been understood to mean "wing," though other possible translations include "flower" (see Vulgate), "signs" from LXX's σημεῖα, or "salt" given the Ugaritic gloss *sisuma* on the Akkadian

---

57. Lust et al., *Greek-English Lexicon*, 337.

58. יתרת is a feminine singular, עשׂה is a masculine singular, and אבדו is a plural so does not agree with either of the preceding words. LXX does not have this problem.

eqlet tabti "fields of salt": *sisuma* is the plural of *ss*, which is considered to be salt.[59]

The translation affects whether the verse is meant in a positive or negative way. For instance it may be a command to make Moab's lands a saline waste, or it may be a summons to help her flee. Certainly it would seem that in LXX, signs appear to be some form of aid or at least warning, though it is hard to make sense of the verse.

To summarize again, my conclusions are as follows: Smothers' observation that salt is always rendered by another word than *ss* in Akkadian and that *ss* only ever means salt marshes is a compelling argument against the comparatively new idea that Moab is to be offered salt. Moreover, that "salt" as a translation for the Hebrew ציץ comes from an Ugaritic gloss on an Akkadian text is a procedure that, to use de Waard's words, seems "farfetched."[60] McKane's and de Waard's comments that signposts are inappropriate for such a chaotic situation are also persuasive. נתן becomes redundant if the sense is sending her out in bloom or taking her crown since Moab is not given anything. Therefore, it seems to me that "wings" becomes the most likely option, in this case, the underlying verb would be נצא "to fly."

So, if Moab is to be given wings to fly away, the question becomes whether it is a straightforward command or an ironic one intended to mock Moab. Either are plausible, but given the command to flee in verse 6 (which is not generally considered to be ironic), I would tend to accept verse 9 as a summons to Moab's neighbors to help her flee away. This understanding seems to cohere with the tenor of LXX, even though the wording differs. It also has the support of traditional interpretation, for example, Rashi.[61] This being said, it is a futile command, for it is clear that Moab will not escape destruction. So, whilst Moab is in need of help and those around are to supply it, such aid can only have a limited effect in the circumstances. Read in this way the verse (in both MT and

---

59. For discussion on this see Allen, *Jeremiah*, 476; Calvin, *Jeremiah*, 13–14; de Waard, *Handbook*, 189–90; Duhm, *Jeremia*, 347; Feinberg, *Jeremiah*, 302; Freedman, *Jeremiah*, 304; Fretheim, *Jeremiah*, 598; Holladay, *Jeremiah, vol. 2*, 341; Jones, *Jeremiah*, 502; Lundbom, *Jeremiah 37–52*, 261; McKane, *Jeremiah, vol. 2*, 1163–65; McKeating, *Jeremiah*, 204; Rudolph, *Jeremiah*, 275; Smothers in Keown et al., *Jeremiah 26–52*, 313–14; Stulman, *Jeremiah*, 362; Thompson, *Jeremiah*, 704; Volz, *Studien*, 208.

60. de Waard, *Handbook*, 190.

61. Rashi, *Complete Tanach*, Online.

LXX) adds to the rhetoric of Jer 48 in terms of the pathos behind such destruction and in the way that divine punishment is meted out with a call for human assistance to the punished. Although both MT and LXX contain the rhetoric on this occasion, overall their literary styles vary slightly.

Literary Form

MT is slightly more poetically phrased than LXX. For instance, in verse 15 MT balances עלה "has come up"[62] with ירדו "have gone down," but LXX does not have an equivalent of עלה. Similarly, in verse 5 MT balances weeping at the מעלה "ascent" with crying at the מורד "descent," while LXX has ἐν ὁδῷ "by way" where MT has מורד. As well, although MT begins both halves of verse 10 with a curse (ארור ... וארור), LXX has only the first (ἐπικατάρατος).

On a couple of occasions, MT's text carries an urgency (even if the sense is one of mockery) that is missing in LXX in that it uses imperatives where LXX does not: עזבו "leave" and היו "be" in verse 28 (though עזבו could be pointed as a perfect), which are rendered by Aorists in the Greek (respectively, κατέλιπον "they left" and ἐγενήθησαν "they became"); and לכו "Come" in verse 2, which is not present in LXX at all.

There are another two verses where a statement is emphatic in MT but not in LXX. The first is verse 9 where πόθεν makes LXX's clause a question, as opposed to MT's statement and the second is the opening to verse 27. LXX has what looks to be quite a literal translation of MT's ואם לוא ... אם, that is, καὶ εἰ μὴ ... εἰ, but the result is that the Greek (which is difficult to understand) has conditional clauses rather than what is generally considered to be an emphatic statement or rhetorical question.[63]

In other words, as well as MT being more poetic than LXX in terms of balancing phrases, it is also a little more urgent and emphatic.

---

62. See footnote 11 re the singular form of עלה.

63. Brueggemann, *Jeremiah*, 447; Clements, *Jeremiah*, 253; Duhm, *Jeremia*, 349; Holladay, *Jeremiah*, vol. 2, 360; Lundbom, *Jeremiah 37–52*, 284; McKane, *Jeremiah*, vol. 2, 1178, 1180; Smothers in Keown et al., *Jeremiah 26–52*, 317.

Conclusion—Differing Theologies?

In summary, then, a comparison of the two has shown that MT's version of Jeremiah's oracle concerning Moab is nuanced slightly differently from LXX's oracle in a number of ways. Each also sheds light on the other, although for the purposes of this work the interest lies in how LXX illumines MT.

The length of the oracle in MT suggests that it is significant, yet its location within the collection does not reinforce the suggestion. However, in LXX both the length and its position at the end of the collection pay tribute to Moab's significance, even though placing the oracle last may have been a literary decision given the subject matter of drunkenness that links to the next chapter. Nevertheless, since Moab is important in LXX, one may reasonably infer the same in MT, which therefore suggests that one is to take the signal from the length of the oracle in MT, rather than from its position in the list. Babylon, it transpires, has a greater prominence in MT than in LXX (for example, see 25:1–13) and her special status eclipses Moab's, as is shown by her final position in the OAN collection.

If Moab has a lower status in MT than in LXX in terms of its place within the OAN collection, the canonical placing of the whole OAN collection within the book suggests the opposite. The nations appear (in increasing detail) at the beginning, the middle and the end of MT Jeremiah. The OANs provide the final chapter to the story as set out in chapter 25.[64] In contrast, all the material on the nations is situated in the first half only of LXX Jeremiah, perhaps because LXX has a tendency to delineate between "poetry" (first half of the book) and "prose" (second half) in a way that MT does not. LXX's structure means that the OANs come before the "new covenant" promises, whereas the reverse is the case in MT. Thus in LXX YHWH pronounces his punishment on all nations before there is restoration for Judah, whereas in MT, he deals with Judah completely (punishment and restoration) before he turns to the nations.

MT's occasional promises of restoration to the nations are not only demonstration that MT gives a fuller account of YHWH's dealings with the nations, but show that individual nations are treated differently

---

64. See also McConville, *Judgment and Promise*, 140.

from one another. On the other hand, Judah's hope stands in clearer contrast to the fate of the nations in LXX, precisely because the OANs (apart from Elam's) do not include such promises.

MT's oracle concerning Moab is more intense than LXX's version. For instance, the end of the oracle builds up to a particularly dramatic climax with the quotation of the taunt song, for its inclusion demonstrates that Moab's history repeats itself. Therefore, there is an inevitability about Moab's destruction (and subsequent reversal of fortunes) that is not there in LXX. The material in verses 40–41 found only in MT also adds to the more striking ending of this oracle in MT, for the strength of the eagle (a metaphor for the destroyer) is contrasted with the weakness of a woman in labor (a metaphor for Moab). Lament, too, finds fuller expression in MT. The nature of divine involvement is also heightened in MT in that there is more speech attributed to the first person and phrases that perhaps reflect a connection between YHWH and Moab, for example, זעקה צעיריה (*qere*) "cry of her little ones." However, there seems to be little difference in the way Moab's offences are presented in the two versions of Jeremiah's oracle over Moab.

Therefore, whilst Moab does not appear in a significant position within MT's OAN collection in Jeremiah, the oracle itself gives, on the whole, a more vivid portrayal of Moab's plight than LXX's does. Such a depiction is further enhanced by the oracle's literary style, which is a little more poetic than LXX in terms of word balance and urgent and emphatic tone. Nevertheless, the dissimilarities do not seem major enough to lead to distinct theologies. Instead, I would be more cautious and talk in terms of varying "nuance" (see the opening sentence to this section) rather than different theologies. In fact, the comparison of the two texts has sometimes confirmed previously detected potential nuances, for example, the extent to which Moab is lamented, particularly by YHWH. Whether the comparison between Jer 48 (MT) and Isa 15–16 (MT) will yield similar results will now be seen.

3

Jeremiah 48 in the Light of Isaiah 15–16

Introduction

ONE OF THE STRIKING CHARACTERISTICS OF JER 48 IS THE EXTENT TO which it shares material with other books (primarily prophetic books) in the OT. Although the primary concern here is with the similarities between Jer 48 and Isa 15–16, it may be helpful to preface this discussion with a table of parallels that sets out all the material Jer 48 shares with other texts. Table 4 does this.

TABLE 4: Parallels between Jer 48 and Other OT Texts

v.	Jer 48	Ref(s)	Parallel Passage
1	לְמוֹאָב כֹּה־אָמַר יְהוָה צְבָאוֹת אֱלֹהֵי יִשְׂרָאֵל הוֹי אֶל־נְבוֹ כִּי שֻׁדָּדָה הֹבִישָׁה נִלְכְּדָה קִרְיָתָיִם הֹבִישָׁה הַמִּשְׂגָּב וָחָתָּה:	Isa 15:1	מַשָּׂא מוֹאָב כִּי בְּלֵיל שֻׁדַּד עָר מוֹאָב נִדְמָה כִּי בְּלֵיל שֻׁדַּד קִיר־מוֹאָב נִדְמָה:
2	אֵין עוֹד תְּהִלַּת מוֹאָב בְּחֶשְׁבּוֹן חָשְׁבוּ עָלֶיהָ רָעָה לְכוּ וְנַכְרִיתֶנָּה מִגּוֹי גַּם־מַדְמֵן תִּדֹּמִּי אַחֲרַיִךְ תֵּלֶךְ חָרֶב:		
3	קוֹל צְעָקָה מֵחֹרוֹנָיִם שֹׁד וָשֶׁבֶר גָּדוֹל:	Isa 15:5bβ–γ Isa 15:8a	כִּי דֶּרֶךְ חוֹרֹנַיִם זַעֲקַת־שֶׁבֶר יְעֹעֵרוּ: (כִּי־הִקִּיפָה הַזְּעָקָה אֶת־גְּבוּל מוֹאָב)
4	נִשְׁבְּרָה מוֹאָב הִשְׁמִיעוּ זְּעָקָה [כ = צְעוֹרֶיהָ] [ק = צְעִירֶיהָ]:		

v.	Jer 48	Ref(s)	Parallel Passage
5	כִּי מַעֲלֵה [כ = הַלֻּחוֹת] [ק = הַלּוּחִית*][1] בִּבְכִי יַעֲלֶה־בֶּכִי כִּי בְּמוֹרַד חוֹרֹנַיִם צָרֵי צַעֲקַת־שֶׁבֶר שָׁמֵעוּ:	Isa 15:5b	כִּי מַעֲלֵה הַלּוּחִית בִּבְכִי יַעֲלֶה־בּוֹ כִּי דֶּרֶךְ חוֹרֹנַיִם זַעֲקַת־שֶׁבֶר יְעֹעֵרוּ:
6	נֻסוּ מַלְּטוּ נַפְשְׁכֶם וְתִהְיֶינָה כַּעֲרוֹעֵר בַּמִּדְבָּר:	Jer 51:6aα	נֻסוּ מִתּוֹךְ בָּבֶל וּמַלְּטוּ אִישׁ נַפְשׁוֹ
7	כִּי יַעַן בִּטְחֵךְ בְּמַעֲשַׂיִךְ וּבְאוֹצְרוֹתַיִךְ גַּם־אַתְּ תִּלָּכֵדִי וְיָצָא [כ = כְּמִישׁ] [ק = כְּמוֹשׁ] בַּגּוֹלָה כֹּהֲנָיו וְשָׂרָיו [כ = יַחַד] [ק = יַחְדָּיו]:	Jer 49:3b Amos 1:15	כִּי מַלְכָּם בַּגּוֹלָה יֵלֵךְ כֹּהֲנָיו וְשָׂרָיו יַחְדָּיו: וְהָלַךְ מַלְכָּם בַּגּוֹלָה הוּא וְשָׂרָיו יַחְדָּו אָמַר יְהוָה:
8	וְיָבֹא שֹׁדֵד אֶל־כָּל־עִיר וְעִיר לֹא תִמָּלֵט וְאָבַד הָעֵמֶק וְנִשְׁמַד הַמִּישֹׁר אֲשֶׁר אָמַר יְהוָה:		
9	תְּנוּ־צִיץ לְמוֹאָב כִּי נָצֹא תֵּצֵא וְעָרֶיהָ לְשַׁמָּה תִהְיֶינָה מֵאֵין יוֹשֵׁב בָּהֵן:		מאין יושב is a common motif in the prophets, particularly in Jeremiah, and is often in conjunction with the noun שמה or verb שמם, e.g. Isa 5:9; 6:11; Jer 4:7; 34:22; 44:22; 46:19; 51:29, 37; Zeph 3:6 (examples where שמה and שמם are not used are Jer 26:9; Zeph 2:5)
		Isa 15:9	כִּי מֵי דִימוֹן מָלְאוּ דָם כִּי־אָשִׁית עַל־דִּימוֹן נוֹסָפוֹת לִפְלֵיטַת מוֹאָב אַרְיֵה וְלִשְׁאֵרִית אֲדָמָה:
		Isa 16:1	שִׁלְחוּ־כַר מֹשֵׁל־אֶרֶץ מִסֶּלַע מִדְבָּרָה אֶל־הַר בַּת־צִיּוֹן:
		Isa 16:4	יָגוּרוּ בָךְ נִדָּחַי מוֹאָב הֱוִי־סֵתֶר לָמוֹ מִפְּנֵי שׁוֹדֵד כִּי־אָפֵס הַמֵּץ כָּלָה שֹׁד תַּמּוּ רֹמֵס מִן־הָאָרֶץ:
		Isa 16:5	וְהוּכַן בַּחֶסֶד כִּסֵּא וְיָשַׁב עָלָיו בֶּאֱמֶת בְּאֹהֶל דָּוִד שֹׁפֵט וְדֹרֵשׁ מִשְׁפָּט וּמְהִר צֶדֶק:
10	אָרוּר עֹשֶׂה מְלֶאכֶת יְהוָה רְמִיָּה וְאָרוּר מֹנֵעַ חַרְבּוֹ מִדָּם:		

---

1. See footnote 4 in chapter 2.

v.	Jer 48	Ref(s)	Parallel Passage
11	שַׁאֲנַן מוֹאָב מִנְּעוּרָיו וְשֹׁקֵט הוּא אֶל־שְׁמָרָיו וְלֹא־הוּרַק מִכְּלִי אֶל־כֶּלִי וּבַגּוֹלָה לֹא הָלָךְ עַל־כֵּן עָמַד טַעְמוֹ בּוֹ וְרֵיחוֹ לֹא נָמָר:		
12	לָכֵן הִנֵּה־יָמִים בָּאִים נְאֻם־יְהוָה וְשִׁלַּחְתִּי־לוֹ צֹעִים וְצֵעֻהוּ וְכֵלָיו יָרִיקוּ וְנִבְלֵיהֶם יְנַפֵּצוּ:		
13	וּבֹשׁ מוֹאָב מִכְּמוֹשׁ כַּאֲשֶׁר־בֹּשׁוּ בֵּית יִשְׂרָאֵל מִבֵּית אֵל מִבְטֶחָם:		
14	אֵיךְ תֹּאמְרוּ גִּבּוֹרִים אֲנָחְנוּ וְאַנְשֵׁי־חַיִל לַמִּלְחָמָה:		
15	שֻׁדַּד מוֹאָב וְעָרֶיהָ עָלָה וּמִבְחַר בַּחוּרָיו יָרְדוּ לַטָּבַח נְאֻם־הַמֶּלֶךְ יְהוָה צְבָאוֹת שְׁמוֹ:	Jer 46:18a Jer 51:57b Jer 50:27a	חַי־אָנִי נְאֻם־הַמֶּלֶךְ יְהוָה צְבָאוֹת שְׁמוֹ: נְאֻם־הַמֶּלֶךְ יְהוָה צְבָאוֹת שְׁמוֹ: (חִרְבוּ כָּל־פָּרֶיהָ יֵרְדוּ לַטָּבַח)
16	קָרוֹב אֵיד־מוֹאָב לָבוֹא וְרָעָתוֹ מִהֲרָה מְאֹד:	Jer 50:27b	(הוֹי עֲלֵיהֶם כִּי־בָא יוֹמָם עֵת פְּקֻדָּתָם:)
17	נֻדוּ לוֹ כָּל־סְבִיבָיו וְכֹל יֹדְעֵי שְׁמוֹ אִמְרוּ אֵיכָה נִשְׁבַּר מַטֵּה־עֹז מַקֵּל תִּפְאָרָה:		
18	רְדִי מִכָּבוֹד [כ = יֹשְׁבִי] [ק = וּשְׁבִי] בַצָּמָא יֹשֶׁבֶת בַּת־דִּיבוֹן כִּי־שֹׁדֵד מוֹאָב בָּךְ עָלָה שִׁחֵת מִבְצָרָיִךְ:	Isa 47:1	רְדִי וּשְׁבִי עַל־עָפָר בְּתוּלַת בַּת־בָּבֶל שְׁבִי־לָאָרֶץ אֵין־כִּסֵּא בַּת־כַּשְׂדִּים
19	אֶל־דֶּרֶךְ עִמְדִי וְצַפִּי יוֹשֶׁבֶת עֲרוֹעֵר שַׁאֲלִי־נָס וְנִמְלָטָה אִמְרִי מַה־נִּהְיָתָה:		
20	הֹבִישׁ מוֹאָב כִּי־חַתָּה [כ = הֵילִילִי] [ק = הֵילִילוּ] [וּזְעָקִי] [ק = וּזְעָקוּ] הַגִּידוּ בְאַרְנוֹן כִּי שֻׁדַּד מוֹאָב:		
21	וּמִשְׁפָּט בָּא אֶל־אֶרֶץ הַמִּישֹׁר אֶל־חֹלוֹן וְאֶל־יַהְצָה וְעַל־[כ = מוֹפָעַת] [ק = מֵיפָעַת]:		
22	וְעַל־דִּיבוֹן וְעַל־נְבוֹ וְעַל־בֵּית דִּבְלָתָיִם:		

v.	Jer 48	Ref(s)	Parallel Passage
23	וְעַל קְרִיָּתַיִם וְעַל־בֵּית גָּמוּל וְעַל־בֵּית מְעוֹן:		
24	וְעַל־קְרִיּוֹת וְעַל־בָּצְרָה וְעַל כָּל־עָרֵי אֶרֶץ מוֹאָב הָרְחֹקוֹת וְהַקְּרֹבוֹת:		
25	נִגְדְּעָה קֶרֶן מוֹאָב וּזְרֹעוֹ נִשְׁבָּרָה נְאֻם יְהוָה:	Ps 75:11 (10)	(וְכָל־קַרְנֵי רְשָׁעִים אֲגַדֵּעַ)
26	הַשְׁכִּירֻהוּ כִּי עַל־יְהוָה הִגְדִּיל וְסָפַק מוֹאָב בְּקִיאוֹ וְהָיָה לִשְׂחֹק גַּם־הוּא:	Zeph 2:10b	כִּי חֵרְפוּ וַיַּגְדִּלוּ עַל־עַם יְהוָה צְבָאוֹת:
27	וְאִם לוֹא הַשְּׂחֹק הָיָה לְךָ יִשְׂרָאֵל אִם־בְּגַנָּבִים [כ = נִמְצָאָה] [ק = נִמְצָא] כִּי־מִדֵּי דְבָרֶיךָ בּוֹ תִּתְנוֹדָד:		
28	עִזְבוּ עָרִים וְשִׁכְנוּ בַּסֶּלַע יֹשְׁבֵי מוֹאָב וִהְיוּ כְיוֹנָה תְּקַנֵּן בְּעֶבְרֵי פִי־פָחַת:	Isa 16:2	וְהָיָה כְעוֹף־נוֹדֵד קֵן מְשֻׁלָּח תִּהְיֶינָה בְּנוֹת מוֹאָב מַעְבָּרֹת לְאַרְנוֹן:
		Jer 49:16	(תִּפְלַצְתְּךָ הִשִּׁיא אֹתָךְ זְדוֹן לִבֶּךָ שֹׁכְנִי בְּחַגְוֵי הַסֶּלַע תֹּפְשִׂי מְרוֹם גִּבְעָה כִּי־תַגְבִּיהַּ כַּנֶּשֶׁר קִנֶּךָ מִשָּׁם אוֹרִידְךָ נְאֻם־יְהוָה:)
29	שָׁמַעְנוּ גְאוֹן־מוֹאָב גֵּאֶה מְאֹד גָּבְהוֹ וּגְאוֹנוֹ וְגַאֲוָתוֹ וְרֻם לִבּוֹ:	Isa 16:6a–bα[2]	שָׁמַעְנוּ גְאוֹן־מוֹאָב גֵּא מְאֹד גַּאֲוָתוֹ וּגְאוֹנוֹ
30	אֲנִי יָדַעְתִּי נְאֻם־יְהוָה עֶבְרָתוֹ וְלֹא־כֵן בַּדָּיו לֹא־כֵן עָשׂוּ:	Isa 16:6bβ[3]	וְעֶבְרָתוֹ לֹא־כֵן בַּדָּיו:
31	עַל־כֵּן עַל־מוֹאָב אֲיֵלִיל וּלְמוֹאָב כֻּלֹּה אֶזְעָק אֶל־אַנְשֵׁי קִיר־חֶרֶשׂ יֶהְגֶּה:	Isa 16:7	לָכֵן יְיֵלִיל מוֹאָב לְמוֹאָב כֻּלֹּה יְיֵלִיל לַאֲשִׁישֵׁי קִיר־חֲרֶשֶׂת תֶּהְגּוּ אַךְ־נְכָאִים:
		Isa 15:2bα	עַל־נְבוֹ וְעַל מֵידְבָא מוֹאָב יְיֵלִיל
		Isa 15:5a	לִבִּי לְמוֹאָב יִזְעָק בְּרִיחֶהָ עַד־צֹעַר עֶגְלַת שְׁלִשִׁיָּה
		Isa 15:8b	עַד־אֶגְלַיִם יִלְלָתָהּ וּבְאֵר אֵילִים יִלְלָתָהּ:

2. Not strictly bα since the Masoretes have not inserted a zakeph katōn at this point.
3. See previous footnote (2) re division of verse.

v.	Jer 48	Ref(s)	Parallel Passage
32	מִבְּכִי יַעְזֵר אֶבְכֶּה־לָּךְ הַגֶּפֶן שִׂבְמָה נְטִישֹׁתַיִךְ עָבְרוּ יָם עַד יָם יַעְזֵר נָגָעוּ עַל־קֵיצֵךְ וְעַל־בְּצִירֵךְ שֹׁדֵד נָפָל:	Isa 16:8	כִּי שַׁדְמוֹת חֶשְׁבּוֹן אֻמְלָל גֶּפֶן שִׂבְמָה בַּעֲלֵי גוֹיִם הָלְמוּ שְׂרוּקֶּיהָ עַד־יַעְזֵר נָגָעוּ תָּעוּ מִדְבָּר שְׁלֻחוֹתֶיהָ נִטְּשׁוּ עָבְרוּ יָם:
		Isa 16:9[4]	עַל־כֵּן אֶבְכֶּה בִּבְכִי יַעְזֵר גֶּפֶן שִׂבְמָה אֲרַיָּוֶךְ דִּמְעָתִי חֶשְׁבּוֹן וְאֶלְעָלֵה כִּי עַל־קֵיצֵךְ וְעַל־קְצִירֵךְ הֵידָד נָפָל:
33	וְנֶאֶסְפָה שִׂמְחָה וָגִיל מִכַּרְמֶל וּמֵאֶרֶץ מוֹאָב וְיַיִן מִיקָבִים הִשְׁבַּתִּי לֹא־יִדְרֹךְ הֵידָד לֹא הֵידָד:	Isa 16:10	וְנֶאֱסַף שִׂמְחָה וָגִיל מִן־הַכַּרְמֶל וּבַכְּרָמִים לֹא־יְרֻנָּן לֹא יְרֹעָע יַיִן בַּיְקָבִים לֹא־יִדְרֹךְ הַדֹּרֵךְ הֵידָד הִשְׁבַּתִּי:
		Isa 16:9b	כִּי עַל־קֵיצֵךְ וְעַל־קְצִירֵךְ הֵידָד נָפָל
		Isa 15:6b	(כִּי־יָבֵשׁ חָצִיר כָּלָה דֶשֶׁא יֶרֶק לֹא הָיָה:)
34	מִזַּעֲקַת חֶשְׁבּוֹן עַד־אֶלְעָלֵה עַד־יַהַץ נָתְנוּ קוֹלָם	Isa 15:4a	וַתִּזְעַק חֶשְׁבּוֹן וְאֶלְעָלֵה עַד־יַהַץ נִשְׁמַע קוֹלָם
	מִצֹּעַר עַד־חֹרֹנַיִם עֶגְלַת שְׁלִשִׁיָּה	Isa 15:5a	לִבִּי לְמוֹאָב יִזְעָק בְּרִיחֶהָ עַד־צֹעַר עֶגְלַת שְׁלִשִׁיָּה
	כִּי גַּם־מֵי נִמְרִים לִמְשַׁמּוֹת יִהְיוּ:	Isa 15:6a	כִּי־מֵי נִמְרִים מְשַׁמּוֹת יִהְיוּ
35	וְהִשְׁבַּתִּי לְמוֹאָב נְאֻם־יְהוָה מַעֲלֶה בָמָה וּמַקְטִיר לֵאלֹהָיו:	Isa 15:2a	עָלָה הַבַּיִת וְדִיבֹן הַבָּמוֹת לְבֶכִי
		Isa 16:12[5]	וְהָיָה כִי־נִרְאָה כִּי־נִלְאָה מוֹאָב עַל־הַבָּמָה וּבָא אֶל־מִקְדָּשׁוֹ לְהִתְפַּלֵּל וְלֹא יוּכָל:

4. Bendavid (*Parallels*, 201) considers that שדד (Jer 48:32) is a parallel of הידד (Isa 16:9) so I have included it for completeness, though it is not one I would necessarily have marked given that הידד occurs in the next verse in Jeremiah.

5. Wildberger (*Isaiah 13–27*, 125) deems there to be no link between Jer 48:35 and Isa 16:12 because the content is too dissimilar (*Isaiah 13–27*, 125). Smothers (in Keown et al., *Jeremiah 26–52*, 310), on the other hand, does link the two.

v.	Jer 48	Ref(s)	Parallel Passage
36	עַל־כֵּן לִבִּי לְמוֹאָב כַּחֲלִלִים יֶהֱמֶה וְלִבִּי אֶל־אַנְשֵׁי קִיר־חֶרֶשׂ כַּחֲלִילִים יֶהֱמֶה	Isa 16:11	עַל־כֵּן מֵעַי לְמוֹאָב כַּכִּנּוֹר יֶהֱמוּ וְקִרְבִּי לְקִיר חָרֶשׂ:
	עַל־כֵּן יִתְרַת עָשָׂה אָבָדוּ:	Isa 15:7	עַל־כֵּן יִתְרָה עָשָׂה וּפְקֻדָּתָם עַל נַחַל הָעֲרָבִים יִשָּׂאוּם:
		Isa 15:5aα	לִבִּי לְמוֹאָב יִזְעָק
37	כִּי כָל־רֹאשׁ קָרְחָה וְכָל־זָקָן גְּרֻעָה עַל כָּל־יָדַיִם גְּדֻדֹת וְעַל־מָתְנַיִם שָׂק:	Isa 15:2bβ	בְּכָל־רָאשָׁיו קָרְחָה כָּל־זָקָן גְּרוּעָה:
		Isa 15:3a	בְּחוּצֹתָיו חָגְרוּ שָׂק
38	עַל כָּל־גַּגּוֹת מוֹאָב וּבִרְחֹבֹתֶיהָ כֻּלֹּה מִסְפֵּד כִּי־שָׁבַרְתִּי אֶת־מוֹאָב	Isa 15:3b	עַל גַּגּוֹתֶיהָ וּבִרְחֹבֹתֶיהָ כֻּלֹּה יְיֵלִיל יֹרֵד בַּבֶּכִי:
	כִּכְלִי אֵין־חֵפֶץ בּוֹ נְאֻם־יְהוָה:	Jer 22:28	הַעֶצֶב נִבְזֶה נָפוּץ הָאִישׁ הַזֶּה כָּנְיָהוּ אִם־כְּלִי אֵין חֵפֶץ בּוֹ
		Jer 19:11aii	(אֶשְׁבֹּר אֶת־הָעָם הַזֶּה וְאֶת־הָעִיר הַזֹּאת כַּאֲשֶׁר יִשְׁבֹּר אֶת־כְּלִי הַיּוֹצֵר אֲשֶׁר לֹא־יוּכַל לְהֵרָפֵה עוֹד)
39	אֵיךְ חַתָּה הֵילִילוּ אֵיךְ הִפְנָה־עֹרֶף מוֹאָב בּוֹשׁ וְהָיָה מוֹאָב לִשְׂחֹק וְלִמְחִתָּה לְכָל־סְבִיבָיו:		
40	כִּי־כֹה אָמַר יְהוָה הִנֵּה כַנֶּשֶׁר יִדְאֶה וּפָרַשׂ כְּנָפָיו אֶל־מוֹאָב:	Jer 49:22a	הִנֵּה כַנֶּשֶׁר יַעֲלֶה וְיִדְאֶה וְיִפְרֹשׂ כְּנָפָיו עַל־בָּצְרָה
		Deut 28:49[6]	יִשָּׂא יְהוָה עָלֶיךָ גּוֹי מֵרָחוֹק מִקְצֵה הָאָרֶץ כַּאֲשֶׁר יִדְאֶה הַנָּשֶׁר גּוֹי אֲשֶׁר לֹא־תִשְׁמַע לְשֹׁנוֹ:

---

6. Smothers (in Keown et al., *Jeremiah 26–52*, 310) suggests a link here and also between Jer 48:41 and Deut 28:52. Deut 28:49 is one of three verses where נשׁר and דאה occur together (the other two being Jer 48:40 and Jer 49:22) and therefore the connection is possible. However, I am less convinced that there is overlap between Jer 48:41 and Deut 28:52 (there is no shared language though the idea is similar), but have included it here for completeness, especially as it is in the same section as Deut 28:49 and therefore the link is more plausible.

Jeremiah 48 in the Light of Isaiah 15–16

v.	Jer 48	Ref(s)	Parallel Passage
41	נִלְכְּדָה הַקְּרִיּוֹת וְהַמְּצָדוֹת נִתְפָּשָׂה וְהָיָה לֵב גִּבּוֹרֵי מוֹאָב בַּיּוֹם הַהוּא כְּלֵב אִשָּׁה מְצֵרָה:	Jer 49:22b	וְהָיָה לֵב גִּבּוֹרֵי אֱדוֹם בַּיּוֹם הַהוּא כְּלֵב אִשָּׁה מְצֵרָה:
		Isa 15:4b	(עַל־כֵּן חֲלֻצֵי מוֹאָב יָרִיעוּ נַפְשׁוֹ יָרְעָה לּוֹ:)
		Deut 28:52	(וְהֵצַר לְךָ בְּכָל־שְׁעָרֶיךָ עַד רֶדֶת חֹמֹתֶיךָ הַגְּבֹהוֹת וְהַבְּצֻרוֹת אֲשֶׁר אַתָּה בֹּטֵחַ בָּהֵן בְּכָל־אַרְצֶךָ וְהֵצַר לְךָ בְּכָל־שְׁעָרֶיךָ בְּכָל־אַרְצְךָ אֲשֶׁר נָתַן יְהוָה אֱלֹהֶיךָ לָךְ:) Pains of childbirth is a common motif (e.g., Isa 13:8; 21:3; Jer 30:6; Mic 4:9, 10)
42	וְנִשְׁמַד מוֹאָב מֵעָם כִּי עַל־יְהוָה הִגְדִּיל:		
43	פַּחַד וָפַחַת וָפָח עָלֶיךָ יוֹשֵׁב מוֹאָב נְאֻם־יְהוָה:	Isa 24:17	פַּחַד וָפַחַת וָפָח עָלֶיךָ יוֹשֵׁב הָאָרֶץ:
		Lam 3:47	(פַּחַד וָפַחַת הָיָה לָנוּ הַשֵּׁאת וְהַשָּׁבֶר:)
44	[כ = הַנִּיס] [ק = הַנָּס] מִפְּנֵי הַפַּחַד יִפֹּל אֶל־הַפַּחַת וְהָעֹלֶה מִן־הַפַּחַת יִלָּכֵד בַּפָּח	Isa 24:18	וְהָיָה הַנָּס מִקּוֹל הַפַּחַד יִפֹּל אֶל־הַפַּחַת וְהָעוֹלֶה מִתּוֹךְ הַפַּחַת יִלָּכֵד בַּפָּח כִּי־אֲרֻבּוֹת מִמָּרוֹם נִפְתָּחוּ וַיִּרְעֲשׁוּ מוֹסְדֵי אָרֶץ:
	כִּי־אָבִיא אֵלֶיהָ אֶל־מוֹאָב שְׁנַת פְּקֻדָּתָם נְאֻם־יְהוָה:	Jer 23:12b	כִּי־אָבִיא עֲלֵיהֶם רָעָה שְׁנַת פְּקֻדָּתָם נְאֻם־יְהוָה:
		Jer 11:23b	כִּי־אָבִיא רָעָה אֶל־אַנְשֵׁי עֲנָתוֹת שְׁנַת פְּקֻדָּתָם:
45	בְּצֵל חֶשְׁבּוֹן עָמְדוּ מִכֹּחַ נָסִים כִּי־אֵשׁ יָצָא מֵחֶשְׁבּוֹן וְלֶהָבָה מִבֵּין סִיחוֹן וַתֹּאכַל	Num 21:28	כִּי־אֵשׁ יָצְאָה מֵחֶשְׁבּוֹן לֶהָבָה מִקִּרְיַת סִיחֹן אָכְלָה עָר מוֹאָב בַּעֲלֵי בָּמוֹת אַרְנֹן:
	פְּאַת מוֹאָב וְקָדְקֹד בְּנֵי שָׁאוֹן:	Num 24:17bβ	וּמָחַץ פַּאֲתֵי מוֹאָב וְקַרְקַר כָּל־בְּנֵי־שֵׁת:
		Isa 16:3	([כ = הָבִיאוּ] [ק = הָבִיאִי] עֵצָה עֲשׂוּ פְלִילָה שִׁיתִי כַלַּיִל צִלֵּךְ בְּתוֹךְ צָהֳרָיִם סַתְּרִי נִדָּחִים נֹדֵד אַל־תְּגַלִּי:)

v.	Jer 48	Ref(s)	Parallel Passage
46	אוֹי־לְךָ מוֹאָב אָבַד עַם־כְּמוֹשׁ כִּי־לֻקְּחוּ בָנֶיךָ בַּשֶּׁבִי וּבְנֹתֶיךָ בַּשִּׁבְיָה׃	Num 21:29	אוֹי־לְךָ מוֹאָב אָבַדְתָּ עַם־כְּמוֹשׁ נָתַן בָּנָיו פְּלֵיטִם וּבְנֹתָיו בַּשְּׁבִית לְמֶלֶךְ אֱמֹרִי סִיחוֹן׃
47	וְשַׁבְתִּי שְׁבוּת־מוֹאָב	Ezek 29:14aα	וְשַׁבְתִּי אֶת־שְׁבוּת מִצְרַיִם
	בְּאַחֲרִית הַיָּמִים נְאֻם־יְהוָה עַד־הֵנָּה מִשְׁפַּט מוֹאָב׃	Jer 49:39	וְהָיָה בְּאַחֲרִית הַיָּמִים [כ = אָשׁוּב] [ק = אָשִׁיב] אֶת־[כ = שְׁבִית] [ק = שְׁבוּת] עֵילָם נְאֻם־יְהוָה׃
		Jer 49:6	וְאַחֲרֵי־כֵן אָשִׁיב אֶת־שְׁבוּת בְּנֵי־עַמּוֹן נְאֻם־יְהוָה׃
		Jer 46:26b	(וְאַחֲרֵי־כֵן תִּשְׁכֹּן כִּימֵי־קֶדֶם נְאֻם־יְהוָה׃)
		Isa 16:13	(זֶה הַדָּבָר אֲשֶׁר דִּבֶּר יְהוָה אֶל־מוֹאָב מֵאָז׃)
		Ezek 25:11a	וּבְמוֹאָב אֶעֱשֶׂה שְׁפָטִים
		Isa 16:14	וְעַתָּה דִּבֶּר יְהוָה לֵאמֹר בְּשָׁלֹשׁ שָׁנִים כִּשְׁנֵי שָׂכִיר וְנִקְלָה כְּבוֹד מוֹאָב בְּכֹל הֶהָמוֹן הָרָב וּשְׁאָר מְעַט מִזְעָר לוֹא כַבִּיר׃

> *Key*
>
> *Emphasis denoting closeness of parallel:*
>
> <u>Same word(s) or root(s). Breaks in the underlining indicate that the words either do not follow the same order in the common material, or are separated by other words.</u>
>
> S̤i̤m̤i̤l̤a̤r̤ ̤w̤o̤r̤d̤s̤ ̤o̤r̤ ̤s̤y̤n̤o̤n̤y̤m̤s̤ ̤(̤t̤h̤a̤t̤ ̤i̤s̤,̤ ̤t̤h̤e̤ ̤s̤a̤m̤e̤ ̤i̤d̤e̤a̤ ̤i̤s̤ ̤p̤r̤e̤s̤e̤n̤t̤)̤.
>
> Wording looks like it has been altered slightly (for example, see Jer 48:31 and Isa 16:7).
>
> (Verse or part verse enclosed by brackets) = possible loose link.
>
> Where a word or phrase in Jer 48 has more than one parallel, it will be emphasised in the "Jer 48" column according to its closest parallel.

> *Table layout*:
>
> To aid the reader, on occasion (when a verse has a parallel in more than one text), the text of Jer 48 has been split across lines so that it lies adjacent to its parallel text.
>
> For each verse of Jer 48, the parallel texts have been arranged according to the following criteria:
>
> 1. the closest parallels are shown first
> 2. the texts follow the order of the verse in Jer 48 as much as possible
> 3. canonical order

Texts are included in the table where there is more than one word in common with a phrase in Jer 48 (for example, Ezek 25:11, Zeph 2:10b). However, those with only one word in common (for example, אש "fire" in Amos 2:2, שרים "chiefs/rulers" in Amos 2:3), or those containing familiar, but general, themes (for example, pride in Isa 25:11 and Zeph 2:10a, and the taunting of Israel in Zeph 2:8), are not included. The table is my own, but I have consulted tables and lists in Wildberger, Bendavid, Smothers, Gray, and Jones as well as NASB's cross-reference column.[7]

The reason for choosing to compare Jer 48 with Isa 15–16 rather than with the words against Moab in other prophetic books is that these other oracles consist only of a few verses each and contain little overlap with Jer 48 in terms of repeated words. Jer 48 and Isa 15–16, on the other hand, not only share a considerable amount of material but they are similar in other ways, too. First, they both refer to a large number of places in Moab, secondly, they are both long oracles, and thirdly, the tone of lament that runs through each of them is striking, if not the most prominent feature of both. These similarities have led commentators to surmise that one author has quarried material from the other, or that both have relied on a common source.

At the same time, there are notable differences between these oracles. For instance, Jer 48 explains that Moab's destruction is YHWH's punishment meted out to Moab because of her offences. The text cites

---

7. Bendavid, *Parallels*, 201, 206, 188; Gray, *Isaiah I–XXVII*, 271; Jones, *Jeremiah*, 499, 505–7; Smothers in Keown et al., *Jeremiah 26–52*, 310; Wildberger, *Isaiah 13–27*, 127–29.

some of these misdeeds. It also communicates Moab's future restoration. In contrast, Isa 15–16 does not depict Moab's calamity in terms of YHWH's punishment and appears disinterested in Moab's sins as well as her ultimate reversal of fortunes. YHWH is also conspicuously absent by name (until the addendum) in Isa 15–16, whereas Jer 48 frequently refers to him. Moreover, there is no equivalent section in Jer 48 to Isa 16:1–5, a passage that is often supposed to be a Moabite appeal to Judah and that looks forward to a righteous Davidic king. As well, Isaiah's oracle concerning Moab concludes with a (self confessed) later addendum, which Jeremiah's does not.

The analysis in this chapter will begin by looking at the similarities between the oracles (that is, shared material, number of place names, length, and lamenting tone) and will then move on to deal with the differences between them. Most of the examination of the differences will concentrate on material found in Jer 48 but not Isa 15–16 (that is, reasons for Moab's sin, her punishment, her restoration, and explicit references to YHWH) whilst the material found only in Isa 15–16 (that is, the supposed appeal with its possible "messianic" allusions, and the addendum) will be given less priority. This is because the key question concerns Jer 48 and the comparison with Isa 15–16 is in order to illuminate Jer 48, not to provide a reading of Isa 15–16.

Having examined the nature and extent of the differences, I shall then investigate the direction of borrowing. Since Isa 24:17–18 is identical in parts to Jer 48:43–44 it is also briefly included. If it can be shown that Jer 48 reuses material from Isa 15–16 (and 24), as the majority of commentators surmise, then the omissions and deletions may illumine the processing behind the text of Jer 48. The final section will pull together all the observations and conclusions, and cautiously seek to answer why the authors of Jer 48 and Isa 15–16 might have shaped their oracles as they did.

Similarities Explored

Shared Material

The shared material tends to take four forms. First, there is a concentrated clustering of equivalent verses; this forms the bulk of the common material between Jer 48 and Isa 15–16, that is, Jer 48:29–38a and

Isa 16:6–12. Secondly, there may be a close correspondence between isolated verses, for example, Jer 48:5 and Isa 15:5b. The third form is less apparent and is when the overlap in the words and phrases is either small enough or general enough to make it unclear whether borrowing has taken place at all, for example, Jer 48:45 and Isa 16:3. Fourthly, there are examples where there is little or no shared language, but where the thoughts are obviously similar, for example, Jer 48:41 and Isa 15:4b. Not only do the third and fourth categories merge, but it becomes difficult to clarify at which point the material ceases to be shared, particularly as the concerns of the oracles are broadly similar (Moab's calamity). This section looks at examples from each category, in descending order of overlapping language.[8]

The closest correspondence is between Jer 48:29–38 and Isa 15:2–7 and 16:6–12, as shown below in the excerpt from Table 4.

29	שָׁמַעְנוּ גְאוֹן־מוֹאָב גֵּאֶה מְאֹד גָּבְהוֹ וּגְאוֹנוֹ וְגַאֲוָתוֹ וְרֻם לִבּוֹ׃	Isa 16:6a–bα	שָׁמַעְנוּ גְאוֹן־מוֹאָב גֵּא מְאֹד גַּאֲוָתוֹ וּגְאוֹנוֹ
30	אֲנִי יָדַעְתִּי נְאֻם־יְהוָה עֶבְרָתוֹ וְלֹא־כֵן בַּדָּיו לֹא־כֵן עָשׂוּ׃	Isa 16:6bβ	וְעֶבְרָתוֹ לֹא־כֵן בַּדָּיו׃
31	עַל־כֵּן עַל־מוֹאָב אֲיֵלִיל וּלְמוֹאָב כֻּלֹּה אֶזְעָק אֶל־אַנְשֵׁי קִיר־חֶרֶשׂ יֶהְגֶּה׃	Isa 16:7	לָכֵן יְיֵלִיל מוֹאָב לְמוֹאָב כֻּלֹּה יְיֵלִיל לַאֲשִׁישֵׁי קִיר־חֲרֶשֶׂת תֶּהְגּוּ אַךְ־נְכָאִים׃
		Isa 15:2bα	עַל־נְבוֹ וְעַל מֵידְבָא מוֹאָב יְיֵלִיל
		Isa 15:5a	לִבִּי לְמוֹאָב יִזְעָק בְּרִיחֶהָ עַד־צֹעַר עֶגְלַת שְׁלִשִׁיָּה
		Isa 15:8b	עַד־אֶגְלַיִם יִלְלָתָהּ וּבְאֵר אֵילִים יִלְלָתָהּ׃

8. Table 4 does not group the verses according to these four classifications; instead, as the Key shows, it highlights where words or roots are the same, where they are synonymous or similar, where it appears that spellings have been altered slightly, and where there is only a possible loose link between texts. Nevertheless, it follows that the level of correspondence can often be seen at a glance.

32	מִבְּכִי יַעְזֵר אֶבְכֶּה־לָּךְ הַגֶּפֶן שִׂבְמָה נְטִישֹׁתַיִךְ עָבְרוּ יָם עַד יָם יַעְזֵר נָגָעוּ עַל־קֵיצֵךְ וְעַל־בְּצִירֵךְ שֹׁדֵד נָפָל:	Isa 16:8	כִּי שַׁדְמוֹת חֶשְׁבּוֹן אֻמְלָל גֶּפֶן שִׂבְמָה בַּעֲלֵי גוֹיִם הָלְמוּ שְׂרוּקֶיהָ עַד־יַעְזֵר נָגָעוּ תָּעוּ מִדְבָּר שְׁלֻחוֹתֶיהָ נִטְּשׁוּ עָבְרוּ יָם:
		Isa 16:9	עַל־כֵּן אֶבְכֶּה בִּבְכִי יַעְזֵר גֶּפֶן שִׂבְמָה אֲרַיָּוֶךְ דִּמְעָתִי חֶשְׁבּוֹן וְאֶלְעָלֵה כִּי עַל־קֵיצֵךְ וְעַל־קְצִירֵךְ הֵידָד נָפָל:
33	וְנֶאֶסְפָה שִׂמְחָה וָגִיל מִכַּרְמֶל וּמֵאֶרֶץ מוֹאָב וְיַיִן מִיקָבִים הִשְׁבַּתִּי לֹא־יִדְרֹךְ הֵידָד הֵידָד לֹא הֵידָד:	Isa 16:10	וְנֶאֱסַף שִׂמְחָה וָגִיל מִן־הַכַּרְמֶל וּבַכְּרָמִים לֹא־יְרֻנָּן לֹא יְרֹעָע יַיִן בַּיְקָבִים לֹא־יִדְרֹךְ הַדֹּרֵךְ הֵידָד הִשְׁבַּתִּי:
		Isa 16:9b	כִּי עַל־קֵיצֵךְ וְעַל־קְצִירֵךְ הֵידָד נָפָל
		Isa 15:6b	(כִּי־יָבֵשׁ חָצִיר כָּלָה דֶשֶׁא יֶרֶק לֹא הָיָה:)
34	מִזַּעֲקַת חֶשְׁבּוֹן עַד־אֶלְעָלֵה עַד־יַהַץ נָתְנוּ קוֹלָם	Isa 15:4a	וַתִּזְעַק חֶשְׁבּוֹן וְאֶלְעָלֵה עַד־יַהַץ נִשְׁמַע קוֹלָם
	מִצֹּעַר עַד־חֹרֹנַיִם עֶגְלַת שְׁלִשִׁיָּה	Isa 15:5a	לִבִּי לְמוֹאָב יִזְעָק בְּרִיחֶהָ עַד־צֹעַר עֶגְלַת שְׁלִשִׁיָּה
	כִּי גַּם־מֵי נִמְרִים לִמְשַׁמּוֹת יִהְיוּ:	Isa 15:6a	כִּי־מֵי נִמְרִים מְשַׁמּוֹת יִהְיוּ
35	וְהִשְׁבַּתִּי לְמוֹאָב נְאֻם־יְהוָה מַעֲלֶה בָמָה וּמַקְטִיר לֵאלֹהָיו:	Isa 15:2a	עָלָה הַבַּיִת וְדִיבֹן הַבָּמוֹת לְבֶכִי
		Isa 16:12	וְהָיָה כִי־נִרְאָה כִּי־נִלְאָה מוֹאָב עַל־הַבָּמָה וּבָא אֶל־מִקְדָּשׁוֹ לְהִתְפַּלֵּל וְלֹא יוּכָל:
36	עַל־כֵּן לִבִּי לְמוֹאָב כַּחֲלִלִים יֶהֱמֶה וְלִבִּי אֶל־אַנְשֵׁי קִיר־חֶרֶשׂ כַּחֲלִילִים יֶהֱמֶה	Isa 16:11	עַל־כֵּן מֵעַי לְמוֹאָב כַּכִּנּוֹר יֶהֱמוּ וְקִרְבִּי לְקִיר חָרֶשׂ:
	עַל־כֵּן יִתְרַת עָשָׂה אָבָדוּ:	Isa 15:7	עַל־כֵּן יִתְרָה עָשָׂה וּפְקֻדָּתָם עַל נַחַל הָעֲרָבִים יִשָּׂאוּם:
		Isa 15:5aα	לִבִּי לְמוֹאָב יִזְעָק
37	כִּי כָל־רֹאשׁ קָרְחָה וְכָל־זָקָן גְּרֻעָה עַל כָּל־יָדַיִם גְּדֻדֹת וְעַל־מָתְנַיִם שָׂק:	Isa 15:2bβ	בְּכָל־רָאשָׁיו קָרְחָה כָּל־זָקָן גְּרוּעָה:
		Isa 15:3a	בְּחוּצֹתָיו חָגְרוּ שָׂק

38	עַל כָּל־גַּגּוֹת מוֹאָב וּבִרְחֹבֹתֶיהָ כֻּלֹּה מִסְפֵּד כִּי־שָׁבַרְתִּי אֶת־מוֹאָב	Isa 15:3b	עַל גַּגּוֹתֶיהָ וּבִרְחֹבֹתֶיהָ כֻּלֹּה יְיֵלִיל יֹרֵד בַּבֶּכִי:
		Jer 22:28	הַעֶצֶב נִבְזֶה נָפוּץ הָאִישׁ הַזֶּה כָּנְיָהוּ אִם־כְּלִי אֵין חֵפֶץ בּוֹ
	כִּכְלִי אֵין־חֵפֶץ בּוֹ נְאֻם־יְהוָה:	Jer 19:11aii	(אֲשַׁבֵּר אֶת־הָעָם הַזֶּה וְאֶת־הָעִיר הַזֹּאת כַּאֲשֶׁר יִשְׁבֹּר אֶת־כְּלִי הַיּוֹצֵר אֲשֶׁר לֹא־יוּכַל לְהֵרָפֵה עוֹד)

It is clear that the majority of equivalent material in Jer 48:29–38a occurs in Isa 16:6–12, whilst the connections with Isa 15:2–7 are less strong. It is also apparent that Jer 48:29–38a reads as an interleaving of Isa 15:2–7 and 16:6–12 and not as if one section follows the other. For example, Jer 48:35 shares language and ideas (Moab's worship on high places) both with Isa 15:2 and 16:12. The overall result is that the intensity of the mourning is concentrated in Jeremiah, but spread across Isaiah. Whichever direction the borrowing took, the original material has been significantly reworked.

An example of close correspondence between isolated verses is Isa 15:5b with Jer 48:5:

Jeremiah 48:5　　　　　　　　　　　　　**Isa 15:5b**

כי מעלה הלחית[9]　　　　　　　　　　　　כי מעלה הלוחית
בבכי יעלה־בכי　　　　　　　　　　　　　בבכי יעלה־בו
כי במורד חורנים　　　　　　　　　　　　כי דרך חורנים
צרי צעקת־שבר שמעו　　　　　　　　　　זעקת־שבר יעערו

For (at) the ascent of Luhith　　　　　　　For (at) the ascent of Luhith
he goes up weeping bitterly;　　　　　　　he goes up weeping
for at the descent of Horonaim　　　　　　for (by) the road to Horonaim
they have heard the distress-　　　　　　　they raise a cry (over their) [lit.
ing cry [lit. distress of cry] of　　　　　　　of] breaking
breaking

---

9. The Qere version; the Ketiv reads הלחות.

Most of the verses either side of Jer 48:5 do not reflect Isa 15–16 (48:3 has echoes of the latter part of Isa 15:5 as well as 15:8a). In Isaiah, the verses either side of 15:5 resonate with Jer 48:34, 36b–7; in fact, Isa 15:5 is located between two verses that are, respectively, akin to Jer 48:34a and 34b. This is seen more clearly in Wildberger's table since he starts by laying out the full text of Isa 15 rather than Jer 48.[10] Thus Isa 15:5 and Jer 48:5 are both examples of close correspondence between isolated verses, as opposed to a larger section that has been reworked.

An instance where the connections are too loose to be strictly classified as shared language, yet may still be weak associations, is the first verse of each oracle.

Jer 48:1	Isa 15:1
למואב כה־אמר יהוה צבאות אלהי ישראל הוי אל־נבו כי שדדה הבישה נלכדה קריתים הבישה המשגב וחתה:	משא מואב כי בליל שדד ער מואב נדמה כי בליל שדד קיר־מואב נדמה:

Although the verses vary considerably from each other, both testify that the cities of מואב have שדד "been destroyed" (both use the Pual). However, where Jer 48:1 lists Nebo and Kiriathaim, Isa 15:1 (the shorter verse) refers to Ar and Kir. Similarly, in Jer 48:3 זעקה "a cry" is heard from Horonaim, whereas in Isa 15:8a הזעקה "the cry" goes round the whole of Moab. While there is only one word common to the two verses, the idea in both is of a loud cry that can be heard from a considerable distance.

An example that demonstrates that the authors expressed the same ideas, but used different language is Jer 48:41 / Isa 15:4b.

Jer 48:41	Isa 15:4b
נלכדה הקריות והמצדות נתפשה והיה לב גבורי מואב ביום ההוא כלב אשה מצרה:	על־כן חלצי מואב יריעו נפשו ירעה לו:

The point of both verses is to express how weak the strong men of Moab have become. However, the strong men of Moab are called גבורי מואב in Jeremiah but חלצי מואב in Isaiah. The weakness runs to the inner core of these strong men, but this inner core is depicted as the לב in

---

10. Wildberger, *Isaiah 1–12*, 127.

Jeremiah, and the נפש in Isaiah. Whereas in Jeremiah their heart becomes כלב אשה מצרה "like the heart of the women in labor," in Isaiah נפשו ירעה לו "his soul trembles in him." The only word common to both sentences is מואב.

Isa 16:11 (Jer 48:36) is a similar example, though in this case there is more shared language and sentence structure and it appears that simple substitution of words has taken place.

Jer 48:36	Isa 16:11
על־כן לבי למואב כחללים יהמה ולבי אל־אנשי קיר־חרש כחלילים יהמה על־כן יתרת עשה אבדו:	על־כן מעי למואב ככנור יהמו וקרבי לקיר חרש:

In both cases the internal organs moan (המה) like a musical instrument, but again, the internal organs as well as the instrument differ. Jeremiah uses חליל "flute/pipe" in Jeremiah whilst Isaiah has כנור "lyre." Interestingly, Jeremiah once more uses לב whilst Isaiah does not, but uses מעה.

In summary, then, the only place where there is substantial commonality is the largely lamenting material of Jer 48:29–38a (Isa 15:2–7 and 16:6–12); otherwise the Isaiah material appears in Jer 48 with "much difference of order."[11] The examples given above demonstrate that the "borrower" has been free in the way he has utilized existing material, sometimes directly quoting from it, at other times reworking it so that it no longer has a one to one mapping with the original, and on yet other occasions using the idea but not the words. Thus, though one author might have relied on the other's work, it was far from blind copying. This variation in the way that the shared material has been used indicates the individual nature of the oracles.

Two points should be noted in relation to the shared material in order to demonstrate the distinct character of each oracle. First, both oracles contain a substantial portion that is not found in the other, (that is, Isa 15:9–16:5 and Jer 48:6–27, 39–46, though see the above discussion on 48:41, as well as the possible slight overlap with Jer 48:45 and Isa 16:3). Secondly, Jer 48 shares material with a number of other passages within the OT (Numbers, Isaiah, Jeremiah, Ezekiel, Amos, and Zephaniah, and possibly Deuteronomy, Psalms, and Lamentations).

---

11. Gray, *Isaiah I–XXVII*, 271.

This is particularly apparent in Jer 48:43–46, which corresponds to Isa 24:17–18a (Jer 48:43–44a); Jer 11:23b and 23:12b (Jer 48:44b); Num 24:17bβ (Jer 48:45b); and Num 21:28–29 (Jer 48:45b–46). Having looked at the specific overlay of material between both passages, it is time to look at more general similarities.

Place Names

Blenkinsopp observes that of the twenty three place names in Isa 15–16, fifteen are mentioned in Jer 48[12] and he notes that whilst many of them cannot be identified, it seems that the most densely populated areas of Moab were affected (Nebo, Medeba, Heshbon, Elealeh, Jazer, Jahaz, and Dibon).[13] Several Isaiah and Jeremiah commentators point out that the place names may be representative of the whole country, "as if he had said that this destruction would not only seize the extremities of that country, but would reach its inmost recesses, so that no one corner

---

12. In order of appearance in Isa 15–16: Moab, Ar, Kir, Dibon, Nebo, Medeba, Heshbon, Elealeh, Jahaz, Zoar, Eglath-shelishiyah, Luhith, Horonaim, Nimrim, Arabim, Eglaim, Beer-elim, Dimon, Sela, Arnon, Kir-hareseth, Sibmah, and Jazer; also Zion. In order of appearance in Jer 48 those that appear in both texts are: Moab, Nebo, Heshbon, Horonaim, Luhith, Dibon, Arnon, Jazer, Sibmah, Elealeh, Jahaz, Zoar, Eglath-shelishiyah, Nimrim, and presumably Kir-heres (for Kir-heres and Kir-hareseth being the same city see Wildberger, *Isaiah 1–12*, 146–7, 150). In addition to these, Jer 48 has Kiriathaim, Madmen, Aroer, Holon, Jahzah, Mephaath, Beth-diblathaim, Beth-gamul, Beth-meon, Kerioth, Bozrah, and Sihon; also Israel. Bethel in 48:13 may well refer to a god rather than a place name, given that it is in parallel with Chemosh in the first half of the verse. LXX renders it ὥσπερ κατῃσχύνθη οἶκος Ισραηλ ἀπὸ Βαιθηλ πεποιθότες ἐπ' αὐτοῖς "as the house of Israel was ashamed of Baithel, when they had confidence in them" (NETS). If a place represents its inhabitants then LXX's plural "in them" (αὐτοῖς) suggests the people of Bethel. In other words, it seems clear that LXX renders Bethel as a town, even if the Greek is not the easiest to read in this verse. Those who consider the possibility that Bethel in MT refers to a deity are: Allen, *Jeremiah*, 480; Carroll, *Jeremiah*, 784; McKane, *Jeremiah, vol. 2*, 1169; Holladay, *Jeremiah, vol. 2*, 358; Lundbom, *Jeremiah 37–52*, 268; McKeating, *Jeremiah*, 205; Smothers in Keown et al., *Jeremiah 26–52*, 315; Sweeney, "Jeremiah," 1021; Thompson, *Jeremiah*, 706; Weiser, *Der Prophet Jeremia*, 406. However, Rudolph (*Jeremiah*, 280) disagrees and deems Bethel to be the place of Israel's shrine, as do: Calvin, *Jeremiah*, 18–19; Duhm, *Jeremia*, 348; Feinberg, *Jeremiah*, 303; Freedman, *Jeremiah*, 30; Fretheim, *Jeremiah*, 599; Jones, *Jeremiah*, 503; Volz, *Der Prophet Jeremia*, 406. Brueggemann, *Jeremiah*, 445 and Miller, "Jeremiah," 891 do not address the issue.

13. Blenkinsopp, *Isaiah 1–39*, 298.

could be exempted."[14] Thus the number of place names may indicate both the intensity and scope of Moab's destruction.

In both Jer 48 and Isa 15–16, the place names often appear more densely in passages of intense lamenting (as well as in the context of judgment in Jer 48:21–24); see Isa 15:1–5, 8; 16:7–9a, 11; Jer 48:5, 31–32, 34, 36.[15] This would suggest that the abundance of towns and cities named is in part to emphasize the breadth and depth of the lament over Moab as well as her destruction. The exaggeration in Isa 15:4 that the cries of Heshbon and Elealeh were heard in Jahaz (which Kaiser notes is 30km/18m away)[16] may also make the same point. In other words, the lament goes wide and deep.

Length

Although the oracles concerning Moab are among the longer ones in Isaiah and Jeremiah, the oracle in Jeremiah is more prominent among its surrounding oracles than its Isaian counterpart. The oracle concerning Babylon is the longest in both books, but in Jeremiah, the oracle concerning Moab is second in length, surpassing even the oracle concerning Egypt. With the exception of Babylon, it is not only longer than Jeremiah's other OANs, but significantly so (it is also somewhat longer than Isa 15–16). In contrast, Isaiah's oracle concerning Egypt is longer (if one includes the oracle directed towards both Egypt and Cush in Isa 20) than its Moabite one. Furthermore, Isaiah's oracles concerning Damascus, Cush, and Tyre are also relatively long, so Isa 15–16 does not stand out from the other oracles in quite the same way that Jer 48 does in its context. This may indicate that Moab has a greater prominence in Jeremiah's OANs than in Isaiah's.

---

14. Calvin, *Isaiah*, 472. See also Isaiah commentators: Kaiser, *Isaiah 13–39*, 66; Widyapranawa, *Lord*, 94, 95; Wildberger, *Isaiah 1–12*, 118; and Jeremiah commentators: Calvin, *Jeremiah*, 8; Clements, *Jeremiah*, 254; Feinberg, *Jeremiah*, 304; Fretheim, *Jeremiah*, 596; McConville, "Divine Speech," 705; McKane, *Jeremiah*, vol. 2, 1177.

15. As noted in chapter 4, Fretheim (*Jeremiah*, 601) points out that five different verbs of lament are used in Jer 48:31–32, 36.

16. Kaiser, *Isaiah 13–39*, 68.

Lament

Despite the element of lament being central to Isa 15–16 and Jer 48, the overall tone of each oracle differs somewhat from the other. This is largely because Isa 15–16 does not have the searing threats of punishment characteristic of Jer 48. For, whilst Isa 15–16 is not homogeneous, it primarily consists of a lament whereas Jer 48 consists of much more than mourning in terms of reasons given for Moab's punishment, etc. In other words, Jer 48 gives a fuller coverage of Moab's downfall. At the same time, whilst lament might be more central to Isa 15–16 than Jer 48, the latter chapter explicitly attributes the first person laments of 48:31–32 and 48:36 to YHWH. Thus the lament here is arguably more intense.

Similar first-person laments to those in Jer 48 are found in Isa 15:5 and 16:9, 11, but they are not explicitly ascribed to YHWH (YHWH's lament in Jer 48:31 is attributed to Moab in Isa 16:7). It is only in the penultimate verse (16:13) that the whole oracle is described as הדבר אשר דבר יהוה "the word which YHWH spoke." Although prophets often represent YHWH in their speech and there is no evidence that this is not the case here, Isaiah leaves open the possibility that the sentiments expressed belong to the prophet only. This is reflected by the way that whilst 16:13 may indicate that the first person singular denotes YHWH throughout, none of the Isaiah commentaries consulted makes this assertion. Some note that the prophet and YHWH are indistinguishable,[17] but most attribute at least some of the first person sayings (15:5, 9; 16:4, 6, 9, 10, 11) to the "author," "poet" or "prophet," "the unknown mourner" (Seitz), or even Moab (Calvin) rather than to YHWH.[18]

Although נאם־יהוה is a literary convention, it is interesting that Jer 48 and Isa 15–16 differ in their use of it. For, Isa 15–16 does not have the occurrences that are in Jer 48:12, 15, 25, 30, 35, 38, 43, 44, and 47

---

17. Goldingay, *Isaiah*, 111; Oswalt, *Isaiah*, 346; Young, *Isaiah*, 46717. Goldingay, *Isaiah*, 111; Oswalt, *Isaiah*, 346; Young, *Isaiah*, 467.

18. Blenkinsopp, *Isaiah 1–39*, 298, 299; Brueggemann, *Isaiah 1–39*, 144; Calvin, *Isaiah*, 473, 476, 493, 494; Childs, *Isaiah*, 131, 132; Clements, *Isaiah 1–39*, 152; Dillmann, *Jesaia*, 158; Gray, *Isaiah I–XXVII*, 272; Hayes and Irvine, *Isaiah*, 242, 245; Kaiser, *Isaiah 13–39*, 73; Kissane, *Isaiah 1–39*, 183, 193; Seitz, *Isaiah 1–39*, 140; Skinner, *Isaiah*, 122, 123, 125, 130, 131; Sommer, "Isaiah," 815; Stacey, *Isaiah*, 111; Tucker, "Isaiah," 169; Watts, *Isaiah 1–39*, 284; Widyapranawa, *Lord*, 99; Wildberger, *Isaiah 1–12*, 118, 120, 138, 148, 151.

(though not all these verses have parallels in both texts). In addition neither does it have כה־אמר יהוה (48:1, 40) and אשר אמר יהוה (48:8). If such conscious shaping has taken place then it might indicate there is more significance behind נאם־יהוה than is usually allowed for, since it would be unlikely that a scribe would make the effort to either remove or add a literary convention. It may be that by placing some of the laments on the lips of YHWH the author has endowed them with more power and force. If this is so, then in this respect too, the tone of lament is more intense in the Jer 48 oracle concerning Moab. However, it must be pointed out that these phrases are much more common in general in Jeremiah than in Isaiah,[19] which may indicate, after all, that there is nothing more than a difference in literary style between the two books.

Summary

In summary, then, there are undoubtedly similarities between Isa 15–16 and Jer 48. The proliferation of place names in both oracles may signify that Moab's calamity is widespread. That they are densely populated places may point to the magnitude of the calamity, and the fact that the places are listed in contexts where verbs for wailing are piled upon each other may indicate the extent of Moab's mourning.

However, a closer look at most of the similarities between the oracles actually reveals divergence between them. First, the overlapping material is not, by and large, laid down in the same form in both oracles; sometimes the author has woven together larger sections, on one occasion he has cited a verse (particularly the case if Jer 48 depends on Isa 15–16), at other times he has used just a couple of words or even incorporated the ideas but not the words. There is also a significant portion of each oracle that is unique to it. In addition, Jer 48 shares material with a variety of other texts in a way that Isa 15–16 does not.

Secondly, whilst both oracles are long and therefore assume a certain significance in their immediate collection, Jer 48 is proportionally much longer than most of its neighbors and therefore has an even

---

19. A quick count in my concordance gives twenty-five occurrences of נאם־יהוה in Isaiah compared to 175 in Jeremiah and thirty-eight occurrences of כה אמר יהוה in Isaiah compared to 150 in Jeremiah.

greater prominence than Isa 15–16. Thirdly, some of the mourning is explicitly attributed to YHWH in Jer 48, which may add force to the grief and importance to the oracle overall. Fourthly, whilst the tone of lament permeates both oracles, it is much more representative of Isa 15–16 as a whole, whereas Jeremiah gives a broader perspective of Moab's calamity. This wider focus means that Jeremiah addresses some issues that Isaiah does not. It is to these that we now turn.

Material in Jeremiah 48 but not Isaiah 15–16

In terms of material present in Jer 48 but absent from Isa 15–16, the most significant differences lie in Jeremiah's attention to Moab's sin, her punishment, and her restoration, and the explicit reference to both YHWH and Chemosh.

Although Jer 48 refers to Moab's sin, punishment, and restoration, equal weight is not given to each and how they are treated differs. That is, the only verse that promises a reversal of fortunes is the last verse and thus the oracle is not infused with hope all the way through. Neither, does the chapter focus heavily in any one place on the reason for Moab's punishment; rather it is punctuated throughout with short explanations of why the calamity befalls her. It is difficult to separate threats of punishment from descriptions of its result, but the idea of punishment seems to run throughout the whole oracle, often twinned with lamentation or the reason for such punishment (for example, 48:7–8, 11–12, 20–21, 32–33, 38, 42, 44).[20]

Sin

Early in the oracle (48:7) the reason given for Moab's predicament is that she trusted in her treasures. In fact, the causal factor in the chapter for Moab's calamity is normally Moab's sin. The other reasons are given in verses 11, 13, 26, 27, 29–30, 42, and possibly 35 but since they are given fuller discussion in chapter 7 they will not be discussed here. It is enough to note that of these sins, Isaiah refers only to Moab's pride, which it phrases (16:6) in the same (though fewer) terms as Jer 48:29–

---

20. Also see Fretheim, *Jeremiah*, 597.

30. Unlike Jeremiah, however, Isaiah does not place Moab's pride in the context of setting herself up against Israel's God.

Punishment

Since Isa 15–16 is largely uninterested in Moab's sins, it is perhaps to be expected that it does not concentrate on the punishment for these wrongdoings. In 15:9 someone threatens to bring further things upon Moab and in 16:10 declares that, הידד השבתי "I have made the shouting cease."[21] As discussed, 16:13 might imply that all first person speeches belong to YHWH but, in Jer 48, YHWH is explicitly connected with the threats of punishment, as he is with some of the laments. Therefore, in Jeremiah there is no question that YHWH is responsible for Moab's downfall. In the following examples, the context (though not cited here) also connects the "I" with YHWH where Isa 15–16 does not:

> ושלחתי־לו "when I will send to him" (48:12) those who will tip him over,
>
> ויין מיקבים השבתי "And I have stopped the wine from the presses" (48:33),
>
> והשבתי למואב "And I will make an end of Moab" (48:35),
>
> כי־שברתי את־מואב "For I have broken Moab" (48:38), and
>
> כי־אביא אליה אל־מואב שנת פקדתם "For I will bring to her, to Moab, the year of their punishment / visitation" (48:44).

The frequent first person references in Jer 48 to YHWH's involvement in Moab's downfall emphasize that it is divinely initiated. Such a focus in Jer 48 on the Divine may explain why Chemosh is targeted in this oracle, but not in the parallel oracle in Isaiah. Certainly, Isa 15–16 does not appear to have the motif of a battle between deities that Miller and Brueggemann regard as a theme running through Jer 48.[22] Neither is YHWH presented in Isa 15–16 as the Divine Sovereign (cf. Jer 48:15) or the God of Israel (cf. Jer 48:1).

---

21. Thomas notes in MT's apparatus for Isa 15:9 that it has been proposed that אַרְיֵה "a lion" be emended to אֶרְאֶה "I see" or יִרְאָה "fear." This would reduce the force of the only explicit reference to YHWH's punishment of Moab in Isa 15–16. Gray (*Isaiah I–XXVII*, 286) also points out that neither the verb (שׁית "to put/set") nor the object (נוספות "things added/additions") really suggest calamity.

22. Brueggemann, *Jeremiah*, 445; Miller, "Jeremiah," 891.

As well as the first person threats, Jer 48 contains several images and metaphors of punishment that are absent in Isa 15–16 and the main ones are as follows. First is the metaphor of the wine that has been allowed to settle but will now be poured out (48:11–12). Second is the metaphor of Moab as a drunkard splashing about in his vomit (48:26). In fact, Moab's humiliation and shame is a key theme in Jer 48, and the terms used by Jeremiah to depict Moab's shame are יבשׁ (48:1 twice, 48:20), בושׁ (48:13 twice, 48:39), and שׂחוק (48:26, 39). In Isaiah, on the other hand, the motif of shame is almost entirely absent in that there are no explicit references to it.

A third image used in Jer 48 (see also Isa 24:17–18) illustrates the inevitability of the coming judgment and is based around word play. If one flees from the פחד "terror" they will fall into the פחת "pit," and if they climb out of the פחת they will be caught in the פח "trap" (48:43–44). Fourthly, Moab is likened to a vessel that is about to be broken (48:38–39). Thus some of the images Jer 48 uses to portray Moab are degrading and the language is harsh, if not shocking. However, arguably, none of these metaphors is as violent as 48:10 in which those who withhold their swords from shedding blood are cursed.

The disaster that befalls Moab is described as משׁפט in Jeremiah (48:21, 47). This reinforces the link between Moab's sin and the destruction brought about by YHWH, and removes any notion that Moab's fate is undeserved. There is no equivalent of these verses in Isa 15–16 and although there is a reference in 16:5 to one who sits on a future Davidic throne שׁפט ודרשׁ משׁפט "judging and seeking justice," the context here suggests that משׁפט has a more salvific meaning.

Restoration

Some Isaiah commentators understand 16:5 to offer hope for Moab (see discussion below), but there is nothing equivalent in Isa 15–16 to the promise of Jer 48:47, which once again is attributed to YHWH: ושׁבתי שׁבות־מואב באחרית הימים נאם־יהוה "'Yet I will restore the fortunes of Moab in the latter days,' says the LORD" (NRSV).

In other words, in Jer 48, YHWH is explicitly mentioned by name and is a central character who plays a greater and more instrumental role in Moab's fortunes than he does in Isa 15–16, where his presence is implicit. That is, in Jer 48, YHWH is the one who judges Moab and brings punishment upon her, he is the one who weeps over her and he is the one who instigates her final re-establishment.

Summary

To summarize so far, then, the text of Jer 48 is more brutal than Isa 15–16 in the way it points out the reasons for Moab's destruction and in the images it uses to portray what it terms Moab's מִשְׁפָּט. Moreover, it explicitly attributes these threats to YHWH. This is not the complete picture, however, for Jer 48 concludes with a future promise of restoration for Moab. In many ways, therefore, Jeremiah's oracle concerning Moab is fuller and richer than Isaiah's, for it encompasses a broader and more complete scope of Moab's catastrophe and calls attention to the nature and extent of YHWH's involvement. At the same time, it is becoming apparent that the two oracles have been shaped for different purposes and the purpose for Isaiah's oracle may be enhanced by its narrower focus. Material in Isa 15–16 that is not in Jer 48 may be part of this focus.

Material in Isaiah 15–16 but not Jeremiah 48

16:1–5

Isa 16:1–5 is difficult to interpret for a number of reasons. For example, Childs points out that the obscurity of the literary structure impedes a "coherent interpretation," and Blenkinsopp cautiously tackles the "many textual problems," which he, with Wildberger, attributes to "extensive damage in transmission."[23] The ancient versions vary widely from each other and MT as well, which may indicate, as Oswalt comments, that "they too were struggling with a difficult passage and were attempting to make sense of it in diverse ways."[24] The subsequent difficulties in interpreting 16:1–5 in MT are as follows. First, it is not clear who addresses whom and whether, if it is Moab who speaks in verses 1–4, is it still Moab in verse 5. The issue mainly turns on how נדחי in 16:4a is pointed:

---

23. Blenkinsopp, *Isaiah 1–39*, 196, 299; Childs, *Isaiah*, 131; Wildberger, *Isaiah 1–12*, 119.

24. Oswalt, *Isaiah*, 341. For a discussion of the major differences see: Gray, *Isaiah I–XXVII*, 287–91; Wildberger, *Isaiah 1–12*, 110–11.

נִדְחַי "my fugitives" (MT), or according to its construct state נִדְחֵי "fugitives of" (Targum).²⁵ Secondly, scholars do not agree on whether verse 5 or verse 6 is the answer (if, indeed, one is given at all) to what might be a Moabite appeal in 16:2–3.²⁶ Thirdly, there is ambiguity over whether 16:5 offers hope to Moab, or merely to Judah.²⁷ Fourthly, there is discussion about whether there are "messianic"²⁸ allusions in this verse, with its reference to the judge who sits on the throne of David.²⁹ It is beyond the scope of this work to attempt to chart a good course through these murky waters, but a look at the map may at least give an indication of what might be considered to be some of the better routes.

Although the commentators do not make the observation, the fugitive state of the Moabites is referred to in the previous chapter, so if one takes Isa 15–16 as a whole, the context would tend to suggest that the versions are correct in their pointing of 16:4a as נִדְחֵי "fugitives of." Therefore, since it makes sense of the text, I accept the weight of recent

---

25. For a discussion on the addressees see: Blenkinsopp, *Isaiah 1–39*, 299–300; Calvin, *Isaiah*, 483; Dillmann, *Jesaia*, 154; Goldingay, *Isaiah*, 109; Gray, *Isaiah I–XXVII*, 288–9; Kaiser, *Isaiah 13–39*, 72; Oswalt, *Isaiah*, 341; Smith, *Isaiah 1–32*, 280; Young, *Isaiah*, 463.

26. For a discussion on the answer see: Brueggemann, *Isaiah 1–39*, 142; Clements, *Isaiah 1–39*, 154; Childs, *Isaiah*, 132; Goldingay, *Isaiah*, 109, 110; Gray, *Isaiah I–XXVII*, 291; Hayes and Irvine, *Isaiah*, 244; Kaiser, *Isaiah 13–39*, 72; Oswalt, *Isaiah*, 341; Seitz, *Isaiah 1–39*, 139; Skinner, *Isaiah*, 129–30; Tucker, "Isaiah", 169; Watts, *Isaiah 1–39*, 287; Widyapranawa, *Lord*, 98; Wildberger, *Isaiah 1–12*, 140.

27. For a discussion on whether the response offers hope see: Brueggemann, *Isaiah 1–39*, 142; Childs, *Isaiah*, 132; Clements, *Isaiah 1–39*, 154; Dillmann, *Jesaia*, 156; Goldingay, *Isaiah*, 110; Gray, *Isaiah I–XXVII*, 291; Hayes and Irvine, *Isaiah*, 244; Kaiser, *Isaiah 13–39*, 74, 71, 73; Oswalt, *Isaiah*, 343; Seitz, *Isaiah 1–39*, 139–40; Smith, *Isaiah 1–32*, 280; Stacey, *Isaiah*, 113; Watts, *Isaiah 1–39*, 287; Widyapranawa, *Lord*, 98; Wildberger, *Isaiah 1–12*, 140.

28. Although commentators frequently use the term "messianic," this is an anachronistic concept. Nevertheless, passages such as Isa 9 and 11 depict an idyllic future for Israel/Judah when a Davidic king will rule in justice and righteousness and where there is transformation generally (for example, carnivorous animals lying peacefully with animals that would normally be considered their prey in 11:6–7). This is the sense in which I use "messianic."

29. For a discussion on possible "messianic" allusions in Isa 16:5 see: Brueggemann, *Isaiah 1–39*, 142; Calvin, *Isaiah*, 485–86; Childs, *Isaiah*, 132; Gray, *Isaiah I–XXVII*, 271–72, 289; Hayes and Irvine, *Isaiah*, 243–44; Kissane, *Isaiah 1–39*, 184, 193; Oswalt, *Isaiah*, 341, 343; Skinner, *Isaiah*, 129; Seitz, *Isaiah 1–39*, 139; Smith, *Isaiah 1–32*, 280; Stacey, *Isaiah*, 113; Tucker, "Isaiah," 167–70; Wildberger, *Isaiah 1–12*, 143–44, 153; Williamson, *Isaiah*, 56–62; Young, *Isaiah*, 464; Widyapranawa, *Lord*, 97, 98.

scholarly consensus that in these verses Moab appeals to Judah for protection, by means of a tribute.³⁰

I am persuaded that the verses do have "messianic" overtones mainly because the language is typical of other "messianic" passages, such as Isa 9 and 11. That is, כסא "throne," באהל דוד "in the tent of David," בחסד "in loving kindness," באמת "in faithfulness," משפט "justice," and צדק "righteousness."³¹ It seems to me, therefore, that what appears to be a promise given in Davidic language might (but not necessarily) indicate that Judah, rather than Moab is the speaker here. Many recent scholars also tend to deem 16:5 to be Judah's response to Moab's request. Thus, since verse 5 seems more appropriate to a Judean speaker and a positive response is in keeping with the overall tone of the oracle with its sympathetic hearing of Moab's cries, I would be inclined to accept that verse 5 is an offer of hope given by Judah to the Moabites.

If Isa 16:5 can be construed as "messianic" then it surpasses the promise of a reversal of fortunes in Jer 48:47, despite its rather elusive nature. At the same time, whether or not Isa 16:5 is "messianic," the hope is expressed in human terms via a human deliverer, whereas in Jer 48:47, YHWH himself is the agent of Moab's restoration.

There are no immediate reasons for the absence of Isa 16:1–5 in Jer 48. If the author of Jer 48 utilized Isa 15–16 (as will shortly be discussed) then it is unlikely that he omitted the first part of Isa 16 because it suggests helping Moab, for Jer 48:9 seems to be an instruction to aid her. As well, Jer 33 is a text that expresses future hope for the house of David, using the same language as the "messianic" passages in Isaiah; משפט and צדק in Jer 33:15–16, חסד in 33:11 and אמת in 33:6, so the book of Jeremiah is not devoid of such material. However, if the author of Jer 48 borrowed material from Isa 15–16 the simpler explanation might be that Isa 15:9b–16:6 was a later addition and unavailable for reuse. This may also be the reason why Jeremiah does not have the addendum in Isa 16:13–14.

---

30. Blenkinsopp, *Isaiah 1–39*, 299; Brueggemann, *Isaiah 1–39*, 141; Childs, *Isaiah*, 131; Clements, *Isaiah 1–39*, 154; Dillmann, *Jesaia*, 154; Goldingay, *Isaiah*, 109; Gray, *Isaiah I–XXVII*, 288; Hayes and Irvine, *Isaiah*, 242; Kaiser, *Isaiah 13–39*, 70; Kissane, *Isaiah 1–39*, 192; Oswalt, *Isaiah*, 341; Seitz, *Isaiah 1–39*, 139; Skinner, *Isaiah*, 127–28; Sommer, "Isaiah," 816; Stacey, *Isaiah*, 112; Tucker, "Isaiah," 168; Watts, *Isaiah 1–39*, 287; Widyapranawa, *Lord*, 97; Wildberger, *Isaiah 1–12*, 119, 140.

31. E.g. Gray, *Isaiah I–XXVII*, 289; Williamson, *Isaiah*, 56–57. See footnote 28 re the term "messianic."

Addendum in 16:13–14

This additional comment in 16:13–14 refers to the main body of the oracle as an "earlier" (מאז) one. Jeremiah's oracle, on the other hand, is presented as the current utterance. Stacey suggests about Isa 16:13–14 that this "final comment is made by an editor who was aware that the prophecy had been in existence a long time, but remained unfulfilled."[32] Perhaps, as Tucker says, it was at a time when Moab was in her "glory."[33] If Jer 48:10 is a gloss inserted by a scribe who saw that the oracle against Moab was not fulfilled (see chapter 6) then it is interesting that in both oracles there is sufficient concern over Moab's flourishing for the scribes to add these prose comments. It would further indicate the ambiguity of the relationship between Israel/Judah and Moab: some authors wrote laments, whilst others called for her destruction.

Direction of Borrowing

There are three obvious possibilities regarding the link between Isa 15–16 and Jer 48. First, that Jeremiah borrowed from Isaiah; secondly that Isaiah depended on Jeremiah, and; thirdly, that both used a common source, at least in part. The latter is a minority view, which is largely rejected even by those who conclude that it is impossible to determine the provenance of the oracle.[34] A handful of Isaiah commentators suggest that Isa 15–16 relies on Jer 48,[35] but the overwhelming majority of Isaiah and Jeremiah commentators are persuaded that it is the Jeremiah author who utilizes Isaiah, even if, like McKane, they are not always

---

32. Stacey, *Isaiah*, 114.

33. Tucker, "Isaiah," 169; see also Blenkinsopp, *Isaiah 1–39*, 300; Skinner, *Isaiah*, 132; Wildberger, *Isaiah 1–12*, 152.

34. Those who accept a common source: Gray, *Isaiah I–XXVII*, 271–72; Oswalt, *Isaiah*, 336; Pfeiffer and van Zyl quoted in Wildberger, *Isaiah 1–12*, 124; Seitz, *Isaiah 1–39*, 138, 140; Skinner, *Isaiah*, 122, 123. Procksch (*Jesaia I*, 222–3) deems 16:6–12 to have come from a common source, though between Isaiah and Jeremiah, he chooses Jeremiah as the author of the Urtext. Isaiah commentators who reject the common source theory: Childs, *Isaiah*, 114; Kissane, *Isaiah 1–39*, 184, 193; Stacey, *Isaiah*, 100. Jeremiah commentators who reject the common source theory: Fretheim, *Jeremiah*, 595, 599, 601, 603; Miller, "Jeremiah," 891; Thompson, *Jeremiah*, 700.

35. Bardtke cited in Wildberger, *Isaiah 13–27*, 124; Blenkinsopp, *Isaiah 1–39*, 296, 298; implied in Smith, *Isaiah 1–32*, 279.

certain in every case.[36] A number of commentators (usually those with shorter commentaries) do not address the issue at all.[37]

However, the situation might not be as simple as the above three options might suggest, for texts themselves are dynamic and shaped over a period of time. Indeed, Holladay remarks that "the literary history of Isa 15–16 is itself tangled: it is not self-evident that the material in Isaiah that duplicates material in the Jer chapter is in every instance antecedent to the duplications in the Jer chapter."[38] Nevertheless, for the sections that have extensive overlap, it can probably be assumed that one or both authors relied on a source and for this reason, the following deals only with the three straightforward possibilities. It is sufficient for the purposes of this chapter to recognize and bear in mind that not all passages were necessarily available to anyone relying on the text of Jer 48 or Isa 15–16.

Demonstrating that Jer 48 depends on Isa 15–16 may be fruitful to the understanding of Jer 48. For example, a citation of lament does not necessarily carry the same weight as an original composition and so might affect how one views the tone. Or the substitution of מורד (Jer 48:5) in place of דרך (Isa 15:5), seemingly to balance it poetically with מעלה, might cast light on Jeremiah's literary shaping and the value he places on such. Alternatively, if it can be established that the author of Isa 15–16 depended on Jer 48, then Isa 15–16 (possibly the first ap-

---

36. Isaiah commentators: Calvin, *Isaiah*, 474; Kaiser, *Isaiah 13–39*, 60; Kidner, "Isaiah," 644; Sommer, "Isaiah," 816; Watts, *Isaiah 1–39*, 284; Wildberger, *Isaiah 1–12*, 124–5. Jeremiah commentators: Allen, *Jeremiah*, 477; implied by Brueggemann, *Jeremiah*, 442; Carroll, *Jeremiah*, 792, 795; Clements, *Jeremiah*, 252; de Waard, *Handbook*, 184; Duhm, *Jeremia*, 349–50, 350–51; Feinberg, *Jeremiah*, 306; Freedman, *Jeremiah*, 312; Holladay, *Jeremiah*, vol. 2, 346, 352; Jones, *Jeremiah*, 499, 505–8; Lundbom, *Jeremiah 37–52*, 287, 290–91, 296, 297; McKane, *Jeremiah*, vol. 2, 1192, cf. 1159, 1170, 1182, 1186–90, 1194; McKeating, *Jeremiah*, 203; Procksch, *Jesaia I*, 208; Rudolph, *Jeremiah*, 281; Smothers in Keown et al., *Jeremiah 26–52*, 310; implied in Stulman, *Jeremiah*, 361; Sweeney, "Jeremiah," 1020; Volz, *Der Prophet Jeremia*, 409, 410, 412, 413; Weiser, *Der Prophet Jeremia*, 403. Also, Schwally, Driver, Schottroff and Alonso-Schökel, cited in Wildberger, *Isaiah 1–12*, 124.

37. Isaiah commentators who do not address the issue: Brueggemann (though see Jeremiah commentary), Clements, Goldingay, Hayes and Irvine, Tucker, Widyapranawa, Young. Dillmann (*Jesaia*, 146) does not discuss the borrowing but deems Isa 15–16 to have been written by an unknown author. Jeremiah commentators who do not address the issue: Kidner and Calvin (though see Isaiah commentary).

38. Holladay, *Jeremiah*, vol. 2, 346.

propriation of Jer 48) might exemplify how Jer 48 was understood in antiquity. For instance, if this is the case then Jer 48:29–38a, in which YHWH weeps and wails (arguably the most intense part of the chapter), has been extensively reused, mainly in chapter 16, but in chapter 15 too, though, interestingly, some of the lament has been taken off YHWH's lips (Jer 48:31) and placed on Moab's (Isa 16:7). In contrast, the reference to YHWH as King (Jer 48:15) has been passed over. If both oracles use a common source, then the situation is similar to that of not knowing which text depends on the other, in that, without the source, analysis is restricted to comparisons. This is by no means valueless, however. For example, comparing Isa 16:6 and Jer 48:29 reveals that עברה (Isa 16:6) seems to have been a suitable synonym for רום לב (Jer 48:29).

Due to the restrictions of space, I will not rehearse all of the arguments for each position (though there are not many), especially as most are not very persuasive. For instance, Gray provides a rationale for a common source based largely on form-critical suppositions (the contrast between the elegiac tone of the common material and the non-shared material).[39] Yet it seems that Gray's case is substantially weakened by his reliance on certain underlying suppositions or assertions, such as his apparent assumption that Isaiah could not have borrowed from Jeremiah.

Wildberger is one of few who provide reasons for the majority position that Jer 48 quarried Isa 15–16. He provides about five reasons (though not systematically) for his view, but again most are less than convincing.[40] For example he supposes that Jeremiah's OANs were salvation oracles for Judah, that Isa 15–16 is carefully structured,[41] and that the fall of Moab in Isaiah is only partial, whereas (if one treats Jer 48:47 as an addition) the oracle in Jeremiah presents it as complete and as a past event.[42] Having given his supporting arguments, Wildberger asserts that, "These observations make clear that Jer 48 depends on Isaiah 15f."[43] To my mind, some of these observations are far from clear indi-

---

39. Gray, *Isaiah I–XXVII*, 271–72; see also Seitz, *Isaiah 1–39*, 138.
40. Wildberger, *Isaiah 13–27*, 14, 122, 124–25.
41. cf. Blenkinsopp, *Isaiah 1–39*, 297.
42. Cf. הנה־ימים באים (Jer 48:12), which suggests that her destruction lies partly in the future.
43. Wildberger, *Isaiah 13–27*, 125.

cators. Nevertheless, I am convinced by his observation that Jeremiah appears to be loosely constructed of material harvested from elsewhere, since, as can be seen from Table 4, Jer 48 shares material with a number of other places.[44] Indeed, Jones also reasons that, "Because so much is quoted, the dependence must be this way round."[45]

Interestingly, one of the few supporting arguments for Isaiah's dependence on Jeremiah uses the same argument; for Blenkinsopp surmises that "the more fragmentary state of Jer 48 suggests that this small collection of anti-Moabite propaganda has provided the raw material for the Isaian poet."[46] Nevertheless, it seems to me more likely, as Wildberger and Jones argue, that a loosely structured text containing material shared with a number of other Scriptures is a passage that has made use of these other sources, rather than a text that others have copied.

Isaiah 24:17–18

Scholars are a little more equally divided regarding the link between Jer 48:43–44 and Isa 24:17–18 than they are between Jer 48 and Isa 15–16. Of the Isaiah and Jeremiah commentators surveyed, only Thompson suggests that there might have been a common source underlying both.[47] Some are of the opinion that Isaiah quotes Jeremiah,[48] many, particularly Isaiah commentators, are undecided,[49] but the majority view is still that Jeremiah quotes Isaiah (Jones' reasoning is the same

---

44. Ibid.

45. Jones, *Jeremiah*, 499, a point he reiterates on p. 507. However, it must be noted that using the term "quoted" in his first clause presupposes his conclusion in the second.

46. Blenkinsopp, *Isaiah 1–39*, 298.

47. Thompson, *Jeremiah*, 713.

48. Blenkinsopp, *Isaiah 1–39*, 356; Holladay, *Jeremiah*, vol. 2, 348–49; Sweeney, "Jeremiah," 1024; Volz, *Der Prophet Jeremia*, 410; Wildberger, *Isaiah 1–12*, 499; Williamson, *Isaiah*, 181–83, 252; also tentatively holding this position are Clements, *Jeremiah*, 204 and Lundbom, *Jeremiah 37–52*, 304.

49. Isaiah commentators: Brueggemann, *Isaiah 1–39*, 194; Goldingay, *Isaiah*, 141; Gray, *Isaiah I–XXVII*, 419; Oswalt, *Isaiah*, 453; Tucker, "Isaiah," 212; Watts, *Isaiah 1–39*, 383; Kissane, *Isaiah 1–39*, 282 is ambiguous on the issue. Jeremiah commentators: Brueggemann, *Jeremiah*, 450–51; Fretheim, *Jeremiah*, 603; McKane, *Jeremiah*, vol. 2, 1196; McKeating, *Jeremiah*, 207.

as for Isa 15–16—see above), although Kaiser is the only Isaiah commentator here to suggest this.⁵⁰

Summary

Ultimately, one cannot fully resolve the direction that the borrowing took. Nevertheless, I am inclined to hold the view that Jer 48 might have been based upon Isa 15–16 and 24:17–18. The weight of scholarly support would indicate similarly. At the same time, the author has substantially changed the existing text for his own purposes and, as the texts stand, the dissimilarities between them highlight the distinct ways in which each has been shaped. In fact, the way an author shapes his work tends to be more apparent when there is a parallel version to act as a comparison. Nevertheless, the greater the divergence between the two texts, the less significant the borrowing becomes in terms of its impact on the new piece. Indeed, as has been shown, the purposes behind Isa 15–16 and Jer 48 appear to be quite separate.

Conclusion: Diverging Purposes

Exploring the similarities demonstrated that, although Isa 15–16 and Jer 48 contain much overlap, the two oracles are quite distinct from each other even in aspects that appear alike on the surface. So, whilst the place names seem to indicate in both oracles that Moab's destruction is widespread and the length of the oracles perhaps represents their importance in their corpora, the shared material demonstrates that the author reworked the secondary text in an unrestricted way, reweaving sections, quoting a single verse, or utilizing just one or two words or an idea.

The shared lament material is concentrated in one place in Jer 48, but spread out across Isa 15–16. Furthermore, Isaiah's oracle is largely a description of Moab's (and sometimes implicitly YHWH's) grief over

---

50. Allen, *Jeremiah*, 487; Carroll, *Jeremiah*, 795; Duhm, *Jeremia*, 351; Feinberg, *Jeremiah*, 307; Freedman, *Jeremiah*, 312; Jones, *Jeremiah*, 499, 506; Kaiser, *Isaiah 13–39*, 190; Rudolph, *Jeremiah*, 283; Smothers in Keown et al., *Jeremiah 26–52*, 310; implied in Stulman, *Jeremiah*, 361; Weiser, *Der Prophet Jeremia*, 410.

the scope and intensity of her destruction, whereas Jer 48 is broader in scope (concerned with Moab's sin, punishment, and restoration) and deeper in intensity (YHWH is explicitly designated as the one who mourns Moab).

Analyzing the material present in Jer 48 but not Isa 15–16 highlights the tensions that are present in Jer 48. First there is the paradox of YHWH as the agent of the punishment, the lament, and the restoration. Secondly, there is the undercurrent of a battle with Chemosh. These tensions may perhaps be detected in Isa 15–16, but to a much lesser degree. Likewise, Moab's sin is not absent in Isa 15–16, but pride is the only offence listed and even then, not in relation to YHWH. Her punishment is also briefly mentioned, but the oracle does not elaborate on it by means of metaphors as Jer 48 does and there is no equivalent to the curse of 48:10. There is also no direct reference to Moab's restoration, though Isa 16:5 seems to be a promise of hope (if not a "messianic" hope) for Moab in answer to a Moabite request to Judah to take pity on her fugitives.

All these observations highlight the diversity between the two oracles and emphasize that, whichever was the borrowed source, Isa 15–16 and Jer 48 bear their own individual stamps. Nevertheless, having addressed the issue of the direction of borrowing, it seems that Jer 48 contains so many references to other texts that its author is probably the one to have harvested the material from elsewhere. This conclusion is in keeping with the consensus among the commentators. However, a more interesting question than which came first might be to ask what those purposes might have been.

Brueggemann asserts regarding Isa 15–16 that mostly, "this song of grief is not interested in blame. The costs and hurts are too massive and acute for moralizing."[51] However, the costs and hurts are massive and acute in Jer 48, yet this oracle is interested in blame. Interestingly, Brueggemann takes a different tack here. He notes the opposing themes of pride and power, and loss, and remarks that "these two incongruous rhetorical elements fight each other."[52] In addition, he sees at the centre of the oracle the process that *arrogance* leads to *loss*, which leads to

---

51. Brueggemann, *Isaiah 1–39*, 145.
52. Brueggemann, *Jeremiah*, 443.

grief.[53] Thus, his approach to Jer 48 somewhat undermines his assertion concerning Isa 15–16. I would suggest that, rather than hurt being too deep for moralizing in Isa 15–16, it may be that issues of blame were not appropriate for the purpose for which Isaiah's oracle concerning Moab was written. Brueggemann also observes that, "The text passes up the chance to make an Israelite point that a Moabite god cannot save."[54] Again, the text may pass up the opportunity because it detracts from its main purpose.

Given its tone and content, one purpose of Jer 48 might be to provide an overall account of the whole perspective of the משפט upon Moab: the reason for it in terms of Moab's sins; who is responsible for it (YHWH by means of שדד "a destroyer"); the nature and scope of it (complete ruin across many of her cities and exile for her god); the reaction to this judgment (Moab's and YHWH's mourning over her); and the final outcome of YHWH's gracious restoration. It is beyond the rubric of this chapter to examine the purposes of Isa 15–16 except to note that scholars have proposed a number of reasons, some of which overlap with those given for Jer 48.[55] However, how scholars have viewed the purposes of Jer 48 is part of the investigation that will now be undertaken as the focus turns to how the U.S. scholars, Fretheim, Miller, and Brueggemann deal with this chapter.

---

53. Ibid., 449.
54. Brueggemann, *Isaiah 1–39*, 145.
55. Goldingay, *Isaiah*, 109; Kaiser, *Isaiah 13–39*, 74; Oswalt, *Isaiah*, 336.

4

An Analysis of Fretheim's, Miller's, and Brueggemann's Readings of Jeremiah 48

Introduction

IN THIS CHAPTER I WILL LOOK AT THE WAY IN WHICH THE THREE contemporary U.S. scholars—Fretheim, Miller, and Brueggemann—approach Jeremiah's oracle against Moab. I will pay particular attention to the hermeneutical moves that they make and will evaluate the respective strengths and weaknesses of such.

I will begin by outlining Miller's, Fretheim's, and Brueggemann's hermeneutical bases, which will be followed by an overview of the main points of their commentaries relating to Jeremiah's OANs and Jer 48 in particular. Then I will assess how the commentators address key issues in the text, such as its tone, the nature of divine involvement, and the content and purpose of the message. The tone is important, not only because it gives an indication of how to hear the message, but also because Jer 48 has quite a distinct note of lament. One reason that the nature of divine involvement becomes an interesting issue is because YHWH expressly interacts with a nation that is not עמי "my people" in the OANs. The OANs are in the strange position of being pronouncements regarding other nations, yet texts included in Israel's Scripture, so the purpose of the message is partly defined by which nation is expected to hear/read it, which adds an intriguing dimension. Therefore, it is pertinent to see how the commentators handle this, as well as what they consider to be the significant aspects of the content of the message. In the final section, I will examine how the three scholars appropriate the text as Scripture in a contemporary context.

Although all commentaries on Jer 48 are short pieces, some of the essential questions are tackled in the scholars' other writings that speak about the OANs, or more general topics, such as divine involvement. Therefore, I will draw on a variety of works throughout. None of the authors engages much with the Hebrew in their commentaries and that is reflected in this chapter.

Hermeneutical Bases

Before noting their individual outlooks, it is worth noting that Fretheim, Miller, and Brueggemann all wrote their commentaries for series whose editors explicitly relate the purpose of the commentaries to the Christian faith. Fretheim wrote for the *Smyth & Helwys Bible Commentary* series, which claims that: "In an unprecedented way, the *Smyth & Helwys Bible Commentary* brings insightful commentary to bear on the lives of contemporary Christians . . . The *Smyth & Helwys Bible Commentary* makes serious, credible biblical scholarship more accessible to a wider audience . . . Our writers are reputable scholars who participate in the community of faith and sense a calling to communicate the results of their scholarship to their faith community . . . Thus the reader can note a confessional tone throughout the volumes."[1]

Miller writes for *The New Interpreter's Bible* series, which describes its intention as follows: "The general aim of *The New Interpreter's Bible* is to bring the best in contemporary biblical scholarship into the service of the church to enhance preaching, teaching, and study of the Scriptures . . . The Reflections [sections] are geared specifically toward helping those who interpret Scripture in the life of the church by providing 'handles' for grasping the significance of Scripture for faith and life today."[2]

Though Brueggemann's commentary is now published independently, it was originally written for the *International Theological Commentary* series. On the back cover of each commentary is written: "The *International Theological Commentary* moves beyond a descriptive-historical approach to offer a relevant exegesis of the Old Testament text as Holy Scripture. The series aims, first, to develop the

---

1. Fretheim, *Jeremiah*, xiv–v.
2. Miller, "Jeremiah," xvii–iii.

theological significance of the Old Testament and, second, to emphasize the relevance of each book for the life of the church."[3]

These are the guidelines to which Fretheim, Miller, and Brueggemann were writing. At the same time, they are all working within their own individual Christian traditions as well.

Patrick Miller, a Presbyterian by tradition,[4] describes himself as a Reformed Theologian,[5] whilst Terence Fretheim studied and now teaches under a Lutheran banner.[6] Brueggemann, who had a "German Evangelical upbringing" and was "a child of the Prussian Union," belongs to the United Church of Christ.[7] Each of these North American scholars sees the Bible as Scripture that is relevant to present societies. Fretheim writes, "Let me suggest a preliminary understanding of the Bible as Word of God: the Bible's unique capacity to mediate God's word of judgment and grace, which can effect life and salvation for individuals and communities."[8] Miller expresses his position in the preface to his collected essays: "The hermeneutics of suspicion is always meant to be followed by a hermeneutics of retrieval, the fresh recovery of the significance of the biblical text for faith and life. I do not know if that is 'the law of the Medes and the Persians,' but it seems to me inescapable if scholarship is to be of service to both the academy and the church."[9]

Brueggemann asserts that the Bible's authority can only be understood in the light of the community it authorizes (that is, the church and synagogue, the academy, and the public arena) and that it is too easily "applied" to contemporary situations. He claims that, "The central thrust of this classic that mediates new life is its offer of an alternative reality of governance that is sure but not dominating, producing new modes of certitude, power, and knowledge."[10]

None of the scholars glosses over or dismisses the "hard texts." Fretheim asserts that "there are some biblical statements about God (as well as other matters) to which the reader simply has to say No! Readers

3. E.g. Widyapranawa, *Lord*, Back Cover.
4. Dobbs-Allsopp, "Teach Me," 26–27.
5. Miller, "God's Other Stories," 9.
6. Lutheran Seminary, "Terence E. Fretheim," Online.
7. Brueggemann, *Book that Breathes*, x, 21.
8. Fretheim and Froehlich, *Bible as Word of God*, 82.
9. Miller, "God's Other Stories," 11.
10. Brueggemann, *Book that Breathes*, 10–16, 17, 41–42.

can no longer simply trust everything that the Bible says, about God as well as other matters, and this makes problematic such an understanding of authority."[11] For: "The texts *themselves* fail us at times, perhaps even often. The patriarchal bias *is* pervasive, God *is* represented as an abuser and a killer of children, God *is* said to command the rape of women and the wholesale destruction of cities, including children and animals. To shrink from such statements is dishonest. To pretend that such texts are not there, or to try to rationalize our way out of them (as I have sometimes done), is to bury our heads in the sand."[12] He insists that we are always in danger of domesticating God, "making God more palatable to modern tastes," especially in relation to the judgment texts. It is therefore particularly interesting to see how he handles such a text as Jer 48, given that he aims to present Jeremiah's challenging image of YHWH in a way that helps "inform faith and life."[13]

Miller acknowledges that "we are before a great and terrible God who is known to be for us but who cannot be domesticated and moralized into a gentle, loving force." Like Fretheim, his solution on occasions is "to protest this savage and ungrounded destruction—as, indeed, we must, for we are moral creatures in God's own image." Yet, at the same time, he asserts that when our questioning is over, we, with Job, may need to repent rather than go home with satisfactory answers.[14]

One of the topics to which Brueggemann frequently returns (and which is most extensively discussed in his *Theology of Old Testament*) is that of the contradictory voices in the texts. Brueggemann perceives that OT rhetoric, particularly as it is found in texts such as Jeremiah, is "endlessly pluri-vocal, subversive, and deconstructive" and his aim is always to give these "'other voices' a serious hearing." Although he argues that suspicion is part of the canonical claim of the OT itself and such "paradigmatic juxtaposition of core testimony and countertestimony" refuse to give closure to the text, he welcomes Jürgen Moltmann's suggestion that Good Friday and Easter Sunday provide a "dialectic of reconciliation." With Miller, he stresses the necessity to retrieve texts after a suspicious reading and he argues that retrieving wounding texts entails honesty in facing the wounding and the wounded, whilst simul-

---

11. Fretheim and Froehlich, *Bible as Word of God*, 61.
12. Ibid., 100.
13. Fretheim, *Jeremiah*, xiii; Fretheim and Froehlich, *Bible as Word of God*, 105.
14. Miller, "Jeremiah," 919.

taneously expecting healing. Like Israel, Brueggemann tries to come to terms with the difficulty that YHWH is "sometimes silent . . . sometimes ashamedly absent . . . sometimes unreliable and notoriously cunning." Therefore, unlike Fretheim and to a lesser extent Miller, Brueggemann is disinclined to say "no" to the problematic texts in this "haunting book," but rather to hold them in tension with the "easier" texts.[15]

In their respective commentaries on Jeremiah, both Fretheim and Miller are sympathetic to Childs' canonical approach and applaud his (and others') attempts to find coherence in the book and to concentrate on the final form whilst not ignoring the process of transmission and earlier levels of the text.[16] Fretheim welcomes the later textual developments because "they reveal an understanding that Jeremiah's words continue to speak to audiences that live on the far side of the original historical context."[17] However, the tension between the historical and literary worlds, between diachronic and synchronic readings, is ever-present and can be observed in the way Miller approaches his commentary on Jeremiah. Whilst he elsewhere proposes that the prophets and their prophecies can only be understood in their social, political and religious contexts, in his commentary on Jeremiah, "oracles and narratives are interpreted as they relate to the picture of the prophet they present without trying to differentiate between the historical prophet and the presented prophet."[18] This is not a reversal of stance, for he does not ignore the historical context in Jeremiah; rather he acknowledges, despite his expansive knowledge of history, that there is a limit to how far one can match the literary and the historical.

Brueggemann refrains from placing too much emphasis on questions of "history" too. As well, he resists the "dominant reality" of our time and place and also the dogmatic theological claims of the Christian tradition. He makes these decisions in order not to "curb the richness, boldness, and complexity of Israel's testimony," and is partly driven by his premise that "fideism and scepticism are twin temptations." Although he considers that preoccupation with historical criticism is responsible

---

15. Brueggemann, *Theology of Old Testament*, 133; Brueggemann, *Jeremiah*, 13; Brueggemann, *Deep Memory*, 48, 55; Brueggemann, *Book that Breathes*, 132, 147, 176; Brueggemann, *Like Fire*, 60, 91, 132–40.

16. Fretheim, *Jeremiah*, 28; Miller, "Jeremiah," 566.

17. Fretheim, *Jeremiah*, 29.

18. Miller, "World," 97; Miller, "Jeremiah," 561.

for severely limiting Jeremiah studies and judges the "hermeneutically innocent" canonical approach of Childs to operate from high ground since it assumes such a reading is self-evident,[19] he acknowledges the merits of both. Nevertheless, Brueggemann, a student of James Muilenburg, claims that OT theology "is essentially a rhetorical analysis ... to see what Israel says about YHWH." He combines the two methods of sociological and literary analysis so that he reads Jeremiah with "*a critique of ideology* and a *practice of liberated imagination.*" He presses the need for a pluralistic interpretation, but at the same time insists that OT theology must also "stand in some interpretive continuity with ancient witnesses who imagined and uttered with radical difference." Brueggemann attempts, in his commentary on Jeremiah, "to 'go inside'" the text with as few prejudices and premature judgments as possible.[20] Thus, Brueggemann asserts, as Miller and Fretheim infer, that one needs to fully enter the literary world of the text to truly understand it.

It is worth including Brueggemann's own admission as a close to this section: "I have come belatedly to see, in my own case, that my hermeneutical passion is largely propelled by the fact that my father was a pastor economically abused by the church he served, economically abused as a means of control. I cannot measure the ways in which that felt awareness determines how I work, how I interpret, whom I read, whom I trust as a reliable voice. The wound is deep enough to pervade everything."[21]

Overviews

Fretheim

Many of Fretheim's general, introductory observations about the book of Jeremiah are reiterated in a more specific way in his remarks on Jeremiah's OANs. For instance, he views the book of Jeremiah as a collage: "That is, the book does not present an argument in any usual sense

---

19. Brueggemann, *Theology of Old Testament*, 729; Brueggemann, *Ichabod*, 88; Brueggemann, *Book that Breathes*, 112–13, 117, 168; Brueggemann, *Like Fire*, 30, 33–34, 91.

20. Brueggemann, *Jeremiah*, xii, 17; Brueggemann, *Deep Memory*, 122; Brueggemann, *Book that Breathes*, 112, 143, 145.

21. Brueggemann, *Book that Breathes*, 32.

or a clear historical development but seeks to achieve its objective by a kaleidoscopic look at a highly complex situation from a myriad of angles. The resultant portrayal is highly impressionistic, perhaps even surreal, and leaves the reader with a sense of the situation that is much more effective than a photograph or a linear argument could achieve."[22] He considers Jer 48 similarly: "The poetry in these oracles is a kind of rhetorical collage, designed to look at Moab's disastrous situation from every angle, as if turning an object in the light and seeing how the light plays off different surfaces."[23]

Other examples of the coherence Fretheim sees between Jeremiah as a whole and the OANs can be found in some of the major themes he detects in both, such as: God and creation; the pathos of God; and, sin and judgment. The theme of creation forms a large part of Fretheim's overall interpretative framework and he claims that, in order to understand Jeremiah as a prophet to the nations, it is imperative to recognize the importance of creation in the book of Jeremiah. He reasons that, "because God is the God of all creation, God is the God of all peoples and nations," and he notes that in Jer 46–51 "again and again the parallels between Israel and the nations are drawn out." Fretheim considers that the function of the OANs is to herald a universal restoration and that the purposes of YHWH are universal in scope. The oracles, such as that concerning Moab, which end with a promise of restoration to the nation are an indication of this. At the same time, he acknowledges that "the particularity of God's work in and through Israel remains intact amid the universality of God's work among the nations" and that Israel has a special place even in the OANs.[24]

Much of Fretheim's commentary on the oracle concerning Moab focuses on the aspect of lament and the pathos of God, which Fretheim sees particularly evident in Jer 48. Indeed, he says, "For God, the internal side of judgment is grief."[25] He also points out that arrogance, not idolatry, is the most common sin in Jeremiah's OANs and is the one for which Moab is condemned in Jer 48.[26] As well, Fretheim draws significant attention to Moab's judgment in terms of her utter destruc-

22. Fretheim, *Jeremiah*, 19, 22 (quote on p.22).
23. Ibid., 597.
24. Ibid., 29–41, 575, 577, 578, 579, 638; Fretheim, *God and World*, 168, 174.
25. Fretheim *Suffering of God*, 112; Fretheim, *Jeremiah*, 597, 602, 603.
26. Fretheim, *Jeremiah*, 576–77, 595.

tion and her shame and humiliation.²⁷ "Certain sounds are interwoven throughout, and they are primarily the sounds of wailing and crying on the part of the Moabites, its neighbors, and God. This theme of weeping is interwoven with the staccato beat of devastation, desolation, and death and their effect on the Moabites and their status in the world. These materials tend to evoke different emotions in the reader: a recognition of what pride, arrogance, and self-satisfaction can lead to as well as a sympathy for those who are suffering in the wake of marauding armies."²⁸

Fretheim's understanding, apparent throughout his commentary on Jeremiah, is that YHWH's judgment is often worked out through consequences inherent in the sin, that is, human רעה "evil" brings רעה "disaster."²⁹

Fretheim notices that Jer 1:1–3 indicates that the fall of Jerusalem has already taken place and therefore that these verses "provide a lens through which the book is to be read." The *preaching* of Jeremiah thus addresses a different audience than the *book* of Jeremiah (even if such audiences are composed largely of the same people). However, he does not appear to allow for an audience for the preaching of Jer 48, since "in their most basic form, these oracles are, of course, not spoken to Moabites but are shaped for exilic readers." Although he considers that the OANs had their own pre-prophetic history of transmission, he is not persuaded by any of the options offered (for example, military, royal, or worship), though he acknowledges that they have been shaped by holy war.³⁰

Miller

Miller also has the Exile and Fall of Jerusalem in mind when he writes of Jeremiah that "no other biblical book so enables readers to compre-

---

27. משפט "judgment" is only used five times in Jeremiah's OANs, two of which are in chapter 48. Therefore, whilst "judgment" may not always be the most appropriate term to use when speaking about Jer 46–51, it appears suitable with regard to the oracle concerning Moab. משפט will be discussed further in chapter 6.

28. Fretheim, *Jeremiah*, 597.

29. Ibid., 34, 576, 579; see also Fretheim, *God and World*, 163. Similar could be said of עון although he does not. Cf. McConville ("Judgment and God," 31, 34) who is wary of this "'mechanistic' worldview."

30. Fretheim, *Jeremiah*, 4, 579, 596.

hend theologically what was going on at that time—to hear both what happened and why it happened." It seems that, for Miller, the OANs help the reader understand the universality of YHWH's dominion, for "the sovereign rule of that God over the whole earth is nowhere more clearly asserted than in the address of oracles to other nations without respect to their relationship to Israel/Judah." He repeats this idea in his section on Jer 48; "even other nations find themselves under the rule of the Lord of Israel." Although he asserts that such a universal reign is good news for both the chosen and unchosen, that God's last word throughout Scripture is not judgment, and that eschatological hope may have universal dimensions, Miller stresses that the restoration promised to Moab and others are specific promises to particular peoples and nations.[31]

Miller notes that Jeremiah's OANs "share neither form nor tone." In some, for example, pathos accompanies the declaration of future destruction, whilst the announcement is given with "fierce intent" in others. He acknowledges that "the sounds and wails and acts of mourning reverberate" in Jer 48, but he does not concentrate on that aspect. Instead, he focuses on the conflict between "'the King, whose name is the LORD of hosts' (v. 15)" and the Moabite gods. Although Miller does not use the terms "Divine Warrior" and "Day of the Lord" with respect to Moab, these are terms he uses throughout his commentary on Jer 46–51 (chapters 46, 47, 49, and 50–51), and the idea is present in his comments on chapter 48, too. For his statement in his "Reflections" on Jeremiah's OANs that, "the divine warrior who goes with sword in hand is the ruler whose kingdom and power are at stake" accords with his portrayal of the God who conquers Chemosh and the Moabite gods.[32] Likewise, he does not mention YHWH's vengeance with regard to Moab, although this is also a common element in his remarks on the OANs in general.

Miller gives both Moab's sin and her resulting punishment considerable attention. The "arrogance and insolence of the nation" leads to destruction and "to the picture of shame and devastation, a nation reduced, is added a nation humiliated." Here, Miller observes, "sin and punishment correspond as they do elsewhere in the prophets." When he talks of a correspondence, he means, loosely, that the punishment fits

---

31. Miller, "Jeremiah," 555, 878, 892, 918–20.
32. Ibid., 878, 883, 885, 886, 890, 900, 915, 919.

the crime. Thus, "the nation that laughed at a destroyed Israel will itself become a laughingstock."[33]

Brueggemann

Since it is difficult to discern the political-historical events, geographical places, and literary intentions in this "disordered" poem of Jer 48, Brueggemann largely restricts himself to the text's claims and its rhetorical effect. He perceives that this literary world is concerned with the power and pride of Moab and her god, Chemosh, all of which are dismantled under the power of YHWH's sovereignty. In less than twelve pages of commentary, Brueggemann uses the word "power" or its derivatives twenty three times (more than he uses any other significant word), six times twinned with "pride." He deduces that the theological conclusion of the wine-making metaphor in 48:10–13 is that Chemosh has failed and the title "the King" in 48:15 provides "a direct challenge to the rule of Chemosh, who is in the process of being dethroned and displaced." Brueggemann points out that both Judah's exile and that of Chemosh, with Moab's priests and princes, are due to trusting in false gods and ideologies.[34]

Much of Brueggemann's work on this chapter focuses on the political nature of Moab's pride and subsequent destruction ("political" is used ten times and variants of "destruction"/"destroy" occur eighteen times). He asserts that, in general, OANs demonstrate that when a nation overreaches itself and "violates the larger dynamic of the political process which has a coherent moral purpose, trouble comes." In Moab's case, the indictment is twofold; first, she raised herself up against YHWH and secondly, she set herself against Israel, making the latter a laughingstock. Her punishment is to be reduced to helpless humiliation. Brueggemann sees the text's assumption that Moab "should be responsive or submissive to YHWH" as "a daring act of rhetoric which insists upon connections where others do not notice or acknowledge them."[35]

Whilst accepting the oft-stated opinion that the OANs declare YHWH's sovereignty over all, Brueggemann argues that this is not their

---

33. Ibid., 890–92.
34. Brueggemann, *Jeremiah*, 442–45.
35. Ibid., 420; 446–47; 453–54.

only purpose and they need more nuanced treatment. Neither is he persuaded that the OANs were intended only for Judah and considers that Jeremiah's oracle against Moab "is too specific and didactic for that to be an adequate explanation of the poem." YHWH "speaks this way because the establishment of YHWH's hegemony over the nations is crucial to their well-being." Thus Jer 48:14–20 urges Moab "to change its speech, in order to bring its speech into contact with the new reality caused by YHWH"—a reality of devastation. Brueggemann expands the idea of unreality and reality (a common theme of his) in his comments on 48:29–33 when he proposes that YHWH is real throughout, but Moab treats him as "unreal," which leads to Moab herself becoming "unreal."[36]

Brueggemann draws attention to the lament and grief in Jer 48, but he does not attribute the weeping to YHWH and his focus, rather than being on the mourning itself, is on Moab's former state and the cause of the mourning, that is, the "exuberant," "extravagant" celebration, no doubt with "exaggerated drinking", which is brought to "an abrupt" end. He understands the poet to be proposing that *arrogance* leads to *loss*, which in turn leads to *grief* (emphasis his).[37]

The restoration promised Moab at the end of the chapter is, he proposes, the newness that follows from YHWH's sovereignty, sovereignty that is only established through Moab's destruction. He asserts that YHWH destroys in order to save, in the same way that governments in the real world of power behave.[38]

Analysis

The analysis that follows looks at how Fretheim, Miller, and Brueggemann deal with the tone of Jer 48, the nature of divine involvement, the contents and purpose of the oracle, and the way it should be appropriated as Christian Scripture today. There is some overlap between sections, partly because the line of delineation between, say, tone and divine involvement, is narrow, but also because the commentators are not work-

---

36. Brueggemann, *Cadences*, 88; Brueggemann, *Jeremiah*, 418–21, 446, 448, 452. The use of the masculine pronoun for YHWH is mine—Brueggemann is careful not to refer to God/YHWH in gendered terminology.

37. Brueggemann, *Jeremiah*, 448–49.

38. Ibid., 452–53.

ing within these categories and their remarks often extend across my divisions.

Tone

There are several major themes that run throughout the oracle against Moab, including lament, destruction, and shame, which are common to the OANs. However, the tone of lament wails louder in the oracle against Moab than in any other of Jeremiah's OANs. Although both Fretheim and Miller point out that mourning is a prominent feature of the chapter, Miller barely discusses the subject, only briefly noting that YHWH is the subject of the lament in verses 31–32.[39] Fretheim, on the other hand, dedicates two sections to the "Divine Lament over Moab," which, together, span three of the total ten pages of his commentary on chapter 48. Brueggemann's commentary lies between the two. He notes that the motif of sadness is adumbrated by the first word of the oracle, "Woe" (48:1), and he discusses the wailing and mourning, but does not offer lament as a *leitmotif* and his commentary reflects this.

I would suggest that the differences may largely be due to the nuances and elements in a text to which the commentators are naturally attuned. Fretheim notices suffering, particularly divine suffering; indeed he has published a book entitled *The Suffering of God*, a work to which he refers the readers of his commentary on Jer 48. His writings are concerned more than Miller's with YHWH's emotions and he asserts in his Jeremiah commentary and in *God and World in the Old Testament* that the God of Jeremiah is not an aloof God. "God is a God of great passions (pathos); deep and genuine divine feelings and emotions are manifest again and again. Sorrow, lament, weeping, wailing, grief, pain, anguish, heartache, regret, and anger all are ascribed to God in Jeremiah."[40] Brueggemann is closer to Fretheim than Miller in his emphases on YHWH's emotions and attributes so it is interesting that he does not note that it is YHWH who wails over Moab in Jer 48.

Fretheim is keen to point out that display of divine emotion is not for sentimentality's sake and in the same way, Fretheim's perceptions of lament in a passage are not due to his own sentimentality. He considers that the tone of 48:30–33 might be ironic, rather than mournful, but he

---

39. Fretheim, *Jeremiah*, 577, 595, 597 (thrice), 600; Miller, "Jeremiah," 890.
40. Fretheim, *Jeremiah*, 33; Fretheim, *God and World*, 173.

reasons from the text that it is a genuine lament. This is partly because YHWH's lamenting corresponds with his summons to the Moabites to flee, but also because lament is a common feature of the OANs.[41]

Fretheim observes (in both his sections concerning divine lament) that five different verbs for weeping and wailing are used in Jer 48:31–33, 36. This range of vocabulary stresses the depth to which YHWH enters into his mourning over Moab, he deduces, emphasizing that "God's lament places the divine wailing over Moab in parallel with the divine lament over Israel."[42] Although, as stated, he acknowledges the particularity of Israel, throughout his commentary on Jer 48 he draws attention, as here, to the similarities between Moab and Israel.

Given that Israel was YHWH's own special people, it is all the more remarkable that YHWH expends such sorrow and mourning over Moab. To have noted that not only were five different funereal verbs used in these verses, but that they were expended on a foreign nation, would have reinforced Fretheim's claim that "this is an intense experience for God."[43] Elsewhere (*The Suffering of God*) he does make this observation: "To hear such mourning on the part of God for a non-Israelite people is striking indeed. Most of this language is also used to describe the weeping and wailing of the Moabites, so that the impression created is that of a God whose lamentation is as deep and broad as that of the people themselves."[44]

A few pages later he calls attention to the parallel between Israel and the nations: "That God is represented as mourning over the fate of non-Israelite people as well as Israelites demonstrates the breadth of God's care and concern for the sufferers of the world, whoever they might be. Israel has no monopoly on God's empathy. All people everywhere have *experienced* the compassion (and judgment) of God, even though they may not realize that fact. There is a universal extension of the compassion of God in these passages that is matched by such texts as Jon. 4:10–11 and Jer. 12:14–15."[45]

That God cares for all people everywhere is undoubtedly a belief held by Christians, and Jer 48 with its strong note of lament lends itself

41. Fretheim, *Jeremiah*, 33, 604–5.
42. Ibid., 601, 605.
43. Ibid., 605.
44. Fretheim, *Suffering of God*, 133.
45. Ibid., 137.

to such an understanding, but I wonder if Fretheim's commitment to his creational model sometimes overshadows the centrality of the concept of election.

Although Miller does not comment on the divine lament in Jer 48 other than noting its existence, neither does he overly seek to converge the paths of YHWH's dealings with Israel and Moab. It is true that he points out the similarity between the fate of Judah and the nations and notes that both Judah and some foreign nations are offered restoration.[46] However, in his commentary, the "foreignness" of Moab remains intact. For instance, the strangeness that Israel's God might relate to Moab at all is reflected in his statement that, "*Even* the other nations find themselves under the rule of the Lord of Israel" (emphasis mine). Also, where Fretheim notices that the restoration promised to Moab uses language used earlier for Israel, Miller points out that no details are given about what Moab's restoration involves, whereas they are for Judah.[47]

Perhaps the best example of the "foreignness" of Moab in Miller's commentary, however, is in the way he concentrates on the centrality of the gods in Moabite culture and reveals YHWH's opposition to them. Miller's ear is attuned to the "conflict between gods that lies beneath the surface of Jer 48" and therefore his commentary assumes a warlike tone.[48] He argues that: "Although there is no explicit conflict between the Lord and the god of Moab, there is an implicit claim that the Lord is sovereign over the gods of Moab. The text combines the reference to Chemosh's going into exile (v. 7) with the identification of the destruction of Moab as 'the work of the LORD' (v. 20), a theme that echoes throughout the rest of the chapter."[49]

He notes that YHWH will bring an end to sacrifices to other gods. In contrast, Fretheim says little about YHWH's opposition to Chemosh and the gods of Moab. This may be because he considers that idolatry is not the focus of Jeremiah's OANs and "even in v. 35 the issue of worshipping other gods is somewhat subdued."[50] However, since chapter 48 implicitly seems to oppose YHWH and Chemosh, a short discussion on the topic might have been helpful.

46. Miller, "Jeremiah," 918.
47. Ibid., 892–93.
48. Ibid., 891.
49. Ibid.
50. Fretheim, *Jeremiah*, 576–77, 602–3.

Although Miller does not explicitly speak in terms of tone, such conflict is a dominant tenor in his work and again it is easy to trace this heightened awareness. Miller has charted the history of Israel's God in relation to the Canaanite gods El and Baal and has a lasting interest in Ugarit and her deities. Therefore, he has given a great deal of thought to the contrasts and connections between the gods of the ANE. In addition, he has written extensively on the topic of YHWH as a divine warrior, who fights holy war for Israel. These two interests combined explain why YHWH should be portrayed in his commentary on Jer 48 as the conqueror of Chemosh, particularly since the imagery of divine warrior is beginning to become more prevalent by the time of Jeremiah: "The language and understanding of God as warrior dominated Israel's faith throughout its course. In prophetic oracles, in psalms of the temple, and especially in the development of eschatological and apocalyptic literature, the centrality of YHWH as the divine warrior and commander of the armies of heaven and earth is very much to the fore and grows out of the earlier theological formulations. It would not be amiss to say that the most elaborated conceptions of the divine warrior come at the end of the Old Testament period."[51]

There is no mention or inference of YHWH as divine warrior in Brueggemann's commentary and while he translates יהוה צבאות as "LORD of the troops" (48:1), his remarks on the verse concern the sovereignty of YHWH, rather than his warrior status (though Brueggemann expounds this military formula elsewhere in his commentary).[52] Perhaps the lack of discussion regarding the divine warrior is largely to do with the fact that Brueggemann focuses not so much on the battle itself, but on the reasons for and the results of it. The first word, "woe" gives the tenor of what follows, he asserts, and writes of verses 34–39: "In grief, this is what the mourner might say: 'How it is broken!' The poet comes close to the edge of language, beyond which nothing dare be uttered. The rhetoric provides no coherent statement, but almost an ejaculation of disconnected words: 'broken, wail, shame, derision.' Moab is completely dismantled; nothing coherent can even be voiced about it."[53]

So, one of the tones in Brueggemann's commentary is brokenness, which is portrayed by the rhetoric of sharp reversals: "Mourning, weep-

---

51. Miller, *Divine Warrior*, 171.
52. Brueggemann, *Jeremiah*, 428.
53. Ibid., 450.

ing, [and] crying" stems from this brokenness along with "humiliation, weakness, helplessness, and instability." However, Brueggemann's concentration on the contrast between the former pride and fortunes of Moab and all she has lost somewhat overshadows the tone of lament. Indeed, he notes how the rhetoric of 48:29 piles up six words, five of which are either derived from the same root or have a similar sound: "'pride, pride, loftiness, pride, arrogance, a haughty heart.'"[54]

In his other writings Brueggemann notes that the proper idiom for a prophet is grief, particularly in Jeremiah, and, "My impression is that one could open Jeremiah's poetry almost anywhere and find this ministry of articulated grief." He also sees in the prophets a God of pathos and suffering, and a God who grieves. Most of Brueggemann's observations and insights regarding YHWH's grief and mourning are in the context of Israel/Judah (for example, grief at their end) and one might conclude that YHWH's pathos is confined to his people in the mind of Brueggemann.[55] Yet, in his chapter "Nations as YHWH's Partner" in *Theology of the Old Testament* he writes: "It is much less explicit that YHWH's governance of the nations is marked as much by *passion* as it is by freedom. Here we move in the realm of inference, but we must at least ponder the rehabilitative utterance of YHWH concerning the nations, which we have noticed in Amos 9:7, Isa 19:23–25, Isa 56:3, 6–7, and Jonah. In each of these, YHWH makes a positive move toward the nations, for which there seems to be no evident motivation."[56]

It is true that *passion* does not necessarily include lament and grief, but YHWH's expressed sorrow over Moab in Jer 48 would support this "inference" of Brueggemann's. It might even allow Brueggemann to say of the nations as he does of Israel, "Without this grief, there is no tomorrow . . . out of God's grief comes utter new possibility." Certainly, such assertions would not be out of place regarding Jer 48 with its strong tone of lament and its final promise of restoration. Similarly, it would have been pertinent in the context of Jer 48 to make his assertion that

---

54. Ibid., 443–51, 453; see also Calvin, *Jeremiah*, 32–33; Feinberg, *Jeremiah*, 305; Fretheim, *Jeremiah*, 601; Lundbom, *Jeremiah 37–52*, 288; Thompson, *Jeremiah*, 710.

55. Brueggemann, *Creative Word*, 12; Brueggemann, *Theology of the Old Testament*, 245, 647; Brueggemann, *Jeremiah*, 5, 7; Brueggemann, *Prophetic Imagination*, 46–48, 79; Brueggemann, *Like Fire*, 69, 192, 199.

56. Brueggemann, *Theology of the Old Testament*, 523; see also Brueggemann, *Creative Word*, 12.

YHWH's purposes for creation become evident in the midst of suffering and the hope of public newness.[57]

Most of Brueggemann's reflections concern Moab, rather than YHWH, and it may be for this reason that he recounts Moab's suffering and lamenting, but not YHWH's. Neither does he talk much about Judah, which may also be why he does not tend to compare and contrast Moab and Judah in the way that Fretheim does. As stated, he makes the comment that Judah and Moab both go into exile because of idolatry, but, like Miller, he retains the foreignness of Moab by keeping her in the context of Chemosh. He writes of 48:7, "It is stunning that this is now 'the people of Chemosh,' Moab as known by its god."[58]

Miller, writing about those nations in Jeremiah that are given no reason for their destruction, asserts, "The reader confronts head-on this terrible God who moves in wrath that cannot be softened or covered up. Its color is blood. Its outcome is death."[59] However, he does not provide a softened image of YHWH that is not blood red for those nations, such as Moab, that are given a reason for their destruction. The oracle against Moab with its plangent wailing is a prime candidate for demonstrating that the "terrible God who moves in wrath" is also, to use Fretheim's words, "a God of great passions (pathos)," "a God whose lamentation is as deep and broad as that of the people themselves."[60] Fretheim recognizes that the holy war tradition has shaped the OANs[61] and acknowledges in *The Suffering of God* that YHWH is sometimes a Warrior, but when speaking of such asks, "what does it *cost* God for God to *be* God?"[62] (emphasis his). He also asserts in several works that YHWH's anger is not a divine attribute and without human sin there would be no divine wrath or violence.[63]

In the light of Miller's and Fretheim's commentaries, the absence of any discussion about what YHWH "feels" for Moab (whether pathos

---

57. Brueggemann, *Like Fire*, 78, 165.

58. Brueggemann, *Jeremiah*, 451.

59. Miller, "Jeremiah," 919.

60. Fretheim, *Jeremiah*, 33; Fretheim, *God and World*, 173; Fretheim, *Suffering of God*, 133.

61. Fretheim, *Jeremiah*, 579.

62. Fretheim, *Suffering of God*, 31–32.

63. Fretheim, "Divine Dependence," 11; Fretheim, "Reflections," 30; Fretheim, "Angry," 365.

or wrath) is even more stark in Brueggemann's commentary. Given that in so much of his work Brueggemann is at pains to hear all the voices in the text, this is somewhat surprising. Whatever his reason, the effect is that YHWH appears remote and even dispassionate. At this point it would be useful to look in more detail at how the commentators view divine involvement in Jer 48.

Divine Involvement

YHWH's relationship to his creation is one of Fretheim's most-discussed topics. Repeatedly throughout his writings he speaks of YHWH interacting with his creation in a relational way.[64] For instance, he writes in *God and World*, "all of the creatures of the natural order are considered to be members of God's own family."[65] That YHWH has a genuine relationship with humanity can be seen in the metaphors that are used in Scripture, for example, king–subject, husband–wife, parent–child, shepherd–sheep, and redeemer–redeemed; even non-personal metaphors, such as a rock, are described in human terms.

> Thus, when we speak of the knowledge of God, the relational and experiential aspects need to be emphasized. God's revelation occurs within the context of a personal relationship, indeed most clearly in connection with a personal encounter, and it is shaped in fundamental ways by the way in which the resultant relationship is understood to engage everyday experience. God does not leave a word and then go, but accompanies that word with a continuing personal presence (cf. the "I am with you" formula in the theophanies—Gen 26:24; Jer 1:8). But even more, that continuing presence is to be interpreted in terms of the theophanic appearance. That presence has essential continuities with what was inherent in the theophany; it is a personal and interpersonal encounter even though the human form is no longer evident (cf. New Testament talk about the work of the Holy Spirit in John 14–16).[66]

---

64. Fretheim, *Suffering of God*; Fretheim, "Color of God"; Fretheim, "Plagues"; Fretheim, "Divine Dependence"; Fretheim, "God Who Acts"; Fretheim, "Reflections"; Fretheim, "To Say Something"; Fretheim, *Jeremiah*; Fretheim, "Response to McConville"; Fretheim, "Angry"; Fretheim, *God and World*; Fretheim & Froehlich, *Bible as Word of God* (the references in each are too numerous to list them all individually).

65. Fretheim, *God and World*, 261.

66. Fretheim, "Color of God," 261.

He observes that the prophets use these relational metaphors more than they do covenantal ones. In Fretheim's view, such a relationship is not confined to Israel but embraces the whole world.[67]

Furthermore, he sees the whole cosmos as interrelated and he often uses the image of a spider web to explain his model.[68] "To live in a relational world inevitably means that every creature will be affected by every other; each individual is involved in the plight of all." This includes YHWH who has chosen to limit himself to work from within the created order. Therefore, YHWH will be affected and caught up by the world's violence, according to Fretheim. At the same time, he argues that YHWH's work with human beings will positively affect the estranged relationship between other humans, the animals, and the natural order in general.[69] He does not make this latter point in relation to Jer 48, although it would suggest that Moab's restoration has, by implication, a good effect on all, which would help support his claims that the purpose of the OANs is about universal restoration. Instead, as mentioned above, he points out that the language used for Moab's restoration of fortunes is that used earlier in the book for Israel (for example, 29:14).

Elsewhere, Fretheim stresses that the intensity of YHWH's presence in the world varies and is partly dependent on human need and experience. He apprehends that this varying intensity also confirms the advantage there is in being the elected people. For, although YHWH engages with the lives of outsiders, blesses them, and even makes promises to them, this is not sufficient for the fullest possible life, a life that Israel has.[70] Nevertheless, this is not a stance he stresses in his Jeremiah commentary on chapter 48.

Fretheim remarks that there is a surprising number of references to "God's daughter" [sic] in Jeremiah's OANs (46:11, 19, 24; 48:18; 49:4; 50:42; cf. Isa 23:12; 47:1) and concludes that, "It is theologically significant that Israel is not the only people who are considered to be the children of God. These references are testimony to God as Creator of all

---

67. Fretheim, *Suffering of God*, 114, 115, 116; Fretheim, "Color of God," 264; Fretheim, "Divine Dependence," 1; Fretheim, "Reflections," 26, 33; Fretheim, *Jeremiah*, 31–34; Fretheim, "Response to McConville," 45; Fretheim, *God and World*, 15, 17, 241.

68. Fretheim, "Divine Dependence," 2; Fretheim, *Jeremiah*, 31; Fretheim, *God and World*, xiv, 19.

69. Fretheim, "Angry," 367; Fretheim, *God and World*, 26, 196.

70. Fretheim, *Suffering of God*, 62; Fretheim, *God and World*, 25, 105, 107.

people; as such, God as parent is concerned about the welfare of all of God's children, not just God's elect."[71]

Jer 48:18 refers to Dibon (an important Moabite city) as ישבת בת־דיבון. However, it is disputable how the בת־ idiom is to be translated ("daughter," "daughter of," "lady," or "inhabitants of") and what precisely it means.[72] The debate partly relates to whether a relationship is implied in the idiom, particularly that with YHWH, or if it is just a way of referring to people of a city or town, that is, "daughter of Dibon."[73] So, while the idiom may imply that YHWH is the father of the people (and Fitzgerald and Caragounis take this to be the case when the idiom is used of Israel), it does not necessarily have that connotation. At the same time, MT Jer 49:4 does not use בת in its construct state as in the idiom and cannot therefore be read as "people of..." Instead, it uses the absolute state and can only be a relational designation for Ammon; הבת השובבה "faithless daughter." However, Jer 48:18 does not actually state that Moab is YHWH's daughter, for example, "my daughter." Therefore Fretheim's presumption on this point suggests that at times his theological schema makes some of his detailed exegesis questionable.

It is, perhaps, also equally theologically significant that, even if the בת־ idiom is used to denote Egypt, Moab, Ammon, and Babylon as YHWH's "daughter" in Jeremiah, the foreign nations are never referred to as his בנים "sons" (a higher status in the ancient world than "daughter") as are Israel and Judah (for example, Isa 1:2). Neither is a marital metaphor employed. In fact a husband–wife relationship is never applied in the OT to describe the relationship between YHWH and the foreign nations. That the higher status terms as well as the most intimate of relational expressions are reserved for Israel/Judah alone suggests that YHWH does not enter into as deep a relationship with the nations.

---

71. Fretheim, *Jeremiah*, 583; also Fretheim, *God and World*, 168 except read "Israelites are" for "Israel is."

72. NRSV translates ישבת בת־דיבון in Jer 48:18 as "enthroned daughter Dibon," NIV "inhabitants of the Daughter of Dibon," NEB and REB "natives of Dibon," NASB "daughter dwelling in Dibon," AV "thou daughter that dost inhabit Dibon," and GNB "you that live in Dibon."

73. Althann, "Jeremiah IV 11–12," 390; Caragounis, "בַּת," 780; Fitzgerald, "Mythological," 403–16; "BTWLT and BT," 167–83; Haag, "בַּת," 335; Tsevat, "בְּתוּלָה; בְּתוּלִים," 341.

So, then, I consider that Fretheim needs to clarify if he is speaking about Israel only when he exhorts his *Ex Auditu* readers, "When thinking of God as judge, remember that the judge behind the bench is the spouse of the accused one in the dock."[74] His overall outlook is in accord with common Christian understanding in that "God is not a suffering-at-a-distance God; God enters into the suffering of all creatures and experiences their life."[75] However, not only is the judge behind the bench not the spouse of the foreign nations, even if he is the parent, he is also the divine warrior who sometimes even acts against Israel/Judah. The relational metaphors are only one facet of divine involvement.

Miller, by contrast, presents a completely different picture to Fretheim of divine involvement. He declares in *The God You Have*:

> The God who speaks to us in Scripture is not friendly except to human beings. The stories of the Lord's war against the other gods (e.g., cutting off the hands and head of Dagon of the Philistines) is a narrative way of telling us that there are all sorts of possibilities out there to lure our worship and obedience, but the maker of heaven and earth is a jealous God and will have none of it. One of the chief ways in which we domesticate God is to assume the kind of friendliness, selflessness, and tolerance on the part of God that we hope is present in each of us. The jealousy and wrath of God are reminders that God is not meant to be likeable but to be God.[76]

As in the case of Fretheim, whilst Miller's general point may stand, I would suggest that he has slightly exaggerated his claim. The God who speaks to us in Scripture might not be friendly to "other" gods, but, as Fretheim observes, "While the people may be the focus for God's suffering, God is anguished over the consequences for all aspects of the created order affected by the devastation."[77] Fretheim proposes that YHWH's lament is more intense for Sibmah than for Jazer because of the vegetation found in Sibmah (Jer 48:32).[78] Miller does not allocate much discussion to the creational aspects and metaphors of Jer 48 and the long quote of Miller's above, where those "except" humans

---

74. Fretheim, "Response to McConville," 45.
75. Fretheim, *Suffering of God*, 166.
76. Miller, *God You Have*, 64.
77. Fretheim, *Suffering of God*, 133.
78. Fretheim, *Jeremiah*, 602.

appear to mean other gods, suggests that Miller does not tend to think in creation-wide terms. Furthermore, when he speaks elsewhere of the universal character of YHWH's sovereignty, it is in terms of YHWH's rule extending to the foreign nations as well as Israel. He also advises that the God of the OT should be understood in political terms, as the creator and governor of both the human and divine worlds.[79] In contrast to Fretheim, then, Miller's work centers on the supernatural rather than the natural world. This is unremarkable given that Miller has written so much on the divine assembly and ANE deities.

Where Fretheim concentrates on the parental and marital metaphors, Miller gives more credence to the metaphor of kingship in Jer 48, noting that the image of YHWH as king predates Israel's own experience of a human king.[80] Fretheim does not elucidate the appellation of YHWH as King in 48:15, but Miller quotes the verse twice and compares the broken scepter and staff of Moabite rule with the rule of the King, the LORD of hosts. For Miller, the reference to YHWH's kingship is an implicit link to YHWH as a warrior. For, "it is the establishment of YHWH's eternal rule and sovereignty that is the ultimate goal of YHWH's wars . . . it is not possible to talk of God as king without talking of God as warrior."[81] It is not possible to determine why Miller does not explicitly refer to YHWH as the divine warrior in his interpretation of chapter 48, when the idea seems so prominent in his mind and prevalent elsewhere in his commentary on Jer 46–51. Perhaps it is due to the confines of space (the commentary on the oracle against Moab is less than three pages in total), or because he does not want to overemphasize his point, or because he feels that he has already been clear enough. Overtly referencing the concept of YHWH as divine warrior might have been beneficial to his reader in establishing Miller's frame of reference, however.

He argues in "God the Warrior," that YHWH is involved with history and does not always reveal himself in ways we would like.[82] In *The God You Have*, he asserts that the proper response of both humans and gods is one of prostrate worship.[83] At the same time, Miller recognizes

79. Miller, "God the Warrior," 45; Miller, "Sovereignty," 141.
80. Miller, "Sovereignty," 142.
81. Miller, *Divine Warrior*, 174.
82. Miller, "God the Warrior," 43.
83. Miller, *God You Have*, 32–33.

that YHWH is not impassible, but is a God of mercy and compassion, who is "tied to moral accountabilities" and that his sovereignty "is power in behalf of justice and compassion."[84] This facet of YHWH's nature does not come to the fore in Miller's work on Jer 48, where he mainly presents the sovereign God as Moab's destroyer, and implicitly portrays him as the avenger of Israel (see Jer 48:26–27). Aside of these examples, there is little in Miller's commentary concerning the interaction between YHWH and humanity. It sometimes seems as if Miller has become used to working with a subset of YHWH's nature, which on occasion leads to a rather narrow presentation of YHWH; a King who is remote.

Miller maintains that a prophet's role is not only to herald YHWH's war, but is one of intercession. In intercessory prayer, the prophet "joins with the will of God to mercy and compassion" to effect a renewal in the world. "Such intercession is expected by God and incorporated into the divine activity."[85] If such intercession is expected, one might ask why Jeremiah, commissioned as a prophet to the nations, does not intercede for Moab (or any other nation). Miller does not ask the question (neither do Fretheim or Brueggemann).

In *The Book That Breathes New Life*, Brueggemann stresses the *relatedness* of YHWH (emphasis his) and in *Theology of OT* he notes that the adjectives used to describe YHWH are primarily relational. At the same time he argues in *Theology of Old Testament* that the central noun metaphors in the OT are ones of governance whilst the less central ones are those of sustenance. "Relational" is a loose term, but he groups what seem to be the most relational metaphors (for example, healer, mother, shepherd) under those metaphors of sustenance, whereas the most frequent metaphors of judge, king, warrior, and father are listed under those of governance. Even the metaphor of father is not nearly as prominent as those of judge, king, warrior, he observes. Given that the three most common metaphors are those of judge, king, warrior, therefore, "relational" does not seem to be the most appropriate adjective to use. This is particularly so in the case of YHWH's dealings with the nations, which Brueggemann treats almost solely under the metaphors of judge and king.[86]

84. Miller, "Prayer," 225, 229.

85. Miller, "Sovereignty," 140; Miller, "Prayer," 225, 217.

86. Brueggemann, *Theology of the Old Testament*, 225, 234–61; Brueggemann, *Book that Breathes*, 148.

The term "relational" does not seem to fit, either, with how else Brueggemann describes YHWH. For instance, he argues that in Jeremiah there is a distance between YHWH and Judah as there is between YHWH and Jeremiah. He also proposes that because YHWH is holy and committed to justice, he is therefore dangerous and subversive and points out that Jer 4–5 describes YHWH as a lion, a wolf, and a leopard. He claims that Jeremiah portrays YHWH's sovereignty in all its rawness, because "Historymakers cannot appeal to an anemic God who is a good buddy or a warm fuzzy. This God is not a God to be 'experienced.'" This is similar to Miller's position that YHWH is not meant to be likeable. In addition, although Brueggemann contends that when YHWH is violent it is normally in order to maintain his sovereignty, he surmises that his violence is sometimes irrational.[87]

In his commentary on Jer 48, YHWH is often referred to as a "dangerous power" who unleashes himself on those who ignore him. As well, however, there are hints of a more "relational" God and Brueggemann attests that YHWH is "the LORD of heaven and earth, the initiator of the Exodus who withstood the Egyptian empire for the sake of the slaves."[88] This idea also comes across in his comments on the final verse of restoration, but although he twice describes YHWH as passionate when speaking of this verse, neither time is in relation to his restorative action. First he writes: "The assertion of v. 47 can of course be understood simply as an editorial maneuver to tone down the awful threat of the foregoing. Read theologically, however, the verse suggests that YHWH's primary business with Moab is not destruction. The destruction so passionately voiced is a 'strategic necessity' in order to establish YHWH's sovereignty, out of which will come YHWH's powerful newness."[89] Then later he adds, "There may be a restoration of destiny (48:47), but first there is an exile (48:7, 11, 46). Because there is a powerful, passionate YHWH, there will be an inescapable exile."[90]

Indeed, the two most prominent metaphors for YHWH in Brueggemann's commentary on Jer 48 are the aforementioned "king" and "judge." As in Miller's commentary, YHWH's sovereignty and rule

---

87. Brueggemann, *Theology of the Old Testament*, 381–83; Brueggemann, *Texts that Linger*, 39; Brueggemann, *Like Fire*, 6, 193–94.

88. Brueggemann, *Jeremiah*, 453.

89. Ibid., 451–52.

90. Ibid., 454.

is the dominant theme and, with Miller, he often depicts YHWH as sovereign over Chemosh. Brueggemann twice quotes the title of 48:15, "the King," and remarks that YHWH defeats Chemosh as he did the Egyptian gods and Dagon. The metaphor of judge is implicit, but apparent, when he speaks of the "verdict of God."[91] He sees the verdict of YHWH—to make Moab disappear—as dominating the entire chapter and one is reminded of the court-scene framework of *Theology of Old Testament*, despite the differing roles of YHWH in the two works.

In the main, however, Brueggemann engages little with the exact nature of divine involvement with Moab. Nevertheless, in *Texts that Linger*, Brueggemann, who is suspicious of certitude, proposes that the OANs challenge Israel's certitude about her relationship to YHWH.[92] He reasons that her natural reply to YHWH's question in Amos 9:7, "Are you not like the Ethiopians to me, O people [lit. sons] of Israel?" (NRSV) is "No." Therefore, "The 'to me' of the question means that YHWH stands outside the cozy reductions of certitude and confidence that marked Israel's theopolitics." He reiterates this in "At the Mercy of Babylon" where he claims that there is a relationship between YHWH and the nations; moreover this relationship finds its way into Israel's theological speech. In *Theology of Old Testament*, he describes this speech as part of Israel's unsolicited testimony and even asserts that, "The way in which Israel is treated by YHWH in the Exodus is the way in which every people may expect to be treated by YHWH." He argues that when similar language is used of Israel and the nations, it shows that Israel's monopoly on YHWH has been broken and he deems Isa 56:7 to show that YHWH finally accepts the nations into his covenant.[93]

Nevertheless, despite the above and although he acknowledges in his commentary that the destiny is the same for Moab and Judah, they receive the same from the hand of YHWH and Nebuchadnezzar, and the metaphor of the broken vessel in 48:38 is used earlier for Jerusalem

---

91. Ibid., 443, 445–47, 449–53.

92. "Certitude" is one of Brueggemann's most common words (it occurs in the third sentence of his "Preface to the CD-ROM Edition" of his *Theology of the Old Testament*) yet he does not seem to define it properly anywhere. Perhaps the closest he comes is in *Theology of the Old Testament* (1997b:75) where he uses it in conjunction with two other phrases that appear to be synonyms of it; "no obvious lines of certitude, no ready formulations of assurance, no self-evident reliabilities."

93. Brueggemann, "Mercy (1991)," 3; Brueggemann, *Theology of the Old Testament*, 520–21, 524; Brueggemann, *Texts that Linger*, 94.

(22:28; 30:12–17),[94] Brueggemann, in his commentary on Jeremiah, does not overstress the similarities between Israel and the nations. It is not possible to see whether this is intentional in his commentary on Jer 48, but he translates the בת- idiom elsewhere as "daughter of," which indicates that he attaches no relational significance to Dibon in 48:18. He also points out that in Isaiah 19:24–25 some, but not all, of the special terms for Israel are used of other nations. Furthermore, he observes in *Theology of the Old Testament* that even scholars who wish to emphasize the sameness between Israel and the nations still retain at least one distinction. "It is odd but worth noting that that 'one respect' is not the same among various scholars but regularly is found somewhere."[95]

It is interesting to observe the language by which Fretheim, Miller, and Brueggemann speak of Moab's restoration. When Fretheim addresses the issue of restoration in his commentary on the oracle concerning Egypt (Jer 46), he uses the term "salvation," but not "forgiveness."[96] He refers to forgiveness only in relation to Israel/Judah in his commentary on Jeremiah's OANs. Likewise, in Miller's "Reflections" on Jer 50:20 where Israel is pardoned, he speaks of YHWH forgiving Israel and contemporary Christians, but he does not use the term "forgiveness" in relation to Moab or the other nations offered restoration. One cannot say whether Fretheim and Miller realize that they, in keeping with the text, have used different language for the nations than for Israel. However, it is possible that they have instinctively and subconsciously distinguished between Israel and her neighbors by their terminology. If so, it is interesting, particularly in Fretheim's case, that despite their stress on universality, their language implies another reality.

Brueggemann asserts in "The Travail of Pardon" that, from its earliest times, Israel has seen YHWH as a God of pardon, even though such pardon is not lightly or readily granted. He seems to use "pardon" (סלח) interchangeably with "forgiveness" and for cases when there has been repentance as well as when there has been none. Contrary to many scholars, he understands that the prophets' function is not to call people to repentance, which is marginal in the prophets, but to proclaim a new

---

94. Brueggemann's claim that God has broken the vessel no one wants is not quite accurate; God breaks Moab *like* a vessel no one wants (48:38) (בו חפץ אין ככלי).

95. Brueggemann, *OT Theology*, 115; Brueggemann, *Theology of the Old Testament*, 521–22; Brueggemann, *Jeremiah*, 444, 450, 456, 472.

96. Fretheim, *Jeremiah*, 586.

truth. Nevertheless, he speaks of forgiveness in relation to the repentant Ninevites in Jonah and, whilst not wishing to push his point, remarks that there is, "it appears to me, a predilection toward forgiveness, restoration, and rehabilitation" even with "the most recalcitrant of nation-partners." Even so, he does not talk in terms of forgiveness/pardon in relation to the nations in Jer 46–51; rather "newness" for Moab and "homecoming" for Ammon.[97]

It is true that, although words for "forgiveness" occur more in Jeremiah than the other prophets (including 50:20), such language is rare.[98] Nevertheless, Jeremiah (along with the rest of the prophets) never offers the nations forgiveness, even when promising restoration as in Jer 48:47; ושבתי שבות־מואב is an idiom for "I will restore the fortunes of Moab" (v. 47). In the case of the Ninevites, the word is the Niphal of נחם "be sorry, moved to pity, have compassion" (Jonah 3:10; 4:2) rather than סלח "pardon, forgive" as in that offered to Judah in Jer 50:20. The lack of forgiveness proffered the nations may (or may not) be a significant distinction between them and Israel/Judah. Given that all interpreters elaborate upon the subject of forgiveness and stress that judgment is not the last word for some of the nations, it would be helpful for a fuller excursus from Brueggemann (and clarification from Fretheim and Miller) on the subject of forgiveness in regard to the nations (Moab in particular, given YHWH's intense lament over her). For example, is it pertinent to view Moab's restoration as evidence that YHWH has forgiven her? If not, how do restoration and forgiveness / pardon differ?

In summary, then, we have seen that Fretheim sees YHWH's involvement with his creation in relational terms (for example, parent-child), whereas Miller and Brueggemann view YHWH's interaction with humanity from the perspective of YHWH as King. Fretheim's interests extend to the natural world of creation: Miller's to the supernal realm of the gods. Brueggemann's interest in the natural realm centers around the political rather than the creational aspects, but he gives more attention to Chemosh than Fretheim. Although I consider each to overemphasize his particular concern at times, when taken together they

---

97. Brueggemann, *Theology of the Old Testament*, 452, 524, 525, 456; Brueggemann, *Creative Word*, 55–56; Brueggemann, "Travail of Pardon," 284–85, 292.

98. סלח "forgive" is used six times in total (which is more than the rest of the prophets combined), כפר "cover, atone" is used once but in a negative way (not forgiving), סליחה "forgiveness" is not used at all, nor is נכה "smite" in the context of forgiveness.

provide quite a wide view of divine involvement. Although Fretheim, more than Miller and Brueggemann, draws out the similarities between Judah and the nations (something the text does not explicitly do), all of them tend to miss the differences between them (also implicit in the text), such as the lack of intercessory prayer for the nations and the fact they are never offered forgiveness. The authors also sometimes omit points or arguments made elsewhere in their works that would either clarify their hermeneutical positions, or would further their claims for Jer 48.

The Message and Its Purpose

Although we have looked at the restoration promised to Moab, the bulk of Jer 48 focuses on the destruction she is about to receive. It is the content of the message and its purpose to which we now turn in order to see how Fretheim, Miller, and Brueggemann handle them and draw out the significant features of the message.

Content

The subject Fretheim most develops is that of mourning and lament. However, he also gives the subject of Moab's sin and her punishment considerable treatment, expounding upon the "language of death and destruction" and the "mocking or taunting of Moab."[99]

That Moab appears to be punished primarily for her pride and arrogance is a good example of a nation judged under what Fretheim calls natural law. For Fretheim understands that nations are judged, as well as against their own laws, according to morality common to humanity (natural law). He explains that arrogance and pride are not normally drawn up into law codes, for "it is assumed that they reflect certain moral orders that people should have known from observation and life experience and for which they would be held accountable." Such a general moral code would also include such matters as social justice, often the motivation for YHWH's judgment. Fretheim sets out this model in the introduction to his commentary, but does not reiterate it in the section on Jer 48. This is a shame, for such a model could explain

---

99. Fretheim, *Jeremiah*, 598, 600.

why hubris is the main sin listed there (as well as in the other OANs).[100] Similarly, Brueggemann also detects in the OT "a kind of international law or code of human standards that seems to anticipate the Helsinki Accords of 1975 in a rough way, a code that requires every nation to act in civility and humaneness toward others."[101] Yet, he too, also does not mention this with respect to Moab.

Neither does Fretheim reiterate the point made in his introduction and his commentary on other chapters of these OANs, that the link between deeds and their consequences is embedded into the moral order, that is, human רעה "evil" brings רעה "disaster." This natural progression from sin to its inherent consequences is, Fretheim argues, the most common agent of divine judgment. In his commentary on Jeremiah's oracle against Babylon, he notices that the language of retribution "is not strictly appropriate for describing" such moral order, since YHWH does not introduce anything new, but utilizes what is already at work. Fretheim also explains in *God and World* that, since this moral order is not a "tight causal weave," the wicked may prosper for a time and the innocent may "unfairly" suffer, including the animals and the land, and even the whole ecosystem. It would have befitted his commentary on Jer 48 to have included this argument, particularly since he suggests that YHWH's weeping is probably, in part, over the animals and the land. Such a suggestion would also have clarified the framework within which Fretheim works.[102]

As Fretheim is interested in the consequences of sin in the natural moral order, Miller's studies have concentrated on the way the texts show the close connections between sin and judgment. As we have seen, Miller finds the same association in the oracle concerning Moab. In fact, he refers the reader of his commentary to *Sin and Judgment in the Prophets*, where he examines such correspondence in detail. In Jer 48, Moab the mocker becomes Moab the mocked. This is a model example of correspondence, and Miller flags it as such. However, he does not

---

100. Ibid., 38; Fretheim, *God and World*, 143, 166. Fretheim notes that natural law is evident throughout the Wisdom literature (Fretheim, *God and World*, 143, 202). Therefore it would be interesting to consider the OANs in the light of Wisdom literature.

101. Brueggemann, *Theology of the Old Testament*, 503. See also McConville, "Judgment and God," 31.

102. Fretheim, *Jeremiah*, 34, 576, 602, 618, 628; Fretheim *God and World*, 160, 163, 165, 636.

identify the correspondence between Moab's sin being arrogant pride and her punishment being shame. This may be because the two are not placed in juxtaposition to each other in the text and therefore do not meet the criteria that Miller has for correspondence. Or it may be because Miller considers the pride–shame notion to be too similar to the mocker–mocked idea to note it separately. Nevertheless, I would suggest that it might have been valuable to make the reader aware of this correlation.[103]

The subtitle of Brueggemann's commentary on Jeremiah is *Exile and Homecoming*. Exile and homecoming are key themes for Brueggemann that are twinned throughout the OT, particularly in communal life. He mainly thinks of the motif in terms of Israel, but, as we have seen, refers to the promised restoration of Ammon as "homecoming." "Homecoming" is not a word he uses in relation to Moab, but he does refer a number of times to her "exile" and the idea of homecoming is probably implicitly present when he speaks of her "restoration of destiny."[104] Whether, in general, this motif is as common as he proposes, it seems to lend itself naturally to Jer 48. In many of his works, Brueggemann plays with the notion of reversals and opposites and his remarks on Jer 48 are no different. He talks about the "massive inversion" of Moab's pride and power, the "dramatic reversal" of her fortunes and status, and how words sounding the same are used to voice "exact opposites" (exile and return).[105] Again, in my view, such motifs are not only in keeping with the text, but draw out some of its key nuances.

However, one motif that is not quite as prominent as Brueggemann presents it, in my opinion, is that of power, particularly political power. He writes (regarding 48:1–9), "The connections between the *centers of power and pride* and the *phrasings of loss* pound at the listener"[106] and he continues such observations throughout the chapter. However, כח "strength, power" is used only once (48:45), as is חיל "strength, efficiency, wealth, army" (48:14), עז "strength" (48:17), and גבור "strong, mighty man" (48:41). It is true that metaphors of power and strength are used (for example, זרע "arm, shoulder, strength" and קרן "horn" in 48:25), as

---

103. Miller, *Sin and Judgment*, 111–19, 126; Miller, "Jeremiah," 892.

104. Brueggemann, *Jeremiah*, 454; Brueggemann, *Ichabod*, 69; Brueggemann, *Word that Redescribes*, 69.

105. Brueggemann, *Jeremiah*, 443, 448–49, 451.

106. Ibid., 443.

all three commentators point out,[107] and that Moab's strongholds and secure places are mentioned (48:1, 18, 41). However, I would propose that the text's main focus is Moab's current situation—weeping in utter brokenness and shame amidst destruction and devastation.

Brueggemann comments that the poet of 48:14–20 "seeks to break the power of ideology which keeps speaking about a reality that no longer exists" and suggests that even the urge to flee in 48:6 and 48:9 may be an urge to flee from royal-urban ideology.[108] It is characteristic of Brueggemann to bring contemporary categories to the text. Sometimes it is illuminating; at other times it is not clear exactly how the category coheres with the original context, that is, in this case, what royal-urban ideology means in a Moabite setting. Nevertheless, it seems to me that the snapshot of the horror of Moab's experience of this new reality eclipses the remembrance (hers and the readers') of the old reality of Moab's power and ideology.

Despite approaching the text through the lens of political power, Brueggemann writes with rhetoric similar to the text itself. He does not diminish the enormity of Moab's sin and presents to his readers the devastating results of her pride and arrogance against YHWH. Brueggemann observes in *Theology of Old Testament* that YHWH approves of human governance but only within his limits (unfortunately, nations are inclined to want to assume too much power for themselves).[109] Such a comment would be helpful regarding Moab.

One strength of Brueggemann as a Christian interpreter, in my opinion, is that when he makes parallels with other parts of Scripture, he includes the NT. So, for instance, when he notes that Moab offends YHWH because she offends his people (48:27), he not only makes references to the language of lament in Ps 59:8, Lam 1:7, and Jer 20:7, but also refers to 1 John 4:20. "Moab does not love the brother whom it has seen, and surely does not love God whom it has not seen."[110] At the same time, an allusion to such a verse is arguably out of keeping with the tenor of the chapter, for the OANs are not concerned with brother loving brother or, indeed, God. Brueggemann does not make a comparable comment regarding Jer 48:10 or 48:26 and it would be interesting

107. Ibid., 447; Fretheim, *Jeremiah*, 600; Miller, "Jeremiah," 892.
108. Brueggemann, *Jeremiah*, 444, 446.
109. Brueggemann, *Theology of the Old Testament*, 518.
110. Brueggemann, *Jeremiah*, 447.

to see how he fits such verses into the framework of 1 John 4:20 that he brings to the chapter. In addition, the OT does not always promote love of the "other" as brother for Israel, either. For instance Isa 60:14 talks about those who had formerly despised Israel bowing down to her and Isa 61:5–6 pictures strangers and foreigners serving her. It does seem clear, however, that YHWH sometimes views offences against Judah as those against himself and it would seem that way here (see chapter 7 for further discussion on this).

I have focused on the main theme of the oracles as found in the respective commentaries, but there are other aspects I could have discussed. For instance, although all interpreters understand differently the concept of the wine settled on its dregs (48:11), they describe the process to which the metaphor refers and thus what they think it means. Fretheim and Brueggemann identify the word play involved in 48:43–44 (פחד "terror," פחת "pit," and פח "trap") and explain that the repetition of the idea is for emphasis. Fretheim recognizes that Moab's restoration has not been fulfilled (not an infrequent occurrence in the prophets).[111]

There are also features of the text that are not overtly theological but may still affect the reading of it. For instance, the oracle against Moab is longer than the other oracles, except that concerning Babylon. Fretheim admits that the reason for its length is unknown, while Miller only acknowledges it is "long, often repetitive" and contains verses identical to material elsewhere. Brueggemann both declares it to be a "long and complicated poem" with a beginning address that "goes on and on" and also admits that it is difficult to determine why it is so long. Although he views the poem as a "catchall" for traditional materials, he suggests that the length may be because Moab was an immediate rival to Judah and thus evoked the most hostility and resentment.[112]

As well, as discussed in the previous chapter, it is notable that Isaiah's oracle concerning Moab (Isa 15–16) is also one of Isaiah's longer OANs (along with Babylon and Egypt) and that, as Fretheim observes, "the oracle in Isaiah has even more the character of a lament!" Miller advises that Jer 48 is to be compared with other oracles concerning Moab, although he himself only remarks on the shared language between Isa 15–16 and Jer 48. Brueggemann does not suggest such a comparison

---

111. Ibid., 450; Fretheim, *Jeremiah*, 599, 603–4; Miller, "Jeremiah," 891.
112. Brueggemann, *Jeremiah*, 442; Fretheim, *Jeremiah*, 595; Miller, "Jeremiah," 890.

and makes only a passing reference to the shared language of Isa 16:6ff. and the oracle against Moab in Amos 2:1.[113] It is interesting that none of the commentators investigates these features a little further, because the length (in Isaiah as well as Jeremiah), combined with the aspect of lament, may indicate that Moab is particularly significant to YHWH. However, the length and nature of their commentaries, particularly Miller's, probably preclude much comparison between the texts.

Another example of an aspect of the text that is not overtly theological is the relationship between poetry and prose. Fretheim asserts in his "Introduction," that "prophetic oracles are often presented in poetic form, but they are also accompanied by prose passages providing interpretative comment." Such an understanding has the advantage of side-stepping, to some extent, the issues of when such prose comments were added, or at least neatly incorporating possible later additions into the core of the oracle. Indeed, Fretheim opines, "let it be noted that problems of coherence are often rooted in the *interpreter's* theological perspective."[114] Miller, on the other hand, referring to Childs and others, warns that: "These salutary efforts to see some coherence in the various 'sources' or tradition complexes and to affirm the significance of the later editorial stages of the book's composition should not cause the interpreter to ignore or smooth over inconcinnities in the text, signs of a less tidy growth that surely was a part of the creation of the book, as is clearly indicated in the different textual forms of Jeremiah."[115]

Neither of them addresses the topic in relation to Jer 48 specifically, however, or remarks on the singular transition from poetry to prose in 48:10. Brueggemann, on the other hand, does comment on this transition, but seems unable to explain the "two incongruous prose verses" around verse 11 (48:10 and 12–13). It is a positive thing for Brueggemann that "the relation between prose and poetry is an endlessly vexed question" because, as he explains in the preface to his Jeremiah commentary, "it is precisely those vexed questions that preclude any final reading . . . The book becomes a place in which to remain and play and listen and notice."[116]

---

113. Brueggemann, *Jeremiah*, 447, 453; Fretheim, *Jeremiah*, 601; Miller, "Jeremiah," 890, 892.

114. Fretheim, *Jeremiah*, 26, 29.

115. Miller, "Jeremiah," 566.

116. Brueggemann, *Jeremiah*, xiii, 445.

Purpose

The Main Purpose(s)—In his commentary on Jer 50–51, Fretheim acknowledges that "it is the kingly rule of Israel's God that will finally prevail over the rule of all earthly kings,"[117] but, he contends, the purpose of the OANs

> is not simply to claim that God rules over the nations (see the language for God as King in 46:18; 51:57), but that God is about the restoration of the entire creation. Jeremiah's God is no local deity, concerned simply about the people of Israel. God is the Creator God, the "God of all flesh" (32:27; see 25:31; 45:5), who works out the divine purposes for the entire creation in and through the movements of all nations and peoples. As helpful as the metaphor of God as King is, it is simply insufficient to encompass these broad-based purposes. Notably, these texts say not a word about these nations honoring the sovereignty of God, as if they would come to "know" that Israel's God is King in and through the experience of disaster (an apparent exception is 16:21 . . .).[118]

Their placement at the end of MT also indicates to Fretheim a "complex eschatological purpose with universal themes," as does the inclusion of an oracle to somewhere as "far-flung" as Elam.[119]

It appears that Miller regards the OANs as having slightly different purposes depending on their audience. He argues that the oracles provide hope for Judah's deliverance, but is ambiguous about the role they played for Moab.

> The nations are an audience for the word of the Lord in their own right. Jeremiah's call at this point is not simply a nationalistic reflex. Whatever good possibilities they may include for the community under judgment—and some good possibilities are definitely indicated—these oracles are not primarily to or for that community. The kingdom of God is universal in scope, and the affairs of all the nations come under its sway. One of the most telling indicators of that in the scriptures is the prophetic propensity for addressing and speaking about the affairs

---

117. Fretheim, *Jeremiah*, 644.
118. Ibid., 575. See also Fretheim, *God and World*, 167–68.
119. Fretheim, *Jeremiah*, 578, 900; see also 617.

and fate of others than Israel and the insistent claim throughout these oracles that what is going on is entirely the Lord's doing.[120]

There are two points of ambiguity in Miller's comments with regard to whether the nations were the intended recipients of the OANs. The first is who is denoted by "the community under judgment," that is, those for whom "these oracles are not primarily to or for." Although the most immediate community under judgment in each of Jeremiah's OANs is the foreign nation itself, which is sometimes offered good possibilities, the previous paragraph talks about the hope for Judah in these oracles and this paragraph begins "But these oracles are not simply to show the elect a way out." The second point of ambiguity is that, although he speaks of the nations as an "audience . . . in their own right," in the next paragraph he concedes:

> It is still not possible to assume that all of these oracles were announced in the hearing of persons who were members of the nation being addressed.
> To that extent, they belong to a cadre of biblical texts that seem to address a larger community that may not or cannot hear them . . . The claim that is inherent in these oracles concerning other nations, oracles that are often addressed quite directly to them, is all the more radical if they were not spoken in their presence. There are indicators that God has other stories with other nations, but Israel's *own* story claims that the Lord is involved with the nations near and far, that they stand under divine judgment for their sins and may also stand under that same divine mercy that so often saved Israel.[121]

Thus it appears that Miller considers the oracles were primarily to and for the nations, even though the audience was largely hypothetical, but their inclusion in Israel's Scripture is Israel's own testimony to YHWH's wider involvement with humanity. Apart from the words of hope offered to Judah, it seems that Miller deems that the main purpose of the OANs is the same for both audiences; to claim YHWH's universal rule, "one that does not depend on the acquiescence of its subjects or even whether they hear the words addressed to them."[122]

---

120. Miller, "Jeremiah," 917.
121. Ibid., 917–18.
122. Ibid., 918. See also p. 878.

Brueggemann thinks the single theme of Jer 46–51 is YHWH's sovereignty and rule over the nations and that the purpose of the book of Jeremiah is to relate the imperial policies and power of Babylon to the claims of Yahwism. Nevertheless, we have seen that Brueggemann, like Fretheim, does not consider that the only purpose of the OANs is to "'Say among the nations, "The LORD is king!"'" (Ps 96:10). He also argues that the purpose for chapters 46–49 (where YHWH triumphs over the nations through Babylon) is different from that of the oracle against Babylon in 50–51, which shows that, ultimately, YHWH's purposes do not converge with Babylon or any earthly power.[123]

The subject of the nations frequently features in Brueggemann's work and thus it is possible, through these other writings, to build up a more comprehensive view of his understanding of the purposes of the OANs. It transpires that there are actually a number of purposes, although most are not mentioned in his work on Jer 48. Some of these overlap with the purpose of prophecy in general or Jeremiah's prophecy more specifically. For instance, he contends that the point of Scriptural prophecy in general is to disrupt the old consensus, while "Jeremiah's call is to *shatter* old worlds (bring them to an end) and to *form* and evoke new worlds (cause them to be)." Such a shattering and reforming takes place through the poetry describing a new reality, by which the listener experiences an alternative world.[124]

Since for Brueggemann, rhetoric is a mediator, and the only way to stop a society's destructive processes, one begins to see why the rhetorical effect of Jer 48 on its listeners is so important to him. Brueggemann is clear in several of his works (including his commentary on Jer 48) that one of the purposes of the rhetoric in the OANs is to crush the absolute self-aggrandizing political power of arrogant and proud nations. He sees this as one of the prime purposes of the oracle concerning Moab: to show that nations cannot act in the way that Moab did, in pride and arrogance, resisting God's authority, magnifying herself instead, and deriding Israel. "There is a terrible accounting."[125]

---

123. Brueggemann, *Jeremiah*, 418, 419, 421.

124. Brueggemann, *Creative Word*, 61; Brueggemann, *Like Fire*, 7, 9, 204; see also Brueggemann, *Jeremiah*, 15, 17; Brueggemann, *Prophetic Imagination*, 3.

125. Brueggemann, *Theology of the Old Testament*, 503–4, 573–74; Brueggemann, *Jeremiah*, 420, 443, 453; Brueggemann, *Texts that Linger*, 13, 43.

OANs do not only challenge the pride of the nation, but the pride of Israel/Judah's particularity, Brueggemann asserts, for they demonstrate that YHWH is involved, even has a relationship, with other nations.[126] "At the end of the Old Testament, prophetic faith knows that Yahwism runs well beyond Israel. Indeed, YHWH, in the end, has more than one chosen people."[127] He even considers what he perceives as Israel's loss of particularity as having a positive element for her; the privilege of normality in being merely one nation among the others.[128] It will be realized from my comments above that I do not accept that the OANs indicate that the nations become other chosen people.

At the same time, Brueggemann sees the OANs as salvation for Israel/Judah because the destruction of her oppressive enemies offers her hope, as well as assures her that she is not singled out for destruction. Fretheim suggests similarly. It is not only Israel/Judah who benefits from this situation, however, for in Brueggemann's mind the OANs can be seen as salvation for the nations as well; as he says regarding Moab, YHWH's hegemony over the nations is for their own well-being. In fact, he claims in *Theology of Old Testament* that Isa 19 shows that, "The ultimate promise 'on that day' for the nations as partners of YHWH is the complete end of hostility and the rule of a shared *shalôm*" though he is more reserved in *Cadences of Home* where he points out that the occasional hope offered to the nations should not be overplayed.[129] Thus Brueggemann considers that the purpose of the OANs is to bring both good and bad news to the nations and Israel/Judah.

Whilst accepting that, within a Christian frame of reference, YHWH's rule over the nations is to their benefit, I would question the assertion that a "complete end of hostility" and "shared *shalôm*" is promised in the OT. First, none of the OANs (including Jer 48) uses this language. Second, there is a paucity of promises of restoration for the nations, as Brueggemann himself notes, and so any positive future is given in muted tones. Thirdly, the book of Jeremiah, at least, does not talk about a complete end of hostility or an idyllic period that includes the nations (for example, Jer 30–31). Brueggemann's language can easily

---

126. Brueggemann, *Texts that Linger*, 13, 102.

127. Ibid., 102.

128. Brueggemann, *Theology of the Old Testament*, 522; Brueggemann, *Texts that Linger*, 13, 102.

129. Brueggemann, *Cadences*, 89; Brueggemann, *Theology of the Old Testament*, 521.

sound as if it stems from a Christian eschatological framework, and while a future shared *shalôm* may be part of the bigger frame of reference, such terminology is out of place in relation to Jeremiah's OANs. Nonetheless, I would agree that Jer 48 spells good and bad news for Moab and possibly good news for Judah (if 48:26–27 are intended to avenge Judah), though there is nothing in the chapter that explicitly indicates bad news for her.

Once more, the outlooks of the three commentators reflect the commentators' own interests. Whereas Miller sees the demonstration of divine sovereignty as the main purpose of the OANs (as does Brueggemann), Fretheim unequivocally asserts that such a perspective is not enough (as does Brueggemann). For Fretheim, the main aim is to announce creation-wide restoration, whilst for Brueggemann it is to show that YHWH will ultimately destroy political pride and absolute power. All positions can be held credibly together as part of a wider purpose. However, Miller appears to paint with a broader brushstroke than Fretheim and Brueggemann, which perhaps blurs the more subtle nuances. For whilst it could be said that renewal and restoration are subsets of divine sovereignty, Miller's explanation does not naturally lead one to think of regeneration.

At the same time, although the OT undoubtedly witnesses to YHWH working out his purposes for the restoration of the entire creation I wonder if it is going too far to see this as the specific purpose of the OANs. I would therefore be inclined to think that Fretheim again overstates his case. This seems particularly so in the case of Jer 48 where, arguably, creation is not the main issue and Moab, not creation, is promised restoration. Brueggemann seems to have the most nuanced understanding and I have presented a variety of his perspectives with their testimony and countertestimony. However, his explanation of the oracle against Moab is much narrower than the views found in his other works and centers around political power: "This poem is exactly the voice of the government of YHWH that intends to re-establish its authority and prerogative."[130] Again, therefore, it seems as if all commentators find in the text confirmation of their overall theological understandings where, in actual fact, the text does not always conform to these.

---

130. Brueggemann, *Jeremiah*, 523.

Other purposes—Both Fretheim and Brueggemann suggest other plausible purposes of the OANs. For instance, Fretheim suggests that "a related purpose of these oracles (at least those in chs. 46–49), depending upon the historical context, may have been to alert Israel that appealing to such nations for help would be a vain exercise. Yet, the texts are remarkably silent about such a purpose."[131] This is similar to Miller's remark quoted earlier (see footnote 76) that the stories of YHWH's war against the nations show that YHWH will not tolerate appeals to other gods. Or, as Miller phrases it in yet another context (the first commandment), "there are other powers at work in the world whose ultimate conquest by the Lord of history is sure but whose power to entice and appeal, to exercise control over our lives . . . is real and constantly present."[132]

When writing about the plagues of Egypt, Fretheim proposes that the purpose of the plagues were for YHWH to raise his name, not just to Israel, but to the whole world.[133] He does not make a similar comment regarding the OANs, but the parallels of judgment on the nations perhaps suggest that he could credibly do so. Brueggemann, on the other hand, does make such an observation. He maintains that the OANs are to suit YHWH's own purposes and argues in *Theology of Old Testament* that these purposes are aside of Israel's needs and in *Cadences of Home* that they are not to do with the destiny of the nations, but YHWH's own glorification.[134] That is, the ultimate purpose of the OANs is to glorify YHWH.

This idea can be compared to Ezek 20 where YHWH withholds judgment from Israel למען שמי "for the sake of my name" (20:9, 14, 22) and restores them for the same reason (20:44; see also 36:22). His concern is that his name should not be profaned in the sight of the nations around. If the idea is that a nation's condition reflects the care or efficaciousness of its deity, then Israel's restoration and the nations' downfall could be seen as two sides of the same coin. As well, when YHWH restores Israel despite her not turning back to him, he tells her וידעתם כי־אני יהוה "then you will know that I am YHWH" (20:44). In

131. Fretheim, *Jeremiah*, 579.
132. Miller, *God You Have*, 22.
133. Fretheim, "Plagues," 392.
134. Brueggemann, *Cadences*, 88; Brueggemann, *Theology of the Old Testament*, 525; see also Brueggemann, *Jeremiah*, 435.

other words, the driving force behind YHWH's actions is his own glorification. This will be discussed further in chapter 7.

Another purpose of the OANs, according to Brueggemann, is to show that, "In the end, the Oracles against the Nations are a theological statement, not to be explained away by historical correlations. In the end, the historical process, the rise and fall of the great powers, is an unmistakable witness to the relentless rule of YHWH." To my mind, this purpose can become quite a key one, particularly in a secular world where political history is not envisaged in terms of God, for, as Brueggemann acknowledges in his commentary on Jeremiah's oracle against Egypt, this claim is not self-evident.[135] Brueggemann also argues that the task of prophetic imagination is to offer adequate symbols to confront the horrors of experience and to give public expression to fears and the reality of death. Given this purpose and that Brueggemann considers the nations were the primary audience for the OANs, then it could be inferred that one intent of the OANs is to provide the nations with such symbols.

Of the three authors, only Brueggemann proposes a purpose for the specific oracle against Moab (to show that nations cannot act in pride and arrogance), but Fretheim and Miller are in good company since most commentators do not suggest a separate purpose for each nation. Nevertheless, both Fretheim and Miller note the differences between the various OANs in Jeremiah and it may be that each individual oracle has no more purpose than to help build up the bigger picture. Thus what Fretheim says about the oracle against Moab, that it is "designed to look at Moab's disastrous situation from every angle, as if turning an object in the light and seeing how the light plays off different surfaces," could be applied to the OANs as a whole.[136] That is, the oracle against Moab would be one surface that would reflect one particular aspect of the disastrous circumstances of the nations; perhaps that of divine lament over such a situation. However, while there is some sense in which the "foreign nations" stand as a whole in opposition to Israel, each nation is a nation in its own right and, in my view, it is one of the strengths of Brueggemann's commentary that he attempts to treat the oracles individually, searching for the specific purpose of each.

---

135. Brueggemann, *Jeremiah*, 424, 426.
136. Fretheim, *Jeremiah*, 577, 597; Miller, "Jeremiah," 38.

In summing up this section on the message of Jer 48, one can see that Fretheim, Miller, and Brueggemann make many insightful observations, expounding the text in a useful way, and pointing out the major themes. In my opinion, Miller's commentary is stronger than Fretheim's in discussing the content of the oracle concerning Moab, whilst Fretheim's gives a better exposition of its purpose (even though his comments relate to Jeremiah's OANs in general). Brueggemann's probably comes somewhere between them; he elucidates both the content and the purpose, but what appears to be his own agenda sometimes detracts from both. He also makes intertextual connections, which is demonstration that he has the whole of the Christian canon in view when he interprets a particular text.

On occasion, all commentators neglect certain things that might be helpful to the reader. For example, neither Fretheim nor Brueggemann talk about natural law in relation to Moab, and Fretheim does not discuss here, although he does elsewhere, the consequences of sin being embedded in the act of sinning. Similarly, Miller neglects to point out the correspondence in the sin of Moab's pride and her concomitant shame, despite correspondence being a frequent theme in other works. Fretheim's view of Jer 48 (that YHWH's ultimate aim is for creation-wide restoration) is more comprehensive than Miller's (that it is a declaration and demonstration of YHWH's sovereignty) or Brueggemann's (that YHWH's power will ultimately dismantle all other political powers), but I doubt that the primary purpose of the OANs, in particular Jer 48, is restoration, or that these OANs always attest to a "creation-wide" scope.

Some of the purposes listed above, such as YHWH's sovereignty over all creation, are timeless, but the following section deals in more detail with how the commentators specifically handle Jer 48 as Scripture, relevant to contemporary Christians.

Scripture for Today

Although the "Connections" and "Reflections" sections of their respective commentaries specifically deal with the application of the text, in the main body of their commentaries both Fretheim and Miller seem to have one eye on the text's present (and even future) relevance. For example, Fretheim says, "for God an internal grieving always accompanies wrath and judgment (as is commonly the case in the breakdown of interhuman relationships)" and Miller writes, regarding the restoration of Moab, "so also will it be with the Lord's judgment against the nations." Similarly, though Brueggemann does not have a comparable section in his commentary regarding application, he too makes generally applicable remarks. For example, regarding 48:40–47 he writes, "Such an act of self-magnification can only bring ruin and devastation." Or, when he articulates the unfeasibility of Moab's policy, he adds, "Nations in the end cannot act in such a way with impunity." Even when Brueggemann elucidates what the God of the text is like, one gets the impression that he is speaking more widely: "the God of the whole Israelite tradition, the LORD of heaven and earth, the initiator of the Exodus . . . the God who destabilizes and deabsolutizes every pretentious and petty political claim for the sake of a larger ordering that makes human life possible." Since Fretheim's and Miller's commentaries do both have a section explicitly geared towards helping those in the church who interpret Scripture, however, it is worth taking a look at how they do this.[137]

In *God and World*, Fretheim writes that "it is not uncommon that communities of faith reduce God to the God of their particular domain. For example, it may be claimed that God's only or primary business is to look after Christian folk." He goes on to argue that the OANs counter this view by showing that YHWH is present and active in all peoples. Brueggemann also understands the OANs to function as "an important critique and warning against a notion of 'God's elect people,' as it pertains both to Jews and Christians."[138] In his "Connections" section on Jer 46 Fretheim propounds this viewpoint and explains how it impacts his ideology of mission:

> The prophetic perspective would claim that all people have had an experience of God before "we showed up with the Bible in our hand." We do not bring God to the world! God is there before we travel to any particular place, indeed before we even thought about reaching out to others. Again, one of our basic tasks is that of discernment. If we listen carefully to these people we may discern specific ways in which God has been active in their lives. Perhaps it has been an experience of unconditional love, or incredible mercy, or a miraculous deliverance at the in-

---

137. Brueggemann, *Jeremiah*, 450, 453; Fretheim, *Jeremiah*, xv, xviii, 603; Miller, "Jeremiah," xviii, 893.

138. Brueggemann, *Texts that Linger*, 100; Fretheim, *God and World*, 167.

dividual or communal level. Our responsibility, then, is to name that experience in terms of the God to whom we witness.[139]

This quote reveals that Fretheim is working within a modern framework from the nineteenth/twentieth century (though this framework reworks a patristic Logos one). However, such an ideology of mission is a long way from the text of Jeremiah's OANs, which do not envisage mission to the nations in any sense like the Christian way. It is also interesting from a missiological view that, as Miller points out, some nations possibly never received "their" denouncing oracles.

Furthermore, Fretheim's imagined experience is a positive one; "love," "mercy," and "deliverance." For some nations that are not promised restoration the only recorded "experience" of YHWH in Jeremiah's OANs is his destruction of them and even for those, such as Moab, that are promised restoration, it is a future event. It is doubtful that, in a contemporary context, it is wise to start from this position and "name that experience in terms of God," not least because it is rarely possible to determine which events are God's judgments. Nevertheless, Fretheim's point may be taken broadly that the OANs counter the assumption that YHWH was not in the nations before the prophet showed up.

In his "Connections" section on Jer 48 (entitled "The Divine Lament over Moab") Fretheim picks up on the theme of lament and says that YHWH mourns with those who mourn: "God enters into the suffering of all peoples, whether or not that suffering has been deserved (as certainly was the case with both Israel and Moab)."[140] Much of what he says in "Connections" repeats what has preceded with regard to both lament and the parallel between Moab and Israel, which is disappointing. Such remarks are general observations and could be read from the viewpoint of either the Moabites, or the Judahites, or a contemporary congregation, although he writes from the position of an observer.

In his article, "Terror All Around," Miller counsels that when surrounded by terror, the point is not to ask about what is happening, but to discern the work of God. He advises that, although we have to be careful about seeing God's judgment in human events, if we assume that it cannot be so, then "we have either forgotten our Bible or allowed the cross to take the sting out of history." Or, in *Sin and Judgment*, he

---

139. Fretheim, *Jeremiah*, 588.
140. Ibid., 605.

writes, "The theological task is not to eliminate this word of judgment in history but to probe more deeply into understanding that reality past and present, for only in this way can the message of the prophets come to life and perdure."[141] In *The God You Have* he also remarks that one's neighbor is to be found in strange and unexpected places (despite the emphasis on neighborliness in Brueggemann's works, Brueggemann does not make this point). Any of these might be suitable conclusions to reach given his comments on Jer 48. The first (not to ask what is happening but to discern the work of God) could be made from the point of view of Moab, though even to speak of "God" is to adopt a frame of reference that would have been alien to Moab. The second point (we cannot rule out that God's judgment is in human events) could be made from Judah's point of view, and the third (that one's neighbors are found in strange places) is a general observation. However, in his "Reflections" on Jer 48 he does not make these points.

He notes, instead, that Moab was not condemned for one single sin, but that pride and mockery of Israel were both reasons for her judgment—judgment that also brought an end to sacrificing to her gods. This suggests to Miller that sin is often a more complex matter than we may realize; "our sins are manifold and complicated but discernible to the eyes of God precisely in all their complexity." This means, for him, that general confession of sin becomes an important liturgical act. He also asserts that the emphasis on shame (in Jer 48 and other nations in Jer 46–51) alerts the contemporary reader, who is probably only aware of personal shame, to corporate shame.[142] To my mind, this application contains insightful observations.

In contrast to Fretheim, therefore, Miller's starting point is the oracle's own frame of reference, that is, Moab is the implied reader rather than Israel. This is not at odds with how he considers the OANs should be interpreted, because, as we have seen, he recommends that they must be heard in their own right. However, he also writes that, "then and now the primary agenda of the listeners to Jeremiah's oracles is set around what happens to the elect community of faith . . . we expect them to have to do with us." Context implies that Miller approves, at least in part, with this expectation. Nevertheless, he does not apply Jer 48 from the stance of the elect, although he does suggest that the OANs can be used to

---

141. Miller, *Sin and Judgment*, 139; Miller, "Terror," 501; Miller, *God You Have*, 18.
142. Miller, "Jeremiah," 918, 920.

warn against national arrogance. In addition, he reiterates the general point that all nations are under YHWH's divine judgment and mercy, and he implies that we must accept the fact that YHWH does battle in this "often messy world . . . as much as within the human soul."[143]

Brueggemann does not think that texts should be "applied" to our contemporary context. "Rather, our situation needs to be *submitted* to the text for a fresh discernment. It is our situation, not the text, that requires a new interpretation." This statement, using the traditional language of "submission," is a clear example that Brueggemann attributes the Scriptures with authoritative power. At the same time his meaning is unclear, for how does submitting a situation to the text differ in practice from "applying" the text? Brueggemann does not see contemporary appropriation of the text as something that happens after the process of analyzing it in its historical context. "Good interpretation surely moves back and forth between *critical historical awareness* and the *pursuit of meaning in contemporary context*." He counsels that if the texts are alive and authoritative then we must ask what they continue to say. So when he talks about the book of Jeremiah's aim being to show that YHWH's dangerous power is released into the public domain and to reshape kingdoms, he continues, "Moab, like all of the nations, must come to terms with YHWH's sovereign resolve. A mocking disregard of this holy intention will bring deep trouble, visible even in the public process."[144]

Although Brueggemann does not have a specific section in his commentary regarding contemporary appropriation of the text, appealing to his wider works yields useful insights. Brueggemann deems many texts to challenge the dominant, consumerist culture of the West, particularly the U.S., a society that is in deep dislocation, despite its excess satiation. According to Brueggemann, such a world is not dissimilar to that of Jeremiah's and he states in his chapter on "The Nations as YHWH's Partner" in *Theology of Old Testament*, "I intend that my analysis of YHWH and the nations should finally settle in the presence of the United States, which has no viable competitor for power." Brueggemann makes the point that grasping after power is not only wrong, but will ultimately fail because "there is simply not enough power in the long

---

143. Ibid., 917, 919–20.
144. Brueggemann, *Jeremiah*, 453; Brueggemann, *Like Fire*, xiii, 37.

run to sustain itself in the face of human restlessness among those who refuse to be eradicated as an inconvenience."[145]

Brueggemann suggests that, like Jeremiah and the prophets, the church should utter speech about hurt and hope to counter this dominant ideology. He contends that peace is not possible "until modes of domination and control are given up." If it is not too late (and it might be), "the only way from here to there, from despair to hope, from death to new life, is by way of weeping, of grief, of exile."[146] The oracle concerning Moab in Jer 48 with its lament, threats of exile (48:7, 12, 46), and promise of restoration seems to be particularly suited to this philosophy of Brueggemann's, so it is surprising that he has not used it for such.

Brueggemann's observations so far have been made from taking Moab as the implied reader. However, one can also ascertain how Brueggemann considers the text should be overheard by its Judahite audience. In *Cadences of Home*, Brueggemann refers to the non-Israelites as second addressees of the text (the Israelites being the first addressee) and makes the point that, "The church in much of the Western world, and surely in U.S. society, has lost its tongue for this second addressee." Thus the OANs function as a reminder to the church that there are second addressees. He reminds the U.S. church that "'the nations as partners' is crucial if we are to recover a biblically informed voice amid the mounting military imperialism of the U.S. government." At the same time, recognizing that other nations are among YHWH's partners does not mean that they should always be highly regarded and Brueggemann cautions the interpretative community to be alert and suspicious of the great political empires (and presumably smaller ones, such as Moab, as well), precisely because the text itself is. He also warns that, "What Jeremiah asserts is that the real danger is not Babylon, or Assyria or the Soviet Union or China. The threat, finally, to our way of life is the sovereign God who will be pushed only so far and then not mocked any further."[147]

---

145. Brueggemann, *Hope*, 105; Brueggemann, *Threat of Life*, 116–17; Brueggemann, *Cadences*, 110–14; Brueggemann, *Theology of the Old Testament*, 113–14, 257; Brueggemann, *Jeremiah*, 18; Brueggemann, *Deep Memory*, 59; Brueggemann, *Like Fire*, xii, 27, 142; Brueggemann, *Word that Redescribes*, 8, 104.

146. Brueggemann, *Like Fire*, 84–85, 177–78.

147. Brueggemann, *OT Theology*, 146; Brueggemann, *Cadences*, 90–98; Brueggemann, *Theology of the Old Testament*, xiii; Brueggemann, *Like Fire*, 171.

Overall, then, Miller's application largely assumes a Moabite frame of reference, whilst Fretheim and Brueggemann make general comments, although Brueggemann in his other works provides readings from the viewpoints of various implied readers. None makes it plain in his commentary that he is starting from the stance he is; it is an implicit hermeneutical move (although since Fretheim considers that the nations were not audiences of the OANs it might be assumed that his application is not concerned with Moab as an implied reader). Since it is quite a big shift in perspective to read the text from a Moabite or Judahite frame of reference, or one that incorporates both, I consider that it would be helpful to declare such a starting point (for example, a brief note in the introduction to the OANs in their commentaries). Reading the text from different viewpoints might also help to create fuller and broader interpretations, as can be seen from the consultation with Brueggemann's other writings. Furthermore, even though many aspects may look similar from any viewpoint (for example, YHWH's sovereignty or YHWH's lament over humanity), the message of Jer 48 would undoubtedly sound different to a Moabite in the sixth century BCE, a Judahite of the same period, and a Christian in today's world (not to mention contemporary Jews as well as the variations that undoubtedly exist across different parts of the contemporary Christian and Jewish worlds).

Conclusions and Reflections

In my opinion, in general, Fretheim, Miller, and Brueggemann do not make unwarranted claims in their commentaries. Nor do they make huge, unjustified hermeneutical leaps. Between them they provide several important insights on Jer 48 and give a wide view of its scope, for example, Fretheim's attention to the realm of the natural world and the tone of lament, Miller's focus on the arena of divine beings, and Brueggemann's concentration on the political nuances and the means and ends of powers. In addition, all authors are bold enough to suggest ways in which the oracle concerning Moab can be understood as Christian Scripture today.

There is some overlap between what each of them says, but their commentaries are more distinctive from each other than one might imagine given the similar backgrounds of the authors (nationality, time of writing, faith, hermeneutical bases). It is possible to discern in their commentaries the issues and themes that have engaged their scholarly thinking over the years. I consider that this is both a strength and a weakness. It is a strength in that it brings out nuances of the text that might be missed or dismissed, such as Miller's emphasis on YHWH's power over Chemosh and his opposition to the Moabite gods with all that worship of them involved. At the same time it is a weakness in that sometimes there is a tendency to overlook elements outside their particular interests and in all commentaries there are one or two aspects of Jer 48 that I consider would have benefited from a fuller treatment. The best example of this is on the subject of tone: Miller and Brueggemann could have expanded upon the aspect of lament, while Fretheim could have given more attention to the impact on the tone that mentions of Chemosh and the Moabite gods might have.

Another weakness is the tendency to see in the text confirmation of the theological models they have formed over the years, such as Brueggemann's emphasis on political power and Fretheim's on creation. Finding such support is not necessarily problematic in itself, for these texts may have contributed to those models in the first place, but I consider that they have overstated their cases at times. For instance, I do not quite see the justification behind Fretheim's assertion that the restoration promised to some of the nations, including Moab, necessarily implies a renewed creation. It is clear from his commentary on Jer 48 that this is not one of the texts of the Bible to which Fretheim "simply has to say No!" However, at times he is perhaps in danger of domesticating YHWH and making him "more palatable to modern tastes."[148]

Miller, on the other hand, touches on YHWH's mercy and his forgiveness, but his overall presentation of YHWH is, to use his words, "a single color: red." Although when Miller depicts YHWH as the color of blood he is not referring to Jer 48, his portrayal of YHWH in Jer 48 still seems to resemble that same color; he is so caught up with the sovereignty of the warrior God that he omits to portray a God who weeps. This outlook may reflect his Presbyterian, Reformed background. Fretheim's Lutheran setting may have provided him with a less rigid/softer view of YHWH, though such suggestions can only be tentative. Ironically, elsewhere, Miller gives a more balanced representation, for example, "The church lives theologically and experientially with the

---

148. Fretheim and Froehlich, *Bible as Word of God*, 82, 105.

question of whether God's anger is always awash with tears, as it was in Jeremiah's time, and whether judgment is no less disturbing to God than it is to those who experience it." He also appreciates that in Jeremiah, particularly in the laments, the anguish of the prophet overlaps with that of YHWH.[149]

Nevertheless, in contemplating Miller's blood-red God, I am reminded of Fretheim's article on *The Color of God*. Too many people are happy with an eight colored crayon picture of God, he opines, whereas even a box of sixty four is not enough.[150] Miller sometimes appears to use too few crayons and, despite his warnings to others, Fretheim himself seems to stick to his favorites. Brueggemann, too, tends to use the same ones over again. Jer 48 uses its own colors (if not sixty four) and I consider that, together, Fretheim, Miller and Brueggemann provide their readers with enough of those colors to get a good picture of Jeremiah's oracle against Moab. In such a portrayal, YHWH is a sovereign ruler who interacts with the whole of creation in a relational way, conquers and crushes false gods, and dismantles self-aggrandizing political powers.

Fretheim, Miller, and, particularly, Brueggemann treat the text as a unified piece and as part of the canonical whole. As such, their commentaries keep Jer 48, and the OANs in general, tightly within the rest of the corpus of Scripture. This I see as a strength, particularly when dealing with them as contemporary Scripture. The OANs might have been a collection of prophecies in their own right before they entered the book of Jeremiah, but a wise handling, in my opinion, interprets them against the rest of Jeremiah and the oracles against Judah. All three commentators do just this, drawing out the parallels between the oracles to the elect and those to the non-elect, and discussing the similarities between their judgments and their restoration.

At the same time, I would suggest that the distinction between Judah and the nations is sometimes lost or overlooked in this approach—in Fretheim's work to a greater extent than in Miller's and Brueggemann's. For instance, in the text the restoration of Moab is not given in detail, as it is to Judah, no forgiveness is offered Moab (or the other nations), the prophets do not intercede for the nations, and metaphors of sonship and marriage are never used in relation to the nations. As well,

149. Miller, "Terror," 501; Miller, "Jeremiah," 563.
150. Fretheim, "Color of God," esp. p. 258.

there is a tendency to lose in Fretheim's and Miller's work a sense of Moab's own identity and to subsume her as one facet of "the nations" (which may be her role). Brueggemann's work is slightly different in this respect in that it gives the oracle against Moab its own purpose, distinct from Jeremiah's oracles against the other nations. In all works, however, I would have welcomed more discussion about the specifics of Moab, particularly in relation to the length of the oracle, especially since Isaiah's oracle concerning Moab is also long.

I suggested throughout that Miller could have said more on different subjects, for example, lament, and the correspondence between pride versus shame, but I am aware that his work is more restricted than Fretheim's and Brueggemann's in terms of space and that he has had to choose what to include and exclude. It must be said that Miller's commentary does not waste space retelling the biblical narrative as some commentaries do, but explains various aspects as it goes along. Fretheim and Brueggemann, more than Miller, tend towards a retelling, but they could probably better be described as explanatory and interpretative walks through the text. All are enlightening commentaries.

I consider that the applicative move from the text to the contemporary world is not the strongest part of any of the authors' works, mainly because their comments tend to be too general or repetitive. At times, Miller writes as if Moab is the implied reader, but most of his comments and those of Fretheim and Miller tend to be quite general, so it is not possible to tell who the implied reader is, if there is one. Whilst general comments are valuable, it would be interesting to look at Jer 48 with different implied readers in mind, i.e., Moab and Judah, and I would suggest that applying some tenets of literary theory might, perhaps, lead to a richer application of the text (despite his lack of a section dedicated to the "application" of the text, it is surprising that Brueggemann does not do this). Interestingly, the Judahite frame of reference is the least discussed, which is strange, not only because Judah would have been the primary audience for Jer 48 (certainly in written form), but also because the Church often sees herself in terms of Israel and Judah, at least metaphorically. Such a reading would raise interesting questions, such as whether it is appropriate to intercede for the nations. In some contexts, the Church might derive from Jer 48 hope that their persecutors will be judged and, perhaps, even be surprised that such judgment might be executed with tears.

YHWH may be sovereign over all and interact with every nation. There may be similarities in his dealings with different nations,[151] and in the language and form of the oracles,[152] but, according to Jeremiah's OANs, YHWH works in different ways with different nations. The oracle against Moab, with its own individual characteristics, demonstrates that one size does not fit all. Between them, Fretheim, Miller, and Brueggemann make the reader aware that this oracle reveals that, on occasion (but not necessarily every time), the Divine Warrior, King of the cosmos, strips a nation of her power and pride, in the same way that he "disrupt[s] all present power arrangements,"[153] but weeps over her individual cities as he does so. Furthermore, amidst the destruction and devastation, alongside the shame and humiliation, and over the weeping and wailing, a whisper of hope for future restoration may be heard.

---

151. See Miller's comments on the similarities between Moab and Ammon ("Jeremiah," 294).

152. Miller, "Jeremiah," 897.

153. Brueggemann, *Jeremiah*, 419.

5

An Analysis of Jones' and Clements's Readings of Jeremiah 48

Introduction

HAVING LOOKED AT THREE CONTEMPORARY U.S. SCHOLARS, I WILL now consider two contemporary UK OT theologians: Douglas Jones (who died in 2005)[1] and Ronald Clements. Like Fretheim, Miller, and Brueggemann, Clements is an active churchman, as was Jones until his death. For comparative purposes, the chapter will follow the same format as the previous one, but it should be noted at the outset that any perceived variations between the UK and the U.S. interpretations are not necessarily due to national or cultural differences. At the same time, any such variations may indicate certain leanings of the two schools of thought.

Hermeneutical Bases

Again, it would be useful to include the editorial statements of Jones' and Clements's respective commentary series regarding the nature and purpose of each. However, the *New Century Bible Commentary* series does not have a separate editorial statement, except for describing itself on the back cover as "scholarly and comprehensive in scope."[2] Therefore, Jones' own comments from the preface will have to suffice.

The editors of the *Interpretation* series write that it "is designed to meet the needs of students, teachers, ministers, and priests for a con-

---

1. Rogerson, "Douglas Jones," Online.
2. Jones, *Jeremiah*, back cover.

temporary expository commentary . . . The series is written for those who teach, preach, and study the Bible in the community of faith . . . It is planned and written in the light of the needs and questions which arise in the use of the Bible as Holy Scripture . . . The task which they [commentators] undertake is both to deal with what the texts say and to discern their meaning for faith and life."[3]

Jones is clearly quoting from information he has from the *New Century Bible Commentary* series when he writes that the series is "to provide guidance for 'students and clergy and also for the interested layman.'"[4] He describes this "as a formidable task, and few have been able to steer a safe course between the Scylla of critical complexity and the Charybdis of uncritical simplicity."[5] However, in contrast to *Smyth & Helwys Bible Commentary*, *The New Interpreter's Bible*, *International Theological Commentary*, and *Interpretation*, there is no mention in this *New Century Bible Commentary* volume on Jeremiah of "faith" or "Christian." Instead Jones gives the main aim of the commentary as seeking to answer the question "what kind of material is this?" and states that, "The aim is to identify each stage of the tradition, of which the ministry of Jeremiah is the first, in order that the total Jeremiah tradition may be understood."[6]

This lack of a specific Christian focus to the commentary does not reflect Jones' approach as an individual, however. For Jones was ordained in the Anglican Church and held various posts within the Church, including that of canon of Durham Cathedral. His final professorship in the Lightfoot Chair of Divinity at Durham University was attached to this canonry.[7] Thus, Jones held together the academic discipline of Theology and Christian faith within a church environment. However, in Jones' mind, such a twinning of "faith and theology" was not the privilege only of those at the top of their profession in academic and / or church fields. For, he writes in the preface to his Torch series' commentary on Haggai, Zechariah, and Malachi: "I believe that biblical scholarship must be justified outside professional preserves. It is important that the ordinary reader shall not only know the results

3. Clements, *Jeremiah*, v.
4. Jones, *Jeremiah*, 7.
5. Ibid.
6. Ibid.
7. Rogerson, "Douglas Jones," Online.

of biblical research, but also to some extent see how they are reached. There is nothing like the discipline of simple language and explanation for exposing weaknesses that can be concealed by impressive technical terminology."[8]

Jones acknowledges that much of the OT is difficult to understand and that the modern world has, in many ways, made such an understanding even harder.[9] Yet his solution is to work harder as a theologian to remove some of these difficulties from his reader, as is seen in the preface to his commentary on Isaiah 56–66 and Joel (also in the Torch series):

> The prophecies of the Book of Isaiah (representative in this respect of all prophecy and, indeed, of the Old Testament) present great difficulties to the modern commentator ... The difficulties are those of communicating the meaning of the text to those who are hungry for the word of God. Until modern days, the reader of a commentary would start to read with the initial conviction that the book contained the treasures of divine wisdom. And this conviction would carry him over the obscurities inevitable in literary forms and ideas of a distant age. He was not worried by the things that deter a modern reader. The modern reader starts from the assumption that the intelligibility and the relevance of the text must be demonstrated to him. He has heard enough, in the air we breathe if not in so many words, to suggest that the Old Testament is full of obscurities. He is not persuaded that the effort to penetrate them is worth making. A universe of thought and progress seems to lie between the prophets and the twentieth century. Above all he looks for relevance and he cannot see that the literature of the Hebrews speaks directly to his condition.
>
> This Commentary seeks to satisfy thoroughly the demand for intelligibility. No pains have been spared to try to show why such and such a form of words was used, what the situation was that evoked them, how they were relevant to the prophet's hearers, what their inner meaning may have been.[10]

---

8. Jones, *Haggai*, 13.

9. While it appears that Jones uses the word "modern" in the sense of "contemporary," his usages also seem to embrace ideas of Enlightenment ideals and historical-critical principles.

10. Jones, *Isaiah 56–66*, 9.

Jones does not lay all the responsibility with the scholar whilst the "ordinary reader" takes a passive role, however. Better understanding often "involves the discussion of issues which, in themselves, are of little interest to most people"[11] and "the price to be paid [for his explaining what lies behind metaphors and images] is that many people, who want help with the reading of the prophets, will turn away from discussions which seem to them so much academic irrelevance. They are asked to believe that the meaning of the prophets cannot be discovered without effort."[12] In other words, his approach to the hard texts of Scripture begins with the contemporary receivers of the text. He advocates that the Christian reader and the academic commentator redouble their efforts and work together in order to grasp a text's meaning and significance.

It is worth noting that whilst Jones often quotes Calvin, "This does not mean that theologically I am a 'Calvinist.' I am not. It does mean that I pay my tribute to one of the greatest of all interpreters of the Old Testament."[13]

Ronald E. Clements is an ordained Baptist minister,[14] who acknowledges that his academic interest in theology stems from his faith:

> That theology is the handmaid of religion, and not necessarily its crowning achievement, is a conviction that underlies this work [*Old Testament Theology*]. Writing from a Christian context, I find myself, in the company of most Christians, committed to the Old Testament as a consequence of the history and genesis of my own faith. To pretend that this is not so, and that some better reasons for studying the Old Testament might be found, would not be intellectually honest. There is a need therefore for seeking to understand the Old Testament theologically from this perspective.[15]

In one of his earliest works, *Prophecy and Covenant*, he states that the two aspects of modern OT study that have most influenced his approach are the importance of cult in Israelite religion and the contributions of form-criticism and tradition-history.[16] Although, in many

---

11. Ibid., 10.
12. Ibid.
13. Ibid.
14. Clements, *Wisdom*, 7.
15. Clements, *OT Theology*, ix–x.
16. Clements, *Prophecy and Covenant*, 119.

ways, he himself is interested in reconstructing OT historical events, for example, see *Abraham and David* and *Isaiah and the Deliverance of Jerusalem* (and even his *A Century of Old Testament Study* shows his natural predilection for such reconstructions), he opines that, "All too easily an overpreoccupation with attempts to reconstruct the biblical history 'as it actually happened' can hide from our eyes the very features which the Bible is at pains to make us see."[17] In fact, he criticizes OT theology for being unbalanced in this area: "Both on account of its own antiquity, and also as a result of the predominantly historical approach to the main subject areas concerned with the Old Testament, the discipline appears to be more a historical, than a truly theological, one. Certainly the study of the history of ancient Israel, and of the history of its religion and literature, creates an impression that the prevailing methodology is historical rather than theological."[18]

He also recognizes that sometimes it is just not possible to reconstruct such history, for: "Questions may be raised concerning the extent which any or all of the prayers ascribed to these biblical figures can be regarded by the modern reader as authentic. It can only be stated quite frankly in regard to such questions that they are unanswerable. The questions themselves therefore are virtually pointless. Not only do we not have the means by which to deal with them adequately, but there would appear to be little gain in attempting to do so, except to satisfy a certain type of curiosity."[19]

In his view, the redaction-critical approach to which he subscribes does not distinguish as sharply as literary criticism between "authentic" and "inauthentic" material. Furthermore, where literary criticism "tends too readily to dismiss the latter as of only slight relevance," redaction criticism sees later textual additions as building on an already established tradition whilst at the same time becoming themselves the basis of further tradition.[20] His definition of a redaction-critical approach, written before Childs had properly developed his "canonical approach" (with *Introduction to the Old Testament as Scripture* in 1979 and *The New Testament as Canon* in 1984) nevertheless resonates strongly with it:

17. Clements, *Prayers*, 6.
18. Clements, *OT Theology*, 179.
19. Clements, *Prayers*, 4–5.
20. Clements, *Prophecy and Tradition*, 6–7.

> What is fundamental to a redactio-critical [sic] approach to the prophetic books is the attempt to understand and interpret the form and intention of these books as a whole. This means both a study of the form and arrangement of the whole book, comprising primary and secondary material, and also a careful appraisal of the structure of the larger units of which the books are composed. It may at times look at the ordering and conjunction of quite short sayings and oracles with a view to discerning in their formal arrangement some clue as to the intention of the editors who have made this arrangement.[21]

A few years later, Clements speaks approvingly of Childs' biblical interpretation, stating that he agrees largely with Childs' account of 2 Kgs 18:17–37.[22] He sometimes even uses terminology favored by Childs, such as the "*shaping* of the book of Isaiah into its present form . . . a very elaborate whole"[23] (emphasis mine). In the preface to his Jeremiah commentary he writes that his aim "has been to try to enable the modern reader to sense how this remarkable book would have been read in ancient Israel and to discern the situation to which it was addressed."[24] Interestingly, though, despite the series' claim that commentators seek to discern in a text meaning "for faith and life," in his preface Clements says nothing about this or, indeed, anything about how the text might function today.

Like Clements, Jones also writes in his Jeremiah commentary that his aim is to identify each stage of the tradition in order that the total may be understood,[25] for "the main benefit of the literary analysis is to help us to understand how the book reached its present form. It is its present canonical form, thus understood, which is finally important."[26] Thus, with their emphasis on the final form, together with their interest in the development of tradition and redactional processes, both Jones and Clements are sympathetic, at least in part, to Childs' canonical approach. At the same time, neither of them purport in their prefaces to read the text from a Christian perspective.

21. Ibid., 6.
22. Clements, *Isaiah and the Deliverance*, 10, 53.
23. Clements, *Isaiah 1-39*, 5.
24. Clements, *Jeremiah*, vii.
25. Jones, *Jeremiah*, 7.
26. Ibid., 47.

Overviews

Jones

Jones deems the OANs to have been "likely to have a liturgical or quasi-liturgical context"[27] and much of his commentary on Jer 48 and the OANs in general is underpinned by the hypothesis that this context was the feast of Tabernacles: "*The restricted interest of the oracles, the recurring and limited themes, the circumscribed pool of vocabulary, suggest that they were composed for a single type of occasion which itself determined the similarities.* It is possible to hazard a guess as to what the occasion was, and to locate it in the feast of Tabernacles. Dogmatic confidence is out of place, for there is no way of avoiding a hypothetical proposal as to the place and purpose of the oracles, itself based on a hypothesis. But there are strong pointers."[28]

One such pointer is the theme of kingship, since it is central to both the OANs and the feast of Tabernacles. As well, he sees the so-called royal psalms with their emphasis on YHWH's triumph over the nations as supporting this idea since they may have been part of the ritual.[29] "What we may imagine to have happened is this. The feast of Tabernacles, when the monarchy had perished, provided the occasion when the theme of kingship of YHWH over all nations was kept alive."[30] Jones' work builds upon that of Bentzen, Reventlow, and Würthwein and, before that, Mowinckel, who pointed out that the New Year Festival (closely linked to the feast of Tabernacles and which Mowinckel termed the Ascension Festival) contained a strong element of judgment against YHWH's enemies; often the foreign nations.[31] Behind the OANs, argues Bentzen, lie the rites of this festival.[32]

Jones writes, concerning Jeremiah's OANs in general that, "The single underlying theme of their message was the sovereignty of YHWH"[33] and the overall thrust of his comments on the oracles against

---

27. Ibid., 34.
28. Ibid., 488.
29. Ibid., 488–89.
30. Ibid., 489.
31. Mowinckel, *Psalmen-Studient II*, 65–77, 268–76.
32. Bentzen, "Ritual," 93.
33. Jones, *Jeremiah*, 490.

the individual nations seems to be aimed at furthering this assertion and demonstrating its validity. His remarks on Jer 48 are no exception and he quotes verse 15, a verse that supports this claim, both in his introduction to the chapter (see below) and in his detailed exposition:[34] "There are also signs that the great feast which we have found to be the most plausible suggestion for the context and occasion of these oracles may be also the context here. Verse 15 has: *says the King, whose name is the LORD of hosts,* cf. 46.18. Here also the real theme is the sovereignty of Israel's God over other peoples."[35]

This hypothesis affects the dating and authorship of the OANs. He considers it unlikely that Isaiah, Jeremiah, or Ezekiel were the authors, but, given the demise in prophecy and that the OANs do not mention the Persian Empire, he thinks it likely that the OANs were written before the fall of Babylon, in the decade before Cyrus.[36] "They are a *genre* and a tradition which belong to the same period between the fall of Jerusalem and the rise of Persia."[37]

In general, as well as offering his hypothesis for the place of the OANs in Israel's cult, Jones is more occupied with the historical-critical and literary components of the text, so that in his introductory section to Jer 46–51 he discusses the differences between LXX and MT, the authorship of the oracles, and phrases characteristic of the Jeremiah tradition, etc. Likewise, in his opening section on Jer 48, he discusses the shared material in this complicated, edited collection of oracles, and attempts to identify which parts belong to the Jeremiah tradition. Interestingly, where Fretheim describes Jer 48 (as well as Jeremiah in general) as a "collage," Jones uses the term "mosaic" to describe the manner in which material found elsewhere within and outside the book of Jeremiah is re-laid to form the OANs generally[38] and Jer 48 in particular.[39]

He recognizes that it is impossible to uncover all the underlying historical events, but gives a brief outline of who the Moabites were and their political status around that time. In his more detailed remarks on the text, he addresses textual, linguistic, and literary issues, as well

34. Ibid., 504.
35. Ibid., 498–99.
36. Ibid., 48.
37. Ibid., 490.
38. Ibid., 34, 486 twice.
39. Ibid., 499, 504, 507.

as clarifying points of geography and history. He observes that the imperative is often rhetorical in the chapter, but does not discuss how that might affect the tone. In fact Jones does not say much regarding the tone. He acknowledges that "The theme of mourning and lamentation is sufficiently pronounced (vv. 5, 17, 31, 37) to suggest that this has something to do with the purposes of the oracles."[40] However, he does not posit a suggestion what this "something" might be and says little concerning the lamentation in this collection of oracles against Moab.

Although he does not think that the holy war tradition is behind the OANs,[41] he does consider that "The ideology of the holy war and particularly the idea of the ban was current in Moab. What was holy to Chemosh was put to the ban in Israel and vice versa."[42] Thus, he explains the references to Chemosh in Jer 48.

Clements

Like Jones (indeed, Jones quotes Clements on this matter[43]), Clements does not deem holy war to have been the setting for all the OANs. He concedes that, "It is a reasonable conjecture that the category of an oracle against a foreign nation owes something to the ideology of holy war."[44] However, he argues that, since not all the foreign nations were Israel's enemies:

> Whatever the category of such prophecy may once have owed to the ideas and practices of the holy war, therefore, must have already receded into the background . . . All in all, therefore, there is no very substantial ground for accepting that the holy war provided the essential setting for prophecies against foreign nations.[45]

Unlike Jones, however, Clements does not consider that the cult provided the setting for the OANS, either.[46] Instead, he concludes: "That any one sphere of Israel's life, the royal court, the cultus or the mili-

40. Ibid., 499.
41. Ibid., 485.
42. Ibid., 502.
43. Ibid., 485.
44. Clements, *Prophecy and Tradition*, 70.
45. Ibid., 71.
46. Ibid., 69.

tary organisation of the state with its inheritance of holy war ideology, formed the exclusive setting of the category of the oracles against foreign powers cannot be regarded as established. Rather we must regard these prophecies as a distinctive genre of their own which drew from many aspects of Israel's life . . . the category in general displays clear signs of having been subjected to an interesting and quite distinctive tradition of development."[47]

Clements is also keen to point out in *Prophecy and Tradition* that whilst there are recurring elements, the collection of OANs in Isaiah, Jeremiah, and Ezekiel show no pattern. For instance, only some are Israel's enemies and some do not contain political threats. "We cannot force these foreign nation oracles into one mould by claiming that they consistently function as a kind of assurance for Israel. Sometimes they do, but often they do not."[48]

For Clements the OANs raise a lot of questions:

> If these close neighbors of Judah were caught up in the same events, was not the same divine purpose that related to Judah also operational for them? . . .
> If, as Jeremiah declared, YHWH the God of Israel was controlling and using Babylon to punish Judah, then what was God's purpose with respect of these other nations who did not worship him as the Lord? Was the same Lord God punishing them also, although they did not know him by name? If so, what were their sins? Were they perhaps simply to be regarded as purely innocent victims of events which concerned them only indirectly? Major questions regarding the morality of God's actions and of the theological implications of monotheism are involved with the answers presented or implied regarding these issues.[49]

Unfortunately, Clements does not provide answers to many of these questions, but in his section on Jeremiah's oracle against Moab he admits that such prophecies may only provide a partial answer to these deeper questions regarding the meaning behind world events.[50]

Given that Fretheim, Miller, Brueggemann, and Jones focus to a greater or lesser extent on YHWH's sovereignty as a key theme of the

47. Ibid., 72.
48. Ibid., 61, 63, 64 (quote on p. 64).
49. Clements, *Jeremiah*, 246.
50. Ibid., 254.

OANs, it is somewhat surprising that Clements, in his albeit short (three page) commentary on Jer 48, does not refer either to the sovereignty of YHWH, or to kingship in any context. As well, he only briefly mentions Chemosh and seems to find more significance in the way that the poem has been built up, for instance, in the number of place names listed.

Clements begins by addressing the literary questions, but the most prominent feature of his commentary on Jer 48 reflects what Clements considers to be one of the primary attributes of the chapter itself; that of tone. He draws attention to the amount of grief expressed by the poem, but finds a diverse range of emotions displayed in the oracle against Moab. In fact, he deems this variety to be characteristic of Jeremiah's OANs in general, for "there is no single emotional tone evident throughout the prophecies, whether of shared grief, vengeful recriminations, or a naïve 'I told you so!' sense of satisfaction. There are many moods expressed in them."[51] How Jones and Clements handle these moods shall now be investigated.

Analysis

Tone

In his preface to his commentary on Haggai, Zechariah, and Malachi, Jones writes (regarding new interpretations he may present), "If sometimes they [the readers] detect a tone of subdued excitement, they are certainly catching the mood of the writer [i.e., Jones] and sharing the intense interest of discovery."[52] Despite Jones' perception that such emotions shine through his written words, this tone of excitement, even subdued excitement, is not immediately obvious to me in either this work or his others. In fact, to my mind, Jones is the most reserved, even detached, of the five UK and U.S. Christian scholars studied here. Therefore, perhaps it is of little surprise that emotion with reference to Jer 48 hardly features in Jones' commentary. Neither does it figure in his general comments on the OANs, although he describes such a message as "a colourful, powerful, condemnatory prophecy."[53]

---

51. Ibid., 247.
52. Jones, *Haggai*, 13.
53. Jones, *Jeremiah*, 486.

It is not that Jones always overlooks the various tones in the oracle; it is simply that he does not expound them. So he notes the shame in 48:1 and 48:13, that destruction (שׁדד) is a theme of the chapter,[54] that in 48:27 the mocker becomes the mocked "by the irony of judgment,"[55] that 48:43–44 communicates the "inescapability of judgment,"[56] and even, regarding 48:14–28, that "the element of anticipatory mourning is strong in this poem, not only in the call to mourning (vv. 17, 20) but also in the use of *'êkāh* (vv. 14, 17) the characteristic opening of the elegy (Isa 1.21; Lam 1.1; 2.1; 4.1)."[57] He also identifies lamentation as one of the elements of 48:1–10 (verse 5), but his comments on 48:5 are solely concerned with the textual aspects of "the ascent of Luhith"; whether it is a corruption of Isa 15:5 and how LXX translates it. The closest he comes to acknowledging the pain that is prevalent in Jer 48 is, rather paradoxically given that it curses those who withhold the sword, in his remarks on 48:10: that judgment "is worked out in the tragedies and vicissitudes of history."[58]

It may be that he plays down the mourning because he does not consider it genuine, for he ignores the weeping and wailing of 48:31–32 and, almost bizarrely, picks up on the tone of celebration instead: "Isa. 15 and 16 are comparatively straightforward laments over the doom of Moab. Here [48:45–47] the lament element is extrapolated and becomes part of an oracle which, like the previous oracles, both celebrates some sort of disaster (the destroyer has fallen, vv. 32, 29) and looks forward to a completion of the judgment (vv. 35, 40–44)."[59]

In fact, the note of celebration is perhaps the strongest tone that comes through in Jones' work, for this is the aspect he chooses to expand regarding 48:45–46, "The heart of the ballad quoted in Numb. 21.27–29, celebrating the destruction of the people of Chemosh, is very much to the author's purpose."[60] On a related note, Jones four times draws attention to the "vintage shouts of rejoicing" of 48:32–34,[61] al-

54. Ibid., 502, 506.
55. Ibid., 505.
56. Ibid., 506.
57. Ibid., 504.
58. Ibid., 502. See chapter 6 for the fuller quote.
59. Ibid., 507.
60. Ibid., 509.
61. Ibid., 499, 506, 508 twice (quote from p. 508).

though the point here is that this celebratory shout (הידד—v. 33) will not be uttered. "The author seems to wish to rub this word in!"[62] "The word *hêdād* occurs three times, as though reinforcing it and playing on it. Is there a play on the Canaanite storm and weather god Hadad, who was expected to guarantee the rain?"[63] Such an emphasis on celebration is less surprising in the context of Bentzen's assertion that "YHWH's advent as judge of the world in the New Year service was considered good tidings ... the theophany of the [sic] God arriving as judge of the world is described as a motive for jubilation."[64]

The scantiness of Jones' discussion on tone may arise from the fact that the tone of the oracles is not crucial to his theory that they formed part of the liturgy of the feast of Tabernacles. In fact, it could be argued that oracles such as Jer 48 that mourn over a foreign nation lend themselves less to such a setting. For this reason, it is a pity that Jones does not address the element of lament and explain its role in relation to this proposed scenario.

Jones' treatment of the tone of Jer 48 may be limited, but Clements gives considerable attention to the subject. As we have seen, he observes a variety of emotions both across the OANs and within each one. Concerning Moab, he writes that: "In ethical and theological content we find a considerable shift of tone and outlook in these sayings addressed to Moab. The final unit portraying Moab as helpless and defeated has a strong feeling of pity for the victims and shares in their fear and confusion (vv. 40–46). The sayings that precede this, however, sharply condemn the traditional pride of Moab . . . Verse 10 adds a touch of brutality by its comment 'cursed is he who keeps back his sword from bloodshed.'"[65]

Acknowledging that verse 10 may be a subsequent addition, Clements nevertheless concludes: "All told, however, there is a mixture of emotions displayed against Moab throughout the chapter and virtually nothing by way of direct allusion to identifiable military actions. We should not therefore rule out the possibility that more explicit historical

---

62. Ibid., 506.
63. Ibid., 508.
64. Bentzen, "Ritual," 94.
65. Clements, *Jeremiah*, 253.

allusions have been deliberately suppressed in building up the whole composite poem."⁶⁶

Clements attributes some of the emotion to the "traditional and deeply felt attitudes" towards these old enemies of Israel and "there is bitter anger expressed against the worship of Chemosh." "Nevertheless," he continues, "all such negative attitudes are totally swallowed up in the larger recognition of the tragedy and horror of Moab's sufferings in the wars against Babylon. The sense is that Moab has suffered far more than it or any people deserve."⁶⁷

Clements clearly does not consider that the mourning is ironic, for he concludes that "By the richness and variety of its poetry, the prophecy as a whole displays a genuine sense of grief shared with Moab in her sufferings (vv. 45–46)."⁶⁸ In *Prophecy and Tradition* he asserts that the strong similarities across the OANs in the invectives against the nations are "the consequence of a particular tradition about YHWH's concern with them."⁶⁹ Interestingly, even though he exposes the negative attitudes towards Moab in the oracle, Clements does not identify any celebratory tones.

Of the five commentators discussed, Clements is the one who most draws out the variety of tones within the oracle against Moab. He is also the only one who proposes that the historical setting has been deliberately understated in order to emphasize the tone. This is an interesting proposal and one to which we shall return when we look at the purpose of the oracle. Now, however, I shall examine how the interpreters handle divine involvement in Jer 48.

Divine Involvement

Jones writes re the OANs that: "They reflect the prophetic conviction, from the time of Amos, that the LORD is the lord of the nations and not of Israel only, that none ultimately escapes the divine judgment, that those who have gloated over Judah's fall will themselves stumble

---

66. Ibid., 253.
67. Ibid., 254.
68. Ibid., 255.
69. Clements, *Prophecy and Tradition*, 66.

and fall, that the LORD is not mocked, and the whole world is in his hand."[70]

As we have seen, Jones views the theme of kingship in the feast of Tabernacles as extending to the nations. He finds such substantiation for this claim in passages such as Zech 14:6, where "it is said that those who survive of the nations that attack Jerusalem on the Day of the Lord, 'shall go up year after year to worship the King, the LORD of hosts, and to keep the feast of booths.'"[71] Thus, for Jones, the primary relationship that YHWH has with the nations is that of divine sovereign.

Jones states that, "The great day of the feast is in a special sense the LORD's day, attracting to itself the ideology of the Holy War. Here Israel receives the promise that, though the nations band themselves against the LORD's people, he will intervene to save them."[72] Nevertheless, Jones cautions that this only applies to OANs "which are really salvation oracles for Judah,"[73] for, as stated above, neither Jones nor Clements subscribe to the theory that the context for the OANs is always holy war, since not all the nations are Israel's enemies. It seems that Moab was not Israel's enemy at the time of the Babylonian rise to power in the sixth century, nor is the oracle a salvation oracle for Judah. Therefore, it seems unlikely that the holy war motif is appropriate in this instance.

Nevertheless, Jones considers that Chemosh is set up in opposition to YHWH in Jer 48, not least because both are cultic gods, but also because Moab as well as Israel/Judah had the concept of holy war and the idea of putting to the ban. Solomon may have made a political alliance with Chemosh, but in 48:7, as Jones implies, it is YHWH who is victorious in the holy war. Jones discerns that in 48:13 the parallels between Moab and Israel are again brought to the fore, for both Moab and Israel were ashamed because of their confidence in false gods (Jones accepts El-Bethel as a deity rather than a place).[74]

However, the real theme of the oracle against Moab, according to Jones, is "the sovereignty of Israel's God over other peoples,"[75] which

---

70. Jones, *Jeremiah*, 486.
71. Ibid., 488.
72. Ibid., 489.
73. Ibid.
74. Ibid., 503.
75. Ibid., 498–99; see also 504.

becomes "crystal clear" in verses such as 48:38b, 42, 44b.[76] YHWH's sovereignty is particularly highlighted, Jones argues, if the oracle is anticipatory or predictive.[77] In Moab's case, this sovereignty, as Jones observes, "looks beyond the destruction of Moab to an ultimate salvation, as also for Ammon 49.6 and Elam 49.39."[78]

Jones does not suggest why Moab might be offered salvation, as he does not for either Ammon or Elam. However, although it is not listed in the quote above, Egypt is also offered restoration (46:26) and Jones is a little more forthcoming in this part of his commentary. He considers that: "At some stage of redaction (after LXX), the ultimate salvation of the nations was envisaged, cf. 48:47 (Moab); 49.6 (Ammon); 49.39 (Elam). For this universalist spirit see also Isa 19.16–25. All are absent from LXX which here represents an earlier text. It should not occasion surprise that this note should be introduced subsequently. It is the inner logic of the teaching on the sovereignty of YHWH and it took time to work it out."[79]

Jones does not elucidate "the inner logic" at work here, which is surprising, for it is quite a big hermeneutical step to start from the sovereignty of YHWH and end with ultimate salvation for all, though Jones would probably see it as more or less self-evident, especially in a post-Enlightenment context. Jones reiterates this view elsewhere in his works and it is apparent that he sees the sovereignty of YHWH in this quite specific way, at least in part. In his commentary on Zech 9:7 he declares, "Even the hated uncircumcised, after judgment, shall be incorporated with the People of God,"[80] although in his commentary on Zech 2:11 he confesses that "We are not told whether this will involve more than the recognition of YHWH as God (Isa 45.23)."[81] However, he realizes that such a stance is problematic, as he articulates in his commentary on Isa 56–66; "Zechariah envisaged many nations 'joined to the LORD,' that is, incorporated in the people of God (2.11; cf. 8:20–23; 14:16–19).

---

76. Ibid., 507.
77. Ibid., 500.
78. Ibid., 507.
79. Ibid., 496. The lack of promise of Moab's restoration in LXX has been discussed in chapter 2.
80. Jones, *Haggai*, 128; see also p.34.
81. Ibid., 66.

But this appeared to raise acute practical problems, and even to lead to contradictions of the law of Moses."[82]

One way that Jones holds this paradox in tension is by appealing to the changing circumstances of history: "When the rise of Assyria in the eighth century B.C. expanded the horizons of Israel, so that her parochial boundaries ceased to be the limits of her concern, the quick sensitiveness of the prophet Amos comprehended the whole known world within the providences of the One God and re-drew the diagram of Israel's special place within it."[83]

Nevertheless, Jones does not nullify the concept of election even whilst he asserts that the non-elect will be incorporated into the people of God. Thus, on one hand, he argues that, "The world is one world, designed for a universal harmony, because the ground and goal of its being is the One God who made it and means to bring all things to perfection" and "the whole world is the world of the One Living God and He never despairs of it."[84] On the other hand, he also asserts that, "we have to reckon with the offensive notion of election, the possibility that He has found and chosen to nourish a heightened sensitiveness to Himself in one set of men, so that through them He may make His will known more clearly to all men."[85] Indeed, the concept of election is fundamental to a universal knowledge of God's will in a Christian understanding and the nature of the nations' incorporation complex. Chapter 7 probes this issue a little further.

Like Fretheim, therefore, it appears that Jones is caught between affirming YHWH's inclusiveness of all people and not denying the exclusiveness of YHWH's covenant with Israel. He clearly feels uncomfortable with the latter and his desire to affirm the former may well be due in part to the culture within which he lived: one that reacts against the dreadful things it has seen, for example, the Nazi regime. That this is the case is indicated, not only in the number of times he refers to the relatively recent term, "racialism," in his works, but also in the way in which he uses it. So, he is quick to proclaim that "Racialism is dead in the thought of Zechariah,"[86] and feels the need to explain that "The re-

82. Jones, *Isaiah 56–66*, 31.
83. Jones, *Instrument*, 10.
84. Ibid., 20, 33.
85. Ibid., 23–24.
86. Jones, *Haggai*, 66.

election of Jerusalem (1:17; 2:12; 3:2; 8:1–8, 22) is not an example of narrow racialism, anticipating Judaism, but a central biblical principle."[87]

We have already seen that in his commentary on Jeremiah, Clements raises the question of whether the same divine purpose was intended for the nations as for Israel since both were caught up in the same events (and he directs his readers to *Prophecy and Tradition*, where he addresses such questions). He also asks if the same God was punishing the nations even though they did not know him by name. A related question, which Clements does not ask, is whether the divine involvement (or even the divine relationship) was also the same between Israel and the nations.

While he draws attention to YHWH's role in history and politics,[88] we have noted that Clements does not mention YHWH's sovereignty in his introductory remarks on Jer 46–51 and in his comments on chapter 48. In fact, although Clements observes that the Jerusalem cult "placed a quite exceptional emphasis upon the cosmic and supra-natural power of YHWH, as the King of the universe,"[89] YHWH's sovereignty is not an overriding theme in Clements's writings and where the idea is present it is often not in the precise terms of "sovereignty." For instance, in his remarks on Jeremiah's oracle against Philistia, he asserts that "at every turning-point the Lord God has remained in control,"[90] that the historical order reveals "a process of re-creating the world under the hand of God,"[91] that "there is more than a hint that some 'grand design' is operative, and that it is important for prophecy to provide a basis for understanding this."[92] Regarding Edom in Jer 49, he states that "the downfall of Edom, as of the other nations made the subject of these prophecies, hangs in the air as a fate decreed by God with virtually no explanation, either moral or historical."[93]

The only time he uses the term "sovereignty" in his commentary on Jeremiah's OANs is in relation to Babylon's fall; "all this will be a result of the providential rule of God, who wields unlimited power and

87. Ibid., 35.
88. Clements. *Jeremiah*, 254.
89. Clements, *Prophecy and Covenant*, 20.
90. Clements, *Jeremiah*, 251.
91. Ibid.
92. Ibid., 252.
93. Ibid., 257.

impartial justice in determining the rise and fall of nations . . . sovereignty over all nations and peoples belongs exclusively to God."[94] Indeed, Babylon's rule is "a demonstration of the sovereign rule of God over the world."[95] Elsewhere, he maintains that Sennacherib, "the Assyrian king had no power than that which had been given to him by God, so that his own boastful claims were an act of blasphemy" and "Isaiah gives a firm implication that the Assyrian king would be punished for this sinful arrogance."[96]

It is clear, then, that Clements recognizes the sovereignty of YHWH over the foreign nations and their kings even if he does not always use such terminology. Nevertheless, if he is reluctant to make too much of YHWH's sovereignty over the nations (and he might not be) then it may be because he is more concerned to discover the divine purpose behind the oracles, rather than to determine the nature of divine involvement. This would explain why, despite Clements's interest in the tone of the oracles and his emphasis on mourning and pain in the oracle concerning Moab, he is silent regarding YHWH's role in the lament and does not address the issue that YHWH himself utters the lament in 48:31–32, 36.

Clements is careful not to diminish Israel's unique position and this may be another reason why he does not stress the universality of YHWH's sovereignty. For in *Prophecy and Covenant*, he claims that, "It is true that the oracles against foreign nations are a large and important part of the prophetic corpus, yet the first interest of the prophets is in God's action towards Israel, and sometimes even the oracles against foreign nations have an indirect concern with Israel."[97] From other works we can see that he acknowledges that "the Hebrew Bible is itself very conscious of the extent to which Israel's experiment in nationhood was closely matched by that of surrounding peoples (as witness the 'foreign nation' oracles of the prophets)."[98] "Yet for all its national and political status Israel is not like any other nation, but is regarded as quite distinct from them." The reason for this, Clements explains, is to be found in

---

94. Ibid., 260.
95. Ibid., 264.
96. Clements, *Isaiah and the Deliverance*, 38.
97. Clements, *Prophecy and Covenant*, 16–17.
98. Clements, "Israel," 7.

Deut 7:6 (cf. Deut 4:20; 14:2; 26:18–19)—simply that YHWH has chosen Israel.[99]

In *Wisdom in Theology*, Clements argues that the wisdom literature in the third century BCE provides a corrective to "the traditional belief in a retributive providence which might be thought to act as a form of natural law,"[100] a "belief in a rather abstract moral order in the world."[101] Such a "traditional belief" would have been operative in the prophets and, although Clements says nothing regarding it in his commentary on Jeremiah's OANs, it is likely that this is the model against which he understands the OANs. If this is so, then he is in company with Fretheim.

Also, like Fretheim, Clements talks about human relationships in terms of a "web," by which he means that: "No one individual can act without what he or she does affecting other people. The whole of humankind live in a remarkable web of relationships in which every individual action has its consequences upon others. The creation of life and the taking of life influence and act upon other people. In families, clans, tribes, and nations; in houses, settlements, villages, and cities, the actions of men and women interact with each other, and thereby human society is experienced."[102]

Unlike Fretheim, however, Clements does not extend this web either to the whole cosmos, or to God. Instead, it seems, Clements envisages a more localized web than Fretheim, one that primarily encompasses those in direct contact with one another; "We are, each one, influenced and molded [sic] by the lives of those around us. In turn, we may assist in the development and formation of the lives of those who know and depend on us."[103] Nevertheless, Clements recognizes a larger scope, even if he does not appear to think of it in terms of a web, for, as he says in his commentary on Jer 48, both Israel and Moab "have been overtaken by the same world-changing events in which the rise and fall of entire nations had been manifested."[104] Whereas Fretheim uses the concept of the web to explain what appears to be violence on the side of

99. Clements, *God's Chosen People*, 32.
100. Clements, *Wisdom in Theology*, 161.
101. Ibid., 164.
102. Clements, *Prayers*, 22.
103. Ibid., 24.
104. Clements, *Jeremiah*, 253. See also Clements, *Ezekiel*, 115.

God and that what God does to one entity will affect another, Clements attempts to show by it that, "A handful of good men and women can become a saving remnant!"[105] He makes no such comment regarding Moab's restoration, however, an event that he regards, instead, as demonstrating that there is always a possibility of hope.[106]

So, then, Clements does not divulge much about how he views divine involvement in the OANs, particularly YHWH's relationship with Moab in Jer 48. Instead he implicitly acknowledges YHWH's sovereignty, but focuses more on the "divine purpose" of the oracles. Jones, too, does not engage a great deal with divine involvement in Jer 46–51, but where he does it is to emphasize YHWH's sovereignty over all peoples. In fact, he considers that the main theme of Jeremiah's ministry, "is the sovereignty of the Word of God over all nations and causes and persons."[107] It is possible that YHWH's sovereignty is the over-arching theme of Jer 48, but the substance of the oracle concerns what can be colloquially termed "blood and tears." It is the contents and message of this oracle and how the commentators handle them that will now occupy us.

The Message and Its Purpose

CONTENT

Jones is attentive to the literary issues in this "*collection* of material,"[108] such as the plays on words, but he also points out interesting phenomena in the content. For example, he notes that an extraordinary amount of place names are mentioned, that there is no reference to the foe from the north, that the theme of the Day of the LORD is implicit only and that there is a "remarkable use of 'scriptural' passages."[109] He discusses whether the prophecies were likely to have been uttered before or after the event of Moab's downfall and concludes that at least some of the sayings are predictive.[110]

---

105. Clements, *Prayers*, 22.
106. Clements, *Jeremiah*, 255.
107. Jones, *Jeremiah*, 42.
108. Ibid., 499.
109. Ibid.
110. Ibid.

Jones' commentary is largely composed of succinct observations and explanations of a historical-critical or textual nature on various points of interest or problematic words and phrases in the text. Therefore, whilst Jones touches on the main themes of the oracle, he does not tend to explore them. So then, he points out that the year of visitation "is a vital motif of all these poems"[111] and he highlights the comparisons between Israel and Moab, for example, 48:13 and 48:14–28.[112] As well, he draws attention to some features in Jer 48 that recur throughout the OANs, for example, shame (48:1, 20, 39), pride (48:2, 7, 29–30, 42), the sword (48:2), and the destroyer (48:8, 15, 18).[113] In fact, he stresses that the repeated use of the root שדד "destroy" forms one of the key themes in the chapter—the destroyer (48:8) destroys Moab.[114] He points out that "there is no indication of who the Destroyer is or from whence [sic] he is expected to come,"[115] but he is "an instrument of the LORD," and "the execution of the destruction of Moab is the LORD's work," although Jones judges the portrayal of such to be simplified.[116] As discussed above, Jones emphasizes the tone of celebration over Moab's destruction.

Like Fretheim, Miller, and Brueggemann, Jones explains the metaphor of Moab having been settled on his lees and the "threat of judgment (v. 12)" that foretells "the reversal of Moab's pride."[117] He also remarks in his notes on 48:27 that, "By the irony of judgment, Moab shall herself become a derision."[118] Yet, he does not draw out the extent and prominence of Moab's shame in the text. Also, like Fretheim, Jones subscribes to some notion of natural law, for as he expresses in *Instrument of Peace*, "When Amos understood that foreign peoples were guilty before God, though they had no knowledge of the law of Moses, he was anticipating the Pauline principle that the Gentiles who do not possess the law have

---

111. Ibid., 506.
112. Ibid., 503–4.
113. Ibid., 498.
114. Ibid., 499, 502.
115. Ibid., 504.
116. Ibid., 502.
117. Ibid., 503.
118. Ibid., 505.

the moral law inscribed in their hearts."[119] Yet, again, he does not discuss such concepts with regard to Jeremiah's oracle concerning Moab.

Clements seems more attuned than Jones to nuances of the content of the message. For example, as we have seen, he observes that there are no specific details about the military actions in the chapter, whilst the range of sentiments is given prominence. He sees the demise and denunciation of Chemosh as striking a "more theological note," whilst the "heavy use" of Moabite place names provides opportunities for word play. For Clements, the content of the message leads him to conclude that "it is evidently the quest for an understanding of the meaning and significance of Moab's downfall that is uppermost in the prophecy."[120] It is not always possible to grasp truly a deeper level of understanding of world-events, but Clements considers that: "Nevertheless, by the manner in which the poems have been composed, often out of earlier fragments and on the basis of very limited acquaintance with the affairs of the nation concerned, there is a careful attempt to bring together the framework in which a fuller understanding is to be sought."[121]

He discerns several key factors in the text: the comprehensiveness, as shown by the list of place names; the characterization of Moab's pride; the anger against the worship of Chemosh; the "tragedy and horror of Moab's sufferings," which eclipse the other key elements; and the promised restoration.[122] Such a list is reflective of features common to OANs in general, for example, the pattern of threatening announcements that sometimes provide a motive for the judgment, which is often hubris against YHWH and pride.[123] Clements says less than one might expect regarding Moab's destruction, which is described in some detail. It is interesting that he does not give Moab's destruction the attention that it perhaps deserves, but focuses instead on the aspect of mourning, whilst Jones brings out the destruction, but not the lament.

---

119. Jones, *Instrument*, 33.
120. Clements, *Jeremiah*, 253.
121. Ibid., 254.
122. Ibid., 254–55.
123. Clements, *Prophecy and Tradition*, 60, 65.

Purpose

Although Jones considers that the OANs are written largely for "the Jews"[124]—presumably Israel and Judah—he appreciates that Jer 48 contains a summons for the Moabites to flee and that it pronounces "a solemn curse on the invader if he is slack in performing what is 'the work of the LORD' (v. 10)."[125] However, as discussed, Jones' primary consideration is not the role of the oracle's message, but how the oracle fits into the festival rituals and liturgy. Therefore, he is not so concerned with questions about a potential original audience. By the same token, he is not interested in subsequent audiences either, such as the Christian reader.

Clements is unclear whether he considers that the nations were ever the recipients of the oracles, for he concludes "that at least some of the prophecies emanate from him [Jeremiah] and that he was truly 'a prophet to the nations.'"[126] Likewise, in *Prophecy and Covenant*, he claims that although the prophets were primarily nationalists, they sometimes delivered oracles outside Israel's borders.[127] At the same time, he avers in *Prophecy and Tradition*, that it is unlikely that OANs were heard by representatives of people they addressed. Instead, "These were apparently preached so as to be heard by Israelites, and hardly, if at all, by the peoples whose downfall they proclaimed."[128] That the nations did not hear the oracles does not necessarily reduce their effectiveness, he avers, since curses were considered effective despite the addressee being absent.

In his Jeremiah commentary, he argues that the oracles had an extensive literary history, though he rejects the idea that Jeremiah's OANs existed as a separate, independent corpus before their inclusion in the book of Jeremiah.[129] He surmises that "the major reason for their inclusion into Jeremiah's book must lie in the fact that the events relating to what Jeremiah had to say about Judah embraced a great many other

---

124. Jones, *Jeremiah*, 486.
125. Ibid., 501.
126. Clements, *Jeremiah*, 247.
127. Clements, *Prophecy and Covenant*, 31.
128. Clements, *Prophecy and Tradition*, 61–62.
129. Clements, *Jeremiah*, 246.

nations also."¹³⁰ This implies that they were intended primarily for Judah, but presumably, whoever heard them would realize that, "If God was at work in these events, then the divine purpose must also incorporate these other peoples in its range."¹³¹ This divine purpose overlaps with the more general purpose of the OANs.

The purpose of the OANs for Jones is, of course, determined by their supposed context of the feast of Tabernacles.¹³² At this point, I will pause and give a short critique of Jones' position, for I am unconvinced that he is correct for the following reasons. First, the feast was a time of celebration (which may be why Jones highlights this sentiment in Jer 48) and not mourning and therefore the tone of lament in Jer 48 does not quite seem appropriate to such a feast. Secondly, mourning over a foreign nation seems particularly inappropriate in a context where Israel celebrates, among other things, her freedom from Egypt (and, as Fretheim argues, at least some of the mourning resists an ironic reading).

Thirdly, none of the so-called royal and Zion psalms that Jones cites as those that "celebrate or anticipate the triumph of YHWH over the nations that threaten Zion and its king," and whose context he argues was the pre-exilic feast of Tabernacles (Pss 2; 18; 46; 47; 48; 68; 72; 76; 93; 97; 98),¹³³ contains any lament or mourning over the nation in question. Neither do those passages he lists as "celebrating" YHWH's sovereignty (Exod 15:8; Num 23:21; Deut 33:5; Pss 22:29; 93:1; 24:7–10; Isa 44:6; Obad 21; Zech 14:9).¹³⁴ In my opinion, therefore, although the content of the OANs and some of the psalms may contain similar material, there is a marked difference in tone between them and I would hesitate before connecting them in the way that Jones, Bentzen, Reventlow, Würthwein, and Mowinckel have done.¹³⁵

Fourthly, one of the presuppositions underlying the concept of holy war, which Jones rejects as suitable for the context of the OANs, underlies the feast of Tabernacles, too. That is, that the nations are

130. Ibid., 247.
131. Ibid.
132. For example, twice on Jones, *Jeremiah*, 504.
133. Ibid., 489.
134. Ibid., 488–89.
135. Bentzen, "Ritual," 93–95; Reventlow, *Amt des Propheten*, 63; Würthwein, "Der Ursprung," 120–22; Mowinckel, *Psalmen-Studien II*, 65–77, 268–76.

Israel's / Judah's enemies; hence the festival celebration over their downfall. Bentzen, Reventlow, and Würthwein all subscribe to this premise, although Würthwein cautions that how much an oracle was spoken in the cult has to be decided in each case.[136] Jones, on the other hand, does not address the issue of the nations as YHWH's enemies, although, as quoted above, he recognizes that not all OANs are salvation oracles for Israel.[137] Instead, he points out that the feast of Tabernacles was the only feast that those from the nations were to attend.[138] Since Jones does not accept the holy war concept partly because not all the nations in the OANs are enemies of YHWH's people, it seems slightly strange that he overlooks this objection in relation to his preferred context.

Nevertheless, Jones is undoubtedly correct that the feast of Tabernacles "was predominantly the feast in which the kingship of YHWH was celebrated," and "hence it was the obvious claimant to be the feast of the world-wide sovereignty of YHWH, attended by all peoples."[139] However, it still does not follow that this feast was the context of the OANs. Within the context of the feast, Jones claims that the purpose of the OANs is "the demonstration and celebration of the sovereignty of YHWH,"[140] particularly "the sovereignty of YHWH over the nations."[141] This is particularly demonstrated in Jer 48:15 in which God is referred to as "the King, whose name is the LORD of hosts."

Clements, as stated above, is not persuaded that the "great Israelite Autumn Festival," or the cult more generally, was the appropriate setting for the OANs, despite the Zion theme running through Isaiah's OANs and the fact that some of the psalms indicate that the cult was involved with political affairs. For, he argues, politics affects so much of life that "in itself, a concern with international affairs and the fate of Israel's neighbors and enemies in prophetic sayings does not necessarily point

---

136. Bentzen, "Ritual," 92, 94; Reventlow, *Amt des Propheten*, 63; Würthwein, "Der Ursprung," 122, 124–25. Würthwein ("Der Ursprung," 122) prefers to use the term "Kultdrama" (cult drama) to refer to the setting, for he considers that the event is acted out.

137. Jones, *Jeremiah*, 489.

138. Ibid., 488; Jones, *Haggai*, 178.

139. Jones, *Haggai*, 179.

140. Jones, *Jeremiah*, 507.

141. Ibid., 504.

to a cultic setting."[142] Perhaps a similar argument could be made with regard to YHWH's sovereignty. Even so, notwithstanding Jones' distinct context, his findings cohere with the other interpreters in that most see the proclamation of "the sovereignty of Judah's God over all peoples" as a crucial purpose of the OANs.[143]

Although I am not persuaded that the OANs were intended for the feast of Tabernacles, such a context does answer Jones' question why this kind of oracle developed "just at the period when Judah was smallest, powerless and utterly at the mercy of foreign powers.[144]" It also provides a setting for these difficult texts and in this way incorporates them firmly into Israelite religion. It is, in my opinion, one of the strengths of Jones' commentary on the OANs that he makes such an attempt, for many commentators do not.

However, a more subtle account of the OANs' development at the time of Judah's weakness might revolve around a theological rather than "psychological" perspective. In the "psychological" move commonly made, the OANs act primarily as a comfort to Judah in her distress because they demonstrate that she is not alone and other nations are experiencing similar disasters. A "theological" reflection, on the other hand, might recognize that in the midst of great darkness it dawns that YHWH is so much greater than has possibly been recognized. In his commentary on Zech 14:5, Jones writes that, "In the worship of the Temple, his coming was hailed as the judgment of all the nations."[145] If there was a similar understanding in pre-exilic times, then it could be argued that a further purpose of the OANs is to herald God's coming.

As we have seen, Clements has a clear idea of how the tone functions within Jer 48. First, he proposes that the oracle against Moab shows that "Israel has not been alone in her sufferings,"[146] which provides an answer to why Israel's scriptures should contain such lamentation over a foreign nation. Secondly: "In the process of piecing together a 'historical map' of the range and savagery of Babylonian conquests among Israel's neighbors, there is a concern to mark out its pattern, to relinquish old grievances and enmities, and to search out in the character and conduct

---

142. Clements, *Prophecy and Tradition*, 69, 67 (quote on 67).
143. Jones, *Jeremiah*, 500.
144. Ibid., 486.
145. Jones, *Haggai*, 173.
146. Clements, *Jeremiah*, 253.

of the nations dealt with some basic clues to understanding historic order. Not least is the concern to draw attention to the powerful currents of historical and political change as a part of the creating and recreating work of God."[147]

Whereas the previous purpose required no action on the part of the people of God, this purpose entails more than passive receptivity. For here they are required to forgive their enemies as well as to understand the changing historic order as the work of YHWH.[148] There is not much debate about the latter point and the very fact that YHWH is seen to be the agent in the histories of foreign nations, as well as in Judah's, would seem to point to this. However, I am not certain that there is anything in the texts to suggest that a "relinquish[ing] of old grievances and enmities" is part of their scope. YHWH, not Israel, grieves over Moab and though Israel's forgiveness of Moab may be a noble act, there is no indication even that YHWH himself forgives the nations, despite the promise of restoration offered to some, like Moab (see chapter 4 for a fuller discussion on forgiveness of the nations). In fact, the nations are sometimes castigated for their treatment of YHWH's chosen people and the ensuing punishment is presented as their just rewards (48:26–27), if not salvation for Israel (49:1–2), a scenario that does not appear to be bound up with relinquishing old grievances. Jer 48:10 would also fit oddly with this reading. Therefore, it seems unlikely that Clements is correct in this respect and I wonder if the Christian emphasis on forgiveness has influenced his thinking here. It is true that the reader is encouraged to share with Moab in her sufferings, but I would contend that empathy and sympathy are not necessarily predicated on forgiveness. Nevertheless, I would agree with Clements that the tone of lament and recognition of Moab's suffering dwarf the "negative attitudes" found in the oracle and that therefore there is "a deeper purpose in history than a simple pattern of retribution"—that of sharing in the grief of Moab.[149]

A third purpose of Jer 48 that Clements gives (he does not list them) is found in the last sentence of his commentary:

> By such a complex range of emotions and images the author of the finished poem has endeavored to see mirrored in Moab's

---

147. Ibid., 254.

148. Clements does not use the word "forgive" but I take it that this term approximately summarizes what is involved by "to relinquish old grievances and enmities."

149. Clements, *Jeremiah*, 254.

> fate a key to understanding the destructive element in human history. Wrapped in the fabric of the historical process an ineradicable element of tragedy is seen and an awareness that all human pride in achievement can be made futile and devoid of lasting greatness. Great triumphs and understandable pride and self-esteem may lead on to an eventual unexplained and terrifying downfall. Even so, hope of renewal and a new beginning is never wholly lost. (v. 47)[150]

From the quotes I have used to demonstrate Clements's second and third points, it is clear that understanding history is important to Clements. The previous quote emphasizes YHWH's role in the historic order and this one highlights the human element. Both are in keeping with Clements's assertion in *Prophecy and Covenant* that "The prophets were first and foremost interpreters of history." His sense that they interpreted events in order to prevent Israel becoming either arrogant or despairing is also reflected in his understanding of the purpose of Jer 48, except that here the lesson can be learned from Moab's downfall, rather than Israel's.[151]

Clements does not emphasize the hopeful ending to Jer 48 as much as I might have expected given that in his chapter on Jeremiah's prayer in 32:16–25 in *The Prayers of the Bible* he presents Jeremiah as "a prophet of hope in a quite special way."[152] He argues: "Outside of God there is no hope, and in a very real sense all other reasons and bases for hope are secondary to this one fact that God means hope, so that all our possibilities for life and for the future derive from God. Jeremiah's prayer [32:16–25] therefore is a prayer about hope, but it is also a prayer about tragedy, suffering, and despair, since it is in the face of these painful experiences that it reveals the true nature of hope in God."[153]

Jeremiah is not the only prophet to offer hope to a specific nation: Egypt and Assyria are assured future blessing in Isa 19:25; Tyre is promised restoration, even if only to prostitution, in Isa 23:17–18; and Egypt can look forward to a time when it is restored to a kingdom, albeit a lowly one, in Ezek 29:14–15. However, hope for the nations is found much more in Jeremiah than in the other prophets (e.g., 12:14–17) and

---

150. Ibid., 255.
151. Clements, *Prophecy and Covenant*, 26.
152. Clements, *Prayers*, 137.
153. Ibid., 137.

Clements's assertion that Jeremiah "was a prophet of hope in a quite special way" is furthered by the fact that Jeremiah offers so much hope to the nations in his OANs. It is also significant that "outside of God there is no hope" even for the foreign nations and Clements's claim that the true nature of hope is revealed in painful experiences could be extrapolated to apply equally to a nation like Moab as to Judah or Israel.

A further purpose of the OANs is one that has been discussed in the previous chapter; that they acted as a warning to Judah not to rely on her neighbors, "since that potential ally will itself fall."[154] Although Clements does not make this point in his commentary on Jer 48, his remarks about the oracle against Egypt in Jer 46 could be said of Moab: "The significance of Egypt's defeat was that it rendered impossible any hope of Egyptian assistance for Judah against Babylon."[155]

Thus Jones and Clements handle the text in different ways, for Clements addresses the questions asked here in a way that Jones does not. Notwithstanding the absence in Clements's own preface to the commentary of any mention of the community of faith, their separate approaches are no doubt indicative of the different foci and purposes of their commentaries as earlier discussed. For the "scholarly and comprehensive in scope" of *The New Century Bible Commentary* is reflected in Jones' detailed verse by verse notes on the text. In contrast, Clements's discursive style that does not deal with any of the textual ambiguities or anomalies is in accord with *Interpretation*'s focus on "the needs and questions which arise in the use of the Bible as Holy Scripture."[156]

That the nature and purpose of the commentary series is partly responsible for their varying perspectives is furthered by the fact Jones has written non-scholarly commentaries in which he has been more free to ask "the big questions," but mainly because Clements wrote the *New Century Bible Commentary* for Isaiah. Parts of Isaiah's oracle concerning Moab (Isa 15–16) are very similar in content to Jeremiah's oracle concerning Moab, thus we are in the fortunate position of being able to compare Jones and Clements on oracles concerning Moab in commentaries for the same series. Clements's commentary on Isa 15–16 is remarkably similar to Jones' on Jer 48. It is unsurprising that he follows the same structure in that he works through all the points of

---

154. Clements, *Prophecy and Tradition*, 64. See also *Isaiah 1–39*, 131.
155. Clements, *Jeremiah*, 249.
156. Ibid., v.

interest on a verse by verse basis. He also says much more in his Isaiah commentary on issues of authenticity and historical-critical issues and not a great deal on the divine purpose. Nevertheless, even in this commentary series he is more aware than Jones of the tone, particularly that of lament.[157]

It becomes clichéd to advocate using both Jones' and Clements's Jeremiah's commentaries in tandem, but together they provide a wider approach to the text. It is interesting that Jones concentrates on the aspect of divine sovereignty, whilst Clements focuses on the pathos and suffering in the text, for this is the same dichotomy that was observed between Miller and Fretheim. One of the main features of Clements's commentary is that he discusses the purposes of the oracle against Moab and one of its strengths is that he takes the oracle seriously in its own right, as opposed to making general comments that could apply to any of the OANs. According to Clements, Jer 48 intends Israel to feel that she is not suffering alone and expects Israel/the reader (Clements is not clear on the differentiation between the two) to share with Moab in her grief. It also encourages Israel/the reader to realize that God is behind human history as well as to acknowledge both that humans can be a destructive influence in shaping this same history and that pride may end in defeat.

Given the differences in the commentary series for which Jones and Clements write and the emphases of each so far, it is not surprising that Jones has less to say than Clements when it comes to handling Jer 48 as Christian Scripture. Nevertheless, it might be possible to extrapolate from his other works how Jones might address the issue; it this that I shall now investigate.

Scripture for Today

Since Jones' setting for the OANs is a specific Israelite/Jewish festival that has not transferred into the Christian calendar, one might expect that a Christian appropriation of them would be limited to extracting general principles. This is perhaps especially the case given that the main purpose of the OANs according to Jones is quite a generic one, namely (to return to a quote I used earlier), that "the LORD is lord of the nations and not of Israel only, that none ultimately escapes the divine

---

157. For example, Clements, *Isaiah 1-39*, 151–53, 156.

judgment, that those who have gloated over Judah's fall will themselves stumble and fall, that the LORD is not mocked and the whole world is in his hand."[158] How much of this can be applied to a contemporary setting is not a question that Jones answers, but most of the above phrases seem tenets applicable to any time or place. The exception might be that which begins with the only clause that is not written in the simple present tense, but the present perfect—"those who have gloated over Judah's fall," which implies that it belongs to a particular sitation. Jones' (also previously quoted) deduction from 48:10 that history includes God's judgment through tragedy could also potentially be applied today.

We glean more about Jones' handling of Scripture from his less scholarly commentaries. In the preface to his commentary on Isa 56–66 and Joel, he appreciates that the prophets do not speak so directly to us as they did to Israel:

> But they spoke of and witnessed to the God of Jesus Christ, who is the same yesterday, and today, and forever. He, therefore, who has ears to hear will hear. It is the recovery of this robust conviction which, with the help of the right kind of clarifying comment, will lead a modern generation to discern anew the spiritual power of the prophets . . . Prophetic witness, apostolic witness and the witness of the contemporary Church are all indispensable for the apprehension of the *whole* truth of God, and that apprehension is imperilled if any of the three is ignored.[159]

Here, then, we see that Jones is comfortable with Christian interpretations of the prophets, but unfortunately we do not have the "right kind of clarifying comment" to know how he might develop such an interpretation for Jer 48. The same commentary gives us a hint, for though Isa 60:22 is not part of Isaiah's OANs, Jones' remark sheds light on his understanding of the response that God desires of the nations; "The nations of the world are to recognize humbly the special place of Zion to reflect the light of God, and to seek that light in the new Israel, the Church of Christ."[160]

Similarly, although Zech 6:8 is not directly relevant to the OAN genre, Jones' exposition is relevant: "This is an affirmation of faith that the power of YHWH is active and present in the very centre of

158. Jones, *Jeremiah*, 486.
159. Jones, *Isaiah 56–66*, 10.
160. Ibid., 72.

the world-power in the north. In the very origin of world disturbance and destruction is the controlling power of the whole earth. There is nothing to unlearn here, once the strange biblical imagery is decoded. According to Christian faith the spirit of God will, if he chooses, rest in the midst of the Kremlin and the Pentagon, for he is the Lord of the whole earth."[161]

This does not mean that Jones sees the Christian faith as universalistic and, as previously discussed, Jones attempts to hold election in tension with God's universal purposes. In the same way, he resists the pressure to deny that Christianity is "*the* religion" or to view election (first Israel's, and then the Church's) as "offensive." Instead, he declares that the fundamental doctrines of Christian faith "cannot be abandoned except the Christian faith is changed into something different from itself." He continues, that "the Christian Church is the bearer of his truth to all men. Paradoxically the concept of election is the clue to the way in which the Christian faith is genuinely the universal religion and the one sure ground of the unity of mankind."[162] In fact, he develops his reasoning, so that later in the same book he argues that:

> The unity of mankind is dependent upon its proper obedience to God, and its recognition of God's universal sovereignty. The New Testament deepens this apprehension, showing that it is in the love of God that men find it possible to love one another beyond the limits of natural love and hate . . . Here, in the love of God, is the ultimate secret of harmony and peace. It rests on the primary prophetic intuition that, without a common allegiance to One who can demand universal obedience, men consult their own sectional interests and fall apart. "When God is left out, all things naturally fall into chaos, since it is He alone who holds them together."[163]

One can therefore argue from the above quotation that if the OANs demonstrate YHWH's universal sovereignty, then Jones may see them as providing a means to attaining one of the first steps to unity.

Like Jones, Clements considers that the theological aspect of the OT is indispensable for Christians: "Since the majority of those who read the Old Testament do so because of its religious interest and concern, it

---

161. Jones, *Haggai*, 89.
162. Jones, *Instrument*, 15–16.
163. Ibid., 41. Jones does not specify whom he is quoting here.

is natural that the questions relating to its theological meaning should have a particular priority."[164] These questions are, as we have seen, at the forefront of his commentary on Jer 48 and his evaluation of the world-changing events that overtake Moab (and Judah) in Jer 48 clearly has contemporary relevance. "The reaction to these changes displayed in this prophecy embraces the fundamental search for meaning in history and for the justification of the ways of God towards humankind that we sense still remain with us in the present. It is one thing to recognize and grasp the nature of what has happened in such major world events, but it requires a much deeper level of understanding to reflect upon their meaning."[165] Clements does not specify what sort of reflection is appropriate and it might be that the reflection is sufficient in itself.

Other general comments in Clements's commentary that I have cited above are relevant to current societies, for instance that historical and political change are part of God's creating and recreating, or that God's and humans' actions combine to shape history, or that triumph may lead to downfall, but that hope is never completely lost.[166] In fact, although in a slightly different context, when exegeting the prayer of Jeremiah in 32:16–25, Clements concludes that "It is only when the depths of human misery and disaster are uncovered that the reality of God and the hope that God brings are shown to be the ground that lies beneath them." The ultimate example of this is to be found in the cross, the "symbol of hope for all Christians."[167] It is also reassuring, even if it is not admirable, for people in distress to know that they are not the only ones who suffer and to take comfort from that.

Another pertinent reflection that can be applied to Jer 48 is found in a statement he makes in *Old Testament Theology* about the OT:

> It has, in fact, become a bridge between the past and the present. In it men have expected to find something more than a history, valuable as this in itself is, and to see lasting and unique expressions of truth. Such a truth has not simply been about the past, or about the conditions and achievements of human existence in the past. Rather, such truth has been about man himself, and his eternal and inescapable confrontation with God. Its very hu-

164. Clements, *Century*, 149.
165. Clements, *Jeremiah*, 253–54.
166. Ibid., 254–55.
167. Clements, *Prayers*, 145.

manity has mirrored more than human values, and affirmed a belief that wherever he goes man is faced with decisions about himself and his world which lead him to recognize the presence of the Spirit of God.[168]

Perhaps Clements's most significant contributions to viewing the oracle against Moab as Scripture are found in his commentary on Ezekiel's OANs and relate to the question of sovereignty: "What appear on the surface, therefore, to be remote and difficult prophecies, with little relevance for us, nonetheless point to an important spiritual truth: God is not the God of one nation only. Consequently, when we look to see the divine hand shaping human affairs, we must not interpret this in any self-centred or narrowly blinkered fashion. God is the God of all nations and peoples."[169] Clements exhorts his readers that, given this premise, the appropriate response is to look beyond nationalism to "establish justice in international affairs."[170] He also warns in his commentary on Ezekiel's prophecy concerning Moab that, "Against such a background we should remember the story of Ruth."[171]

What is clear is that both Jones and Clements are at ease in moving from the OT to the NT as well as from the world of the OT to their own world. This is less clear in Jones' commentary on Jeremiah, but more than evident in his other commentaries. Most of the homiletic comments I have made based on the works of both commentators tend to be quite generalized and could have been made from many passages in the OT (and, indeed, have been in the cases where I have extrapolated). Some, such as the recognition of YHWH's universal sovereignty, are more specific to the OANs, or at least to texts in which the foreign nations feature prominently, but not to Jer 48 in particular.

That a foreign nation is threatened with destruction as well as promised hope of a restoration is not unique to Jer 48, but such texts are not common. However, this predicament is a frequent one for Israel, so, in many ways, contemporary applications of it are not new. What is unusual is that these applications (such as hope stemming from despair) can arguably be made concerning people who are not currently incorporated into the people of God. God's involvement in a nation's

---

168. Clements, *OT Theology*, 200.
169. Clements, *Ezekiel*, 115.
170. Ibid.
171. Ibid., 119.

history is not dependent on the status of its relationship to him. At the same time, YHWH obviously has enough of a relationship with Moab that he mourns over her downfall. Therefore, it is a little disappointing that neither commentator suggests a possible theological significance for YHWH's tears over Moab.

Conclusions and Reflections

Having assessed these two scholars, I am once more surprised that given the similarities between them, they, like their U.S. counterparts, have produced two such different commentaries. Part of this is due to the different purposes between the commentary series; Jones' is primarily intended to be scholarly, whereas the main purpose of Clements's is to be "faithful to the text and useful to the church."[172] Nevertheless, despite their stated hermeneutical stances, in Jones' commentary on Jer 48, there is little explanation of what its "inner meaning may have been"[173] and in Clements's commentary there is not much evidence of the redaction-critical approach that he considers characterizes his work, in terms of "a study of the form and arrangement of the whole book, comprising primary and secondary material, and also a careful appraisal of the structure of the larger units of which the books are composed."[174] That this is entirely due to the constraints of the style of commentary series is doubtful and may point to a tendency to veer in the direction of either a historical-critical approach, or an expository one. The strengths and weaknesses of their commentaries lie, respectively, in the direction they do and do not take.

Despite the style of Jones' commentary, neither he nor Clements treat the text in isolation from their own faith (as can be seen in the way that Jones engages with the text in other commentaries). Not only do they approach the text from a position of faith, but they approach it from a specifically Christian faith, in that they look at it not simply in the context of the rest of the OT, but through the lens of the NT and the cross (as do the U.S. scholars). In this the outcomes of their works cohere with their hermeneutic intentions.

---

172. Clements, *Jeremiah*, v.
173. Jones, *Isaiah 56–66*, 9; see also p. 10.
174. Clements, *Prophecy and Tradition*, 6.

In looking at the UK scholars in conjunction with the U.S. ones, it is interesting that all interpreters appear to stress either the aspect of YHWH's universal sovereignty, or the element of lament in this chapter (this is less the case with Brueggemann): Fretheim and Clements emphasize lament whilst Miller and Jones (who are both less concerned with the tone in general) focus on sovereignty. However, since the two facets of the text are by no means mutually exclusive, it is somewhat surprising that the commentators are predisposed to one or the other. It perhaps reflects the unexpressed presuppositions of the commentators who might not imagine a Divine Sovereign (who is closely linked with the idea of holy war) who cries, or envisage a weeping God as the King of all creation. That this is not pure conjecture on my part might be found in the fact that I have not discovered the two characteristics of YHWH discussed in tandem by any of the commentators. In fact, not all the scholars (in this case both Jones and Clements) even comment on the fact that YHWH is the subject of the mourning over Moab in Jer 48.

Not only are the two UK scholars different from each other in their remarks, but in some aspects each is distinct from the three U.S. scholars as well. For instance, Jones alone holds to the feast of Tabernacles as the context, whilst Clements is the only interpreter to emphasize the variety of tones within the oracle and to suggest that the historical aspect is downplayed in order that these tones might be further accentuated.

I noticed no significant difference between the U.S. and the UK scholars, though the UK ones (or perhaps just Clements, since Jones did not publish a great deal) seemed less inclined to repeat material from their other works and to find in the texts confirmation of their already-held views. Almost ironically, the concept of cult and the idea of tradition, particularly prophetic tradition, underlie much of Clements's work and yet he rejects the cult as being the context for the OANs.[175] Wisdom is another topic in which Clements is interested, yet he does not attempt to apply to the OANs lessons he finds in the wisdom literature. A third area in which Clements is sometimes engaged is that of historical reconstruction, yet, again, he refrains from attempting to provide a historical reconstruction of the OANs. This is no doubt due,

---

175. In *Prophecy and Tradition* (p. 87) Clements confesses that his earlier book, *Prophecy and Covenant* "did not allow sufficiently for the diversity of the various cultic and covenantal traditions in ancient Israel."

in part at least, to his awareness that such endeavors can become too consuming, to the cost of other elements.

Although both UK commentators perhaps highlight one aspect of the text at the expense of another, I do not consider either commentator to overstate his arguments. Jones, in particular, is tentative about his own conclusions and does not promote them as much as he might. Rather, he presents his thoughts with an openness that his reader might not accept them. I may not be convinced by Jones' hypothesis, but in my view, neither he, nor Clements, makes any unjustifiable hermeneutical moves in his commentary.

Clements asks many pertinent questions, but does not answer most of them. Although he acknowledges at the outset that he cannot answer them all, it is unfortunate that he does not attempt to address more, such as the morality of God. He also concentrates on the divine purpose of the oracle, whereas I think a little more emphasis on divine involvement might be helpful. However, he covers quite a range of subjects given that his entire commentary on Jer 48 spans less than three pages.

Both Jones and Clements view the OANs as intended primarily for the Jews and this may reflect the fact that the principle of election is important to them both. Nevertheless, Jones also considers that the nations are offered ultimate salvation and incorporation into the people of God, but he is not too clear on how he holds together the notions of election and particularity. It is therefore disappointing that in his commentary on Jeremiah's OANs he does not elucidate his position, for this seems an appropriate place to do so. In addition, in my opinion, like their U.S. colleagues, neither commentator draws out the distinction between Judah and the nations as clearly as he might have done. Nevertheless, once again, they each provide a unique slant on the text and together provide further possibilities for understanding Jeremiah's oracle concerning Moab.

At this point I begin my own reading of the text, starting with Jer 48:10. Although it probably is a later addition to the text, I commence with this verse because it stands apart from the rest of the chapter. Since it is probably a commentary on the text it also introduces the rest of the chapter.

6

The Curious Curse in Jeremiah 48:10

ארור עשׂה מלאכת יהוה רמיה וארור מנע חרבו מדם

Cursed (is) the one doing (the) work of YHWH (in) slackness and cursed (is) the one holding back his sword from blood.

Introduction

VERSE 10 IS AN ANOMALY IN ITS IMMEDIATE CONTEXT FOR SEVERAL reasons. First, it introduces an abrupt change in tone, in that the harshness of the curse comes after a call for others to help Moab, which in turn follows a general survey of the extent of Moab's destruction. Secondly, verse 10 references a new, unnamed party. Thirdly, it appears that it might be a prose sentence in the midst of poetry. It is also to be noted that YHWH is mentioned in the third person in verse 10, whereas the chapter begins with כה־אמר יהוה and up until this point, YHWH appears to be the speaker.

Since the verse seems so awkward in its context, one naturally wonders if it is, as most see it, a later addition to the text.[1] If this is the case, then it would partly explain the change in tone. As well, the identity of the potentially cursed sword bearer in verse 10 may depend on whether the verse is part of the original text. In a sixth century context, one of the main contenders might be Babylon, but if the verse was inserted at a later time when Babylon herself had fallen, then some other wielder of the sword is presumably intended. It should be noted at the outset that there is no consensus on the question of dating and Duhm is a

---

1. Carroll, *Jeremiah*, 783; Duhm, *Jeremia*, 347; Fretheim, *Jeremiah*, 597; Holladay, *Jeremiah, vol. 2*, 342; Lundbom, *Jeremiah 37–52*, 262; McKane, *Jeremiah, vol. 1*, 1170; Rudolph, *Jeremiah*, 279; Smothers in Keown, et al., *Jeremiah 26–52*, 309; Thompson, *Jeremiah*, 704; Volz, *Der Prophet Jeremia*, 405; Weiser, *Der Prophet Jeremia*, 405.

rare exception when he attempts it (and suggests the time of Alexander Jannaeus).[2]

This chapter seeks to find a possible explanation for the seemingly strange placement of verse 10 and also to propose how it might function in the wider context of Jer 48. In order to do so, I will investigate various aspects of the verse in order to build up a picture. First, I will analyze textual and literary aspects (textual variants, poetry versus prose, tone, the identity of YHWH's worker/sword wielder, and whether the verse is a gloss). Secondly, I will consider pertinent intertextual resonances (Ps 149:6b–9; Jer 25:13; Judg 3) that may contribute to the understanding of the verse. Finally, I will evaluate how Jer 48:10 might be appropriated as Christian Scripture.

Textual and Literary Analysis

Textual Variants

The only textual variant in Jer 48:10 is that the equivalent of וארור (the second curse) is missing from LXX (31:10). However, this variant may impact on whether the verse is seen as poetry or prose, for the repetition of ארור in MT creates symmetry between the openings of the two halves of the verse. If it is poetry, then it would reinforce the argument for seeing the two halves of the verse as equivalent, that is if the one עשה מלאכת יהוה רמיה is the same as the one מנע חרבו מדם, and the work of the Lord is equated with brandishing the sword.[3]

Poetry or Prose

Many Bible translations and commentators deem Jer 48:10 to be prose rather than poetry, although some, such as Brueggemann and Holladay are tentative in their stance.[4] Even Rudolph's assertion that it "is hardly

2. Duhm, *Jeremia*, 347.

3. Both מלאכת and רמיה are unusual words to use in this context. מלאכה normally refers to creational/building work and often used in the context of what should not be done on the Sabbath. It is not common in the prophets and occurs five times in Jeremiah. Interestingly, one is in 18:3—the "work" that the potter is making on the wheel—and the other is in 50:25 in relation to YHWH bringing out his weapons. רמיה normally is translated "deceitfully."

4. Allen, *Jeremiah*, 480; Bright, *Jeremiah*, 314, 320; Brueggemann, *Jeremiah*, 444;

to be read metrically"[5] does not make it clear whether the verse is to be read as non-metrical poetry or prose. Surprisingly, it seems that these commentators do not tend to *argue* for the prosaic nature of the verse, but instead simply *state* their conclusion.

The prosaic nature of 48:10 is not self-evident, however, and although most modern English versions format the text as prose, NASB, NEB, NIV, and REB lay it out as poetry. Lundbom, Jones, Feinberg, Clements, and McKane are among exegetes who consider that it could be poetry.[6] Clements and Jones are a little ambiguous when they do not count it as, respectively, a "prose insertion"[7] or "prose addition."[8] For there are two issues at stake in these phrases: prose versus poetry; and addition/insertion versus original material. Nevertheless, it would seem that they do deem the verse to be poetry, particularly Jones, who describes it as having a "distinct, but nicely balanced form."[9] It is Lundbom, however, who gives the most comprehensive (and persuasive) argument for it being poetry. For, he argues, "If it were prose, one would expect one or more of the common prose particles in a reading such as ʾārûr hāʿōśeh ʾet-mĕleʾket yhwh (bi)rmiyyâ, wĕ ʾārûr hammōnēaʿ ʾet-ḥarbô middām."[10]

At the same time, not only is LXX, with its omission of וארור, less poetic than MT, but Targum Jonathan is too. For whilst the accusative marker is not applicable in Aramaic, some of the prose particles that Lundbom notes are absent from MT, such as the definite article and ב, are present in the Targum:

ליט דיעביד עלה עבידא מן־קדם יוי בנכל בנכלא
וליט דימנע חרביה מקטול

> Cursed be he who makes the deed *done from before* the Lord into deceit, and cursed be he who withholds his sword from *slaughter*.[11]

Fretheim, *Jeremiah*, 597; Holladay, *Jeremiah*, vol. 2, 342, 347; Rudolph, *Jeremiah*, 274; Smothers in Keown et al., *Jeremiah 26–52*, 304, 308.

5. Rudolph, *Jeremiah*, 279 [my translation].

6. Clements, *Jeremiah*, 252; Feinberg, *Jeremiah*, 301; Jones, *Jeremiah*, 501; Lundbom, *Jeremiah 37–52*, 257; McKane, *Jeremiah*, vol. 1, 1155, 1170.

7. Clements, *Jeremiah*, 252.

8. Jones, *Jeremiah*, 501.

9. Ibid.

10. Lundbom, *Jeremiah 37–52*, 257.

11. Hayward, *Targum of Jeremiah*, 172.

That the verse seems to be rendered as prose in LXX and Targum may be an indicator that Jer 48:10 in MT is also to be conceived as prose.

Furthermore, whilst there is some balancing in the structure of MT's text in that ארור opens both halves, and the two participles in the first and second "cola" are potentially parallels of one another, the symmetry is not complete.[12] For רמיה acts adverbially ("slackly") and so is not balanced by מדם "from blood."[13] Moreover, as Kugel points out, "parallelistic lines" are not necessarily an indication of poetry and neither is regularity of writing.[14] As well, the meter is not regular throughout, though McKane does not consider it to be non-metrical enough to "stand out like a sore thumb."[15]

It is probably these mixed signals that lead Carroll to describe it as "a prose commentary (with poetic traces?)," and Thompson as "almost poetic."[16] In fact, Thompson conjectures that it may originally have been poetic.[17] Nevertheless, despite the difficulties in classifying Hebrew as poetry or prose, it seems that, overall, verse 10 cannot be strictly categorized as poetry.[18] Therefore, I would agree that it is "almost poetic" prose, but prose nevertheless.

Interestingly, it seems that there is a general consensus among commentators, even those who accept Jer 48:10 as prose, that the two halves of Jer 48:10 speak of the same thing.[19] That is, either explicitly or implicitly, they equate the wielding of the sword with the LORD's work,

---

12. Holladay (*Jeremiah*, vol. 2, 342) deems that the second ארור is "likely to be a clarifying expansion."

13. I am grateful to Stuart Weeks for pointing out that רמיה is not otherwise used adverbially and that the lack of preposition in the phrase could lead to an alternative translation something along the lines of "Cursed be the one making the work of YHWH slackness." However, the sense is still strained (how does one make YHWH's work slackness/deceit, particularly in the context of wielding swords?), but more pertinently, the slight adjustment in translation does not make a significant difference to the points made here. Therefore, I have retained the usual translation.

14. Kugel, *Idea*, 3, 70.

15. McKane, *Jeremiah*, vol. 1, 1170.

16. Carroll, *Jeremiah*, 782; Thompson, *Jeremiah*, 704.

17. Thompson, *Jeremiah*, 700.

18. See Kugel, *Idea*, especially chapter 2 (pp. 59–95) for a full treatment of this, including the acknowledgement that the terms "poetry," "prose," and "parallelism" are terms unknown to the Bible (p. 69).

19. E.g., Rudolph, Brueggemann, Fretheim, and Smothers.

and think it is one person who performs both duties.[20] Since there is no dispute over this matter and both halves of the verse make sense when so understood, this is the interpretation accepted here.

There is also agreement among most commentators, even among those who consider that the verse might be poetry, that the verse "intrude[s] upon the continuity of the text."[21] How much the verse "intrudes" in terms of tone is now the focus of our investigation.

Tone

McKane is an exegete who is not persuaded that verse 10 is prose, yet considers it a misfit. He explains why scholars take this view: "The verse has been viewed with suspicion and it has been thought to co-exist uneasily with the general sentiments of the chapter (Giesebrecht, Duhm, Cornhill, Volz, Rudolph, Weiser, Bright, Nicholson). Attention is directed to the hotness of the thirst for revenge which is expressed (Giesebrecht, Cornhill, Volz) and also to the circumstances that v. 10 is a *non sequitur* in relation to what precedes."[22] Since he is not convinced that verse 10 is prose (his normal deciding factor in determining a verse as secondary material in Jer 48),[23] McKane concludes that, "The main case against v. 10 would seem to me to be that it is a *non sequitur* after vv. 8ff (Duhm) and is poorly connected with what follows. Its isolation may be an indication that it is a gloss, but the discreteness of chapter 48 makes this difficult to judge."[24]

Not all commentators agree with McKane's assessment of the verse, however, for as Kidner claims, 10b "chimes in with the note of un-

---

20. Brueggemann, *Jeremiah*, 445; Calvin, *Jeremiah*, 15; Carroll, *Jeremiah*, 780, 782; Feinberg, *Jeremiah*, 302; Freedman, *Jeremiah*, 304; Fretheim, *Jeremiah*, 599; Jones, *Jeremiah*, 501, 502; Kidner, *Message*, 142–43; Lundbom, *Jeremiah 37–52*, 262–63; McKane, *Jeremiah, vol. 1*, 1165; Miller, "Jeremiah," 891; Rudolph, *Jeremiah*, 279; Smothers in Keown et al., *Jeremiah 26–52*, 314; Stulman, *Jeremiah*, 362; Thompson, *Jeremiah*, 704; Weiser, *Der Prophet Jeremia*, 405–6; Holladay, Clements and McKeating do not discuss the relationship between the sword and the LORD's work.

21. Holladay, *Jeremiah, vol. 2*, 346; see also McKane, *Jeremiah, vol. 1*, 1165; McKeating, *Jeremiah*, 204; Lundbom, *Jeremiah 37–52*, 257; Rudolph, *Jeremiah*, 279; Smothers in Keown et al., *Jeremiah 26–52*, 314; Stulman, *Jeremiah*, 362; Weiser, *Der Prophet Jeremia*, 405–6.

22. McKane, *Jeremiah, vol. 1*, 1165; see also Lundbom, *Jeremiah 37–52*, 257.

23. McKane, *Jeremiah, vol. 1*, 1170.

24. Ibid., 1170–71.

sparing judgment which coexists in the chapter with the note of grief."[25] This position coheres with Fretheim's overall view of the chapter as "a kind of rhetorical collage" of destruction and grief,[26] though Fretheim himself deems verse 10 to be a gloss. However, the fact remains that while observations may be made that lessen the incongruity of the verse, it contrasts more starkly with its surrounding verses than does any other in the chapter. Moreover, whilst there are other examples of harsh words (for example, the command in 48:26 to make Moab drunk so that he will splash in his vomit), none other goes as far as cursing the one who might hold back on such commands.

At this point, it is time to look at the identity of the swordsman of verse 10, for this may cast light on the purpose of the verse.

Identity of the Sword Wielder

Although the addressees in the previous verse are also unnamed, it seems clear that they are not the same as the cursed in verse 10. For those in verse 9 are called to give wings (or perhaps salt)[27] to Moab so that she might flee, while the one in 48:10 is cursed if he (the participles take the masculine singular form) holds back his sword, from shedding presumably Moabite blood. As well, the imperative in verse 9 is in the plural (תנו) whereas the curses in verse 10 are in the singular (ארור עשׂה . . . וארור מנע). There are three main proposals for the identity of the sword wielder of 48:10: Babylon; another enemy, such as an Arab tribe; or Judah.

If the verse is not a later addition, then the context would be that of the rest of the chapter (as it might be even if the verse is a scribal gloss). Babylon was the empire of the time, which was conquering smaller nations, and passages such as Jer 25 indicate that Babylon was the tool used by YHWH to subdue Moab and others. Therefore, if verse 10 is original material then it is likely that Moab's enemy in verse 10 would be Babylon. In fact, Calvin and Fretheim seem to be in no doubt that Babylon is meant here.[28]

---

25. Kidner, *Message*, 143; see also Brueggemann, *Jeremiah*, 444; Clements, *Jeremiah*, 253; Jones, *Jeremiah*, 501; Volz, *Der Prophet Jeremia*, 405.

26. Fretheim, *Jeremiah*, 597.

27. See chapter 2 for a discussion of the translation of Jer 48:9.

28. Calvin, *Jeremiah*, 14; Fretheim, *Jeremiah*, 599; see also Rudolph, *Jeremiah*, 278; Lundbom, *Jeremiah 37–52*, 263.

On the other hand, as Jones notes, "There is no independent evidence of a conquest of Moab at this time," and "the absence of any reference to a foe from the north makes it precarious to assume that this is the Babylonians."[29] Furthermore, as Duhm, Rudolph, and McKane recognize, Babylon would not have needed the spur of a curse in order to wield the sword against Moab.[30]

Jones and Carroll suggest that the enemy could have been Arab tribes, though they also think it possible that the oracle did not have a particular people in its purview.[31] Others propose that the author had in mind a Judean conflict with Moab, though when this might have occurred is open to question. Rudolph speaks vaguely of "later hatred against Moab,"[32] but more specific suggestions include: Josiah's campaigns (Carroll thinks this is unlikely);[33] when Moab joined the marauders against Judah in 2 Kgs 24:2;[34] or even "when Moab was actually being attacked by Nebuchadnezzar, being a projection of Judah's own hostility at having suffered at the hands of the same devastator herself."[35]

Carroll, with Lundbom, concludes that the verse has been glossed with holy war motifs,[36] though, Smothers disagrees, explaining his reasoning thus: "If this verse was inserted by a glossator to incite Judean vengeance against the Moabites, as suggested by Carroll (783), it is out of keeping with the rest of the oracles concerning the nations in Jeremiah, except for the Babylonian oracles, which evidence remarkably little hatred for the nations."[37] However, if the verse is a later gloss, then one might expect it to be "out of keeping with the rest."

It seems to me that Duhm, Rudolph, and McKane are correct that the exhortation in 48:10 is unnecessary if the Babylonians are the target audience. Though not incontrovertible, when this observation is put

---

29. Jones, *Jeremiah*, 500.
30. Duhm, *Jeremia*, 347; McKane, *Jeremiah*, vol. 1, 1165; Rudolph, *Jeremiah*, 279.
31. Jones, *Jeremiah*, 500; Carroll, *Jeremiah*, 786; see also Bright, *Jeremiah*, 322; Brueggemann, *Jeremiah*, 445; Thompson, *Jeremiah*, 704.
32. Rudolph, *Jeremiah*, 279 [my translation].
33. Carroll, *Jeremiah*, 782.
34. Lundbom, *Jeremiah 37–52*, 263.
35. Ibid.
36. Carroll, *Jeremiah*, 782.
37. Smothers in Keown et al., *Jeremiah 26–52*, 314.

together with the lack of historical evidence for a Babylonian invasion, I am led to suspect that the Babylonians are not the focus of verse 10. In fact, one could argue that no serious enemy needs a prompting to withhold the sword, far less a threat to do so; it is perhaps more conceivable that such an injunction is issued to an audience that is not much more powerful than Moab. Judah would fit this profile. However, since the identity of the people largely seems to rest on whether the verse is a gloss, it is worth investigating this possibility next.

Gloss

As we have seen, it is mainly the harsh tone of verse 10 that persuades some commentators that the verse is not original to Jeremiah, but is an editorial comment.[38] Yet those, like Jones and Kidner who deem that verse 10 is congruous in its context, do not judge it a gloss, or, like Clements, are not sure of its status.[39] In other words, whether verse 10 is considered a gloss is largely dependent on how well the text is seen to fit into the surrounding context.

Such a move is not unwarranted, for incongruity is one clue to a text's insertion. The problem comes when there is disagreement over what is incongruous. For instance, as well as the disparity in opinion regarding tone, the switch in focus from those who are to help Moab to those who are to destroy her does not necessarily mean that verse 10 is out of keeping with the preceding ones. For Jer 48 characteristically swaps and changes between those it addresses or references. That is, as shown in detail below, it moves between addressing a general audience, Moab, Moab's allies, Moab's enemies, and her neighbors as well as switching between second and third person references to Moab. On a number of occasions the speech is in the first person.

   v. 1 third person reference to Moab
   v. 2 second person address to Moab
   vv. 3–5 third person reference to Moab
   vv. 6–7 second person address to Moab
   v. 8 third person reference to Moab
   v. 9 second person command to Moab's allies

---

38. Carroll, *Jeremiah*, 783; Fretheim, *Jeremiah*, 597; McKane, *Jeremiah, vol. 1*, 1170; Smothers in Keown et al., *Jeremiah 26–52*, 309; Thompson, *Jeremiah*, 704.

39. Clements, *Jeremiah*, 253; Jones, *Jeremiah*, 501; Kidner, *Message*, 143.

> v. 10 third person address to Moab's enemies
> vv. 11–13 third person reference to Moab
>> v. 12 YHWH speaks in the first person
> v. 14 second person address to Moab
> vv. 15–16 third person reference to Moab
> v. 17 second person command to Moab's neighbors
> vv. 18–19 second person address to Moab
> v. 20 begins in the third person but is also a second person address to Moab
> vv. 21–25 third person reference to Moab
> v. 26 second person command to Moab's enemies
> vv. 27–28 second person address to Moab
> vv. 29–38 a first person speech
>> vv. 29–31 third person reference to Moab
>> v. 32 second person address to Moab
>> vv. 33–38 third person reference to Moab
> v. 39 third person reference to Moab
> v. 40 third person reference to Moab's destroyer
> vv. 41–42 third person reference to Moab
> v. 43 second person address to Moab
> v. 44–45 third person reference to Moab (first person speech in v. 44)
> v. 46 second person address to Moab
> v. 47 first person speech that refers to Moab in third person

Therefore, it is pertinent to ask if there are other indications in the text that point to its being a gloss. For instance, if the verse is prose, as it seems to be, then it is more likely that Jer 48:10 is a gloss, particularly since the surrounding verses are poetry. The vocabulary and language might also signify whether the verse is part of the original.

However, in the same way that it is not clear-cut whether the verse is poetry or prose, the language indicates both continuity and discontinuity. On the one hand, as Holladay notes, the mention of YHWH in the third person in 48:10 comes out of context.[40] On the other hand, as Miller points out, there is "imagery of the bloody sword" in verses 2 and 10 and "the destruction of Moab as 'the work of the Lord' (v. 10), [is] a theme that echoes throughout the rest of the chapter."[41] Taking a wider view, the sword is a motif running through Jeremiah's OANs, and Fretheim and McKane both draw attention to the personification

---

40. Holladay, *Jeremiah, vol. 2*, 347.
41. Miller, "Jeremiah," 891.

of the sword in 46:10 and 47:6–7.[42] In fact, the sword terminology runs through the book of Jeremiah as a whole. Indeed, it is noticeable how much more frequently חרב is employed in Jeremiah (and Ezekiel) than in other OT books.[43] At the same time, חרב is a common word throughout the whole of the OT, and its use in 48:10 does not necessarily indicate that the verse belongs to the chapter.

As well, the Qal passive participle of ארר, ארור "cursed," is employed six times in Jeremiah (11:3; 17:5; 20:14, 15; and twice in 48:10);[44] only Deuteronomy contains more such occurrences.[45] Yet, once again, ארר is a normal Hebrew word and consequently cannot be classed as Jeremianic language.[46]

Although there are indicators pointing in both directions, it seems to me that the factors that point to the verse being a gloss (that is, that it is probably prose and the reference to YHWH in the third person) seem stronger than those that indicate it is part of the original material (use of common words and motifs, even if they are more common in Jeremiah). Therefore, I would cautiously conclude with Duhm, Rudolph, and others, that verse 10 may be a gloss.[47] However, it does not follow that it therefore should be deleted as some have suggested,[48] for, as McKane reminds us, "There is no text-critical evidence to support its deletion."[49] Instead of deleting the verse, then, I would propose that one tries to understand it.

42. Fretheim, *Jeremiah*, 598; McKane, *Jeremiah, vol. 1*, 1165.

43. Seventy times in Jer, ninety-one times in Ezek, cf. twenty-four times in 1 Sam, twenty-three times in Judg, twenty-two times in Isa, nineteen times in Josh, eighteen in Pss; fifteen in 2 Sam; and around ten times in each of 1 Kgs (eleven times), 2 Kgs (eight times), 1 Chr (nine times), and 2 Chr (twelve times).

44. None of these instances is generally thought to be a later addition.

45. Genesis also contains six occurrences of ארור.

46. Interestingly, cursing and Moab are twinned elsewhere in the OT. For Moab attempts (via Balaam) to curse (קבב, ארר) Israel in what could be termed as the first OAN in the canon (Num 22:6, 11, 12, 17; 23:7, 8, 11, 13, 27; 24:10). As far as I can tell, Moab is the only nation to curse Israel; Shimei curses (קלל) David (2 Sam 16:7, 10, 11, 12, 13; 19:21; 1 Kgs 2:8), but he is an Israelite (of the house of Saul) and although David as king represents Israel, it is David in particular whom Shimei curses.

47. Duhm, *Jeremia*, 347; Holladay, *Jeremiah, vol. 2*, 347; Lundbom, *Jeremiah 37–52*, 262; Rudolph, *Jeremiah*, 274, 279.

48. Holladay, *Jeremiah, vol. 2*, 347; Rudolph, *Jeremiah*, 274; Volz, *Der Prophet Jeremia*, 405–6.

49. McKane, *Jeremiah, vol. 2*, 1166.

As a gloss, the verse is removed from the Babylonian context and thus ties in with my previous conclusion that Judah may have been the intended recipient of the curse in 48:10. Holladay asserts that it is not possible to determine a setting for glosses like verse 10,[50] but although there may be no way to definitively determine its setting, I would suggest that a canonical reading may provide one possible way of accounting for this verse. That is, there are intertextual resonances between Jer 48:10 and other parts of the OT that give 48:10 a plausible context and a reason for its writing.

Intertextual Resonances

Psalm 149:6b–9

Perhaps the most striking intertextual resonance is that with Ps 149:6b–9.[51] For Jer 48:10 with its curse against those who withhold their swords from Moab resounds with echoes of Ps 149:6b–7, which envisages godly ones

וחרב פיפיות בידם	and two-edged swords in their hands,
לעשות נקמה בגוים	to execute vengeance on the nations
תוכחת בל־אמים	and punishment on the peoples (NRSV).

Like Jer 48:10, the sword wielded against a foreign nation is portrayed as a positive thing in Ps 149:6b–7. Might it have been that a scribe, writing out the oracle concerning Moab in Jer 48, perhaps writing at a time when Moab was relatively prosperous, realized that the prophecy had not been fulfilled and, recalling Ps 149, called on his[52] godly countrymen to help fulfill it?[53]

---

50. Holladay, *Jeremiah*, vol. 2, 354; see also Clements, *Jeremiah*, 253; McKane, *Jeremiah*, vol. 1, 1165–6, 1170.

51. I am grateful to Walter Moberly for pointing out this Psalm and its resonances to me.

52. I use the masculine personal pronoun simply because the scribe was more likely to have been male.

53. I am grateful to Jeremy Corley for suggesting I compare Jer 48:10 with Ps 137:7–9. Here Edom is razed and the one who dashes Babylon's little ones against the rock are blessed. It is also interesting that Jer 50:15 (the oracle against Babylon) "fulfils" the desire in Ps 137:8 for Babylon to be recompensed according to her deeds. The link

Such a scenario is strengthened by the intertextual echoes that then bounce back from Ps 149 to Jer 48. For Ps 149:9 reads, לעשות בהם משפט כתוב "to execute on them the judgment decreed" (NRSV). Such a reference to the משפט כתוב may have reminded the scribe of the OANs, which are written judgments, but specifically, of Jer 48:21 and 48:47, which refer to the disaster falling upon Moab as her משפט "judgment." In fact verse 47 ends with עד־הנה משפט מואב "Thus far (the) judgment upon Moab."

In order to test out the plausibility of this conjecture, it is pertinent to examine several aspects: the usage of the psalms in Jeremiah; how Ps 149 has been interpreted, particularly whether the commentators refer to Jer 48, and what they understand to be משפט כתוב; and the usages of משפט "judgment" in the OT.

Jeremiah and the Psalms

Holladay points out in his article on Jeremiah and the Psalms that, "Parallels between passages in Jeremiah and the Psalms have long been noted" and that, "Borrowing did take place in both directions." He continues:

> There are a large number of passages in Jeremiah that are dependent on prior expressions in the Psalms. The crucial element in my argument is the contention that in almost every case the expression in the psalms [sic] is simple and open to general use, while in Jeremiah's employment of the expression in question there appear to be marks of some distinctive, personal adaptation, whether it be greater specificity, or irony, or deformation, or some other variation. I suggest sixteen psalms whose parallels in Jeremiah offer marks of his distinctive usage; they are Pss 1; 2; 6; 7; 9–10; 22; 35; 38; 64; 78; 79; 83; 84; 122; and 139.[54]

Ps 149 is not among those Holladay cites, perhaps because he is only concerned with what he considers to be authentic material in Jeremiah. Nevertheless, despite the fact that 48:10 may well have been inserted at a later date by a non Jeremianic author, if the author has appropriated the psalm then he has done so in the same vogue (including that of psalms'

---

between Ps 137:8 and Jer 50:15 strengthens the possibility that the OANs have some relationship to the Psalms, an idea that might fruitfully benefit from further research.

54. Holladay, "Indications," 245, 246, 248 (long quote on p. 248).

usage in chapters 46–51). For not only has he used it with "greater specificity" than was originally intended, but the psalm has also been "deformed" in that it has been employed as a curse (as well the sword in Jer 48 is not two-edged—a matter that will be addressed below). At any rate, there is a precedent in Jeremiah for quoting the psalms, which a scribe might recognize and perhaps even follow. It may even have been the trigger that led him to think in terms of the psalms.

Psalms Commentators and Jeremiah 48

Nevertheless, it appears that Psalms commentators do not find parallels between Ps 149 and Jer 48, although some of the remarks about Ps 149:6b–9 are strikingly reminiscent of those made by exegetes of Jer 48:10 in terms of the "bellicose tone" and "unedifying spirit" (to use Oesterley's words) that sit awkwardly in their context.[55]

Broadly, there are four main views regarding the nature of the psalm: an eschatological hymn; a song in the context of (possibly postexilic) battle; a metaphorical depiction; and cultic worship. However, there is overlap between these views, which will be indicated in the footnotes. Determining the setting may help to assess how a scribe of Jer 48:10 may have appropriated the psalm.

Of those who see Ps 149 as looking forward to eschatological judgment,[56] Allen gives one of the most comprehensive explanations for this position, reasoning mainly that it is similar to other eschatological passages:

> Most probably the psalm is an eschatological hymn that looks forward to a future victory wrought by YHWH on Israel's behalf . . . this is why the ground for praise in vv 7–9 looks to the future. In support may be cited the relationship of the psalm to Pss 96 and 98, which are eschatological in tone. The "new song" (שיר חדש) of v 1 accords with Pss 96:1; 98:1, which praise the coming dynamic intervention of YHWH into history in an unprecedented and final manner. As in Pss 96:10; 98:6, the king-

---

55. Broyles, *Psalms*, 517; Kraus, *Psalms 60–150*, 566, 568; Oesterley, *Psalms 2*, 584–85; Terrien, *Psalms*, 925.

56. Allen, *Psalms 101–150*, 397–98 (Allen considers that the eschatological hymn may have been sung in a cultic setting); Gunkel, *Psalms*, 365; *Introduction*, 260; Kidner cited in Allen, *Psalms 101–150*, 397–98; Kittel cited in Buttrick, *Psalms*, 757; Terrien, *Psalms*, 926.

ship of YHWH is invoked in v 2. Divine ישועה "salvation," is celebrated in Pss 96:2; 98:2–3; 149:4 and כבוד, "glory," in Pss 96:3; 149:5; YHWH is "to judge" (לשפט) the earth in Pss 96:13; 98:9, while Ps 149:9 gives a longer expression. Another common factor is the linkage of both those psalms of the divine king and this one with Isa 40–66 . . . Also significant is the prospect of the nations' submission or, failing that, destruction in Isa 60:12, 14; the root חרב, "destroy," Isa 60:12, may be echoed in its homonym חרב, "sword" in v 6 . . . It is difficult to avoid the conclusion that, like Pss 96 and 98 and Isa 40–66, this psalm is building on the motifs of the future victory of YHWH over the nations and the exaltation of Israel.[57]

Kraus, on the other hand, deems the language of Ps 149 to correspond so well with the other warlike passages in the Psalter that he thinks an eschatological placement is unreasonable.[58] Oesterley, too, claims that, "it must be insisted, eschatology usually expresses itself in a more definite and detailed manner than is offered in this late psalm."[59] Unfortunately, Oesterley does not elaborate on what a more definite and detailed manner entails.

Oesterley is among those scholars who consider that the psalm was written for a (perhaps holy) war setting, although the precise purpose varies: whether it is a call to war (as found in Isaiah, Jeremiah, and Micah) before it begins; a war song sung on the eve of a battle against the foreign nations; or a victory song intended for afterwards.[60] There are a number of hypotheses regarding the dating of the psalm,[61] but it is normally dated as post-exilic, due to post-exilic language and syntax and references to post-exilic situations.[62] Within this period, the most popular settings given for this psalm are those of Nehemiah[63] and, historically, the Maccabees,[64] though the Psalms are now thought to have

---

57. Allen, *Psalms 101–150*, 397–98.
58. Kraus, *Psalms 60–150*, 567.
59. Oesterley, *Psalms 2*, 585.
60. Briggs and Briggs, *Psalms*, 543; Buttrick, *Psalms*, 757, 759; Dahood, *Psalms 101–150*, 356; Duhm, "Die Psalmen," 301–2; Oesterley, *Psalms 2*, 585.
61. Allen, *Psalms 101–150*, 398; Kraus, *Psalms 60–150*, 566–67; Weiser, *Psalms*, 839.
62. Buttrick, *Psalms*, 757.
63. Broyles, *Psalms*, 517; Kraus, *Psalms 60–150*, 567.
64. Duhm, "Die Psalmen," 301–2; Kraus, *Psalms 60–150*, 566; Oesterley, *Psalms 2*, 585–86.

been written down before Maccabean times.⁶⁵ However, Broyles argues that a Persian context was unlikely since "Judah had no standing army under the Persian Empire."⁶⁶

He considers that the psalm was intended metaphorically, as does Terrien. Broyles likens the two-edged sword in Ps 149:6b to the praise of God in 6a, whereas Terrien considers that it "is probably a metaphor for designating the powerful word of God."⁶⁷ This understanding largely solves the problematic nature of the verse. It is also a position that is supported by Berman's recent study on "the sword of mouths," in which he argues that the term חרב פיפיות always "bears an overt oral reference"⁶⁸ (even in Judg 3) or is a metaphor that portrays the potency of words (Ps 149 included).⁶⁹ However, whilst Judg 3 may include a play on the double-speaking of Ehud and his sword of mouths,⁷⁰ the חרב פיפיות is also used physically to slay King Eglon (Berman does not deny this). One wonders how a song of praise or the word of God effectively executes נקמה "vengeance," תוכחת "punishment," and משפט "judgment" on the nations and I would suggest that Ps 149, like Judg 3, has more than a metaphorical sword in mind.

Finally, there are those who see the psalm as written for cultic worship, and incorporating a sword dance.⁷¹ Usually this cultic occasion is understood to take the form of a feast; either a feast of YHWH or the feast of Tabernacles, the latter (the principle festival of the autumnal new year) perhaps indicated by שיר חדש "new song"⁷² and comparable to the fire dance at Tabernacles as described in Mishnah.⁷³ This under-

---

65. Allen, *Psalms 101–150*, 398; Terrien, *Psalms*, 925.

66. Broyles, *Psalms*, 517.

67. Ibid., 517–18; Terrien, *Psalms*, 926 (Terrien holds together this metaphorical setting with an eschatological one); see also Allen's discussion on this (*Psalms 101–150*, 517).

68. Berman, "Sword of Mouths," 302.

69. Ibid. 291–303.

70. Ibid., 291–93.

71. Goulder, *Psalms*, 299; Allen, *Psalms 101–150*, 398; Dahood, *Psalms 101–150*, 357; Eaton, *Psalms*, 314–15; Eaton, *Historical*, 482–83; Kraus, *Psalms 60–150*, 567, 568; Leslie, *Psalms 60–150*, 87–88; Limburg, *Psalms*, 503; Mowinckel cited in Kraus, *Psalms 60–150*, 566; Schmidt cited in Kraus, *Psalms 60–150*, 566; Weiser, *Psalms*, 839, 37–38.

72. Eaton, *Psalms (Historical and Spiritual)*, 482.

73. Goulder, *Psalms*, 299.

standing, too, at least resolves some of the tension in the psalm in that the sword is not wielded for real against an enemy.

Nevertheless, I am most persuaded that the psalm is to be understood as referring to an eschatological or, at least, future event, for I am not convinced that an entirely metaphorical setting does justice to the text,[74] particularly with its reference to משפט כתוב. The same would apply to the sword dance in a cultic setting. At the same time, as Broyles points out, the lack of military power in the time of Nehemiah seems to suggest that this setting is not quite right either.

If the author of the psalm anticipated an eschatological or future event, then it is natural that my hypothetical scribe of Jer 48:10 would use it in the way I have suggested, that is, as a call to the godly (perhaps at the time of the Maccabean wars) to usher in this future glorious day by fulfilling the משפט כתוב. However, before accepting this construal too quickly, it is necessary to examine more carefully what scholars deem משפט כתוב to be and whether Jer 48 does, in fact, fall under its rubric.

משפט כתוב

There is a variety of opinions about what constitutes the משפט כתוב "written judgment" in Ps 149:9 and scholars tend to cite the various alternatives, being cautious about which option they accept. These include: YHWH's own decrees that are written in the books of heaven;[75] texts prescribing the destruction of the pagan Canaanite nations (Deut 7:1ff; 20:13);[76] and prophecy, including that against Israel / Judah (Isa 45:14 is a popularly quoted text, but also Isa 24:21–22; 41:15–16; 49:7, 23; 60; 66; Ezek 38; 39; Hos 7:14; 8:14; Joel 4[3]:9–16, 19–21; Mic 4:13; Zech 14; even Deut 32:41–43).[77]

---

74. I am not opposed to a metaphorical reading strategy, but this is a different issue.

75. Allen, *Psalms 101–150*, 400; Buttrick, *Psalms*, 759; Eaton, *Psalms (Historical and Spiritual)*, 483; Oesterley, *Psalms 2*, 586.

76. Allen, *Psalms 101–150*, 398; Dahood, *Psalms 101–150*, 400; Gunkel, *Psalms*, 366; Weiser, *Psalms*, 839.

77. Allen, *Psalms 101–150*, 400; Briggs and Briggs, *Psalms*, 543; Buttrick, *Psalms*, 759; Eaton, *Psalms (Historical and Spiritual)*, 483; Oesterley, *Psalms 2*, 586; Terrien, *Psalms*, 925; see also Gunkel, *Psalms*, 366.

Dahood says that "others see here an allusion to the prophetic oracles against the nations,"[78] but he does not name these "others" and it seems from the above references that these oracles (usually considered prophecies of judgment) are not typically cited. This is despite the fact that some of Jeremiah's written prophecies concerning the nations talk in terms of משפט (Jer 48:21, 47; 49:12; 51:9). In fact, as we have seen, Jer 48:47 seems to refer to the whole oracle as משפט, when it concludes the chapter with עד־הנה משפט מואב. At this point, therefore, it is prudent to look at how משפט is utilized in Jer 48 to see whether it is likely that the author of 48:10 could have made the mental link between Ps 149's משפט כתוב and the משפט upon Moab in Jer 48 (though the term משפט כתוב itself is not used in Jer 48).

משפט IN JEREMIAH 48

Although not common, it is not unusual for the OANs to be described by the texts themselves as YHWH's judgment. As seen above, apart from Jer 48, משפט is used twice in Jer 46–51: Jer 49:12 and 51:9 where Babylon's judgment is said to have reached the heavens. Elsewhere the OANs are described as משפט in Isa 34:5 and Ezek 39:21, and the plural noun, שפטים, is used in Ezek 25:11; 28:22; 30:14 and 19. The root שפט is used in relation to all the nations in general (Jer 25:31; Ezek 39:21; Joel 4[3]:2, 12), but it is also employed with regard to specific nations: Moab (Jer 48:21, 47; Ezek 25:11); Babylon (Jer 51:9); Edom (Isa 34:5; Ezek 35:11);[79] Sidon (Ezek 28:22); Thebes (Ezek 30:14); Egypt (Ezek 30:19); and Gog (Ezek 38:22).[80] In other words, a fair representative of the nations across Isaiah, Jeremiah, Ezekiel, and Joel can be said to fall under YHWH's "judgment."

Most dictionaries consider that משפט is used both in terms of judicial justice and punishment, but consider that the punitive sense

---

78. Dahood, *Psalms 101–150*, 358.

79. This oracle is against Mount Seir in particular.

80. It is generally accepted that this refers to the judgment of Gog and its allies (or evil in general), rather than Israel (Allen, *Ezekiel 20–48*, 208; Clements, *Ezekiel*, 173; Cooke, *Ezekiel*, 415; Darr, "Ezekiel," 1522; Eichrodt, *Ezekiel*, 524–25; May in May and Allen, "Ezekiel," 276; Sweeney, "Ezekiel," 1116; Wevers, *Ezekiel*, 290; Zimmerli, *Ezekiel 2:25–48*, 314; also the *Tanchuma (Va Eirah 22)* and the Jewish "sages" cited in Eisemann, *Ezekiel*, 591.

is less common.⁸¹ According to Johnson, Jer 48:21, 48:47, and Ps 149:9 are examples where משפט is used punitively: "When the oracle of disaster against Moab in Jer 48:47 ends with the words 'thus far is Moab's *mišpāṭ*,' this refers not just to the verdict, the decision reached concerning Moab, but also to all the disasters listed, the entire fate of Moab."⁸² Like Johnson, the author of the article on משפט in *The Dictionary of Classical Hebrew* also deems these three verses to use משפט to mean the execution of judgment.⁸³ Johnson asserts, as well, that when משפט denotes the nature of the judgment, that is, the punishment or deliverance, the singular form is normally employed.⁸⁴ Jer 48:21, 47, and Ps 149:9 all use the singular form.

Among the texts that Niehr cites where שפט is used in the context of "condemn" or "punish" are: 1 Sam 3:13; Ezek 5:10, 15; 11:9–11; 16:41; 21:35(30); 25:11; 28:22, 26; 30:14, 19; and 35:11. Interesting for our purposes is that in Ezek 5:10, 15; 11:9–11; 16:41; 21:35(30); 28:22; 30:14, 19 the חרב again seems to be (at least in part) the method of שפט, and, furthermore, that in Ezek 21:35(30); 25:11; 28:22; 30:14, 19, the threat is against the foreign nations, including Moab in 25:11. Thus, in Niehr's examples, as well as in Ps 149:6b–9 and Jer 48, judgment is linked with punishment by the sword.⁸⁵

In addition, in Ezek 5:15, judging appears to be equated with punishing/rebuking (יכח), for it reads, בעשותי בך שפטים באף ובחמה ובתכחות חמה "when I execute judgments on you in anger and fury, and with furious punishments" (NRSV). In arguing that YHWH can use the enemy, למשפט, for his own punitive ends, Johnson cites Hab 1:12.⁸⁶ In fact (though Johnson does not say this), in Hab 1:12 משפט is also in parallel with the Hiphil of יכח "to rebuke / correct":

---

81. Clines "מִשְׁפָּט," 556–64; Enns "מִשְׁפָּט," 1142–44 (though Enns barely touches on the punitive side); Johnson "מִשְׁפָּט," 87–88; see also the articles on שפט, which say the same—Niehr "שָׁפַט; "שָׁפַט" 421; Schultz "שפט," 214.

82. Johnson "מִשְׁפָּט" 90–91 (quote on p. 90).

83. Clines "מִשְׁפָּט," 558.

84. Johnson "מִשְׁפָּט," 89–90. He notes that when it is used in this way it is synonymous with *šepeṭ* and *šᵉpôṭ* "both of which only have this negative sense" (p. 90).

85. Allen (*Psalms 101–150*, 400, 398) connects Ps 149:6b–9 with Isa 66:15–16, which also contains both חרב "sword" and משפט "judgment."

86. Johnson "מִשְׁפָּט," 91.

יהוה למשפט שמתו	You, (O) YHWH, have marked him for judgment
וצור להוכיח יסדתו	And you, (O) Rock, have established him for rebuke

Thus, what is not quite so apparent in Ezek 5:15 is made clear in Hab 1:12; that judgment and the disciplinary execution of its verdict are sometimes twinned.[87]

When it is used punitively, משפט is often in conjunction with the idea of deliverance because, as Johnson observes, judgment is "positive for those who are just and innocent, but negative for the wicked and sinful." In Johnson's mind, Ps 149:9 is an example of this.[88] However, in the case of Jer 48, there is no apparent deliverance for Israel or others. In fact Jer 48:4 even implies that, far from being delivered, the innocent are instead caught up in the suffering, since השמיעו זעקה צעיריה[89] "her little ones have sounded out a cry [of distress]."

All in all, therefore, it seems clear that משפט is often used in the OT to denote punishment and that this is how it is used in Jer 48:21 and 47 as well as in Ps 149. In other words משפט does not carry overtones of deliverance in Jeremiah's oracle concerning Moab. It has been frequently noted that what are commonly termed, for ease of reference, "OANs" may not all be oracles *against* a nation, but rather oracles concerning a nation (the Hebrew uses על, אל, and ל). However, it seems clear that Jer 48 can be designated as an oracle *against* Moab. At the same time, it is clear from the rest of the chapter that although Jer 48 lacks the idea of deliverance, Moab's משפט is nevertheless, "not the kind a judge imposes with coolness and impartiality" to use Goldingay's phrase, for it is accompanied by YHWH's tears.[90]

Having established that משפט can mean bloody punishment, and that this is how it appears to be intended in Jer 48 as well as Ps 149:9, we can be more confident in claiming a link between the two passages and suggesting that a scribe perceived that link. However, one further text

---

87. McConville ("Judgment and God," 29–30) also remarks that parallelism often helps open up a word's meaning, though he draws attention to the instances where משפט is linked with words such as צדקה "righteousness" (e.g., Isa 9:7).

88. Johnson "מִשְׁפָּט," 99, 91, 93. In fact, Goldingay (*OT Theology*, 169–70) claims that this is its sole meaning in the OT, though the above demonstrates that this is not so.

89. I have quoted the *qere* version; the *ketiv* reads צעוריה.

90. Goldingay, *OT Theology*, 170.

will be examined in the light of Jer 48 as written punishment, the like of which is to be carried out in Ps 149, and that is Jer 25:13.

Jeremiah 25:13

Jer 25:31 uses the Niphal form of שפט to say that YHWH is "entering into controversy" with all flesh. Thus, if chapter 25 is the precursor to chapters 46–51, then all Jeremiah's OANs may be seen as falling under the rubric of YHWH's judgment. Furthermore, perhaps *prima facie* the most obvious example in the OT where the OANs might be seen as משפט כתוב is in Jer 25, although the text does not contain the phrase itself and משפט does not occur at all. For, in Jer 25:13, YHWH declares that he will bring על־הארץ ההיא את־כל־דברי אשר־דברתי עליה את כל־ הכתוב בספר הזה אשר־נבא ירמיהו על־כל־הגוים "against that land all (the) words which I have spoken against it, everything written in this book which Jeremiah prophesied concerning all the nations."

However, a longer look shows that the link between this verse and the OANs is less evident, for this verse is beset with difficulties, not least because LXX inserts Jeremiah's OANs part way through it, after כל־הכתוב בספר הזה. The rest of MT's verse 13 (re Jeremiah's prophecies) occurs as a superscription to the OANs in LXX's 32:1. As well, Jer 25 starts with Judah and her judgment, so whilst the reference to הארץ ההיא "that land" initially looks like it denotes Babylon (that is, one of the nations), the context suggests it might be otherwise. As it stands, verse 13 can thus be read either that YHWH is going to do to Judah all that he has done to the other nations, or that YHWH is going to bring upon Babylon all that has previously been prophesied against it/the nations. Some scholars are sharply divided on the issue; Fretheim and Jones are sure that it is a reference to Babylon[91] whilst Carroll is as certain that it denotes Judah.[92]

There are various ways of approaching what appears to be a threat of punishment against Babylon in an oracle of judgment against Judah. In his apparatus for BHS, Rudolph (who deletes אשר־נבא ירמיהו על־כל־הגוים)[93] suggests changing ההיא to הזאת to correspond to הארץ הזאת in verse 11, that is, Judah. He also sees verse 12 (with its

---

91. Fretheim, *Jeremiah*, 356; Jones, *Jeremiah*, 327; see also Freedman, *Jeremiah*, 167.
92. Carroll, *Jeremiah*, 496; see also Nicholson, *Jeremiah 1–25*, 212.
93. See Rudolph's apparatus in BHS.

reference to Babylon) as out of place.⁹⁴ Duhm, on the other hand deems verse 13 to be the conundrum, although he does not suggest deleting it.⁹⁵

Holladay's proposal is that: "If the skeleton of v. 13 was present in the second scroll (so the assumption of the present study), then the 'land' must have been Judah. The easiest assumption then is that the text was originally 'the land' (compare v. 11) and that the demonstrative 'that' was added when v. 12 was added, so that the reference of the verse shifted from Judah to Babylon (Rudolph's emendation of 'that land' to 'this land' has the same intention, but is less plausible)."⁹⁶

Although these are strategies intended to ease the problem, in Jones' eyes there is no problem. For he sees verse 13 as following the natural prophetic order: first YHWH judges Israel/Judah by means of an agent that acts as his servant, and then he turns to judge the agent itself.⁹⁷

Unsurprisingly, how את כל־הכתוב בספר הזה is to be taken is also disputed. Scholars who understand "that land" to refer to Babylon are apt to deem בספר הזה to refer to Jeremiah's OANs as a whole,⁹⁸ perhaps Jer 50–51 in particular,⁹⁹ the scroll Seraiah was to take to Babylon (51:60),¹⁰⁰ or all the words spoken by Jeremiah against the nations.¹⁰¹ Exegetes who judge the verse to relate to Judah tend to think that בספר הזה includes everything up to this point (that is, Jer 1:1—25:12),¹⁰² or one of Baruch's scrolls (Jer 36).¹⁰³ Drinkard is of the opinion that Baruch's scroll included the OANs.¹⁰⁴ Brueggemann and Jones are inclined to think

---

94. Rudolph, *Jeremiah*, 160.

95. Duhm, *Jeremia*, 202.

96. Holladay, *Jeremiah*, vol. 1, 669.

97. Jones, *Jeremiah*, 327–8.

98. Drinkard in Craigie et al., *Jeremiah 1–25*, 368; Duhm, *Jeremia*, 202; Freedman, *Jeremiah*, 167; Fretheim, *Jeremiah*, 356; Kessler, "Function," 65; McKane, *Jeremiah*, vol. 1, 627.

99. Rietzschel cited in Holladay, *Jeremiah*, vol. 1, 664. Jones, *Jeremiah*, 328 and Carroll, *Jeremiah*, 492 also give this as a possibility.

100. Rudolph, *Jeremiah*, 162.

101. Duhm, *Jeremia*, 202.

102. McKeating, *Jeremiah*, 129; Thompson, *Jeremiah*, 514.

103. Carroll, *Jeremiah*, 492; Holladay, *Jeremiah*, vol. 1, 667; Jones, *Jeremiah*, 328; Miller, "Jeremiah," 761.

104. Drinkard in Craigie, et al., *Jeremiah 1–25*, 368.

בספר הזה incorporated some, if not the entire, book of Jeremiah as existed at the time of writing.[105] In summary, then, the book in Jer 25:13 may have been the OANs in chapters 46–51, but it is by no means certain. The situation in LXX is easier, for as LXX has it, πάντα τὰ γεγραμμένα ἐν τῷ βιβλίῳ τούτῳ naturally reads as a reference to the OANs that immediately follow.[106]

It seems, then, that there are no unequivocal arguments either for whether הארץ ההיא denotes Babylon or Judah, or for what את כל־הכתוב בספר הזה represents. However, despite what appears to be distinct redactional histories between Jeremiah's OANs in LXX and MT, I am most persuaded that Jer 25:13 refers to Babylon by LXX's placement of the OANs. For it indicates that, for LXX authors at least, the focus at this point has moved definitively from Judah to Babylon, rather than that verse 12 is a passing reference to Babylon. In LXX's reading, too, πάντα τὰ γεγραμμένα ἐν τῷ βιβλίῳ τούτῳ would suggest the OANs. Furthermore, as it stands without textual emendation, הארץ ההיא most naturally refers to the preceding ארץ כשדים in verse 12.

It is impossible to say conclusively that Jer 25:13 was written before 48:10, but it seems likely that it was. Therefore, if 25:13 existed first and the author of 48:10 recognized the scroll in 25:13 as relating to the OANs, then it is not inconceivable that such a reference to this scroll may have acted as an additional reminder of Ps 149's משפט כתוב. Nevertheless, whenever they were written, as they stand now the passages come together canonically and so are open to intertextual reading.

A further resonance that may have influenced the author of 48:10 (particularly if he had Ps 149 in mind) and inspired him to refer to the wielding of the sword as מלאכת יהוה "YHWH's work" is Judg 3.

YHWH's Work and Judges 3

Lundbom appreciates that Jer 48:10 introduces the idea that Moab's coming catastrophes are YHWH's work[107] and Carroll is reminded of other texts in which humans are expected to carry out YHWH's work

---

105. Brueggemann, *Jeremiah*, 224; Jones, *Jeremiah*, 328.
106. See also McKane, *Jeremiah*, vol. 1, 627.
107. Lundbom, *Jeremiah 37–52*, 263.

of judgment (Jer 50:25) and even cursed for not doing so (Judg 5:23).[108] To these, Smothers adds Deut 7:16, where the people are commanded not to show mercy to their enemies.[109] However, one text that the commentators do not mention, but which is arguably even more applicable, is Judg 3:12–30, for here (as mentioned above) the human sword is used in divine judgment against the king of Moab.

Although משפט does not occur in this passage, Ehud, one of the שפטים that YHWH raised up for Israel (Judg 2:16–19) and strengthened (3:12), kills King Eglon of Moab with a two-edged sword. Ehud therefore sets a precedent for Moab being judged with a sword. If Berman is correct that the חרב ולה שני פיות can be used metaphorically, then the lack of a reference to a sword with two edges in Jer 48:10 could be due to the fact that a metaphorical interpretation is not appropriate in this context. Whether one can interpret 48:10 metaphorically as a Christian reading strategy is another matter and one that will be addressed shortly.

Summary of Proposal

My tentative proposal is that Jer 48:10 may have been added by a scribe/redactor who was struck by the fact that this prophecy against Moab had not been fulfilled. He may then have recalled the words of Ps 149:6b–9, where Israel is encouraged to wield a two-edged sword to execute judgment on the nations, according to כתוב משפט. This led him to insert a command to wield the sword so that the משפט כתוב of Jer 48 might be fulfilled, perhaps in order to hasten the advent of the day of celebration and honor for the godly (Ps 149:9b). The reference in Jer 25:13 to Jeremiah's written words against the nations may have helped establish the association between Jer 48 and Ps 149. This connection could have been confirmed by the story recorded in Judg 3 where not only does the Judahite, Ehud, take a sword against the Moabite king Eglon, but does so as one of YHWH's deliverers. At any rate, the implicit connection between the Lord's work and the sword in Judg 3 is made explicit in Jer 48:10.

Whilst this hypothesis may amount to nothing other than speculation, it is one that is supported by various factors and is, therefore, at

---

108. Carroll, *Jeremiah*, 780, 782.
109. Smothers in Keown, et al., *Jeremiah 26–52*, 314.

least plausible. That the verse might be a gloss is suggested by the third person reference to YHWH and the fact that it is probably prose located in the midst of poetry. What we know of history also backs up the theory that this oracle had not been completely fulfilled, since there are no accounts of a Babylonian invasion of Moab at that time. Moreover, the threat is incongruous if issued against the great empire of Babylon, but not so if it is intended to spur later Judah into action against one of her old enemies. The Maccabean wars may provide a suitable setting for this. As well, the possible allusion to Ps 149 is in keeping with the rest of Jeremiah, in that not only are psalms used in the book of Jeremiah, but they are also utilized in a similar manner (transforming the psalm in some way as well as making it more specific). In fact, it seems to me that one of the strongest arguments in favor of the proposal is that it ties together conclusions and observations that other scholars have made.

Furthermore, the way the scribe seems to understand Ps 149 concurs with the purpose for which many Psalms commentators think it was written, that is, as anticipating a future or eschatological day. That the scholars deem משפט to mean punishment in both Ps 149 and Jer 48 also gives weight to the connection between the two passages. The advantage of such a construal is that it makes sense of some of the incongruities of verse 10, such as a call for bloodshed in what is an otherwise largely lamenting chapter. How Christians have made sense of the chapter is a different matter.

Christian Interpretations of Jeremiah 48:10

This section gives a very brief overview of the history of the Christian reception of Jer 48:10 and the kinds of moves that Christians have made.

In his commentary on Jer 48:10 Calvin denounces overly metaphorical interpretations:

> This passage has been very absurdly explained, and it is commonly quoted as though the Prophet had said, that special care ought to be taken by us, not to omit anything of what God commands. But they thus misrepresent the meaning. We ought therefore to bear in mind what I have already said, that these words are addressed to the Chaldeans, as though he had said, "Spare not, but shed blood, and let no humanity move you, for

> it is the work of God; God has armed you, that ye might fully execute his judgment and spare no blood: ye shall then be accursed, except ye execute his vengeance." It is not indeed a common mode of speaking; but as to the subject and the meaning there is no ambiguity. It is the same thing as though he had said, "Go on courageously, and boldly execute God's vengeance, inasmuch as punishment has been denounced on them."[110]

It seems therefore as if Calvin is proposing that the verse should be kept in its context of vengeance and bloodshed. Calvin, in a sense, stands between two traditions. Behind him are the fathers and pre-modern interpreters who do read the verse "metaphorically" and in front of him are the modern exegetes who tend to take the "plain sense" of Scripture.

Sulpitius[111] Severus (born c. 360, died c. 420–425)[112] interprets Jer 48:10 metaphorically in the second letter dubiously attributed to him, where he uses the verse in loose connection with the psalms.

> When you repeat a psalm, consider whose words you are repeating and delight yourself more with true contrition of soul, than with the pleasantness of a trilling voice . . . Display diligence in all your doings; for it is written, Cursed (Jer 48:10) is the man who carelessly performs the work of the Lord. Let grace grow in you with years; let righteousness increase with age; and let your faith appear the more perfect the older you become; for Jesus, who has left us an example how to live, increased not only in years as respected his body, but in wisdom and spiritual grace before God and men.[113]

It is interesting that the references to the sword and bloodshed are absent in Severus's reinterpretation of the verse and seemingly replaced with "grace," "righteousness," and "faith." Sulpitius does precisely what Calvin rejects, for his phrase "Display diligence in all your doings" is similar to Calvin's "not to omit anything of what God commands." The difference is that Sulpitius encourages such a reading, where Calvin warns against it.

---

110. Calvin, *Jeremiah*, 14–15.

111. His name is spelled "Sulpitius" in the translation of his "Dubious Letters," and "Sulpicius" by the Catholic Encyclopaedia. For consistency, I always use the former spelling.

112. Weber, "Sulpicius Severus," online.

113. Severus, "Letter 2," online.

The advantage of Sulpitius's use of 48:10 as an aphorism is that it keeps the verse within a Christian rule of faith and protects it from wooden, literalistic reuses of which Pope Gregory VII (Hildebrand) is accused. The verse seems to have been a favorite of this "dominant personality" who, as well as dedicating his life to ecclesiastical reform, made an alliance with the Normans that included military aid, and campaigned for a crusade with himself at the head.[114] In fact, he quoted Jer 48:10 in at least eight letters,[115] though in all but two of these he qualifies his quotation with an explanation that what is meant is keeping back the word of preaching, reproof, or admonition from rebuking the carnally minded.[116] Nevertheless, if Rudolph is correct then Gregory's use of 48:10 "has worked itself out fatally even if he himself (cf. Condamin and Lauck) did not want to understand it in a literal sense. We have here an object lesson for the false usage of the OT in Christian religion."[117] For, it seems, Gregory's metaphorical reading was lost in his frequent citation of the verse in conjunction with his emphases on military warfare in other areas of life.

Modern interpreters tend to shy away from usages that work themselves out fatally, but they tend to avoid as well the kind of metaphorical usage with which Sulpitius is comfortable. Jones' insight on the verse may provide a suitable example of a modern interpreter who works with the "plain sense" of Scripture without being literalistic: "The execution of the destruction of Moab as the LORD's work (cf. 50:25) is presented in an over-simplified way. But that a judgment is worked out in the tragedies and vicissitudes of history is part of the insight into history which is Israel's gift to the thought of mankind."[118]

Thus, as part of the wider canon of Scripture the verse contributes to the general witness to the mysteries of God and his dealings with the world. Jones has at least attempted to read Jer 48:10 as Christian Scripture. However, the result is a very general comment that could be made about Jer 48 as a whole or the OANs in general. So then, we return to Calvin. How does Calvin suggest a Christian read Jer 48:10

114. Gregory, *Correspondence*, xxiv; Oestereich, "Pope St Gregory VII," Online.
115. Gregory, *Correspondence*, 8, 11, 15, 40, 82, 101, 104, 155.
116. Ibid., 11, 40, 82, 101, 104, 155.
117. Rudolph, *Jeremiah*, 279 [my translation]; see also Feinberg, *Jeremiah*, 302; Volz, *Der Prophet Jeremia*, 405.
118. Jones, *Jeremiah*, 502.

well? Unfortunately, although Calvin tells his readers how one should not read Jer 48:10 he does not provide them with an example of what he considers is a good interpretation.

What we do have, though, is Calvin's reading of Ps 149:9, a verse that I have argued throughout may have been the catalyst for the scribal gloss of Jer 48:10. Calvin warns that all God's children, like the Jews in the Psalm, must only execute vengeance at God's command. He continues to say that this jurisdiction is peculiar to the offices of rulers and magistrates, but:

> As to the Church collective, the sword now put into our hand is of another kind, that of the word and the spirit, that we may slay for a sacrifice to God those who formerly were enemies, or again deliver them over to everlasting destruction unless they repent (Eph. vi. 17). For what Isaiah predicted of Christ extends to all who are his members,—"He shall smite the wicked with the word of his mouth, and shall slay them with the breath of his lips." (Is. xi. 4) If believers quietly confine themselves within these limits of their calling, they will find that the promise of vengeance upon their enemies has not been given in vain.[119]

Thus, in Calvin's reading, the sword remains in the hand of the godly, but it is no longer a real sword, but a metaphorical one. By doing so, Calvin maintains the "plain sense" of the context of vengeance, but does not take the text literalistically. Today this would be called a figural reading (figural readings will be discussed in a little more detail in the next chapter).

Eaton, too, metaphorically likens the two-edged sword of Ps 149:6–9 to the sword of the Spirit in Eph 6:17 and the word of God in Heb 4:12.[120] Both Calvin and Eaton follow in the wake of Augustine's interpretation: "This sort of weapon contains a great mystical meaning, in that it is sharp on both sides. By swords sharpened on both sides, we understand the Word of the Lord: (Heb 4:12) it is one sword, but therefore are they called many, because there are many mouths and many tongues of the saints."[121]

Interestingly, although some Psalms commentators understand the battle in Ps 149 to be symbolic (for example, a sword dance), in Calvin's,

---

119. Calvin, *Psalms*, 316–17.
120. Eaton, *Psalms (Historical and Spiritual)*, 315.
121. Augustine, *Exposition on Psalm 149*, online.

Eaton's, and Augustine's interpretations, the battle is a real one, albeit not one of flesh and blood. Neither is the battle an internal struggle of the human heart against evil inclinations, or against principalities and powers, but, as in Ps 149, one where the godly are avenged and punishment comes upon their wicked enemies.

In the same way that Pope Gregory VII's usage of Jer 48:10 led to bloodshed, Weiser notes that Ps 149 was also utilized as a battle cry on behalf of the princes in the Thirty Years War and "misused by Thomas Münzer to sanction his lust for vengeance."[122] Again, analogical readings steer away from these kinds of dangers.

At the same time, a metaphorical reading appears more suitable for Ps 149:6b–9 than Jer 48:10 because of its less specific language. Jer 48, on the other hand, contains detailed references to places in Moab, the reason for her sin, and the subsequent form her punishment will take. Thus, it seems, that the moves that are made in metaphorically appropriating Ps 149:6b–9 cannot be made with equal facility with respect to Jer 48:10, which is ironic given that Ps 149 may be the text behind Jer 48:10.

To summarize, then, both literalistic and metaphorical interpretations of Jer 48:10 have been abused. Taking the text woodenly has led to tragic bloodshed, but too free a metaphorical interpretation that removes the text from its context, such as Sulpitius's, is also arguably unwarranted, as Calvin points out. Jones' interpretation avoided both pitfalls but the corollary was a very general statement that could have been made from Jer 48 even if verse 10 was omitted. Calvin's metaphorical reading of Ps 149:9 might act as a model for Jer 48:10; on the other hand, the psalm's non-specific language encourages a good metaphorical reading in a way that Jer 48 does not. At the same time if the verse is a later comment from a "zealous voice" that "breaks in" from the sidelines,[123] then perhaps it lends itself to being extracted from its context to be taken more figurally.

An alternative approach is to set aside completely the verse in the light of the cross and resurrection. In the garden of Gethsemane, Peter cuts off the servant's ear and Jesus rebukes him and tells him to put back the sword, for those who take up the sword shall perish by the sword (Matt 26:51–52). Here the work of the Lord is not to be executed with

122. Weiser, *Psalms*, 839.
123. Stulman, *Jeremiah*, 362.

the sword and it could be argued that, since Jesus' breaking into the world, the work of the Lord no longer requires the sword. At any rate, it is a generally accepted Christian principle that discipleship entails less wielding the sword and more turning of the other cheek.

At the same time, it should also be noted that the context in Matt 26 is as specific as that of Jer 48. In fact, the NT is diverse in its witness as the OT and speaks with a multitude of voices as is shown by the martyrs who cry out for vengeance in Rev 6:10. Jer 48:10 and Rev 6:10 both show that those behind such outbursts are not automatically met with a rebuke, nor are their words silenced. Nevertheless, it does not follow that these cries are normative or even legitimate.

The nature of the verse as a scribal addition might itself be an indication of how to read the OT as Scripture in that although the scribe probably did not appreciate some of the text he was writing (e.g., the call for others to help Moab in verse 9 and the promise of restoration in verse 47), he did not delete anything. The hard texts remained as part of the whole. How Jer 48 as a whole should be read as Christian Scripture is the quest of the next and final chapter.

7

A Christian Reading of Jeremiah 48

Introduction

THIS CHAPTER OF THE BOOK ATTEMPTS TO GIVE A CHRISTIAN READING of the oracle concerning Moab in Jer 48. It begins with an outline of my own Christian perspective and hermeneutical position since these affect the reading I give. After this follows a short introduction to figural reading, for this is one of the approaches that I take to Jer 48, along with making value judgments within a Christian frame of reference. Then the chapter gives a brief overview of Jer 48 and introduces the idea of Easter as the ultimate horizon, before dealing with the text in five logical discrete blocks: verses 1–10; verses 11–13; verses 14–28; verses 29–39; and verses 40–47. Whilst there is no consensus on how Jer 48 should be divided, these section breaks cohere with those of the major commentators who also divide their commentary according to groups of verses (as opposed to those who give a verse by verse explanation), as can be seen from Table 5. The chapter ends with some concluding reflections on the text, followed by two codas that give an imaginative portrayal of Jer 48 by means of literary storyboards.

These codas are included because a kaleidoscopic representation of Jer 48 may lend itself more easily to a visual rather than written medium. Thus the standard way of interpreting the text in commentaries may be supplemented by a filmic montage. Coda 1 gives a representation of the chapter in its sixth century context whilst Coda 2 portrays it within a Christian frame of reference.

Fretheim, Miller, Brueggemann, Jones, and Clements all offer a Christian reading of Jer 48, though the U.S. scholars do so more explicitly. As discussed elsewhere in this work, Fretheim draws out from the chapter the aspect of lament and YHWH's suffering, Miller concentrates on YHWH's sovereignty, and Brueggemann focuses on Moab's pride and abuse of power and the judgment that follows as a consequence. Nevertheless, it must be said that none of the scholars cited deals with his preferred theme to the exclusion of the others. In my reading I am particularly interested, as well as in the laments over Moab, in the reasons given for her judgment, since these are a key characteristic of the oracle (as shown by their absence in Isa 15–16) and therefore impact its interpretation. Thus I attempt to build upon Brueggemann's work, which is specifically interested in Moab's pride and Fretheim's, which focuses on lament. These issues will be dealt with throughout within the sections that raise them, rather than as separate sections. At the same time, I seek to pick up and draw together a number of ideas from all these scholars (as well as others) in order to give a sense of the whole. Due to these emphases, for reasons of space I cannot always engage with the many technical difficulties with the text, nor justify the decisions I have made for reading it a certain way.

TABLE 5: Commentators' Breakdown of Jeremiah 48 into Sections

Fretheim	Miller	Brueggemann	Jones	Carroll	Rudolph	Thompson
1–10	1–13	1–9	1–10	1–10	1–10	1–10
11–17		10–13	11–13	11–17	11–20	11–17
	14–28	14–20	14–28			
18–28		21–28		18–28	21–28	18–28
29–39	29–39	29–33	29–47	29–39	29–31	29–39
		34–39			32–39	
40–47	40–47	40–47		40–47	40–46, 47	40–47

Hermeneutical Bases

My perspective is that of a Western Protestant, who lives in that strange time where modernism and post-modernism coexist, if not always in harmony. That both aspects have shaped me is demonstrated by this paragraph. For although I consider it a helpful exercise to classify myself, I am unable to do so in the way that I can classify my conversation partners in chapters 4 and 5, since I am part of the increasing number of Christians who have no denominational affiliation or loyalties. At the moment I happen to attend an Anglican church.

It is easier to clarify my hermeneutic position with regard to the text. I try to enter the literary world of the text and take it on its own terms. For example, the speaking voice of Jer 48 is Jeremiah's since in the literary world of the text the OANs are attributed to Jeremiah (Jer 46:1). At the same time, I appreciate that much of what at times I might take for granted is only available to me because historical-critical scholars have gone before and up-turned the stones, revealing what is underneath. This is the case concerning both the broader understanding of the context of the text and also the more intricate details of Hebrew roots and word usages.

Nevertheless (apart from the fact that there is often little consensus among scholars, for example, how much of Jeremiah is "authentic"), it seems to me that such research does not lead to a satisfactory reading of the text as "Scripture." However, I would reiterate what Rendtorff says regarding the Book of the Twelve; that "there is no simple alternative between a 'diachronic' and a 'synchronic' reading."[1] Therefore, in areas of the text where I deem the historical critical observations to make a significant difference to the interpretation of the text, I have addressed them (for example, the work on the curse in verse 10 in chapter 6).

A Figural Reading Strategy

There are various ways of recontextualizing a passage within a Christian frame of reference. For the Church Fathers a metaphorical interpretation was a normal way of reading the texts, but after the Reformation and Calvin, metaphorical readings received less explicit attention and the emphasis was on the literal meaning. In recent years there has been renewed interest in "figural" reading (a term that seeks to bypass the potential definitional problems with "metaphorical," "allegorical," or "typological"). The sheer difficulty of Jer 48 with its bloodshed and violent imagery raises the possibility that a figural reading might be one good way of recontextualizing Jeremiah's oracle concerning Moab.

---

1. Rendtorff, "How to Read," 87.

There appear to be no established rules for what a figural reading should or should not be. However, there are several aspects that seem to be generally agreed upon even if implicitly. First, figural readings are seen as extracting additional meaning from a text, often by reusing it in a new context.[2] In fact, Seitz claims that a Scriptural text contains "the seeds of its own extension."[3] Or, as he puts it elsewhere, "Figural interpretation has assumed there is a surplus of intended meaning in every divine revelation."[4]

Secondly, Christian figural readings view the text through a Trinitarian lens so that the additional meaning often points to Christ or finds Christ in the text, for as Carter asserts, Jesus Christ is the "subject matter of the Bible as a whole."[5] Though he does not explicitly state it, in Carter's view, the second person of the Trinity is often behind the text and the third person of the Trinity is the one who guides the interpreter to see Christ in the text and in the right way.[6]

Thirdly, there is a concern with how such readings should function in the life of the Church and Christian faith. For example, Radner is of the opinion that "the figural reading of the Bible is in part bound up with our own need to be changed, be challenged in our hearts, to be judged, condemned, and remade."[7] At the same time he warns against simply making something in the text "stand for" something else, since this quickly leads to reducing the text to moralistic homilies.[8] Carter cautions that while all interpreters will "read into the text" something that is not "there," the question to ask is what should be "read in" in order to avoid an arbitrary interpretation.[9] Likewise Davis also addresses the "difficult imaginative task" of recontextualization and concludes that, like all artists, "biblical interpreters and preachers must submit their work to standards of precision and functionality as well as those of imagination and beauty."[10] She thus speaks of "imaginative precision."

2. Walters, "Finding Christ," 33, 38.
3. Seitz, "History," 6.
4. Seitz, *Figured Out*, 32.
5. Carter, "Karl Barth," 134.
6. Ibid., 135–36; see also Davis, "Abundance of Meaning," 83.
7. Radner, "Truth," 27.
8. Radner, "Leviticus," 119.
9. Carter, "Karl Barth," 135.
10. Davis, "Abundance of Meaning," 64, 68.

One way of exercising this, she argues, is to "read the Old Testament text in relation to the story of Jesus *before* we can discover its meaning for the Christian life."[11]

She also makes the point that, "We can interpret the Bible for the Christian life—and interpret it accurately, skillfully, even beautifully—only because others have consistently done so before us."[12] It is this tradition of Christian exegesis that shapes Davis's view of interpreting OT passages christologically:

> Does it violate their literary, historical, and above all their theological integrity to read and preach them as pointing to and illumining the person, work, death, and resurrection of Jesus the Christ? My short answer is no. The freedom to make that move and the ability to make it with some precision are gifts that come to us out of the theological tradition, and it is essential that we continue to exercise them in preaching that takes the full measure of the gospel. But that does not mean that every sermon must or should be explicitly Christological. The freedom to preach Old Testament texts christologically is, in my judgment, just that; a freedom that the Christian preacher may exercise at any time and should exercise sometimes, not a requirement for preaching any particular text responsibly.[13]

Fourthly, interpreters draw attention to inner-biblical examples of figural readings and use them as formative case studies in terms of noting which moves are and are not made.[14] Whilst Walters asserts that, "'Scripture' is the premier example of the re-use of texts,"[15] it should be noted that "reuse" is not necessarily "figural reading," though the examples where Jesus sees himself in the Psalms can be classed as such.[16]

It could be argued that Jer 48:45–46 is an example of inner-biblical figural reading with its recontextualization of the taunt song in Num 21:28–29. For the old song refers to fire and flames whereas Moab's

---

11. Ibid., 76; see also Louth, *Discerning the Mystery*, 115–17.

12. Davis, "Abundance of Meaning", 65; see also p. 69.

13. Ibid., 72.

14. Carter, "Karl Barth," 133–36; Davis, "Abundance of Meaning," 64, 65, 69, 76, 83; Louth, *Discerning the Mystery*, 116–17, 120–21; MacDonald, "Gone Astray," 53–60; Radner, "Truth," 27; Radner, "Leviticus," 115, 119; Seitz, *Figured Out*, 32; Seitz, "History," 4–6; Walters, "Finding Christ," 33, 38, 40–46.

15. Walters, "Finding Christ," 39.

16. Ibid., 40–46.

judgment is not described in these terms elsewhere in Jer 48. It seems more likely that the fire that previously destroyed Heshbon is now used to refer to Moab's breaking, desolation, destruction, and capture, rather than to introduce the notion that Moab's destruction will be partly by fire. However, I would tend to see this as "reuse" of a text, rather than a "figural reading."

Structure and Overview

As stated above, the structural breakdown of Jer 48 given here closely follows that of Brueggemann and the general consensus (see Table 5). A more detailed outline is as follows:

1–10 Overview of Moab's current and future predicament with a reason
    1–5 description of destruction, shame, and tears plus warning / threat
    6–9 urge to flee, reason for Moab's destruction, command to help
    10 curse on those withholding their swords from blood
11–13 Moab is settled wine about to be poured out
14–28 Description of extent of judgment and commands to various parties
    14–20 question, statement, threat, and 10 commands (17–20)
    21–25 judgment upon many places—Moab's strength broken
    26–28 Moab to be made a drunk laughingstock and urged to leave
29–39 Moab's pride leads to YHWH's lament, threats, and Moab's lament
    29–30 Moab's pride
    31–32 YHWH's lament
    33–35 YHWH's threatened destruction
    36 YHWH's lament
    37–39 Moab's lament
40–47 Inescapability of Moab's destruction followed by a promise of restoration
    40–42 destroyer like an eagle coming upon the arrogant Moab
    43–44 inescapability of terror, pit, and trap
    45–46 reuse of taunt song found in Num 21
    47 promise of restoration

The oracle opens with a description of Moab's destruction in terms of its severity and scope, Moab's shame, and her mourning over the catastrophe that has befallen her. Moab is urged to flee, others are commanded to help her, and another audience is cursed if it does not pursue her. The first ten verses set the tone of the oracle as a whole. These themes are expanded in verses 11–28 by means of various metaphors and rhetorical questions and reasons are given for Moab's punishment. The intensity steps up a pace, too, with the imperatives of verses 14–28. However, the climax of the oracle seems to be in verse 31 where YHWH castigates Moab for her pride and then weeps over her. From this point on there is a slight shift in focus, for YHWH's presence becomes more overt and Moab's less. This is demonstrated not only by the attention given to YHWH's mourning, but by the increase in first person references to him in this second half of the chapter. The final few verses (40–47) reiterate the inescapability of Moab's destruction and many of the same themes as were introduced in verses 1–10 recur, perhaps indicating an unending cycle of sin and destruction. However, the last verse ends on a somewhat surprising note of restoration.

Lament, Judgment, and the Cross

Two important themes in Jer 48 are judgment and lament. Other key motifs in Jer 48 are pride (and its corollary, shame) and destruction. Overarching all is the idea of YHWH's sovereignty. All these ideas come together in the NT nowhere more clearly than in the death and resurrection of Jesus Christ.

Different voices utter lament through Jer 48. However, all of them primarily mourn the broken state of Moab. Her little ones are first heard to cry out over Moab's brokenness (the Niphal of שבר—v. 4) and the people of Moab continually weep over Moab's destruction (שבר—v. 5). Her neighbors are called to mourn over her brokenness (the Niphal of שבר) in verse 17 and the inhabitants are called to wail over her destruction (שדד) in verse 20. Whilst YHWH weeps and wails for Moab's pride in verses 29–32, his weeping in verse 32 is implicitly over what the destroyer (שדד) has done to her. The Moabites bemoan their desolation (משמה) in verses 33–34 and it is Moab's end that causes YHWH to wail in verses 35–36, though no specific words of destruction are used. Again, in verses 37–39 the inhabitants of Moab lament their broken state (שבר).

Although the lament that takes place in the Passion narratives is not explicitly centered around brokenness, but is due to a number of causes, Christ's death is the driving force behind most of it. Christ is deeply grieved in the Garden of Gethsemane over his coming trial (Matt 26:38; Mark 14:34), the disciples fall asleep from sorrow in the garden (Luke 22:45), Peter weeps bitterly over betraying Jesus (Matt 26:75; Mark 15:1; Luke 22:62), the crowds and women lament and mourn Christ before his death (Luke 23:27, 48) and Mary weeps outside the tomb afterwards (John 20:11–15). Though Judas does not lament as such, he hangs himself from remorse over his betrayal (Matt 27:3–5).

When the lament over Moab's brokenness in Jer 48 is compared with the Passion narratives, the question arises to what extent Christ and Moab can be linked figurally. For Moab's sin, given the significance that it has in the chapter, is a major obstacle in drawing an analogous relationship between Moab and Christ and it is doubtful that such a move portrays the required imaginative precision of which Davis speaks. Perhaps a better way of construing the parallel is to see, instead, Christ as embodying Moab (as one among many), or simply taking the burden of Moab's lament, at the Cross. This would be a similar move to that made frequently within Christianity that YHWH's judgment of the world falls on the shoulders of Christ on Good Friday.

In fact, the understanding of judgment in Jer 48 might be made richer by viewing it through this lens. Judgment (משפט) in Jer 48 is in the direction from YHWH to Moab. Whilst the portrayal of judgment in the Passion narratives is more complex and judgment is not explicitly mentioned, the direction is that human judgment is passed on Christ, for example in Jesus' trial. Human judgment on Christ unwittingly opened the way to YHWH's judgment on sin, thus enabling restoration for humanity, although this restoration is not akin to Moab's restoration in Jer 48:47. Nevertheless, the promise made to the Moabites witnesses to the same hope as the empty tomb on Easter Sunday; God's ability to bring new life from death.

Easter can thus be seen as the ultimate horizon of a Christian reading of Jer 48. However, this is to paint with a broad brush and a closer reading might suggest other Christian "parallels." The following reading seeks to bring out some of these, whilst keeping the idea of Easter as the background against which all stand.

Verses 1–10: Destruction, Lament, Inescapability

As indicated above, the first ten verses give an overview of Moab's predicament and introduces the reader to several key themes in the chapter: Moab's destruction (vv. 1–6, 8–9); her shame and the irony of a shattered stronghold (v. 1); her lament (v. 4–5); a reason for her catastrophe (v. 7); the totality of the disaster (v. 8); and an implicit acknowledgement that YHWH is the instigator of this (vv. 1, 8, 10). In this way, the first section acts as an introductory summary of the entire chapter. Whilst they do not speak in terms of an introductory summary, Fretheim and Miller also note that the major themes of the chapter appear in these first few verses.[17]

Superscription (v. 1)

The oracle begins by introducing the two main actors who will dominate this chapter; Moab and YHWH; למואב כה־אמר יהוה צבאות אלהי ישראל. Brueggemann remarks that these are two unlikely parties to be linked.[18] The title יהוה צבאות אלהי ישראל, is a Jeremianic term, which occurs thirty five times in MT Jeremiah, as opposed to five times in the rest of the OT (2 Sam 7:27; Ps 59:5; Isa 21:10; 37:16; Zeph 2:9 35). It is never used to introduce another of Jeremiah's OANs, though it appears both in the oracle concerning Egypt (46:24) and twice in that against Babylon (50:18; 51:33). Thus it is interesting that this extended title is employed in the three longest oracles in Jer 46–51 and that it is reserved for the start of the oracle concerning Moab. It is worth noting at this juncture that both יהוה "YHWH" and אלהים "God" are used in the OANs, the preference being יהוה, as is usual in prophecies. Thus there appears to be no difference in the way that God is presented to the foreign nations, that is, the Tetragrammaton is not reserved only for prophecies concerning Israel / Judah.

---

17. Fretheim, *Jeremiah*, 597; Miller, "Jeremiah," 890–91; see also Volz, *Der Prophet Jeremia*, 410.

18. Brueggemann, *Isaiah 40–66*, 443.

Place names

Whilst it is common for the OANs to open by naming the nation in question, Moab is mentioned by name proportionally more times in Jer 48 than most nations are in their respective oracles, as Table 6 demonstrates (unsurprisingly, the shortest oracles contain proportionally the highest occurrence).

TABLE 6: Number of times a Country is Named in Jeremiah's OANs

Jer Ref	Country	No. of times named
ch. 46	Egypt	11
ch. 47	Philistia / Philistines	3
ch. 48	Moab	34
49:1–6	Ammon / Ammonites	3
49:7–22	Edom + Esau	4 + 2 = 6
49:23–27	Damascus	3
49:28–33	Kedar + Hazor	2 + 3 = 5
49:34–39	Elam	7
chs. 50–51	Babylon + Chaldea / Chaldeans	55 + 10 = 65

Thus not only, as we have seen previously, are there numerous place names in the chapter, but מואב itself is repeated.

Rudolph includes an appendix to his commentary on Jer 48 in which he attempts to provide, as best as possible, a location for each of these places. Though many are unknown and others disputed, it is apparent that the places are not grouped according to geographical location in these sections; for example, Heshbon in the South and Horonaim in the North appear in both verses 1–5 and verses 31–36. Nor do they obviously represent the extremities of Moab's borders.[19] What is obvious is that there is word play on these place names, though it is not always apparent what that is. For example, מדמן may be a play on דם "blood,"

---

19. Rudolph, *Jeremiah*, 284–88. For a discussion on place names see also Allen, *Jeremiah*, 479; Feinberg, *Jeremiah*, 304; Ferch, "Nimrim," 1116; Fretheim, *Jeremiah*, 596, 597; McKane, *Jeremiah*, vol. 2, 1157–58, 1176; McKeating, *Jeremiah*, 203; Volz, *Der Prophet Jeremia*, 411.

דמם "silence," or מדמנה "dung pit" though it is generally understood to refer to Dibon (or Dimon).[20]

While Levine observes that citing "numerous towns and locales" as Isa 15–16 and Jer 48 do "seems to be typical of laments, in general,"[21] there are an unusually high number of place names mentioned in Jer 48. This may be, as previously discussed, to demonstrate the comprehensiveness of Moab's destruction.[22] This comprehensiveness becomes clearer as the oracle progresses and more and more of Moab is affected one way or another.

Woe (v. 1)

The opening word of YHWH's oracle is הוי. It is the language of a funeral lament but when used in prophetic literature as a cry over those still alive, it becomes a chilling threat. In fact, in his detailed article on הוי in *TDOT* Zobel argues that the prophets borrowed from laments over the dead in order "to make the point that judgment is inescapable."[23] The inescapable nature of Moab's judgment is clear throughout Jeremiah's oracle, particularly verses 8, 43–44, as commentators regularly point out.[24] Therefore, if Zobel is correct, the first word of the oracle adumbrates the tenor of what is to follow. הוי, then, becomes the ominous death knell that sounds for Moab.

---

20. Allen, *Jeremiah*, 479; Carroll, *Jeremiah*, 778, 799; Clements, *Jeremiah*, 253; Duhm, *Jeremia*, 345; Feinberg, *Jeremiah*, 301; Freedman, *Jeremiah*, 302; Fretheim, *Jeremiah*, 597; Holladay, *Jeremiah, vol. 2*, 356; Jones, *Jeremiah*, 501, 502; Lundbom, *Jeremiah 37–52*, 249; McKane, *Jeremiah, vol. 2*, 1157; McKeating, *Jeremiah*, 203; Rudolph, *Jeremiah*, 274–75, 278–79; Smothers in Keown et al., *Jeremiah 26–52*, 306, 311; Thompson, *Jeremiah*, 703; Volz, *Studien*, 306; Volz, *Der Prophet Jeremia*, 409, 411; Weiser, *Der Prophet Jeremia*, 404.

21. Levine, *Numbers 21–36*, 102.

22. Calvin, *Jeremiah*, 8; Carroll, *Jeremiah*, 781; Clements, *Jeremiah*, 254; Fretheim, *Jeremiah*, 596, 602; see also Brueggemann, *Isaiah 40–66*, 444; Miller, "Jeremiah," 891; Rudolph, *Jeremiah*, 283.

23. Zobel, "הוי" 362–64.

24. Brueggemann, *Isaiah 40–66*, 450–51; Calvin, *Jeremiah*, 45, 48; Feinberg, *Jeremiah*, 307; Fretheim, *Jeremiah*, 603; Jones, *Jeremiah*, 506; Lundbom, *Jeremiah 37–52*, 259, 306–7; McKane, *Jeremiah, vol. 2*, 1196; Miller, "Jeremiah," 892; Rudolph, *Jeremiah*, 283; Stulman, *Jeremiah*, 365–66.

Language of Destruction (vv. 1–5)

Verses 1–5 are primarily concerned with Moab's destruction and the cry in verse 3 could act as a one line summary of these five verses: שד ושבר גדול "Devastation and a great breaking!" A look at the language of destruction shows that it is not different to that used against Israel/Judah. That is, there do not seem to be specific words used for the nations as opposed to Israel/Judah. For instance, given that the Israelites are "to put to the ban" (חרם) the Canaanites when they enter the land (Deut 7:2; see also passages in Joshua where they חרם the people), one might expect חרם to feature in the context of the OANs. Yet חרם is only found in Jeremiah's oracle concerning Babylon (50:21).

Jer 48 is no exception and though some words tend to be used more for the foreign nations (שדד, לכד, and שד) and some less (for example, שבר), the following words of destruction found in this oracle are used in the context of both Israel and the nations: לכד "to capture, take, seize" (48:1); שדד "to destroy" (48:1, 8, 15, 18, 20, 32), and its noun, שד "violence, havoc, devastation, ruin" (48:3); שבר "to break, break in pieces" (48:4, 17, 25, 38); the Niphal of שמד "to be exterminated" (48:8, 42), נפץ "to shatter; (Pi.) dash to pieces" (48:12) (this word is used predominantly by Jeremiah in the hammer poem in 50:20–23); the noun טבח "slaughter" (48:15); גדע "to hew down/off," (Niph.) "to be hewn off" (48:25); the Hiphil of שבת "to cause to cease" (48:33, 35); the nouns שמה "waste/horror" (48:9) and משמה "devastation, waste; horror" (48:34); חתת "to be dismayed" (48:1, 20, 39) and its noun form, מחתה "terror, destruction, ruin" (48:39); תפש "to lay hold of, wield," (Niph.) "to be seized arrested caught" (48:41); צרר "to suffer distress" (48:41); בוש "to be ashamed" (48:13, 39); אבד "to perish" (48:8, 36, 46); איד "distress, calamity" (48:16); and שבי (48:46) and שביה (48:46) "captivity, captives." Even terms such as שכר "to be/become drunk" (48:26) are common to both. As noted, although משפט "judgment" is not frequently used in relation to the nations (that is, in terms of YHWH's judgment), Jer 48 uses משפט twice (48:21, 47) and it is found twice more in the same book (49:12; 51:9).

Thus the common vocabulary would seem to imply that when it comes to YHWH destroying there is no difference in treatment between Israel and Moab (or the other nations). If this analogy is right then it might be one way in which YHWH metes out justice with impartiality (cf. Rom 2:9–12). That there is a plethora of terms used to describe Moab's destruction indicates the serious nature of Moab's wrongdoing in YHWH's eyes. Where the numerous place names seem to suggest the scope of YHWH's judgment against her, the abundance of terms denoting destruction adds to its intensity. That many of these terms (אבד, חתת, לכד, שבר, שד, שדד, שמד, and שמה) occur in the first ten verses means that the chapter begins with a forceful note, for the way that the rhetoric works here is in piling up the words.[25] The force of the rhetoric is enhanced by the long title given to YHWH in the superscription and the introductory הוי. Although this list may suggest alliteration, the text does not tend to use this rhetorical tool in that alliterative terms of destruction are not used together.

Whilst the first two verses focus solely on the portrayal of Moab's destruction and a number of words are used to depict Moab's breaking, in verses 3–5 several terms are used to describe the Moabites' lamenting over her situation: קול צעקה "sound of an outcry" (v. 3)[26]; זעקה "cry/outcry" (v. 4); בבכי יעלה־בכי "he goes up weeping bitterly" (v. 5); and צרי צעקת־שבר "distressing cry of breaking" (v. 5). The first five verses thus paint a vivid picture that almost compels emotional involvement in the onlookers, especially if Moab's tears amidst horror spring from צעיריה[27] "her little ones" and not the place, Zogora (v. 4).

Rhetorical Kaleidoscope

Changing Agent and Means of Punishment

The agents and the means of Moab's punishment do not remain static as the oracle progresses, though the anonymous שֹׁדֵד makes his appearance in verses 8, 18, and 32. In the first ten verses, those in Heshbon (v. 2) and the destroyer (v. 8) are the implied agents of Moab's punishment, whilst the sword (v. 2), along with capture and shaming (vv. 1, 7) are the means. The sword also figures in verse 10, though it is not again mentioned in the chapter. In verses 11–13 the means of punishment is expressed via

---

25. See also Brueggemann, *Isaiah 40–66*, 443.

26. קול may be used as an exclamation. This is how NRSV understands it when it translates it "Hark!"—see also Gen 4:10. Nevertheless, the sense is not significantly affected whichever way it is translated.

27. Qere cited here; the Ketib reads צעוריה.

the metaphor of wine being poured out. The agents of the punishment are YHWH, indirectly, and those who tip the wine. In verses 14–28 the agent is once more the destroyer and the means are through slaughter and being made a drunken laughingstock. The destroyer continues to be the agent in verses 29–39, although YHWH claims responsibility by use of the first person as the primary agent. The means of judgment are through cessation of agricultural processes and, again, by Moab being made a laughingstock. In the final verses in 40–47, YHWH continues to take responsibility for Moab's fate (via the eagle in v. 40) and the means are through the metaphor of terror, pit, snare, fire, and captivity. Thus whilst ideas do recur within the oracle, it is not as vainly repetitive as Weiser seems to think, for new ideas are introduced even up to the final verses.[28] Clements is therefore perhaps more accurate when he refers to "the richness and variety of its poetry."[29]

Swapping of Audiences

In verse 2, the poem swaps from speaking about Moab in the third person to addressing her in the second, which raises the question of whether she was ever the intended recipient of the address. As has been discussed earlier, opinions are divided on this issue, although most consider that Moab was not the intended recipient. As Raabe points out (see chapter 1) it is not beyond the realms of possibility that she was. Nevertheless, it is clear from other OT passages that the nations were not always expected to hear the oracles, even if they were addressed in the second person within the oracle. YHWH's answer to Hezekiah's

---

28. Weiser, *Der Prophet Jeremia*, 403: "Wiederholungen, Widersprüche, störende Unterbrechungen des Gedankenzusammenhangs, Wechsel von poetischen mit prosaischen Stücken, auffallende Anlehnungen und Entlehnungen aus anderen alttestamentlichen Texten führen zu der Annahme eines auf Jeremia zurückgehenden Kerns, der durch verschiedenartige Zusätze nicht gerade glücklich ergänzt worden ist, so daß der Gesamteindruck eines Mosaiks entsteht. Auch die Textüberlieferung läßt zu wünschen übrig." ("Repetitions, contradictions, irritating interruptions of the overall content, swapping between poetic and prosaic parts, notable imitations and borrowing from other OT texts lead to the assumption that there is a core from Jeremiah, which has rather unfortunately been extended by various additions, so that the overall impression is that of a mosaic. The tradition of the text leaves much to be desired.") [my translation].

29. Clements, *Jeremiah*, 254; see also Brueggemann, *Isaiah 40–66*, 446.

prayer concerning Sennacherib in 2 Kgs 19:21–28 is a case in point.³⁰ Balaam's curses in Num 24:15–24 are another.³¹ As well, it is highly unlikely that the animals of the Negev were the intended recipients of Isa 30:6 (though admittedly, this is not written in the second person).

Moreover, it is improbable that all the audiences addressed in Jer 48 (Moab's allies in verse 9, her enemies in verses 10 and 26, her neighbors in verse 17, and her destroyer in verse 40) were intended to hear it. Instead, it seems that these second person speeches have a rhetorical purpose, for the effect is that the hearer/reader is pulled into the midst of the action. Although most of the commentators surveyed here do not make such observations, Volz notes that this formula is effective at maintaining the vividness.³² In verse 6 it seems as though even the writer himself has become involved for he urges the Moabites to flee and save their lives and to become like a ערוער in the wilderness. It is worth noting that most commentators do not deem this verse to be ironic, though Duhm considers it is a summons to live in poverty.³³

Varying Metaphors

In the same way that the agents and means of punishment change throughout the chapter, and the texts swap between audiences, the metaphors also vary. Verse 6, with the imperative to the Moabites to be like a ערוער in the wilderness, is the first of several metaphors in the chapter. The next is the reference to wings in verse 9, but from verse 11

---

30. Brueggemann, *1 and 2 Kings*, 509–11, 516–17; Fritz, *1 and 2 Kings*, 377; Gray, *1 and 2 Kings*, 690–91; Hobbs, *2 Kings*, 279, 283 (though his comment, p. 284, that we do not hear Sennacherib's response implies that Hobbs considers it possible that Sennacherib heard at some point YHWH's response to Hezekiah); Montgomery, *Kings*, 494.

31. Ashley, *Numbers*, 506; Budd, *Numbers*, 271; Gray, *Numbers*, 373. Even the Jewish authors who deem Balaam to have perhaps beheld the Kenites from afar, i.e. Levine, *Numbers 21–36*, 204 and Milgrom, *Numbers*, 209, do not suppose that they heard his words.

32. Volz, *Der Prophet Jeremia*, 411. Compare David's lament over Saul and Jonathan in 2 Sam 1:19–27, which similarly changes between rhetorical addressees.

33. Allen, *Jeremiah*, 479–80; Brueggemann, *Isaiah 40–66*, 443–44; Calvin, *Jeremiah*, 10–11; Carroll, *Jeremiah*, 782; Duhm, *Jeremia*, 346; Feinberg, *Jeremiah*, 301; Freedman, *Jeremiah*, 303; Fretheim, *Jeremiah*, 597; Holladay, *Jeremiah, vol. 2*, 350; Jones, *Jeremiah*, 501; Lundbom, *Jeremiah 37–52*, 251, 254; Rudolph, *Jeremia*, 279; Smothers in Keown et al., *Jeremiah 26–52*, 312; Stulman, *Jeremiah*, 362; Volz, *Studien*, 307–8; Volz, *Der Prophet Jeremia*, 411–12; Weiser, *Der Prophet Jeremia*, 405.

onwards, the metaphors become common, beginning with the image of undisturbed wine finally being poured out and then the bottle broken in verses 11–13. In verses 14–28 Moab's strong men are described as going down to the slaughter (v. 15), and Moab herself is described as a formerly mighty scepter and staff of splendor (v. 17), which now has a broken horn and arm (symbols of strength—v. 25), as a drunk wallowing in its vomit (v. 26), and as a nesting dove (v. 28). Verses 29–39 speak of Sibmah as a vine with extraordinarily long tendrils (particularly if the "sea of Jazer" is the Dead Sea in v. 32), YHWH's wailing is likened to flutes (v. 36), and Moab is described as a broken undesirable vessel (v. 38) as well as one who has turned his back (v. 39). Verses 40–47 compare Moab's enemy to an eagle (40), the inevitability of Moab's destruction as a terror, pit, and snare (v. 43–44), and refer to Moab's forehead and scalp (v. 45).

Commentators tend not to discuss the metaphors as rhetorical tools, though Brueggemann acknowledges their rhetorical power.[34] However, given that the subject matter is Moab's destruction, it would seem as if the purpose is to demonstrate that Moab's punishment is inevitable. They also show that her judgment will be widespread in the same way that the multitude of place names listed does.

The language throughout, therefore, whilst telling the same story, does so in a variety of ways, all of which are vivid.

Moab's Sin (v. 7)

The first explanation for Moab's predicament is introduced in 48:7; יען בטחך במעשיך ובאוצרותיך "because of your trust in your achievements and in your treasures." Most commentators consider that Moab's punishment is caused by her misplaced trust as explicitly stated by the text,[35] some noting that it is specifically self-assurance, pride or hubris for which she is judged.[36] Others deem Moab's trust in Chemosh to be part of the indictment itself since Chemosh is included in the result-

---

34. Brueggemann, *Isaiah 40–66*, 449.

35. Brueggemann, *Jeremiah*, 444; Duhm, *Jeremia*, 346; Fretheim, *Jeremiah*, 595, 598; Rudolph, *Jeremiah*, 279; Smothers in Keown et al., *Jeremiah 26–52*, 312; Stulman, *Jeremiah*, 362; Thompson, *Jeremiah*, 703–4.

36. Calvin, *Jeremiah*, 12; Feinberg, *Jeremiah*, 301; Volz, *Der Prophet Jeremia*, 412; Weiser, *Der Prophet Jeremia*, 405.

ing punishment in the second part of the verse.[37] However, מעשׂים and אוצרות (or even LXX's fortresses) do not naturally extend to the inclusion of deities, though it could be argued that "treasures" envisage a shrine, given that temples often housed the most valuable commodities. Nor does Chemosh's exile directly follow Moab's trust in her treasures in the text; Moab's own capture does. Furthermore, if worship of Chemosh is at the centre of Moab's trust here, it seems strange that the text does not explicitly state it, but rather refers to what seem lesser charges of trust in herself. Nevertheless, the reference to Chemosh in the second half of the verse may well allude to his impotence.[38] It may also be in order to demonstrate the seriousness of the consequences of Moab's misplaced trust, or to reveal that her sins have unforeseen consequences. For, due to her imprudence, not only will the common people of Moab be taken captive, but her god Chemosh will also go into exile and not even his priests will be spared.

The idea that treasures are a snare is not a foreign idea to either the OT (for example, Prov 11:28) or the NT (for example, the famous verse about the love of money in 1 Tim 6:10) and in this respect Jer 48:7 with its castigation of trusting in riches is an easier theme to appropriate in a contemporary context than some other notions in the chapter might be. Furthermore, the NT also exemplifies this idea in the parable of the rich fool in Luke 12:13–21, which addresses the double sided aspect of trusting in one's deeds and one's treasures.[39] The inappropriate trust of the rich fool does not explicitly bring down God's judgment (Luke 12:20), but as Calvin says, "such persons will suffer the penalty of their own folly."[40] Jas 1:11 also remarks that the rich man will wither away in the middle of his busy life, again linking the works with the treasures. True treasure, according to Luke 12, appears to be selling possessions and giving to charity (12:33). Though Jer 48 does not make this point, a Christian interpreter might use this observation from Luke 12 in order to suggest what Moab's behavior should have been. If Dives had Moses

---

37. Allen, *Jeremiah*, 480; Clements, *Jeremiah*, 254. Whether "idolatry" is the appropriate term to use with respect to the nations will be addressed in relation to v. 35.

38. Calvin, *Jeremiah*, 12; see also Thompson, *Jeremiah*, 703–4.

39. As stated, previously in chapter 2, LXX differs from MT at this point and there is less correspondence between LXX 31:7 and Luke 12:13–21. There is also no overlapping Greek between the two that is worth noting.

40. Calvin, *Jeremiah*, ii, 151.

and the Prophets (Luke 16:29), then contemporary Christians also have the four Gospels.

One of the purposes suggested for the OANs in general is that they acted as a warning to Israel/Judah not to put her trust in the other nations. That is, God's people should not trust what is not of God, whether it is other deities, a nation's military power or economic security. The parable of the wise and foolish builders who respectively built their houses on rock and sand (Matt 7:24–27; Luke 6:47–49) depicts the consequences of building on the wrong foundation. Whilst the parable is not explicitly about trust, but concerned with whether one chooses to act on the words of Christ, the inherent warning is not to trust in any party other than Christ. Therefore, a Christian interpreter of the OANs (including Jer 48) looks beyond the OT to the NT where Christ's words are the foundation for trust.

The rabbis taught that the nations only had to keep a few basic moral laws, whereas Israel had to keep the whole Torah. "Therefore, they argued, there was no advantage to becoming a Jew and there was no point in encouraging converts."[41] However, the OANs, particularly verses like Jer 48:7, demonstrate that even without a law, nations are not exempt from punishment just as severe as Israel's even if they "only had to keep a few basic moral laws."

Moab's Sins in the Context of the Other OANs

Lundbom asserts that, "Reasons for divine judgment occur now and then in the Foreign Nation Oracles, but they are not common."[42] This is not quite the situation, however, for most nations are castigated somewhere in the prophets either for arrogance and pride (Egypt, Philistia, Moab, Ammon, Edom, Babylon, Tyre, and Assyria), misplaced trust (Egypt, Moab, Ammon, Babylon, the valley of vision,[43] Assyria, Lebanon, and seemingly Kedar and Hazor), or for sins against Israel / Judah (Egypt, Philistia, Moab, Ammon, Edom, Damascus, Babylon, and Tyre and

---

41. Cohn-Sherbok, *Judaism*, 28.
42. Lundbom, *Jeremiah 37–52*, 255.
43. Although the valley of vision (Isa 22) probably refers to Jerusalem (e.g., Watts, *Isaiah 1–39*, 337), it is included here since it is contained in what is generally regarded as the main body of Isaiah's OANs, i.e., chapters 13–23.

Sidon). See Table 7 and Table 8 for the references for each of these. Indeed, these three offences are the most frequently cited in the OANs.

Just a couple of notes to explain the tables:

1. Nations that are not accused of any sins are not included in Table 7 and Table 8, e.g., Elam in both tables, Sidon (as its own entry) in Table 7, and Kedar and Hazor, Valley of Vision, Assyria, and Lebanon in Table 8.

2. If *italicized*: sin is *implied*.

Strangely, idolatry is not often listed as one of the reasons; so Jer 50:38 and the possible allusion to Moab's idolatry in Jer 48:35 are unusual in this respect. Nonetheless, Moab's main offences are those that are common to the foreign nations. For, apart from trusting in her own deeds and treasures (v. 7) Moab's offences are that: she had been at ease since her youth (v. 11); relied on Chemosh (v. 13); magnified herself against YHWH (vv. 26, 42); mocked Israel (v. 27); and was proud (vv. 29–30). בדים in verse 30 may also indicate boasting and the reference to sacrificing on high places in verse 35 may imply that Moab is judged for idolatry. In addition to these specific reasons, verse 44 reveals that Moab's destruction was punishment and verses 21 and 47 that it was משפט.

The book of Jeremiah does not always provide a reason for a nation's catastrophe (see the oracles concerning Philistia, Damascus, and Elam). Sometimes it alludes to a nation's wrongdoing or refers to it in general terms, such as YHWH's יום נקמה "day of vengeance" upon Egypt when he would avenge (נקם) himself on her (46:10—see also 46:21, 25), or what seems (particularly given Jer 48:11) to be an implicit condemnation of Kedar and Hazor's ease (שלו) and security (49:31) (בטח). At other times nations are accused, like Moab, of specific sins. That is: Ammon is indicted for mistreating Judah (49:1–2), boasting (49:4)[44] and trusting in her treasures (49:4); Edom is accused of losing her wisdom (49:7) and being arrogant (49:16); and Babylon is blamed for mistreating and oppressing Israel (50:7, 17, 33; 51:24), sinning against YHWH (50:14, 24), wronging others (50:15, 29, 49), arrogance (50:31, 32, 44), idolatry (50:38) and being abundant in treasures (51:13). Although it

---

44. The Hebrew uses the Hithpael of הלל for boasting in Jer 49:4; this is different from the possible allusion to Moab's boasting (בדים) in Jer 48:30 and Isa 16:6.

TABLE 7: Nations' Sins in the OANs Other than Those against Israel/Judah

	Arrogance/ Pride/Boasting	General unrighteousness	Misplaced Trust
Ammon	Jer 49:4; Zeph 2:8, 10	Amos 1:13	Jer 49:4
Assyria	Isa 10:12, 13–14, 15, 33; Zeph 2:15	Nah 1:15; 3:19	
Babylon	Isa 13:11, 19; 47:7, 8, 10; Jer 50:29, 31, 32, *44*		*Isa 47:8, 10*
Damascus		Amos 1:3	
Earth (Isa) / General (Joel) / Jerusalem's enemies (Zechariah)			
Edom / Mount Seir	Jer 49:16, *19*; Ezek 35:10; Obad 3	Amos 1:11	
Egypt	Isa 20:5; Ezek 29:3, 9; 30:6, 18; 31:10, 14; 32:2, 12	Ezek 32:2	Isa 20:6
Kedar and Hazor			*Jer 49:31*
Lebanon	*Zech 11:2–3*		
Moab	Isa 16:6; 25:11, 12; Jer 48:29, 30; Zeph 2:8, 10	Amos 2:1	Jer 48:7, 13
Philistia	Zech 9:6	Amos 1:6	
Tyre (+ Sidon and Philistia in Joel)	Isa 23:9; Ezek 27:3; 28:2, 5, 6, 17	Ezek 28:15; Amos 1:9	
Valley of vision[45]			Isa 22:8

---

45. See footnote 43.

	Wronging/Slaying others (not Israel at least, not specifically Israel)	Sin against YHWH (usually arrogance)	Violence, Anger, Envy, Hatred	Foolishness
Ammon				
Assyria	Nah 2:12; 3:4	Nah 1:11	Nah 3:1	
Babylon	Isa 14:5–6; Jer 25:14; 50:15, 29; 51:7, 49;	Jer 50:14, 24		
Damascus				
Earth (Isa) / General (Joel) / Jerusalem's enemies (Zechariah)	Isa 24:16	Zeph 1:17		
Edom / Mount Seir		Ezek 35:13	Ezek 35:6, 11; Amos 1:11	Jer 49:7
Egypt				Isa 19:11, 13
Kedar and Hazor				
Lebanon				
Moab	Amos 2:1	Jer 48:26, 42		
Philistia	Amos 1:6; Zech 9:7			
Tyre (+ Sidon and Philistia in Joel)			Ezek 28:16; (Jonah 3:19—in context of Judah)	Ezek 28:17
Valley of vision*				

	Having amassed wealth	Idolatry	Scorning temple
Ammon			Ezek 25:3
Assyria	Nah 3:16	Nah 1:15	
Babylon	Jer 51:13	Jer 50:38	*Jer 51:51*
Damascus			
Earth (Isa) / General (Joel) / Jerusalem's enemies (Zechariah)			
Edom / Mount Seir			
Egypt			
Kedar and Hazor			
Lebanon			
Moab		*Jer 48:35*	
Philistia			
Tyre (+ Sidon and Philistia in Joel)	Zech 9:3		
Valley of vision			

	Wronging own country	Astrology	Transgressing laws, covenant	Not celebrating feast
Ammon				
Assyria				
Babylon	Isa 14:20	Isa 47:12–13		
Damascus				
Earth (Isa) / General (Joel) / Jerusalem's enemies (Zechariah)			Isa 24:5	Zech 14:17–18
Edom / Mount Seir				
Egypt				
Kedar and Hazor				
Lebanon				
Moab				
Philistia				
Tyre (+ Sidon and Philistia in Joel)	Ezek 26:17			
Valley of vision				

TABLE 8: Nations' Sins in the OANs against Israel / Judah

	Possessing land of Judah	Oppressing / Doing violence to / Taking captive / Selling / Plundering Israelites	Taking vengeance on Judah	Delivering Israel to sword	Not showing mercy to / helping Israel	Being unreliable allies of Israel	Mocking / Scorning Judah / Rejoicing at her downfall	Thinking Judah is like all the nations
Ammon	Jer 49:1-2	Amos 1:13					Ezek 25:3, 6; Zeph 2:8, 10	
Babylon		Isa 14:2; Jer 50:7, 17, 33; 51:24			Isa 47:6			
Damascus		Amos 1:3						
Earth (Isa) / General (Joel) / Jerusalem's enemies (Zechariah)		Jonah 3:3; Zech 14:12						
Edom / Mount Seir		Amos 1:11; Obad 10, 13–14	Ezek 25:12	Ezek 35:5	Amos 1:11; Obad 11		Ezek 35:15; Obad 12–13	
Egypt						Ezek 29:6–7		
Moab					(cf. Deut 23:4)		Jer 48:27; Zeph 2:8, 10	Ezek 25:8
Philistia		Zech 9:8	Ezek 25:15	Amos 1:6?				
Sidon							Ezek 28:24, 26	
Tyre (+ Sidon and Philistia in Joel)		Jonah 3:5, 6, 19		Amos 1:9	Amos 1:9		Ezek 26:2	

is not an indictment as such, in 51:51 Israel grieves that aliens have entered YHWH's holy place. Thus there is no standard pattern regarding whether the grounds for a nation's punishment are specified in Jeremiah or, if they are, how explicitly they are presented. This same variety exists generally in the OANs (for example, Isa 13–23, Ezek 25–32, Amos 1–2, Obad, and Nah).

It can be seen from the above that Babylon and Moab are accused in Jeremiah of having committed most of the common sins of all the other nations combined (both in Jeremiah—see Table 9 also—and the OT OANs in general) and thus stand out from the rest of the nations in terms of the extent of their wrongdoing as well as in respect to their predicament being a result of YHWH's משפט (see chapter 6). If commentators are correct that Babylon should be treated separately from the other nations then it could be argued that Moab stands as a "model" OAN in chapters 46–49 and Babylon stands on its own at the end. Babylon is also conspicuous in Isaiah in terms of the number of indictments given (Isa 13:11, 19; 14:2, 5–6, 20; 47:6, 7, 8, 10), as in Ezekiel are Tyre (Ezek 26:2, 17; 27:3; 28:2, 5, 6, 16, 17), Mount Seir (Ezek 35:5, 6, 11, 13, 15), and Egypt (Ezek 29:3, 6–7, 9, 16; 30:6, 18; 31:10, 14; 32:2, 12). As well, as Table 9 shows, Jer 48 incorporates most of the sins of which Moab herself is accused elsewhere in the OT OANs (pride, arrogance, oppression of Israel/Judah, setting herself up against YHWH) and in this respect provides a comprehensive summary of the rest.

The reasons for Moab's destruction are interspersed throughout the oracle, although the centre of the chapter (48:26–30) contains the core of them. Similarly, the explanations in Jeremiah's other OANs for a nation's catastrophe tend to be scattered over the oracle rather than appearing all together in one place. In fact, apart from Amos, there is no set formula where the reasons appear in the OANs in other prophetic books though, like Jeremiah, they tend to occur at intervals throughout the oracle except at the end. Although some prophets do display a preference for a certain structure, this is not universally applied. For instance Ezekiel begins some oracles with an indictment of a specific offence (25:3, 8, 12, 15; 26:2) and ends some of these (as Jer 48 does) with a general reminder that their predicament is due to YHWH's שפטים "judgments," נקמה "vengeance," or תוכחות "reproofs" (25:11, 14, 17).

In summary, then, Jeremiah's oracle against Moab is typical (as are Jeremiah's OANs in general) of other OT OANs in several ways. First, Moab is accused of sins that are common to the OANs. Secondly, the oracle appears in a collection where some oracles provide a rationale for the calamities and some do not. Thirdly, the reasons tend to be individually introduced at intervals as the oracle progresses. Fourthly, as seen, its use of משפט is not unusual, particularly in the way that the oracle ends with a reference to it.

At the same time, it is an oracle that contains more condemnations than most. Indeed, of all the prophetic passages that speak against Moab, Jeremiah's oracle contains the most reasons for her judgment. So, then, Jer 48 is not only comprehensive in terms of the scope of the places cited, but also with regard to the reasons provided for Moab's judgment. Hence, in this respect, it would seem that Moab may function as an example OAN for Jer 46–49 (as it seems Babylon does in Isaiah and Tyre, Edom, and Egypt do in Ezekiel).

Sword (v. 10)

The rhetoric of the first few verses of Jer 48 finds its climax in verse 10 with the harsh curse, as has been discussed at length in chapter 6. As the text stands now, if verse 9 is a call to help Moab, then verse 10 is a striking reversal and thus this first section of the oracle concludes with a surprise. This is not the only part of the oracle to end this way, for, as has already been pointed out, the entire chapter ends on a startlingly positive note for Moab.

Summary

Perhaps the most striking element to come out of these verses is the rhetoric employed to portray the seriousness of the words of the Lord of hosts, the God of Israel, upon Moab. That this is a communication specifically between YHWH and Moab is indicated by the superscription in which these two actors are named. The first word of the oracle, הוי, sets the tone: Moab's time is up. The amount of place names and the repeated references to מואב make it clear that Moab's destruction extends across all her land and the ominous, even macabre, word plays on the place names (for example, Madmen and blood) is a further way of

TABLE 9: Reasons for Moab's Judgment in Jeremiah 48 Found Elsewhere in OANs

Jeremiah's Reasons for Moab's Judgment (48)	Other Nations Accused of the Same Sin in Jer 46–51	Moab Accused of the Same Sin in Other Prophetic Books
Trusting in treasures	Ammon	
Being at ease	Kedar and Hazor	
Confidence in her god / idolatry	Babylon	
Making herself great against YHWH	Babylon	(cf. Ps 83:6)
Boasting	Ammon	Isa 16:6
Taunting / mocking Israel / Judah	Ammon, Babylon	Ezek 25:8; Zeph 2:8, 10
Pride / arrogance	Edom, Babylon	Isa 16:6; 25:11–12; Zeph 2:8, 10

linking Moab inextricably with destruction. The various terms used to denote her devastation emphasize the inevitability and intensity of the catastrophe and the reference to Chemosh's exile show that it affects all aspects of Moabite society. That Moab is addressed in the second person (common to the OANs) brings an immediacy to the oracle, as does the second person address to other parties. Swapping between audiences and switching between literary styles (description, threat, lament, summons to help, curse) results in swift scene changes that draw the hearer / reader into the chaotic situation. A variety of vivid metaphors increase this effect, as does the change in agent and means of punishment. It is apparent that Jer 48 does not so much tell a sequential story as paint a picture. Therefore a reading of the chapter may best be represented as a film rather than as text (see Codas 1 and 2).

The reasons for Moab's judgment are typical of those given in other OT OANs, though Jer 48 contains more than the average. In verse 7 she is punished for misplaced trust in her own deeds and treasures. This reading is enriched for the Christian by the parable of the rich fool, the rich man and Lazarus, the wise and foolish builders, and verses such as Jas 1:11. The NT spells out that the underlying foundation of confidence should be Christ and his words and that one should seek to store up treasures in heaven, not on earth.

Verses 11–13: Undisturbed Wine Tipped Out

One of the most interesting features about the wine metaphor in verses 11–13 is that it is split across poetry and prose, though modern English translations and commentators are not always agreed on which verses are which.[46] Kugel has famously drawn attention to the difficulty in distinguishing poetry from prose, and when, in conclusion to *The Idea of Biblical Poetry*, he avers that "the whole notion of biblical poetry is both right and wrong," one wonders that there is any consensus at all.[47] Since the mix does not detract from the metaphor as a whole or create a break in subject, it will not be discussed further here. That the metaphor is composed of both poetry and prose, however, does perhaps reflect the fluid way in which Jer 48 has been constructed.

In Jer 25, YHWH threatened that the nations would be forced to drink the cup of the wine of his wrath, an image that is used later in Jer 48. Wine imagery is utilized a number of times in Jer 48 and on each occasion Moab assumes a different metaphorical role in the viniculture process. Here, in verses 11–13 she is the wine, in verse 26 she is the one who will drink the wine of YHWH's wrath in keeping with chapter 25, whilst in verse 32–33 she is the wine producer. Whereas the winemaking process has been successfully completed in verses 11–13, by the time the oracle has passed the half way point, Moab's grapes are not even being harvested. This may indicate a progression in YHWH's judgment on Moab, perhaps even an intensification of it. At any rate, the recurrence of the wine metaphor is one method by which the theme of judgment runs through the oracle.

---

46. Those who consider verses 11–13 to be all poetry: NIV; Feinberg, *Jeremiah*, 302; Freedman, *Jeremiah*, 304–5; Miller, "Jeremiah," 887; Thompson, *Jeremiah*, 705. Those who deem verse 11 to be poetry and verses 12–13 as prose: NASB; NRSV; Jewish Study Bible; REB; Allen, *Jeremiah*, 474; Brueggemann, *Isaiah 40–66*, 444–45; Carroll, *Jeremiah*, 785; Clements, *Jeremiah*, 252; Lundbom, *Jeremiah 37–52*, 263; McKane, *Jeremiah, vol. 2*, 1168; McKeating, *Jeremiah*, 204. Those who see only verse 13 as prose: Holladay, *Jeremiah, vol. 2*, 342, 346; Rudolph, *Jeremiah*, 276, 280; Smothers in Keown et al., *Jeremiah 26–52*, 304, 315; Volz, *Studien*, 309; Volz, *Der Prophet Jeremia*, 406; Weiser, *Der Prophet Jeremia*, 406. NEB has only verse 12 as prose.

47. Kugel, *Idea*, 286.

If the first ten verses do act as a kind of introductory summary to the chapter, then it makes sense that they are written in plainer language and that once the scene has been set, more pictorial forms can be used. YHWH (described in the first person for the first time in verse 12) is the one to cause Moab to be poured out. YHWH as the one who controls Moab's fate is in contrast to Chemosh and Bethel in verse 13 and their impotence highlights YHWH's omnipotence (though this is not the language of the Hebrew text).

Moab's Ease (v. 11)

Verse 11 does not accuse Moab of any obvious misdemeanor, but the ease in which Moab dwells. This key concern is emphasized by a piling up of terms, which is characteristic of Jeremiah. In fact her undisturbed state is described in six different ways: Moab has been at ease (שאן); undisturbed on his dregs (שקט . . . אל־שמריו); not been emptied (לא־הורק); not gone into exile (בגולה לא הלך); and thus retains his flavor (עמד טעמו); and his aroma has not changed (ריחו לא נמר). It would seem here, at least, that Moab's ease is the sole reason why YHWH will send his cohort to tip him over, empty his vessels and shatter his[48] jars.[49]

Most commentators use either "complacent" or "complacency" at some point in their exegesis of this verse.[50] This is possibly because, like Holladay, they consider that the phrase ושקט הוא אל־שמריו "(and) undisturbed on his dregs" is proverbial for complacency.[51] Certainly, complacency would cohere with the theme of Moab's pride that seems to run through the chapter, such as her self-confidence in verse 7 and smug certainty of her own ability in war in verse 14. Alternatively, commentators may have been influenced by a common understanding of

---

48. The MT has "their" rather than "his" at this point.
49. See also Carroll, *Jeremiah*, 784–85; McKane, *Jeremiah*, vol. 2, 1167.
50. Brueggemann, *Jeremiah*, 444; Clements, *Jeremiah*, 253; Fretheim, *Jeremiah*, 599; Holladay, *Jeremiah*, vol. 2, 358; Jones, *Jeremiah*, 499, 503, 504; Kidner, *Message*, 142; Lundbom, *Jeremiah 37–52*, 266; McKeating, *Jeremiah*, 205; Miller, "Jeremiah," 891; Smothers in Keown et al., *Jeremiah 26–52*, 314; Stulman, *Jeremiah*, 362; Sweeney, "Jeremiah," 1021; Thompson, *Jeremiah*, 705. Duhm, Rudolph, and Volz do not speak about verse 11 in terms of complacency, but Weiser (*Der Prophet Jeremia*, 406) uses the word "selbstsicher" (self-confident, self-reliant).
51. Holladay, *Jeremiah*, vol. 2, 358.

הקפאים על־שמריהם in Zeph 1:12, as "the people who rest complacently on their dregs" and read one text in the light of the other.

There is a strong rhetorical element in verse 11 for it exaggerates Moab's undisturbed history according to the rest of the OT. For instance, David subjugated Moab during his reign (2 Sam 8:2), and Ahab exacted annual tribute from her (2 Kgs 1:1; 3:4–5). Even Jer 48 itself reuses a song (found in Num 21:28–29) concerning Moab's change of ownership (48:45–46). In other words, even before Israel had seriously started to settle in Canaan, Israel's tradition portrays Heshbon as having been tipped from vessel to vessel.[52] So then, the only part of Jer 48:11 that really can be said about Moab is that she was not taken into exile. In fact, though some commentators assert or imply that Moab had had an untroubled existence,[53] most understand the claims of 48:11 to mean merely that Moab had been spared exile (or, with Lundbom, that she had had peace for a while).[54]

That exile is not solely envisaged in Jer 48:11, however, is hinted at by the use of שאן and שקט. For, whilst Miller notes that "being at ease" is ambiguous in its meaning,[55] שאן (a word employed only in the prophetic literature of the OT) means being quiet, without anxiety, secure, at rest; a sense that the dictionaries ascribe to its use in Jer 48:11.[56] In other words, it seems clear that the rhetoric of verse 11 gives "an idyllic and unreal description in view of the troubled history of all the small nations during the Assyrian period," to use Carroll's words.[57] Such a skewed perspective is typical of anger, jealousy, or resentment and thus

---

52. This coheres with the account of history given by Maxwell Miller ("Moab," 883), including Moab's own tradition according to the Moabite stone.

53. Calvin, *Jeremiah*, 15–16; Jones, *Jeremiah*, 503; McKane, *Jeremiah*, vol. 2, 1166–67; Stulman, *Jeremiah*, 362.

54. Brueggemann, *Jeremiah*, 445; Duhm, *Jeremia*, 347; Feinberg, *Jeremiah*, 303; Freedman, *Jeremiah*, 304; Fretheim, *Jeremiah*, 599; Lundbom, *Jeremiah 37–52*, 265; Smothers in Keown et al., *Jeremiah 26–52*, 314; Rudolph, *Jeremiah*, 279; Sweeney, "Jeremiah," 1021; Thompson, *Jeremiah*, 705; Weiser, *Der Prophet Jeremia*, 406.

55. Miller, "Jeremiah," 891.

56. BDB 983; Ludwig and Baumgartner, "שאן," 1375; Oswalt, "שאן," 10; Thiel, "שאן;שַׁאֲנָן," 265. The adjectival form, שאנן, tends to be defined in dictionaries as "carefree self-confidence" or describing "illusionary security" (Ludwig and Baumgartner, "שאן," 1375; Thiel, "שאן;שַׁאֲנָן," 265, 267) or even "careless, wanton, arrogant" (BDB 983). Ludwig and Baumgartner translate it "carefree" in Zech 1:15 and "self-confident" in Ps 123:4.

57. Carroll, *Jeremiah*, 784.

the unrealistic description of Moab in verse 11 may hint at YHWH's anger. Might it be that YHWH cannot bear to look on wicked nations still at ease when his punishment of Israel and Judah has involved totally uprooting them and sending them into exile?

Zech 1:14–15 is a text that "attests to a divine announcement that the Lord is jealous for Jerusalem and Zion and very angry with the nations 'that are at ease' (שאנן). They made the disaster of the Lord's anger against Jerusalem even worse."[58] Though there is no mention of YHWH's anger in Jer 48:11, in Zech 1:15 it is explicit: וקצף גדול אני קצף "(and) I am greatly angry *with* anger," as is the link to Israel and Judah. Most Zechariah commentators consider that YHWH's anger stems from the nations overstepping the limits of their divine commission to punish Israel.[59]

Ps 123:4 may further illumine Zech 1:15 and Jer 48:11 (and 48:27) when it attributes the "scoffing" (לעג) of YHWH's people to השאננים "those who are at ease." A final text worth noting is Ezek 16:49 in which Sodom is described as guilty because she had exaltation (גאון),[60] abundant food, and lived in quiet ease (ושלות השקט) yet did not help the poor and needy. This demonstrates that responsibility towards the poor was not only the rubric of Israel/Judah. Given the OT's concern for the poor and needy, the implicit assumption behind Jer 48:11 might be that Moab did not share her wealth appropriately.

Chemosh and Bethel Shamed (v. 13)

Israel is only mentioned by name three times in Jer 48: in verses 1, 13, and 27. The first instance seems almost incidental, for it is in an appellation of YHWH; אלהי ישראל. However, this designation assumes a greater significance in the light of verse 13, for here, despite 48:1 having explicitly stated that YHWH is Israel's God, we learn that Israel has placed her confidence elsewhere. One implication of verse 13 seems to be that YHWH was not the object of Israel's shame and that her exile

---

58. Miller, "Jeremiah," 891.

59. Jones, *Haggai*, 60; Mitchell, et al., *Haggai*, 126; Thomas in Thomas and Speers, "Zechariah," 1062; Zvi, "Zechariah," 1251.

60. Though NRSV and other versions translate גאון "pride," in this context it seems to be better translated by "exaltation" since the other descriptions in the list (abundant food and ease) are not necessarily negative qualities.

was not due to his failure to protect her. Instead, the inference is that YHWH himself was the cause of Israel's predicament. Pre-empting such possible objections to YHWH's potency paves the way for the declaration of his sovereignty in verse 15.

In verse 1, Israel's God shamed Moab, which, presumably, evoked in Moab a sense of shame concerning herself. In verse 13, the shame is turned outwards towards the deity who has failed her. The message of verse 7 with its indictment about false trust resounds in this verse and similar points could be made. Verse 13 also makes explicit Chemosh's impotence, whereas this is only implied in verse 7. The presentation of misplaced trust in verse 13 is also more subtly nuanced for whilst trust in self and hubris might be part of what Fretheim calls "natural law," trust in one's deity is less obviously an offence. The same cannot be said of Israel, for she had trusted in a deity other than her own, a sin she had been repeatedly warned against (including on the tablets of stone). Therefore, whilst Moab's predicament is placed in parallel with Israel's in verse 13, and Chemosh and Bethel are both shamed, Moab's and Israel's offences are somewhat different.

Furthermore, whilst verse 13 might appear to be an equalizer between Moab and Judah because it juxtaposes their shame of Chemosh and Bethel, verse 27 disabuses one of such an idea. Israel may have been ashamed of Bethel, but she is not to be made a laughingstock by Moab. In this third and final reference to Israel in the chapter, it is plain that YHWH is still Israel's God as announced in verse 1 and that he has not ceased to look after her interests, despite sending her into exile.

Summary

In summary, then, the wine metaphor in Jer 48:11–13 is especially ominous given the threat in Jer 25. It seems clear that Jer 48:11 is primarily concerned with what it sees as Moab's ease. This is indicated by the piling up of terms used to emphasize this undisturbed state and the exaggerated account of Moab's history in language that implies peaceful security. Moab's undisturbed condition might have disturbed YHWH because of jealousy for Israel, but it seems that at least in part it is due to Moab's complacency. The intertextual resonance in Zech 1:15 affirms that the nations at ease made YHWH angry whilst that of Ps 123:4 implies that this might have been because they scoffed at Israel. Ezek 16:49 might also suggest that Moab was irresponsible with her wealth.

Although Jer 48:13 places Israel and Judah side by side in their shame due to their misplaced trust, verses 1 and 27 are indicators that YHWH is still Israel's God and will avenge her. Verse 27 will be discussed more fully in the next section. There is also an implicit claim in verse 13 that Israel's exile was at YHWH's behest, and not because YHWH had been conquered by a more powerful deity. Such a clarification opens the way for verse 15's declaration of YHWH's sovereignty.

Verses 14–28: The King Commands

The section begins with a rhetorical question asking Moab how she can say she is strong and ready for battle (v. 14) when the strongest of them has been destroyed (v. 15). The words of destruction are given immediate force by the fact they issue from the mouth of המלך יהוה צבאות שמו "the King whose name is YHWH of hosts" (v. 15) and, as some point out, YHWH's power is in contrast to Moab's.[61] Stulman notes that in verse 15, the first become last and that this inversion of categories recurs throughout the chapter.[62]

Then, as Carroll observes, the imminence of Moab's distress is made plain by the words of verse 16, קרוב איד־מואב לבוא ורעתו מהרה מאד "The calamity of Moab is coming near, And his distress hastens exceedingly." This imminence is further reinforced by the style of the verses that follow (vv. 17–20), that is, the imperatives given to Moab and her neighbors regarding how they are to respond to the disaster. For, as discussed above, the constant swapping between addressees and referring to Moab in the third and second person brings an immediacy and urgency to the text, as Volz recognizes, as well. Yet verses 14–28 increase the intensity since here the text not only moves between addressing Moab's neighbors (v. 17), Moab herself (vv. 14, 18–19, 27–28), and Moab's enemies (v. 26), but it also piles imperatives one on another: נֻדוּ . . . אִמְרוּ "Mourn . . . Say" (v. 17),[63] וּשְׁבִי . . . רְדִי "Come down . . . and sit" (v. 18), עִמְדִי וְצַפִּי

---

61. Brueggemann, *Isaiah 40–66*, 447; Calvin, *Jeremiah*, 21; Lundbom, *Jeremiah 37–52*, 272; Miller, "Jeremiah," 891–92.

62. Stulman, *Jeremiah*, 363.

63. Qere quoted: Ketib is יֹשְׁבֵי.

"Stand and keep watch" (v. 19), אִמְרִי[65] . . . שַׁאֲלִי[64] "Ask . . . say" (v. 19), הֵילִילוּ וּזְעָקוּ הַגִּידוּ "Howl and cry out, Declare" (v. 20), הַשְׁכִּירֻהוּ "Make him drunk" (v. 26), וְהָיָה . . . וְשִׁכְנוּ . . . עִזְבוּ "Leave . . . and dwell . . . and be" (v. 28).[66]

Verses 21–24 explicitly describe Moab's predicament as משפט "judgment" and highlight the extensive nature of the damage to be inflicted by citing the places affected. The loss of Moab's power is reiterated in verse 25 by the breaking of her horn and arm. This verse is an ironic reminder that whereas Moab had thought herself strong and powerful (v. 14), nothing could be further from the truth. This theme of pride coming before a fall runs through the Old and New Testaments, from Israel (Prov 16:18) and Moab (Jer 48:14–15, 25) to the church (1 Cor 10:12). All these passages paint a rather metaphorical picture of pride leading to shame, so it is less a matter of Christians doing a figural reading of Jer 48:14–15, 25 at this point and more that these verses give a vivid depiction of the metaphor in 1 Cor 10:12.

It appears that disrobing Moab of her power is not enough, for verse 26 commands her enemies (presumably) to make her drunk so that she will roll in her vomit and become a laughingstock. The reference to making Moab drunk in 48:26 is undoubtedly part of the motif about making the nations drink of the cup of wine of YHWH's wrath in Jer 25. This motif is an enduring theme that is picked up again in Rev 14 (in relation to Babylon). It occurs in the oracles concerning Edom (49:12) and Babylon (51:39, 57), though only Moab is made to vomit (Babylon sleeps forever and the oracle concerning Edom does not divulge particulars) in keeping with 25:27. Moreover, not only does Moab vomit, but she ספק "claps" in her vomit, though ספק is a strange word in its context.[67] Nevertheless, the picture is vivid (as it is throughout Jer 48) and if verses 14–24 are intense with regard to the extent and the imminence of Moab's destruction, the portrayal of Moab's shame here in verse 26 is equally forceful.

---

64. Qere quoted: Ketib is הֵילִילִי.
65. Qere quoted: Ketib is וּזְעָקִי.
66. See also Volz, *Der Prophet Jeremia*, 411; Carroll, *Jeremiah*, 785.
67. Carroll, *Jeremiah*, 787; Lundbom, *Jeremiah 37–52*, 283; McKane, *Jeremiah*, vol. 2, 1179.

Making Herself Great against YHWH (vv. 26, 42)

Whilst 48:26 at least presents us with a tangible wrongdoing of Moab's, once again this is a verse that tells only half a story. First, it does not explain in what way על־יהוה הגדיל "(s)he made herself great against YHWH" (see also 48:42). Secondly, as chapter 4 noted, Brueggemann points out:

> The indictment, on the face of it, is more than a little curious, because Moab would not have imagined itself in any way in relation to YHWH. The text, however, never reflects upon or explains why Moab should be responsive or submissive to YHWH. The text simply assumes this to be the case, and further assumes that Moab should know about this definitional relation. That Yahwistic claim, which is foundational to all these "Oracles against the Nations," is a daring act of rhetoric which insists upon connections where others do not notice or acknowledge them. Moab's failure is a failure to come to terms with the rule of YHWH, a rule which is the driving power of this poetry.[68]

Whilst Brueggemann is surely correct that the daring rhetoric insists that Moab is also under YHWH's rule, Jeremiah's language need not imply that Moab should know about this relationship. There may not have been any intentionality behind Moab's behavior, but she is nevertheless accountable.

Although verse 26 does not explain what it means by Moab making herself great against YHWH, verse 27 continues with the pointed remark, ואם לוא השחק היה לך ישראל "Now surely Israel was a laughingstock to you."[69] Thus, it seems, Moab's mockery of Israel might be associated with making herself great against YHWH. That is, by exalting herself over Judah, Moab exalts herself over YHWH.[70] In fact, sin

---

68. Brueggemann, *Jeremiah*, 446.

69. This verse "has caused much difficulty for translators" (Lundbom, *Jeremiah 37–52*, 284) and Lundbom's rather unique translation will be discussed in due course. For the rest, the problems lie mainly in how to make sense of the verse, whether one translates אם לוא as an asseverative or an interrogative and whether ה is to be translated as the definite article or an interrogative. However, Holladay (*Jeremiah, vol. 2*, 360) argues that there is little difference in meaning whether one translates it, "Surely for you Israel has become a laughingstock" or as a rhetorical question, "Has Israel *not* been for you a laughingstock?" (emphasis mine).

70. Allen, *Jeremiah*, 482; Brueggemann, *Jeremiah*, 447; Calvin, *Jeremiah*, 29–30, 47; Carroll, *Jeremiah*, 788; Fretheim, *Jeremiah*, 601; Lundbom, *Jeremiah 37–52*, 283, 305;

against Israel/Judah is the sin in both verses in the Targum, for verse 26 accuses Moab of [71] על עמא דיוי אתררבו "making himself great against the people of YHWH." The Targum may be harmonizing its translation with Zeph 2:10. For Zeph 2:8–10 is a short oracle against Moab and Ammon that threatens to punish them for reproaching/taunting (חרף) Israel, for their גאון "pride," and because ויגדלו על־עם יהוה צבאות "(and) they made themselves great against the people of YHWH of hosts." Whether or not Targum harmonizes the texts, Zeph 2:8–10 may itself be a clue that pride against YHWH's people is pride against himself, for in both this text and Jer 48:27, Moab is condemned for taunting Israel. Zeph 2:8–10 also brings the whole into the context of Moab's and Ammon's גאון, an explicit reference to the pride that is implied by על־יהוה הגדיל in Jer 48:26.

In fact, it is hubris that Carroll thinks is the root of the accusation in verse 42, a verse that also accuses Moab of על־יהוה הגדיל.[72] In the immediate context of verse 42 there is no equivalent verse to 27 and therefore no further illumining of what exaltation against YHWH might entail. Therefore, as Miller asserts, "The clues must be taken from the earlier context."[73] That is, despite the fact that verse 42 may well have been the original one and verse 26 the copy, in the final form of the canon, verse 42 seems to act as a reference back to verses 26–27.

If arrogance against YHWH is to be equated with arrogance against Israel, then verse 26 is perhaps a less "daring act of rhetoric" than Brueggemann supposes, for Moab could have "known better" than to shame another nation by making it a laughingstock and should have been responsive to Israel, if not YHWH. Even so, it is still daring for the text to elevate this offence to the level of a sin against YHWH, which is largely Brueggemann's point. For, as in verse 7, the consequences of Moab's sin in 48:27 turn out to be bigger than she might have imagined.

McKeating, *Jeremiah*, 206; Miller, "Jeremiah," 892; Rudolph, *Jeremiah*, 281; Smothers in Keown, et al., *Jeremiah 26–52*, 317; Sweeney, "Jeremiah," 1024; Weiser, *Der Prophet Jeremia*, 407–8.

71. Sperber, *Bible in Aramaic*, 244 (Qere version).

72. Carroll, *Jeremiah*, 795.

73. Miller, "Jeremiah," 891.

Caught among Thieves (v. 27)

As normally translated, the rhetorical question in verse 27, אִם־בַּגַּנָּבִים נִמְצָא, expects the answer, "No, Israel was not caught amongst thieves."[74] However, not only does the text dare to imply that Israel is undeserving of Moab's mockery, but the metaphor used to describe her "innocent" status is that used elsewhere in the book to denote her guilt (though it is possible that the text refers to a time other than 721 BCE). In 2:26 she is described as a thief and in 2:34 she is accused of treating others as robbers. It may simply be that the two texts are making different rhetorical points in the way that Deut 7:7 and 10:22 do. For Israel is described as a small nation in Deut 7:7 in order to demonstrate that her election was YHWH's initiative, whereas in Deut 10:22 she is described as a large nation as demonstration of fulfillment of the Abrahamic promise.

On the other hand, the reuse of this metaphor in 48:27 may be to indicate that Israel's guilt before YHWH does not mean that she is guilty before Moab (also see the above remarks on verse 13). If this is the case then it is almost a reverse of what has just been discussed (that Moab's guilt before Israel is guilt before YHWH). In this way, then, these two verses seem to invert what Moab's common perception might have been. Her own offences are portrayed as worse than she had probably anticipated, whilst the sins of the other (Israel) suddenly become non-existent, at least as far as Moab is concerned. Commentators do not point out this inversion, although they note Israel's innocence and / or the inappropriateness of Moab's mockery of her.[75]

Lundbom's approach is distinct from that of most because it relies on a translation of verse 27 that addresses Israel, not Moab (I can find no version that translates the text in a similar way);[76]

וְאִם לוֹא הַשְּׂחֹק הָיָה לְךָ יִשְׂרָאֵל	Then surely the joke is for you, Israel,
אִם־בַּגַּנָּבִים נִמְצָא	if among thieves he has been found.

---

74. Whether translated as a rhetorical question or strong indicative (see footnote 69), the sense is the same.

75. Calvin, *Jeremiah*, 30; Carroll, *Jeremiah*, 789.

76. ASV, AV, ESV, Geneva Bible, JPS, NAB, NASB, NEB, REB, NET, NIV, New Jerusalem Bible, New Living Translation, (RSV and) NRSV, Holladay, McKane, Smothers and Freedman.

כי־מדי דבריך בו תתנודד	For more than all your words against him, you will shake your head![77]

Lundbom explains that this translation can make sense if אם לוא is translated "surely," the ה as a definite article ("the joke") and not an interrogative, ישראל is taken as a vocative, and the second אם has the usual meaning of "if." He argues that his translation is more logical than the usual rendition since "It makes little sense to ask if Israel has been caught among thieves, because it has (cf. 2:26, 34)."[78]

However, there are two linguistic considerations to be noted, one of which would tend away from Lundbom's proposal and the other which would support it. The first is the presence of היה, for if Lundbom is correct that the present tense is intended, then one would expect no verb to represent "to be." Secondly, Lundbom accepts the Qere נמצא "he has been found," whereas the Ketiv reads נמצאה "she has been found." The masculine form, נמצא, coheres with the masculine pronouns for Moab used in verse 26 and would therefore suggest the same party. However, there are no other positive comments directed towards Israel, nor is she addressed elsewhere in the oracle. Thus, there are no precedents in the chapter to lend support to Lundbom's translation. Therefore, whilst not dismissing Lundbom's alternative translation, I would tentatively accept the translation of the consensus.

Summary

In summary, then, the pace quickens and the intensity deepens in verses 14–28 in terms of the multiple voices and moods, in the graphic metaphors, and by means of the word קרוב "near at hand" in verse 16. This intensity is increased with the imperatives that follow from verse 17. Moreover, Moab's predicament is a result of (YHWH's) judgment. YHWH's משפט is explicit in verse 21 and implicit in verses 26–27 where there appears to be an allusion to YHWH's cup of wrath. Moab's pride has resulted in her shameful fall, a lesson that is easily transferable to a Christian setting, particularly as the NT itself contains warnings of

---

77. Lundbom, *Jeremiah 37–52*, 282.
78. Ibid., 284.

such. The rhetoric of verses 26–27 seems to invert the way Moab would likely have seen her own sins and those of Israel.

Verses 29–39: Pride, Lament, Destruction

Pride (vv. 29–30)

Verse 29 reads, שמענו גאון־מואב גאה מאד גבהו וגאונו וגאותו ורם לבו, which the NRSV translates "We have heard of the pride of Moab—he is very proud—of his loftiness, his pride, and his arrogance, and the haughtiness of his heart." In this short verse of ten words, eight are words or phrases that describe Moab's pride: גאון "pride"; גאה מאד "exceedingly proud"; גבה "haughtiness"; גאון "pride"; גאוה "pride"; and רם לב "haughtiness of heart." Verse 30 adds another two words that depict Moab's problem: עברה and בד. There is debate over the translation of both words, but with McKane and the majority, I accept עברה as "arrogance" and בדים as "boasting" as fitting the context.[79] Who the "we" are in verse 29 is also open to debate,[80] but I would be inclined to view it as including YHWH, given that the "I" in the next verse denotes him.

It is not surprising, given the eight ways in which Moab's pride is described in verses 29–30, that the next verse begins על־כן, for surely she will "therefore" be punished in some way. Such expectation does not account for Jeremiah's daring acts of rhetoric, however, and instead of a torrent of threats, YHWH's tears stream down the next few verses. Such surprises are perhaps characteristic of YHWH.

The first person singular in verse 30 is explicitly designated as YHWH and from verse 31 he suddenly becomes the focus, eclipsing Moab's pride with his grief:

---

79. For a discussion on this see: Allen, *Jeremiah*, 482; Calvin, *Jeremiah*, 33, 34; Carroll, *Jeremiah*, 789; Duhm, *Jeremia*, 350; Feinberg, *Jeremiah*, 304; Freedman, *Jeremiah*, 308; Fretheim, *Jeremiah*, 601; Holladay, *Jeremiah*, vol. 2, 343; Jones, *Jeremiah*, 505; Lundbom, *Jeremiah 37-52*, 286; McKane, *Jeremiah*, vol. 2, 1183; Rudolph, *Jeremiah*, 280; Smothers in Keown et al., *Jeremiah 26-52*, 305; Sweeney, "Jeremiah," 1022; Thompson, *Jeremiah*, 709; Volz, *Der Prophet Jeremia*, 407; Weiser, *Der Prophet Jeremia*, 401.

80. For a discussion on this see: Calvin, *Jeremiah*, 32; Feinberg, *Jeremiah*, 305; Freedman, *Jeremiah*, 308; Fretheim, *Jeremiah*, 601; Holladay, *Jeremiah*, vol. 2, 352; Kidner, *Message*, 142; McKane, *Jeremiah*, vol. 2, 1182; Lundbom, *Jeremiah 37-52*, 288; Rudolph, *Jeremiah*, 282; Thompson, *Jeremiah*, 710; Volz, *Der Prophet Jeremia*, 407; Weiser, *Der Prophet Jeremia*, 408.

אייליל "I will howl" (v. 31);

אזעק "I will cry out" (v. 31);

יהגה "he will moan," though most translations accept the variant reading, אהגה "I will moan" (v. 31);

אבכה "I will weep" (v. 32);

לבי . . . יהמה "my heart moans" (v. 36); and, again,

לבי . . . יהמה "my heart moans" (v. 36).

Nevertheless, despite the twist in the על־כן of verse 31, verses 32–36 inform us that Moab's pride will be punished. Commentators of Jer 48 appear to have little to say regarding the significance of על־כן "upon ground of such conditions/therefore" that begins 48:31, which is surprising given that it is such a departure from the tone of the preceding verses. The situation in Isa 16:7 is slightly simpler since it is Moab who mourns and commentators generally understand her pride to have led to her fall and "therefore" she mourns.[81]

I would suggest that verses 29–38 form the climax of the oracle for three main reasons. First, nowhere else in the chapter is there such a diatribe of Moab. Secondly, this is the only place where YHWH pours out his grief over Moab. That one follows from the other creates acute tension at this point. Thirdly, the sharp change in focus from Moab to YHWH creates a turning point in the chapter. Before this point, there has only been one reference to YHWH in the first person: ושלחתי־לו "(and) I will send to him" (48:12) those who will tip him over. From verse 31, however, there are ten (if one accepts the variant reading in verse 31); in addition to his expressions of mourning (see above) there are:

ויין מיקבים השבתי "(and) I have stopped the wine from the presses" (48:33);

והשבתי למואב "(and) I will make an end of Moab" (48:35);

שברתי את־מואב "I have broken Moab" (48:38); and

אביא אליה אל־מואב שנת פקדתם "I will bring to her, to Moab, the year of their punishment / visitation" (48:44).

---

81. E.g., Goldingay, *Isaiah*, 111; Gray, *Isaiah I–XXVII*, 291; Wildberger, *Isaiah 13–27*, 146.

As Fretheim points out, in these verses "God hears and knows (vv. 29–30); God laments (vv. 31–32, 36), and God judges (vv. 33, 35, 38)."[82] Moab's arrogance (עברה) and pretentious idle talk (בדים) have indeed come to nothing (לא־כן). Not only is Moab destroyed, but even the rhetoric itself gives her less space as Moab's pride gives way to YHWH's moaning heart and his judgment.

Lament (vv. 31–36)

The verses in 48:31–36 are perhaps the most poignant of the whole chapter and, as stated, the only ones in which YHWH himself is said specifically to mourn over Moab. Interestingly, in the Targum, YHWH has been removed altogether from the weeping and the wailing of 48:31–36 and, instead, it is Moab herself that is said to mourn. Similarly, in LXX, YHWH's involvement is drastically reduced in these verses; only in 31:32 (a different text to MT in a number of ways) is the weeping attributed to the first person (YHWH)—see chapter 2 for a fuller discussion on LXX. Turning back to MT, however, it is worth considering whether the lament is genuine or ironic.

Genuine or Ironic Lament

The question over the genuineness of the lament arises because of the incongruity of mourning in the midst of such a harsh oracle of judgment. In addition, in the literary context, the lament is sung before the death of Moab, which might indicate that it is intended as a taunt. If the lament is intended in mockery, then it retains the harshness of the oracles; if the grief is genuine and also sincere (the two are not necessarily synonymous, as will be discussed), then mourning becomes the predominant tone, since it pervades the whole of the oracles. However, it seems to me that Jer 48 is not intended as a mocking taunt for the following reasons.

First, Isa 14:3–21 is an explicit example of a taunt over a foreign nation (Babylon) but Jer 48 is not comparable to it. Tucker similarly points out regarding Isa 15–16 that "It lacks the marks of a taunting or ironic poem seen in the taunt song over the king of Babylon (14:3–21)."[83]

82. Fretheim, *Jeremiah*, 601.
83. Tucker, "Isaiah," 167–68 (quote on p. 167).

Tucker does not elucidate what these markers might be, but his commentary on 14:3–21 suggests that the main marker is the use of משל to describe the oracle. For, as Eissfeldt argues, משל is the name for a mocking saying as well as a proverb.[84] Jer 48 does not use משל. Another marker in Isa 14:3–21 is that it ironically uses איך "how," characteristic of funeral dirges.[85] This brings me to my second point.

איך is characteristic of laments, yet when it is used in the prophets (apart from as an interrogative) it is employed more often in sarcastic mockery, usually in the context of OANs. That is: "How the oppressor has ceased" (Isa 14:4), "How you are cut down to the ground" (14:12), or in Jeremiah in the context of Moab as a laughingstock, "How shattered it is! . . . How Moab has turned his back" (48:39); see also Jer 49:25; 50:23 (twice); 51:41 (twice); possibly Ezek 26:17 if it is a mock dirge; Obad 1:6; Mic 2:4 (the only time it is used against Israel); and Zeph 2:15.[86] Given that איך is so appropriate in the context of taunts against foreign nations and that it is used this way elsewhere in Jer 48, its absence in the lament parts of Jer 48 might indicate that they are not taunts.

Thirdly, if the author is mocking Moab and her grief, then describing in detail the depth and extent of her mourning does not seem to be the best way to convey it. For surely mockery requires a certain amount of distancing from the mocked in order to be effective, whilst depictions of weeping are more appropriate in a text that invites sympathy. Indeed, although mock funeral dirges often ape genuine laments in the way that they compare the former greatness that existed before death with the current state at death,[87] they tend not to express sorrow or pain (ironic or otherwise) to the same extent. For instance, of the mocking dirges listed by Eissfeldt, Isa 14:3–21 and Ezek 28 do not contain any such sentiments and Isa 32 only commands the women to mourn (32:11–12). Ezek 27 is the sole one to communicate bitter wailing and even then it is only in three verses towards the end (vv. 30–32). On the other hand, all those Eissfeldt lists as genuine laments (2 Sam 1:17–27; 3:32–35; Jer 9; Lam 1; 2; 4; Amos 5) do convey sadness and grief. Thus if expression

---

84. Eissfeldt, *OT*, 66, 93.

85. Tucker, "Isaiah," 158. See also Eissfeldt, *OT*, 94, 95; Wildberger, *Isaiah 1–12*, 50, 56.

86. The instances where it is not used in this way are Jer 3:19 (though it is used ironically here), 9:18(19), and Obad 1:5.

87. Eissfeldt, *OT*, 95–96.

of grief is an indicator of genuine mourning or mockery, it is likely that Jer 48 is a legitimate lament.

Fourthly, I cannot find examples where mourning attributed to YHWH, as it is in Jer 48, is meant as insincere or in mockery. Fifthly and finally, there is a lack of scholarly support for understanding the laments as mocking.[88] Nevertheless, Brian Jones in his book *Howling Over Moab* argues strongly that the lament in Isa 15–16 is meant ironically and many of his observations and arguments are relevant to this study. Therefore, whilst it is not possible here to rehearse all his arguments, the following is a disputation of his salient points.

Response to Brian Jones

Jones observes that the OANs frequently use the "sarcastic imperative," for example, Flee! Turn aside! Hide! Go down and mourn! Sit in the dust![89] However, the OANs also use such imperatives for Judah in ways that do not indicate sarcasm. There are three, possibly four, such examples in Jer 50–51, none of which are generally taken to be ironic by commentators. Perhaps the most obvious is the call to the Judahites in 51:6 נסו מתוך בבל ומלטו איש נפשו אל־תדמו בעונה "Flee from the midst of Babylon and escape each with his life; do not be silenced in her punishment"; 51:45 says similarly; see also 51:50, and possibly 50:8.[90] Jones

---

88. Allen, *Jeremiah*, 485; Brueggemann, *Jeremiah*, 443, 448, 449 (though he thinks v. 17 is mockery—p. 445); Calvin, *Jeremiah*, 9, 35–36, 41–44 (though he thinks vv. 17 and 20 were not intended to evoke sympathy—pp. 22–23, 26—and that the prophet gives voice to Moab's feelings rather than his own in these verses); Carroll, *Jeremiah*, 785, 792–93, 796; Clements, *Jeremiah*, 1, 254–55; Duhm, *Jeremia*, 348, 350; Feinberg, *Jeremiah*, 301, 305–6; Freedman, 309–11, and implied in 306; Fretheim, *Jeremiah*, 595, 597, 600–605; Holladay, *Jeremiah*, vol. 2, 349–53, 355, 361; Jones, *Jeremiah*, 499, 501, 504; Kidner, *Message*, 142; Lundbom, *Jeremiah 37–52*, 253, 256, 277, 289, 290–91, 295, 299, 301 (though Lundbom is unsure whether the weeping in vv. 31–32 is genuine); McKane, *Jeremiah*, vol. 2, 1178, 1186, 1191 (though he sees the lament in vv. 31–32 as incongruous—p. 1186—and v. 17 as gloating—p. 1174); McKeating, *Jeremiah*, 206–7; Miller, "Jeremiah," 890–91; Rudolph, *Jeremiah*, 280–81; Smothers in Keown et al., *Jeremiah 26–52*, 308, 319 (though he sees v. 17 as a taunt and vv. 31–32 as a means of announcing judgment rather than expressing sorrow); Stulman, *Jeremiah*, 362, 364; Thompson, *Jeremiah*, 712; Volz, *Der Prophet Jeremia*, 387, 389, 410, 413; Weiser, *Der Prophet Jeremia*, 404–5, 408–9.

89. Jones, *Howling*, 127.

90. Allen, *Jeremiah*, 513, 530; Brueggemann, *Jeremiah*, 466, 474, 480–81; Carroll, *Jeremiah*, 823–24, 842, 850; Clements, *Jeremiah*, 260; Feinberg, *Jeremiah*, 317, 329;

does not explain why imperatives to the nations should be considered sarcastic whilst those to Judah should not be.

Part of Jones' understanding of Isaiah 15–16's laments as satirical is based on the assumption that Jer 48 is unmistakably ironic.[91] This is despite the fact that "Admittedly, the prophets present no obvious examples of ironic first-person expressions of sympathy, while straightforward, first-person expressions of sympathy do occasionally occur."[92] However, since it seems far from clear that Jer 48:31–32 is ironic, his premises are questionable.[93]

Furthermore he claims that "All the foreign nations are, with but a few exceptions, portrayed negatively in the HB. Moab, however, is cast in an *exceptionally* negative light, as will be apparent in the following survey of those texts in the HB that mention Moab."[94] He continues:

> Ruth alone among all the texts in the HB has been construed as presenting Moab, or at least the Moabite woman Ruth, in a positive light. Such an interpretation of the story probably misses the point, however. Part of the narrative tension in Ruth derives from the danger involved in Elimelech's family seeking refuge in Moab during a famine and the even greater threat presented when Elimelech's two sons marry Orpah and Ruth, Moabite women. These dangerous decisions bear fruit when not only Elimelech, but also his two sons, die in the land of Moab. Moreover, the narrator subtly calls to mind the Moabite primal scene of origin (Gen 19) in his account of Ruth lying down by the drunken Boaz on the threshing floor (Ruth 3). Quite probably the story assumes and plays upon the contempt the Israelites felt toward the Moabites. At the very least, the story presents a complex picture, as difficult to interpret as it is intriguing. It does not, however, give any solid evidence of a positive attitude

---

Freedman, *Jeremiah*, 327, 337, 346–47; Fretheim, *Jeremiah*, 624, 634, 643; Holladay, *Jeremiah*, vol. 2, 416, 422, 430; Jones, *Jeremiah*, 528, 536, 544; Lundbom, *Jeremiah 37–52*, 439, 480 (though Lundbom thinks 50:8 has an ironic slant—p. 382—and 51:50 is a command to hurry into exile—p. 487); McKane, *Jeremiah*, vol. 2, 1258, 1299, 1340, and implied in 1335; McKeating, *Jeremiah*, 215, 222–23; Miller, "Jeremiah," 914–15; Smothers in Keown et al., *Jeremiah 26–52*, 365, 369, 371–72; Stulman, *Jeremiah*, 381; Thompson, *Jeremiah*, 734, 750, 765, 767.

91. Jones, *Howling*, 130.
92. Ibid., 134.
93. See footnote 88.
94. Jones, *Howling*, 137.

toward Moab and in no way suggests that amicable relations existed between the nations at the time it was written.[95]

Jones' position is an unusual one and slightly skewed for he ignores the praise given to Ruth by the Israelite characters in the text itself: Boaz in 2:11–12 and 3:10, and the women in 4:15.

As well, when David is fleeing from King Saul and it is presumably no longer safe for his parents to live in Israel, it is the king of Moab who shelters them (1 Sam 22:1–4). Yet again, Jones does not draw out the positive light in which the king of Moab is portrayed; rather he proposes that David's later harsh treatment (2 Sam 8:2) was a deuteronomistic attempt to counter this favorable account in 1 Sam 22 (as well as that in Ruth 4:18–22).[96]

He points out that Moab is derisively portrayed by means of sexual and/or scatological imagery in at least four instances: the story of Ehud; that of Lot and his daughters; Isa 25:10–12, and Jer 48:26.[97] This is a valuable observation and Moab's "beginnings" may explain why the prophets later used such imagery. However, these passages persuade Jones that the tone of the oracle is one of hatred throughout, whereas this is not necessarily the case.

He proposes that: "If we are to place ourselves among the poem's original audience (in so far as this is possible), we must be ready to hate the Moabites, to wish them destroyed, to rejoice and gloat over their misfortune. Then we shall be suitably prepared to catch the poet's meaning in the confession, 'My bowels growl like a lyre for Moab' (16:11)."[98]

However, one could argue that the reverse is true: if we are ready to hate the Moabites and wish them destroyed, to rejoice and gloat over their misfortune then we shall be suitably ill-prepared for the poet's confession of lament. In fact, such reversal of expectations is common in the Bible.

Jones considers that "'I drench with my tears Heshbon and Elealah,' paints a ridiculous picture" in 16:9a (cf. Jer 48:32) for the verb used, רוה, indicates complete saturation.[99] However an alternative way of look-

---

95. Ibid., 151–52.
96. Ibid., 148.
97. Ibid., 154.
98. Ibid., 161.
99. Ibid., 268–69.

ing at it is to see the larger than life language as being for emphasis. Similarly, whilst Jer 48 does not employ רוח, it piles up five different verbs in 48:31–36 (ילל "to howl," זעק "to cry, cry out, call," הגה "to moan, growl, utter, speak," בכה "to weep, bewail," המה "to murmur, growl, roar"). As stated above, most commentators of Jer 48 do not take these verses to be intended ironically.[100]

All in all, then, I am not persuaded by Jones that the lamentation over Moab in Isa 15–16 (and Jer 48) is satirical. It is at this point that my reading strategy determines that if laments are not ironic, then they are likely to be heart-felt. This would particularly seem so when the lament is uttered by YHWH, for my reading strategy is to read with the grain of the text as best as this can be discerned. As well, the text, written about Israelites for Israelites, is composed sympathetically. This is demonstrated by the psalms of lament, whether community laments (for example, Pss 44, 60, 74, 79, 80, 83, 85, 137) or individual ones (for example, Pss 6, 22, 38, 39, 41, 42–43, 55, 59, 64, 69, 70, 77, 86, 88, 102, 109, 140, 142, 143), which have been revered for millennia and used liturgically as sincere utterances. Though Moab, not Israel, is the object of lament in Jer 48, it seems unlikely that expressions of grief are used as purely stylistic devices when they are not elsewhere. This view is in contrast to McKane who asserts of Jer 48, "Lament is ancillary to oracle [*sic*] in vv. 29–39 and its presence does not show that YHWH's compassion is awakened or his grief engaged but only that a disaster of great dimensions is to engulf Moab."[101] At the same time, bringing the lament into the realms of the divine may well be another way to portray the comprehensive nature and depth of Moab's destruction.

Idolatry? (v. 35)

Jer 48:35 reads: והשבתי למואב נאם־יהוה מעלה[102] במה ומקטיר לאלהיו "And I will cause Moab to cease, declares YHWH; *the* one offering *sacrifices on* a high place and making sacrifices to his gods." Before analyzing the question of idolatry in this verse, it is worth noting a textual point: שבת is used in conjunction with ל. This is an unusual construction and as far

---

100. See footnote 88.
101. McKane, *Jeremiah, vol. 2*, clxvi.
102. The lack of the definite article on מעלה is puzzling and may be due to haplography (see Rudolph in BHS).

as I can see, the only other occurrence where this occurs is in Ruth 4:14 where the people say to Naomi that YHWH has not left her without (שבת ל) a kinsman-redeemer (context suggests that probably the next of kin is implied). It is ironic that in Ruth 4, a Moabite is one half of a relationship that YHWH uses not to leave Naomi without offspring whilst in Jer 48 he causes Moab herself to cease.

The reference to Moab's worship of her gods in Jer 48:35 is confusing in that it is not clear whether the text wishes to convey Moab's idolatry as a cause of YHWH's punishment (and therefore an indictment of Moab at this point) or whether the termination of her worship forms part of the penalty for other sins, including the aforementioned pride in verses 29–30. It is also questionable whether idolatry is even the correct terminology to use in relation to the OANs; certainly the concept of idolatry does not play a major role in them. At this point, it is worth briefly defining idolatry.

Barton explains that "Worshipping gods other than YHWH, and using images in worship, are essentially two different phenomena, not merely two different aspects of the same aberration."[103] In other words he separates the command in Exod 20:3 (and Deut 5:7) from that in Exod 20:4–6 (cf. Deut 5:8–10). When considering the possibility of "idolatry" in Jer 48, the question relates to the first phenomenon; was Moab condemned for worshipping a god other than YHWH? Moberly points out that the OT distinguishes between אלהים and יהוה in that only Israel is expected to worship יהוה whereas everyone is expected to acknowledge and fear אלהים. The latter is worked out by means of exercising moral restraint, such as refusing to take advantage of a weaker party.[104] According to Provan, taking advantage of a weaker party would constitute idolatry since "Idolatry, then, is more than merely the practice of a certain type of ritualistic religion. It is a matter of the whole orientation of a person's (or nation's) being, as it impinges on social, economic, and political life."[105] However, as Schultz notes, Provan's definition of idolatry is broad and thus the term becomes less useful and all sin could be labeled idolatry.[106]

---

103. Barton, "Work of Human Hands," 64.

104. Moberly, *Bible, Theology and Faith*, 92–94.

105. Provan, "To Highlight," 25.

106. Schultz, "Response to Provan," 40. At the same time, the OT in general paints a picture where right living follows from right worship and the reverse. Thus in a general way it could be said that idolatry is at the root of all wrongdoing.

Whatever its exact definition, Pharaoh does not get the attention of YHWH because of idolatry, but because YHWH hears the cries of his people under Pharaoh's oppression (Exod 2:23–25). Even when YHWH desires that Pharaoh/the Egyptians will know who YHWH is (Exod 7:5, 17; 8:10; 9:14, 29; 14:4, 18; see also 8:22), worship of other gods is not mentioned. YHWH's response to Hezekiah's prayer is also concerned with Assyria's treatment of Judah, not Sennacherib's misplaced worship (2 Kgs 19:21–28). Nebuchadnezzar is humbled at the point he boasts of building Babylon by his own strength (Dan 4:30) until he acknowledges it is the Most High who gives and takes away power (Dan 4:25; 5:34–36).

In fact, there seems to be only one verse in Jeremiah that implies that a nation is judged for worship of "idols," though whether this relates to worshipping gods other than YHWH or worshipping through images is not clear. This is 50:38 in the oracle concerning Babylon:

חרב אל־מימיה	A drought against her waters,
ויבשו	that they may be dried up!
כי ארץ פסלים היא	For it is a land of images,
ובאימים יתהללו	and they go mad over idols.

On the whole, the only times Jeremiah's OANs speak of a nation's gods are when they specify that the deities are punished or destroyed along with the people of the nation (46:25; 48:7; 49:3; 50:2; 51:18, 44, 47, and 52)—see also 10:15; 43:12–13.

There is more interest in Moab's deities than in some others in Jeremiah's OANs, for Chemosh is mentioned three times as well as there being a reference to Moab's gods in general. As previously stated some commentators do hold the opinion that Moab is condemned for her idolatry (particularly in v. 35), though they tend to be reserved in propounding their position.[107] Nevertheless, even in Jer 48 the focus tends

---

107. Calvin (*Jeremiah*, 40) is not reserved. Nor does he comment on the fact that idolatry is rarely condemned in the OANs, probably because idolatry is a common motif of Calvin's, which he draws out from many texts. Calvin is also working within a framework that is mainly concerned with giving a contemporary application, rather than conducting a historical exercise. Moreover, Calvin lacks religio-historical insights into ANE religion. Whilst he does not call it idolatry, Duhm ("Die Psalmen," 348) in his comments on 48:13, also ascribes Moab's decline as due to her "Heidentum" "heathenism." Those who are more reserved are: Brueggemann, *Jeremiah*, 449; Feinberg, *Jeremiah*, 305; Fretheim, *Jeremiah*, 602–3; Holladay, *Jeremiah*, vol. 2, 304.

to be on the conflict between YHWH and the people rather than their gods.¹⁰⁸ However, the rhetorical shaping of 48:35 serves to highlight the tension between the opposing deities, for the first person address and יהוה stand at the start of the verse whilst לאלהיו "to her gods" is placed at the end. That YHWH overpowers Chemosh is another way in which the attention shifts from Moab to YHWH at this point. Having concluded that idolatry is probably not a central concern in Jer 48, if one reads Jeremiah in a more developed/canonical context, that is, in the light of passages such as Isa 45–55, it becomes natural to read Moab's behavior as idolatrous. Thus more than one reading of the text is possible.

What Causes YHWH's Tears? (vv. 31–36)

Whether or not verse 35 is a reference to idolatry, one does not expect YHWH's deep felt sorrow over Moab to על־כן follow an allusion to Moab's worship of her gods any more than one supposes YHWH's tears will fall as a result of Moab's pride. As with the על־כן that begins verse 31, however, the commentaries do not have much to say on the על־כן between verses 35 and 36. It could be argued that in both verse 31 and 36 YHWH's weeping is because of the pathos/poignancy of the futility of Moab's actions. For 48:30 informs that Moab's idle boasts have accomplished nothing, whilst it becomes clear in Jer 48:37–38 that Moab's misdirected efforts in verse 35 extend to the whole population. In considering this futility, I am reminded of the conclusion to Jeremiah's OANs in 51:58b, ויגעו עמים בדי־ריק ולאמים בדי־אש ויעפו "So peoples toil only for emptiness and nations only for fire. And they are weary."

If the futility of Moab's actions is the issue in these verses, then על־כן in 36b can be seen to follow on from 35 in that both her worship and her acquisition of riches has been in vain. Then the sense of these verses becomes, "I will make an end of Moab (and therefore all she does is futile). Her sacrifices, though earnest are pointless. Therefore my heart wails over the futility. (I will make an end of Moab) and therefore all she has gained will perish." This reading makes more sense if the כי in the next clause (v. 37) is translated "though," that is, Moab has lost the abundance it produced

---

108. Feinberg, *Jeremiah*, 1; Fretheim, *Jeremiah*, 1; Holladay, *Jeremiah*, vol. 2, 352; Jones, *Jeremiah*, 1; Miller, "Jeremiah," 892; Volz, *Der Prophet Jeremia*, 406; and tentatively McKane, *Jeremiah*, vol. 2, 1168.

| כי כל־ראש קרחה | though every head (is) bald |
| וכל־זקן גרעה | and every beard has been shorn (lit. diminished) |

Although כי can be translated "though,"[109] an example being NRSV's and ESV's translation of Jer 50:11, no commentator or modern English translation appears to translate it "though" in Jer 48:37.[110] Nevertheless, translating כי as "though" maintains the theme of the futility of Moab's actions.

The response of the Moabites in verse 37 is similar to that of the Ninevites in Jonah who dress in sackcloth and fast (though there is no mention that the Moabites fast) and whose king sits in ashes (Jonah 3:5–6, 8—again, not present in Jer 48). In both cases the mourning/repentance extends to everyone. In Jonah this is conveyed by the narrative, which tells us that מגדולם ועד־קטנם "from the greatest of them to the least of them" (3:5), האדם והבהמה הבקר והצאן "the (hu)man, and the beast, the herd, and the flock" (3:7), and האדם והבהמה "the (hu)man and the beast" (3:8). In Jer 48, it is expressed by a repetition of כל and its variants: כל־ראש ... וכל־זקן ... כל־ידים ... כל־גגות ... כלה "every head ... and every beard ... all their hands ... all the roofs ... all of him" (48:37–38).

However, there is a big difference between the Ninevites and the Moabites. Though both react in a similar way and this reaction involves the whole of the country, the king of Assyria calls the Ninevites to call on God and turn from their wicked ways (Jonah 3:8), whereas the Moabites call on their own gods (at least metaphorically by way of sacrifices) and there is no mention of a turn from wickedness. Nineveh does turn from her evil ways and God relents, but Moab does not and so God continues with his plan.

Although the story of Jonah reveals that YHWH has compassion on Nineveh (Jonah 4:11) there is no indication (as far as I can see) that he mourns over other "foreign" nations.[111] YHWH/the prophet does not

---

109. BDB 471, though BDB states that כי is normally followed by an imperfect (rather than perfect) verb when translated "though," but in Jer 48:37aα, there is no verb and in 48:37aβ there is only a participle.

110. Including ESV, JPS, KJV, NASB, NET, NEB, REB, NIV, NLT, RSV, NRSV, JPS Tanakh.

111. In Isa 21:3, the prophet is in anguish over the "wilderness of the sea," but here

even mourn over Israel/Judah as much as one might imagine, though it is interesting that in Jer 13:17 he weeps over Judah's גוה "pride."[112] Why Moab in particular is singled out and given so much space in Jeremiah may always remain a puzzle. However, again, a canonical reading strategy might allow the reader to make links between texts in order to try to do justice to the canonical space given to Moab.

In the book of Ruth, the heroine is described as רות המואביה "Ruth the Moabite" five times and referred to as a Moabite or from Moab another five times. Contrary to Brian Jones' assertions, it seems that the text portrays her as an exemplary model; that she is a foreigner is all the more remarkable, therefore. Her role, effectively, is to rescue Elimelech's bloodline and his land (Naomi's inheritance). The book ends with the genealogy of Boaz's line from Perez to David. Joel Lohr has pointed out in his dissertation that Pharaoh's daughter, by saving Moses, saves the race of Israel (or at least is a catalyst for the Exodus).[113] Thus, Pharaoh's daughter stands at the start of Israel's life under YHWH as their sovereign. This stage is coming to an end by the time of Ruth's context and it is another foreign woman who emerges to provide the means for the next stage of Israel's history; that of Israel as a kingdom. As well as enabling Elimelech's blood-line to continue and, as a great-grandmother of David, providing the means for Israel's golden age, might she also in some way, as an exemplary representative of Moab, have provided YHWH with a favorable memory of Moab that could not easily be forgotten? It is also interesting that whilst YHWH does not weep over Egypt, she is offered restoration in the major oracles concerning her in Isaiah (19:21–25), Jeremiah (46:26), and Ezekiel (29:14–15).[114] Moab, on the other hand is only offered restoration here in Jer 48, despite the strong element of lament in both Isaiah and Jeremiah.

Moab is significant, too, for the fact that Moses died in the land of Moab (after seemingly communicating his last recorded words from there—Deut 33:1–34:1) and YHWH himself buried him in that

---

the context (21:3–4) suggests that it is the prophet himself, as distinguishable from God, who speaks in 21:6.

112. See also Isa 22:4, Jer 8:21; 9:1; and 14:17 for examples where God/the prophet mourns over בת־עמי "the daughter of my people" (Israel/Judah).

113. Lohr, "Chosen," 121–31.

114. In Isa 19 she will be as great as Israel and Assyria while in Ezekiel she can only hope to become a lowly kingdom. In Jeremiah the promise is to restore her as she was previously.

land (Deut 34:5–6). Laying Moab to waste disturbs the resting place of YHWH's servant Moses, אשר ידעו יהוה פנים אל־פנים "whom the Lord knew face to face" (Deut 34:10). In fact, Maxwell Miller writes, in his article on Moab in ABD, "The plains of Moab provide the setting for a considerable portion of the Genesis–Joshua narrative . . . from Numbers 21 through Joshua 3."[115] When reading Jer 48 against these other texts, YHWH's weeping and wailing over Moab perhaps seems less strange.

Jesus' Sorrow over Jerusalem

Nevertheless, if YHWH enters into such deep mourning over a recalcitrant foreign nation, it might indicate that he will mourn much more over his own people. Indeed, YHWH's mourning over Moab brings to mind Jesus' anguished cry over Jerusalem in Matt 23:37–39 (and the parallel in Luke 13:34–35) and although in the text Jesus is not said to mourn over the city, it is generally considered that he did; in fact the NIV's subtitle for Luke 13:31–35 is "Jesus' Sorrow for Jerusalem."

Jerusalem is portrayed as complacent and heedless (13:26–27) and therefore it did not receive Christ and his teaching. In actual fact, according to Christ, she killed the prophets and stoned others sent by God (13:34). Her complacency is reminiscent of Moab's undisturbed state like unopened wine and her pride akin to Moab's. In both cases, pride and complacency blinded them to their true state of vulnerability and need in the same way as the rich fool. In Luke 13:34, Jesus expresses his desire to gather the children of Jerusalem as a hen gathers her chicks, but Jerusalem would not have it. From the context it seems likely that Jerusalem would not have it partly because she did not see herself in terms of a defenseless little chick, but perhaps saw herself as strong in the way that Moab did (48:14). A Christian reading might ask whether the Church also sees herself in self-satisfied terms.

Jesus warns complacent Jerusalem that the first will be last and the last first (Luke 13:30), an idea that recurs in Luke. For example, those who exalt themselves and choose the esteemed seat at the wedding banquet will be humbled and vice versa in 14:7–11, as well as the parable in 16:19–31 in which the rich man goes to Hades whilst the poor man, Lazarus, is carried by angels to Abraham's bosom. Though these reversals are part of God's justice, they are sometimes meted out

---

115. Maxwell Miller, "Moab," 887.

with tears as Jer 48 and Luke 13 demonstrate. However, it is doubtful that when Judah heard the words uttered against Moab, she would have joined YHWH in weeping over her (see Jer 48:10). The history of the Church shows that, to her discredit, she has not shed many tears over Jerusalem. Jerusalem is an "other" to the Church as Moab was an "other" to Judah. A Christian reading might challenge these responses and seek to redress the balance and to show compassion for those who are outside of the Church.

Jesus' grief is not common in the NT, as YHWH's is not in the OT. When contemplating this and realizing that Jesus' sorrow is reserved for Jerusalem, YHWH's wailing over Moab is all the more remarkable. This is particularly so given that YHWH's weeping over Moab is described in much greater detail and given considerably more space than Jesus' sorrow over Jerusalem. A Christian reader might see in Jer 48 a reminder of the mystery that God's purpose includes Gentiles; see for example Rom 11:25.[116]

Broken and Shamed (vv. 37–38)

If YHWH weeps over Moab's destruction, Moab does so no less. Verse 38 tells the reader that there is lamentation everywhere in Moab because YHWH has broken her like a pot that no one wants. Moab is shattered, wails, and is ashamed of being a laughingstock. Since the beginning of the oracle, Moab has wept with shame over her destruction, but in these verses her lamentation and humiliation are magnified. Six words were used to describe her pride at the beginning of the section and now, at the end of it (v. 39), four expressions are used to depict her shame:

הפנה־ערף מואב	Moab has turned his back (of the neck)
בוש	he is ashamed
והיה מואב לשחק	And Moab has become a laughingstock
ולמחתה לכל־סביביו	And a horror to all those surrounding him

116. Dunn, *Romans 1–8*, 678.

Summary

Verses 29–39 therefore begin with Moab's pride and end with her shame. In between are YHWH's and Moab's tears and YHWH's lament over Moab acts as the pivot point for the chapter. For from this point, YHWH takes more of an active part in the oracle. I argued that idolatry is not the focus of verse 35 and suggested that it may be the futility of Moab's efforts that cause YHWH's weeping, which I also argued is heartfelt. At the same time, YHWH does not turn back from executing the punishment planned for Moab, perhaps because she has shown no repentance. His mourning over Moab is less puzzling if one takes a reading strategy that includes other texts in which Moab is significant. That is, Ruth the Moabitess was the great-grandmother of David and Moab was the resting place of Moses. It is no surprise that Moab weeps and is shamed over her fate and this section ends where the oracle started; Moab is trapped in a cycle of destruction, shame, and tears. A Christian reading might consider YHWH's weeping over Moab in the light of Jesus' weeping over Jerusalem; both Jerusalem and Moab were complacent and confident and both met their reversal to the accompaniment of divine tears. Heavenly weeping over nations is rare so Moab is privileged, particularly as a Gentile nation. Moab's downfall would likely have been good news for Judah, but a Christian reading might encourage a different response, for instance one of weeping. It might also wish to highlight the mystery that God's purposes extend to Gentiles.

Verses 40–47: Inevitable Destruction Plus Promise

In this last section of Jer 48, Moab is once again threatened with the destroyer (likened to an eagle in verse 40) and with inescapable punishment described in terms of the terror–pit–snare metaphor. שנת פקדתם "the year of their visitation / reckoning" (48:44) is "a vital motif of all these poems"[117] and a reminder that these verses are YHWH's punishment. The final verses of the oracle quote an old song, after which comes the promise of restoration.

---

117. Jones, *Jeremiah*, 506.

Echoes of Verses 1–10

Though commentators do not address it *per se*, this final part of the chapter reiterates many of the ideas in this first section, though much of the actual wording is different. As the oracle starts with a reference to the two main characters (YHWH and Moab), so it also ends with one: נאם־יהוה עד־הנה משפט מואב (v. 47).[118] The first word of the oracle itself is הוי "Alas" (v. 1) and the last words (before the final verse of restoration) begin with a similar word, אוי "Woe" (v. 46).[119] Calamity is planned in Heshbon in verse 2, whilst the outcome of previous such planning is sung in the taunt song in verse 45 (the song might even have been included in order that Heshbon be mentioned at the end). Moab and her cities are captured (לכד) in verses 1, 7, 41, 44, and 46 and exterminated (שמד) in verses 8 and 42, despite her strongholds, which are also referred to in both sections, though in verse 1 the word is משגב whilst in verse 41 it is מצד. In verse 2 Moab is cut off from being a nation (מגוי), whilst in verse 42 she is destroyed from being a people (מעם). In fact, verse 8 informs that no city will escape, whilst verses 43–44 make the same point by means of the metaphor of trap, pit, and snare. The Moabites are urged to flee (נוס) in verse 6, but warned in verse 44 that it is futile to do so. Both passages give a reason for her calamity; in verse 7 it is because she trusts in her own achievements and treasures and in verse 42 it is because of her arrogance towards YHWH. Chemosh makes an appearance in verse 46 as well as in verse 7. Arguably, there are mentions of flying in both passages, though in verse 9 Moab is called to fly away (נצא תצא) whilst in verse 40 it is her enemy who will fly swiftly (דאה). Thus there is a sense in which, by the end of the chapter, Moab has come full circle. She is trapped in the cycle of death and destruction—that is, until the final verse. YHWH is the only one who can break the cycle.

Jer 48:45–46 was discussed in chapter 2 in relation to LXX. In this chapter, the conclusion was that the taunt song from Num 21:28–29 acts as a rhetorical tool to intimate that what had happened to Moab would happen again. Given the above, it seems that this reading particularly fits with the tenor of this section of Jer 48 that appears to pay tribute to the perpetuation of the endless cycle of sin and destruction.

---

118. Lundbom, *Jeremiah 37–52*, 243.
119. Brueggemann (*Isaiah 40–66*, 451) also makes this observation.

Restoration (v. 47)

In the opening scenes of the book of Jeremiah, the prophet is depicted as a prophet to the nations (1:5, 10) לנתוש ולנתוץ ולהאביד ולהרוס לבנות ולנטוע "To pluck up and to pull down, And to destroy and to throw down, To build and to plant" (Jer 1:10). There are four verbs for tearing down and two for building up. This does at least pay literary tribute to the imbalance between the two ideas, for Jeremiah mainly tears down nations by delivering prophetic oracles of judgment to them. He is more positive towards Judah (notably chapters 31 and 33, particularly 31:27–28), but apart from the brief promises of restoration to four of the nine nations and the conditional promise of 12:14–17, he does not build them up.

There is no reason in the text itself why YHWH should choose to restore Moab. It might be for the same reasons as he weeps over her. However, could it be that the ultimate purpose that Fretheim considers to be behind the Exodus is also that of the OANs? "Generally for Exodus, God's liberation of Israel is the primary but not the ultimate focus of the divine activity. The deliverance of Israel is ultimately for the sake of the entire creation. The issue for God finally is not that God's name be made known in Israel; the scope of the divine purpose is creationwide, for all the earth is God's. God's purpose is to so lift up the divine name that it will come to the attention of all the peoples of the earth."[120]

Exodus makes clear that the hardening of Pharaoh's heart is in order that YHWH may multiply his signs and wonders in the land of Egypt (for example, Exod 7:3; 10:1; 11:9) so that וידעו מצרים כי־אני יהוה "(and) the Egyptians will know that I am YHWH" (Exod 7:5; 14:4, 18). Though in Isa 19:21 ונודע יהוה למצרים וידעו מצרים את־יהוה ביום ההוא "YHWH will make himself known to Egypt, and the Egyptians will know YHWH in that day," there is little in the OANs about "knowing" YHWH, particularly in Jeremiah's OANs. This includes Jer 25 (considered the introduction to chapters 46–51). In addition, although both Exodus and the OANs deal with foreign nations and portray YHWH's punishment of them, the OANs do not contain the "signs and wonders" that are part of YHWH's revelation of himself in Exodus. Therefore, if YHWH's ultimate purpose is to lift up his name in Jer 48:47 then it is subtle and at best implicit in a canonical reading. Moreover, it could be

---

120. Fretheim, "Plagues," 392.

said that in many texts God's purpose is ultimately to glorify himself, in a similar way that the OANs can be read against the backdrop of his universal sovereignty.

The final words of Jer 48, עד־הנה משפט מואב "Thus far the judgment of Moab" are generally considered to be an editorial comment to denote the end of the oracle, since "The sheer length of the oracle against Moab has constrained an editor to add a note indicating its termination."[121] However, there are some who see a theological purpose behind these words, though interestingly, there are two contrasting (but not contradictory) ways in which this can be viewed. Feinberg represents the first when he asserts that, "Finally, Jeremiah proclaims that God's judgment still hangs over Moab."[122] Brueggemann, Miller, and Kidner are proponents of the second in their claim that the promise of restoration demonstrates that judgment is not the last word for the nations, but rather that restoration is (as it is for Judah), and Kidner quotes Jas 2:13b "mercy triumphs over judgment."[123] Once again, a combination of the two would seem to do justice to the text, for although restoration is a reality, it belongs to the future, whereas the משפט is for Moab's present.

When MT and LXX Diverge

As noted in chapter 2, LXX does not have the equivalent of either the taunt song in MT's 48:45–46, or the final verse of restoration. How does one handle a verse that is included in one tradition but not another, especially if the more widely accepted version looks as if it is the addition, as verse 47 does here?

The pragmatic approach is to choose one and work with that one alone, acknowledging that there are variant traditions. If the intent of Scripture is, in part, to lead to a transformation of life, then the substantive issues remain much the same. For, in the main, the differences between MT and LXX are unlikely to transform lives in diverse ways.

---

121. Carroll, *Jeremiah*, 795; see also 797; Freedman, *Jeremiah*, 313; Fretheim, *Jeremiah*, 604; Holladay, *Jeremiah, vol. 2*, 345; Lundbom, *Jeremiah 37–52*, 311; McKane, *Jeremiah, vol. 2*, 1201.

122. Feinberg, *Jeremiah*, 307.

123. Brueggemann, *Jeremiah*, 451–52; Kidner, *Message*, 143; Jones, *Jeremiah*, 507; Miller, "Jeremiah," 893.

Jer 48:47 is not one of the more commonly read texts in any tradition, it seems, and its inclusion or exclusion would barely be noticed by most. Nevertheless, whilst the choice of canon is unlikely to be of much consequence to the overall life of faith, omissions and additions do nuance a particular passage.

So then, an alternative approach is to work primarily with one canon but consult the others and adjust the primary one accordingly. A variation of this is to refuse to adopt any particular textual tradition as a "canon" and to search for the Christian OT among the various traditions. This is Wagner's approach.[124] Wagner follows Childs when he suggests that the search for the Christian Bible should start with the outer perimeters of tradition, that is the more expansive Greek, and move in towards the Hebrew MT. Wagner also considers Childs' theological model of interpreting the OT can be applied to LXX. That is, hearing the voices of LXX and NT are heard as distinct, but complementary witnesses.[125]

In relation to Jer 48:47, one could search for the "best" witness perhaps based on a number of factors. For instance, by choosing the more original (probably LXX at this point), by deciding that the chapter with the broadest range of responses to Moab is most conducive to the verse (in which case MT would take priority), by taking as the norm the level of indictment in the OANs as a whole (where LXX would seem to be more in keeping), or by keeping to the general idea of the OT that God is good (in which case retaining the promise with MT would appear to be the better option). Yet, as complicated as this may sound, looking at the verse in the context of ever widening concentric circles is not enough.

The comparison of MT's Jer 48 with LXX 31 (in which the promise is absent) in chapter 2 showed varying nuances that stemmed in part from the placement of the oracle within the OANs and also the position of the OANs within the book as a whole. In other words, as one searches deeper for the "solution" to verse 47 (MT), more permutations and combinations emerge as contributory factors in the quest, until it becomes a question of which Jeremiah one chooses; LXX or MT. Jeremiah is the book most at variance between LXX and MT so is particularly susceptible to such unraveling. Moreover, there is a danger that searching for

124. Wagner, "Septuagint," 23–26.
125. Ibid., 23–25.

the best Christian witness becomes analogous to forming one gospel from the four. Therefore, I would suggest that LXX and MT are not to be dove-tailed into a distilled third but that they remain as two separate documents, drawing attention to the omissions/additions in the other. The verse of restoration in MT Jer 48 stands out precisely because of its absence in LXX, so the question becomes, What role does it play within the chapter?

Jer 48:47 is not simply MT's Judeo-Christian equivalent of the hope at the bottom of Pandora's box. It is a promise to a recalcitrant nation (whether or not she heard it) that YHWH will punish but that he will restore; one will follow the other. It is demonstration to Judah that YHWH's restoration is as plausible for the nations as it is for them. Similarly, from the perspective of the Church, it is demonstration that God is gracious to those who are not his people, though reading other OANs shows that grace is not a certainty. For the Church itself, the verse carries the promise of Easter Sunday.

Grace

In *Prophecy and Discernment,* Moberly discusses the conundrum of holding in tension passages in Jeremiah that speak about God's response to human transformation with those that assert that God will bring about restoration regardless of human actions. In the face of repentance meeting rebuff and restoration being offered as an act of complete grace, Moberly points out that, "We are faced by the fundamental issue of the relationship of divine sovereignty and initiative with human moral responsibility and accountability. Can one articulate the one without misrepresenting or downplaying the other?" His answer is that, whilst as a general rule, God is responsive to humans, there are occasions when God's freedom allows him to act outside this general maxim.[126]

His comments relate to a tension in the larger presentation of Jeremiah as a book, which is the reason for the excursus. Thus it may not be extrapolating too far to apply such reflections to Moab, particularly since, as noted above, the Moabites do not "repent" or confess their transgressions in the way that the Judahites do (though the Judahites themselves are not said to *shūv* in Jer 14:7–9, 19–22, passages where

---

126. Moberly, *Prophecy and Discernment,* 96–97.

they acknowledge their sins; משובות "apostasies" in 14:7 is the only time the root is used). Given that there is nothing to suggest that by the end of the oracle the Moabites have either turned to God or away from their wickedness, the promise of restoration demonstrates even more clearly the divine grace.

Summary

In this last section of the oracle, then, the emphasis seems to be on Moab's story repeating itself because it contains many of the same themes that were present in the first ten verses. In addition, the inclusion of the ancient song may also be intended to point to the cyclical nature of Moab's story, whilst the inevitability of Moab's plight is emphasized through the terror–pit–trap metaphor. If the purpose of the promise of restoration in 48:47 is to glorify God, then there are only whispers of it emanating from other parts of the canon. Instead, in restoring an unrepentant nation, YHWH's sovereignty and grace come to the fore. For a Christian, these themes meet at the Cross. The absence in LXX of this verse of restoration complicates the reading of MT, but I suggested that the two traditions are too different for a quest for the "best reading" to be fruitful. That is, the verse of restoration suits MT where the lack of it is fitting in LXX.

Reflections

Having analyzed the passage exegetically and given a suggested reading of it from a Christian perspective, a few reflective thoughts regarding a Christian appropriation of Jer 48 are in order. Some of these will arise out of reading the text analogically.

Response to Moab's Downfall

It is unlikely that Jer 48 functioned as a salvation oracle to Judah since Babylon was oppressing both these small countries, meaning that Moab was not strong enough to oppress others and Judah had her eyes on deliverance from a much greater enemy. Nevertheless, Judah may still have obtained hope from the fact that she was being avenged for having been made a laughingstock by Moab. For whatever the *Sitz im Leben*, as stated above, the downfall of an enemy was surely good news to Israel.

In the light of the NT and against the background of Jesus' exhortation to love one's enemies (Matt 5:44) the right Christian reaction to a similar scenario when misfortune befalls another party or an enemy might be (as also stated above) to show compassion for them rather than to gloat. The second half of Matt 5:44 might even indicate that intercession is the right response, though verses such as Jer 7:16 and Jer 15:1 indicate that intercession is not always what is required. Showing compassion for, or interceding on behalf of, others does not imply that their sin will not be judged. There may even be a place for desiring the downfall of one's enemies (Nazi Germany comes to mind), providing these desires are held in tension with the notion that judgment begins with the household of God (1 Pet 4:7).

Alternatively, a Christian reading might take a more figural route and see Moab as representing one's own sins, and therefore hope for its downfall and rejoice when it is conquered. The problem with this reading is that the last verse of restoration does not fit the analogy well. Such an analogy can therefore be made better from LXX, which does not have this promise, though the tone of lament lends itself to neither.

Substituting Moab

As we have seen Brueggemann asserts that "I intend that my analysis of YHWH and the nations should finally settle in the presence of the United States, which has no viable competitor for power."[127] In other words, when he reads the oracle concerning Moab he reads it with the U.S. in mind. Such a reading is in keeping with the Christian principle of taking the log out of one's own eye before looking for the speck in another's and the acknowledgment that judgment begins with the household of God (1 Pet 4:7). Brueggemann's stance may be commendable (and brave) in that he himself is from the U.S., but one of his reasons for using the U.S. as a substitute seems to be because it has no "viable competitor for power." If this is the premise then it becomes viable for anyone from any nation to read Jer 48 with the U.S. in mind. However, if a non-U.S. person reads in this way then they themselves are open to the charge of trying to take the speck out of another's eye and ignoring

127. Brueggemann, *Theology of the Old Testament*, 527.

the plank in their own. It would perhaps be more legitimate to do as Brueggemann does and turn the critique upon one's own people, even if they are a small nation with relatively little political power, for example, Sweden.

Calvin's solution is more nuanced than Brueggemann's and enables such a move to be made more easily. In his interpretation of Jer 50:40 where Babylon is likened to Sodom, he writes: "The destruction of Sodom is as it were a mirror in which we behold God's vengeance on all the ungodly. God overthrew Sodom; but he does not proceed in the same way with other lands and nations; yet the same is the lot of all the unbelieving, of the despisers of God, and reprobates."[128]

Calvin's concept of the mirror neither affirms that we can substitute Babylon with the nation of our choice, nor denies us that move. Rather, it allows us to view any nation against the reflection of any OAN and see which parts of the images overlap. In other words, we are not limited to the U.S. because it "has no viable competitor for power" nor to the OANs concerning Babylon and/or Assyria because these nations are the most notorious.

Furthermore, if the text is a mirror then it can be used not only for any nation, but for the Church (or any other group). Indeed, it is natural that a Christian reader, as part of the Church, reads Jer 48 as a critique of the Church rather than of a nation. This is a bold move in that God's people are equated with those who are not his people, yet the premise for doing so still lies with the idea of removing the plank from one's own eye. Trusting in treasures, relying on one's own accomplishments, mocking others (particularly God's people), arrogance before God, pride, and idolatry (if such it be in Jer 48) are generic offences that anyone may commit as an individual or as part of a larger community. The idea that a party cannot look at judgment towards others without first doing so with regard to itself is developed in the NT in a way that it is not in the OT.

Universality versus Israel's Uniqueness

Although commentators agree that Israel is peculiar among the nations, it seems that they are tempted to stress instead the similarities between Israel and "the rest." Kaminsky warns that, "one must provide a correc-

---

128. Calvin, *Jeremiah*, 183.

tive to the tendency to read the Bible through the lens of current popular notions of race, ethnicity, and multiculturalism when such readings lead to serious distortions of the biblical text, especially those that deal with the idea of election."[129]

That Israel is "special" among the nations is nowhere overturned in the OT. Even the shocking claim in Amos 9:7 starts fading by the next verse and has almost disappeared by 9:15 (the end of the book of Amos). Amos 9:7 consists of a rhetorical question, הלוא כבני כשיים אתם לי בני ישראל נאם־יהוה "'Are you not as the sons of the Cushites to me, sons of Israel?' declares YHWH." The implied answer is "yes" (after the immediate reaction of "No, of course not!"), for it transpires that YHWH has engineered exoduses for the Philistines and the Arameans. However, the prophet rather undermines his point by effectively saying over the next few verses, "Well, no not really—in fact you're not at all." For in the next verse YHWH declares that he will not completely destroy the house of Jacob and by verse 12 this house is possessing וכל־הגוים אשר־נקרא שמי עליהם "(and) all the nations who are called by my name." The last few verses are completely concerned with Israel's restoration (described in idyllic terms) and YHWH's last words in Amos, אדמתם אשר נתתי להם "their land which I gave to them," brings Israel full circle right back to their beginnings in Gen 12:1—YHWH's call to Abraham to go to the land that YHWH would show him. In other words, the prophet does not sustain the rhetoric that ignites Amos 9:7 and it fizzles out in a matter of verses. Despite the fact most commentators take this passage to demonstrate that YHWH's relationships with other nations are "just like" his one with Israel,[130] it seems to me that what Amos 9:7–15 actually demonstrates is that not even rhetoric can give credence for long to an implication that the other nations are on a par with Israel.

The nations are the "unchosen" virgin daughters (for example, Jer 48:18), too remote for a relationship that involves forsaking, but close enough for YHWH to have compassion on them. Ultimately, though, the precise nature of YHWH's involvement with Moab and the other nations is not given. Maybe this is how it should be; after all, these are Israel's Scriptures and the intimate details of YHWH's involvement with

---

129. Kaminsky, "Concept of Election," 35.

130. E.g., Anderson and Freedman, *Amos*, 863; Cripps, *Amos*, 264; Mays, *Amos*, 156–57, 159; Stuart, *Hosea–Jonah*, 393. Wolff (*Joel and Amos*, 347) is an exception.

the others are not necessary for Israel to know. Perhaps all they need to realize is that the nations are not outside YHWH's perimeters.

Moreover, as I have made clear throughout, the diversity of content and form in the OANs (for example, with regard to restoration) prohibits any sure way of calculating how God might act. Their consistent message is that God punishes wrong-doing, or at least, wrong-doing runs a high chance of being punished, but beyond this, there is an element to God's freedom that cannot be fathomed. Nevertheless, in the glimpse that the OANs give us into God's "hidden histories" (to use Brueggemann's term) with the other nations, we can see that in at least one case, his punishing has caused him pain.

Conclusion

When taken on its own terms in a sixth century context, Jer 48 is a passionate piece of writing, centered around a few themes; Moab's destruction, shame, pride, offences, punishment, lament, and impotence in the face of YHWH. For Christians, the comprehensive and intense way in which YHWH judges sin meets the mystery of his compassion at the foot of the Cross.

Having looked at the individual reasons for Moab's disaster in Jer 48, several themes stand out. First, the text often makes striking rhetorical moves: in verse 7 the consequences for misplaced trust are destruction of the nation's god; in verse 11 Moab is described as "at ease" despite her troubled history; in verse 26 mockery of Israel seems to be classed as making herself great against YHWH; verse 27 implies that Israel is innocent in terms that indict her in other parts of Jeremiah (2:26, 34); and following the condemnation of Moab's pride in verse 29–30, the על־כן of verse 31 introduces not only punishment, but also weeping. Secondly, the text often piles up language for emphasis, such as Moab's undisturbed state (v. 11) and her pride (vv. 29–30). Thirdly, the consequences of sin are more than Moab might expect, that is, misplaced trust leads to exile (v. 7) and mocking Israel is equated with exaltation against YHWH (vv. 26–27). Finally, the references to the שנת פקדתם "year of punishment" and משפט "judgment" express the inevitability and inescapability of the judgment, and the comprehensive and exhaustive nature of it. The language of destruction in Jer 48:1–5 is the same for Israel as for the nations, which perhaps points to the impartiality of which Rom 2:9–12 speaks.

Misplaced trust (Jer 48:7, 13) is a mode of behavior that is widespread and a number of biblical passages address it (for example, Luke 12). Pride coming before a fall (Jer 48:14–15, 25) is also a common sin and one that receives a warning in the NT (1 Cor 10:12). There are at least two possible ways in which a Christian interpreter can handle Moab's fall in Jer 48:26–27. The first is to respond with compassion to another who is under judgment (though in practice it is not possible to tell whether something is "judgment"). The second is to see Moab as representing one's sins and therefore to rejoice over its destruction. However, this seems a less viable interpretative option in a chapter that contains a verse of promise as well as resounds with the note of lament.

Jer 48 and the accounts of Jesus weeping over Jerusalem show that whilst the Deity's judgment turns pride and complacency into shame, he occasionally does so with tears. In fact, on both these occasions when he cries over a nation, it is in the context of judgment, seemingly demonstrating Fretheim's notion that the internal side of God's judgment is grief. Moab as a foreign nation is particularly privileged to be a recipient of the divine passion, a privilege that has deeper resonances in the light of the NT. If verses 31–36 figurally adumbrate Good Friday, then verse 47 carries with it the seeds of hope for Easter Sunday. This final verse of restoration is a witness that YHWH is gracious to those who are not his people, though grace is not to the exclusion of judgment.

There is more than one way to read Jer 48 as Christian Scripture, but one possibility is to read it as a critique of the Church; that is to use the text as a "mirror" to use Calvin's term. This would be in keeping with the idea in the NT that a party judges itself before judging others.

It is clear that not everything is spelled out in the chapter; we are not told why YHWH disapproved of Moab's ease, or what על־יהוה הגדיל means in concrete terms. It is not even clear how significant idolatry is in 48:35. However, this in itself may be an interpretative key, for there is a sense that the rhetoric delivers its blow and then moves on. If the shrapnel left behind causes consternation or angst then it is in keeping with the tone of Jer 48. There is also an element of mystery to YHWH's judgment; at times it is more severe than one might expect, but on other occasions, just when one might anticipate fire raining down on the head of Moab (cf. 48:45), YHWH's tears fall instead (though the two are then mingled). Thus, YHWH's justice and his compassion hold surprises.

Coda 1

Literary Storyboard of the Film of Jeremiah 48 (6th Century Context)

The rubrics are in italicized script. The viewer's description is in normal font.

[vv. 1–9] The film begins in silence and in black and white. A long camera shot shows what is obviously a devastated city. Smoke rises from crushed buildings and the crumbled ring of stones surrounding them shows that this had been a walled city.

The camera slowly moves in. Strewn everywhere are crushed and broken human and animal bodies. Already a light film of dust has begun to cover them. Some appear to have been victims of the falling buildings and lie trapped; others have been struck with the sword, with heads and limbs severed from the rest of their bodies.

The view quickly becomes a long shot again before the camera races across the screen in a blur to portray another scene similar to the first; then another and another. Demolished city after demolished city; all that remains of a country is rubble, dust, smoke and silent corpses.

The camera moves in once more on another shattered city. Then, for the first time, there is movement other than falling dust and rising smoke. There is also the first expression of color as well as sound. A three or four year old little girl in a scarlet tunic walks along, alone, sobbing.

The atmosphere is transformed: silence gives way to a burst of noise and there is accompanying activity. A bleeding woman screams hysterically as she holds two small limp bodies to her. The sound seems to frighten a small child nearby, for he immediately begins wailing, his head thrown back, a lone wolf cub howling to the moon. The pack responds and one by one the little ones begin crying out in pain and fear. Some of the women hold them in vain attempts at comfort. For others it is too late and soon there is the rhythmic chant of wailing and swaying as the women mourn their dead families.

A man walks into the picture, bare headed, wearing sackcloth and holding a bowl of ashes. He periodically takes a few ashes between his fingers and sprinkles them upon his head. He remains with his back to the camera throughout. A man in sackcloth touches a tall, anguished Moabite on his arm and says clearly and with some compassion, "Flee, save yourselves. Survive against the odds, just as juniper trees do in the wilderness." The Moabite turns and with bitterness asks, "Why? Why this?" The man in sackcloth replies steadily, "Because you trusted in your own achievements and treasures."

The scene changes and the figure in sackcloth, his back still to the camera, now stands in front of a crowd who are dressed differently to the Moabites. An interested crowd has gathered to gaze on the scene and the bare headed man beseeches them. "Help him flee. Give wings to Moab so that she might fly away."

[v. 10] *The scene changes to a bare room, though everything in this scene is in color. A young man sits at a wooden desk writing on a scroll and the angle shows clearly the text. That it is an account of the previous scene indicates that the film has moved forward in time.* A scribe sits writing what is obviously an account of the previous scene, but when he has written, "Give wings to Moab that she might fly away," he throws down his pen, jumps up, away from his desk, and cries out, "What about OUR pain, Lord? Who gave US wings to flee? Moab didn't! Moab scorned us! Don't give her wings! Cut her down! Finish the job! Moab prospers still—the sword has not yet done its work!" Then he moans, looking upward, "WE are your sons. Judah. Remember us. Take pleasure in your people. Beautify the afflicted ones with salvation. Let the godly ones exult in glory; Let them sing for joy on their bed. Let the high praises of God be in their mouth . . . " He pauses with a sharp intake of breath of sudden enlightenment and then continues slowly, "And a two-edged sword in their hand, to execute vengeance on the nations and punishment on the peoples." He pauses once more, looks down at his scroll, and then breathes softly, "To execute on them the judgment written ... This is an honor for all His godly ones." Rushing back to his desk and sitting down, with a bright look in his eyes, he proclaims, "Praise the Lord!" and seizing his pen, he continues writing, "Cursed be the one who does the Lord's work negligently, and cursed be the one who withholds his sword from bloodshed."

[vv. 11–16] The next scene is the most colorful so far. It is a harvest scene at the end of the day and a happy group of laughing men are standing together, including the anguished (Moabite) man from above, which shows that this is a flash-back to former times. The joyful harvest scene is a relief from the passion of the previous scenes and recognizable is the anguished man who had been called to flee, but how different he looks now. "Another good year!" he exclaims, brightly. "Another good decade. Thanks be to Chemosh! And may we build ever bigger barns!" There is a cheer and two small boys bring pitchers of wine to the group of sweating men. Everyone fills a jar, but then freezes for without warning the man in sackcloth appears. They watch him as he approaches one of the pitchers of wine and tips out the red liquid onto the harvested land, before smashing the pitcher. Finally, he speaks. "You have been undisturbed wine from your youth but Adonai declares that he will tip you over and smash you, and your blood will water the land of Moab. How can you say, 'We are mighty warriors?' Choice young men like you are already going down to the slaughter." The tall man steps forward. "Dear Chemosh!" he ejaculates, but the other swiftly cuts in, forestalling any further utterances. "You will be ashamed of Chemosh as Israel was ashamed of Bethel!" he retorts sharply, adding, "says the King, whose name is Adonai of hosts."

[vv. 17–28] The camera cuts back to a previous scene of devastation. The strong, quick beat of the sound track indicates a change in pace. A series of black and white scenes follow in quick succession, none longer than a few seconds. The man in sackcloth addresses the crowd of onlookers that he had previously summoned to help Moab flee. Now he implores them to mourn her; clearly it is too late for aid to be given her now. It is not clear whether his tone is one of mockery.

Then he is standing in front of part of a wall that has not been destroyed. On it sit a few young soldiers, dejected with minor wounds. Now it is clear that he ridicules them. "Come down from your glory and sit on the parched ground, O daughter Dibon, for the destroyer has reached even this most central city and the fight is over." The little girl in the scarlet tunic appears from behind the wall where she has been hidden and she is still crying. She sits down with her legs folded up, her hands around her knees, and she rocks herself to and fro.

A family is huddled together by the roadside, looking dazed. The man in sackcloth approaches them. "Stand there and watch, O inhabitants of Aroer," he says, in a gentler tone, "Ask those who are still trying to run and they will tell you that the whole of Moab has been shattered. Wail and cry out for she has been destroyed." "It's so . . . total" the husband says, overwhelmed. "Every city, every town . . . " His voice trails off as his wife begins to weep and he looks on helplessly as his children's shrill voices soon join hers.

The camera pans through city after city in silence and, as each scene is shown, a subtitle provides the appropriate memorial caption: Holon, Jahzah, Mephaath, Dibon, Nebo, Beth-diblathaim, Kiriathaim, Beth-gamul, Beth-meon, Kerioth, Bozrah. Then the camera zooms out again to display an ever wider, but less distinct, view of the country. The father is correct; every city, every town has been destroyed; the whole land of Moab, far and near has been broken. Charred remains of burnt cattle punctuate black landscapes.

The next scene (in color) is a flash-back depicting another harvest celebration. The tall man is even younger in this scene. The tall man is standing in the midst of a group of inebriated men lounging on the ground and, with slurred speech, is thanking Chemosh for the harvest. Suddenly, he stops mid-sentence and a sneer crosses his face, for a young Judahite shepherd is herding a few sheep across the land a short distance away. The tall man approaches him. "You think this is disputed land, do you?!" he taunts, "You think this Moabite city still belongs to your great king David, do you?" The men behind are obviously amused. "Your god couldn't hold onto the land could he? He couldn't even stop Israel from going into exile into Assyria, could he?" Several of the men clap behind him. "You should worship Chemosh, instead, Judahite. Go on, down on your knees and worship Chemosh. Let me hear you say it. 'Praise be to Chemosh'—say it—say it!" He pushes the young man down, but the Judahite remains silent.

There is a pause in the laughing as someone else catches the Moabites' attention. It is the man in sackcloth who now stands before them, quivering with rage. He does not address the Moabites, however—he addresses the youth on the dusty soil beside him, but points to the tall Moabite man. "Make him drunk," he orders him, "for he has become arrogant against Adonai." When the Judahite remains motionless several of the inebriated farmers cheerfully rise to what they perceive as a high-spirited game. One grabs the tall man and grapples him to the ground and another puts a jar to his lips and pours wine down his throat. When they step away, the tall man turns to one side and vomits. Then he falls back into the spreading pool of red, fetid liquid that he has just expelled.

The Judahite is still on his knees. "Leave the cities and run away to the cliffs," he murmurs, looking at the semi-conscious tall man. "Run away, be like a dove that nests in the crags. It is safe there and no one can humiliate you."

[vv. 29–38] Once more the present condition of Moab is portrayed in black and white. The arrogant smirk has disappeared from the face of the tall man and, in shame, he looks at the ground. He does not see the man in sackcloth until the latter turns to him and declares, "We have all heard of your pride, Moab; your arrogance is widely known; you are proud and haughty, but your boasts have accomplished nothing." In the distance the little girl in the scarlet tunic is stumbling away from the city, her progress slow and ineffectual. The man in sackcloth pauses as he looks at her, then in barely audible tones he sighs, "Therefore, I will weep for you, Moab" and looking back towards the tall man he says in a louder voice, "Even for all Moab I will cry out."

There are very quick scene changes showing various cities in turn. The man in sackcloth is no longer in view, but his voice continues. "I will moan for the men of Kir-heres" he intones as a group of men can be seen wailing. "For the fruitful vine of Sibmah," he cries as a mixed crowd of people lift up their voices and all but drown out his voice, "How your fruits, your grapes, your harvest have been destroyed." *There is a momentary flashback that shows (in color) the same crowd of people identically positioned, but differently clothed and instead of wasteland, they are surrounded by choice vines and orchards. They are still crying out, but their cries are the joyful shouts of harvest.*

The inhabitants of another city are wailing and the sound merges with the weeping of the man in sackcloth until the two are indistinguishable. In yet another town, the inhabitants are dressed in sackcloth and ashes, crying to Chemosh, holding their wounded offspring, kneeling over a dying spouse, screaming in pain. The man in sackcloth's voice can just about be heard, reeling off names in memorial of the cities that had once existed: Sibmah, Jazer, Heshbon, Elealeh, Jahaz, Zoar, Horonaim, Eglath-shelishiyah, Nimrin, Kir-heres.

The wailing fades as the camera once more changes to an increasingly wider lens. Finally, the only sound is that of the choking sobs of the man in sackcloth and his disjointed speech as he tries to express a heart that cannot be translated into words. "Moab . . . Moab . . . Moab. My heart aches for you. Oh Moab. Kir-heres . . . " He dissolves into desolate sobbing once more. "I have broken Moab like a pot that no one wants" he repeats again and again, a broken man himself.

[vv. 39–47] The pace slows down and the familiar scene, portrayed in black and white, is that of a destroyed city. For the first time Moab's destroyer can be seen, for guards surround the city and some are beginning to rebuild a few of the fortified booths on the higher places. One of the guards is beating the tall man, whilst his comrades idly watch, half amused, half bored. When the man collapses, the guard kicks him outside the city. The little girl in the scarlet tunic joins him without a word and they sit together, shaking slightly. The man in sackcloth appears behind them and, unseen by them, looks for a long time. Then he states, before turning quickly away, "The hearts of the mighty men of Moab in that day will be like the heart of a woman in labor. Moab will be destroyed from being a people because he has become arrogant towards Adonai."

It is the same city (still black and white), but now the conquering guards are rounding up Moabite survivors. A number of refugees are hiding in terrified silence in nearby caves, but one by one, with a triumphant shout, the guards find them. Most come meekly out to be tied up and deported as slaves. Others try to flee, but are overtaken by bloodthirsty soldiers on horses who then round them up, in the process trampling some underfoot. Still others, many severely wounded, make their way to the desert, but they are not juniper trees or doves and most are obviously perishing from lack of water and the heat. In a brief interlude in the action, the man in sackcloth's voice can be heard. "Terror, pit and snare are coming upon you, O inhabitant of Moab. The one who flees from the terror will fall into the pit and the one who climbs up out of the pit will be caught in the snare."

The man in sackcloth now comes into view, walking silently and purposefully. In the background the slow singing of a taunt song against Moab can be heard. The man in sackcloth walks along surveying the destruction, to the accompaniment of a song, "A fire from Heshbon has devoured Moab. The people of Chemosh have been taken captive." If it was once a taunt song, the effect now is somewhat lost; instead it has an ironic sadness about it.

Violins continue playing the tune. The man in sackcloth stops. On the ground in front of him is a small, scarlet tunic. Horses' hooves can be seen imprinted in the ground around. He drops to his knees, with a long, heart-rending moan and clutches the tunic to his chest. "Yet I will restore the fortunes of Moab in the latter days," he finally promises quietly, holding the tunic tightly to him and then burying his face into it.

Coda 2

Literary Storyboard of the Film of Jeremiah 48 (with a Christian Frame of Reference)

The rubrics are in italicized script. The viewer's description is in normal font.

[vv. 1–9] The film begins in silence and in black and white. A long camera shot shows what is obviously a devastated city. Smoke rises from crushed buildings and the crumbled ring of stones surrounding them shows that this had been a walled city.

The camera slowly moves in. Strewn everywhere are crushed and broken human and animal bodies. Already a light film of dust has begun to cover them. Some appear to have been victims of the falling buildings and lie trapped, others have been struck with the sword, with heads and limbs severed from the rest of their bodies.

The view quickly becomes a long shot again before the camera races across the screen in a blur to portray another scene similar to the first; then another and another. Demolished city after demolished city; all that remains of a country is rubble, dust, smoke and silent corpses.

The camera moves in once more on another shattered city. Then, for the first time, there is movement other than falling dust and rising smoke. There is also the first expression of color as well as sound. A three or four year old little girl in a scarlet tunic walks along, alone, sobbing.

The atmosphere is transformed: silence gives way to a burst of noise and there is accompanying activity. A bleeding woman screams hysterically as she holds two small limp bodies to her. The sound seems to frighten a small child nearby, for he immediately begins wailing, his head thrown back, a lone wolf cub howling to the moon. The pack responds and one by one the little ones begin crying out in pain and fear. Some of the women hold them in vain attempts at comfort. For others it is too late and soon there is the rhythmic chant of wailing and swaying as the women mourn their dead families.

A man with a tonsure walks into the picture, wearing a brown habit and holding a string of rosary beads. He periodically takes the next one between his fingers, his lips moving silently. He remains with his back to the camera throughout. A tonsured man in a brown habit walks purposefully towards the lone wolf cub. The child falls silent as the tonsured man picks him up in his arms and carries him towards the bleeding woman who is still hysterical; she too calms down as the tonsured man approaches. Putting the child down before her, he looks directly at her and says, "Woman, behold your son." He takes the child's hand and pulls him towards the woman, "Behold your mother."

Then he touches a tall, anguished Moabite on his arm and says clearly and with some compassion, "Flee, save yourselves. Survive against the odds, just as juniper trees do in the wilderness." The Moabite turns and with bitterness asks, "Why? Why this?" The tonsured man replies steadily, "Because you trusted in your own achievements and treasures. You said to yourselves, 'What shall we do, since we have no place to store our crops? We will tear down our barns and build larger ones. We have many goods laid up for many years; let's take our ease, eat, drink, and be merry.'" The tonsured man pauses before adding, "You fools! This very night your souls are required of you."

The scene changes and the tonsured figure, his back still to the camera, now stands in front of a crowd who are dressed differently to the Moabites. An interested crowd has gathered to gaze on the scene and the tonsured man beseeches them. "Help him flee. Give wings to Moab so that she might fly away." He takes a bleeding Moabite by the arm and leads him to a nearby onlooker. "Take him," he says softly. The stranger looks around uncomfortably before sighing and moving towards his donkey. He takes a cloth from his provisions, rips it into strips and throws them at the Moabite. "These should help the cuts," he barks and catching the tonsured man's eye, he nods to the water bottle hanging from the donkey's back and adds in a kinder tone, "Help yourself to water." He begins to walk swiftly away, beckoning to the Moabite to join him, but the Moabite is limping slowly and cannot keep up. With an exaggerated exhalation of breath and what is obviously ungracious resignation, the stranger helps the injured man onto his donkey and they both begin their journey. As they pass the tonsured man the stranger says, unsmilingly, "I have family in Ammon; I'll take him there and give them money to look after him. I'll pass this way again in a couple of weeks and I can give them more if they need it."

[v. 10] *The scene changes to a bare room, though everything in this scene is in color. A young man sits at a wooden desk writing on a scroll and the angle shows clearly the text. That it is an account of the previous scene indicates that the film has moved forward in time.* A scribe sits writing what is obviously an account of the previous scene, but when he has written, "Give wings to Moab that she might fly away," he throws down his pen, jumps up, away from his desk, and cries out, "What about OUR pain, Lord? Who gave US wings to flee? Moab didn't! Moab scorned us! Don't give her wings! Cut her down! Finish the job! Moab prospers still—the sword has not yet done its work!" Then he moans, looking upward, "WE are your sons. Judah. Remember us. Take pleasure in your people. Beautify the afflicted ones with salvation."

Two phantoms rise up before him. One stands to his left; an armored man wielding a sword boldly proclaiming, "There is an appointed time for everything. And there is a time for every event under heaven. A time to uproot what is planted, a time to kill, a time to tear down, a time to tear apart, a time to hate, a time for war." On his right is a prisoner with a crown of thorns and surrounded by hostile soldiers. The prisoner says to the scribe, "Those who take up the sword shall perish by the sword." The scribe looks from one to the other and then finally he bursts out, "Beautify the afflicted ones with salvation. Let the godly ones exult in glory; Let them sing for joy on their bed. Let the high praises of God be in their mouth. And a two-edged sword in their hand, to execute vengeance on the nations and punishment on the peoples, to execute on them the judgment written . . . This is an honor for all His godly ones." Rushing back to his desk and sitting down, he seizes his pen and continues writing, "Cursed be the one who does the Lord's work negligently, and cursed be the one who withholds his sword from bloodshed." Even having made the decision, however, his agonizing is not over and he hovers with his pen over the scroll. Then, suddenly, he leaps to his feet with a roar, pushes over the chair in his anger, splutters, "What I have written, I have written!" and rushes from the room.

[vv. 11–16] The next scene is the most colorful so far. It is a harvest scene at the end of the day and a happy group of laughing men is standing together, including the anguished (Moabite) man from above, which shows that this is a flash-back to former times. The joyful harvest scene is a relief from the passion of the previous scenes and recognizable is the anguished man who had been called to flee, but how different he looks now. "Another good year!" he exclaims, brightly. "Another good decade. Thanks be to Chemosh! And may we build ever bigger barns!" There is a cheer and two small boys bring pitchers of wine to the group of sweating men. Everyone fills a jar, but then freezes for without warning the tonsured man appears. "You build on sand," he says, "and you rich men will wither away in the middle of your busy lives." They watch him as he approaches one of the pitchers of wine and tips out the red liquid onto the harvested land, before smashing the pitcher. Finally, he speaks. "You have been undisturbed wine from your youth but Adonai declares that he will tip you over and smash you, and your blood will water the land of Moab. How can you say, 'We are mighty warriors?' Choice young men like you are already going down to the slaughter." The tall man steps forward. "Dear Chemosh!" he ejaculates, but the other swiftly cuts in, forestalling any further utterances. "You will be ashamed of Chemosh as Israel was ashamed of Bethel!" he retorts sharply, adding, "says the King, whose name is Adonai of hosts."

[vv. 17–28] The camera cuts back to a previous scene of devastation. The strong, quick beat of the sound track indicates a change in pace. A series of black and white scenes follow in quick succession, none longer than a few seconds. The tonsured man addresses the crowd of onlookers that he had previously summoned to help Moab flee. Now he implores them to mourn her; clearly it is too late for aid to be given her now. It is not clear whether his tone is one of mockery.

Then he is standing in front of part of a wall that has not been destroyed. On it sit a few young soldiers, dejected with minor wounds. Now it is clear that he ridicules them. "Come down from your glory and sit on the parched ground, O daughter Dibon, for the destroyer has reached even this most central city and the fight is over." The little girl in the scarlet tunic appears from behind the wall where she has been hidden and she is still crying. She sits down with her legs folded up, her hands around her knees, and she rocks herself to and fro.

A family is huddled together by the roadside, looking dazed. The tonsured man approaches them. "Stand there and watch, O inhabitants of Aroer," he says, in a gentler tone, "Ask those who are still trying to run and they will tell you that the whole of Moab has been shattered. Wail and cry out for she has been destroyed." "It's so . . . total" the husband says, overwhelmed. "Every city, every town . . . " His voice trails off as his wife begins to weep and he looks on helplessly as his children's shrill voices soon join hers.

The camera pans through city after city in silence and, as each scene is shown, a subtitle provides the appropriate memorial caption: Holon, Jahzah, Mephaath, Dibon, Nebo, Beth-diblathaim, Kiriathaim, Beth-gamul, Beth-meon, Kerioth, Bozrah. Then the camera zooms out again to display an ever wider, but less distinct, view of the country. The father is correct; every city, every town has been destroyed; the whole land of Moab, far and near has been broken. Charred remains of burnt cattle punctuate black landscapes.

The next scene (in color) is a flashback depicting another harvest celebration. The tall man is even younger in this scene. The tall man is standing in the midst of a group of inebriated men lounging on the ground and, with slurred speech, is thanking Chemosh for the harvest. Suddenly, he stops mid-sentence and a sneer crosses his face, for a young Judahite shepherd is herding a few sheep across the land a short distance away. The tall man approaches him. "You think this is disputed land, do you?!" he taunts, "You think this Moabite city still belongs to your great king David, do you?" The men behind are obviously amused. "Your god couldn't hold onto the land could he? He couldn't even stop Israel from going into exile into Assyria, could he?" Several of the men clap behind him. "You should worship Chemosh, instead, Judahite. Go on, down on your knees and worship Chemosh. Let me hear you say it. 'Praise be to Chemosh'—say it—say it!" He pushes the young man down, but the Judahite remains silent.

There is a pause in the laughing as someone else catches the Moabites' attention. It is the tonsured man who now stands before them, quivering with rage. He does not address the Moabites, however—he addresses the youth on the dusty soil beside him, but points to the tall Moabite man. "Make him drunk," he orders him, "for he has become arrogant against Adonai." When the Judahite remains motionless several of the inebriated farmers cheerfully rise to what they perceive as a high-spirited game. One grabs the tall man and grapples him to the ground and another puts a jar to his lips and pours wine down his throat. When they step away, the tall man turns to one side and vomits. Then he falls back into the spreading pool of red, fetid liquid that he has just expelled.

The Judahite is still on his knees. "Leave the cities and run away to the cliffs," he murmurs, looking at the semi-conscious tall man. "Run away, be like a dove that nests in the crags. It is safe there and no one can humiliate you."

[vv. 29–38] Once more the present condition of Moab is portrayed in black and white. The arrogant smirk has disappeared from the face of the tall man and, in shame, he looks at the ground. He does not see the tonsured man until the latter turns to him and declares, "We have all heard of your pride, Moab; your arrogance is widely known; you are proud and haughty, but your boasts have accomplished nothing." In the distance the little girl in the scarlet tunic is stumbling away from the city, her progress slow and ineffectual. The tonsured man pauses as he looks at her, then in barely audible tones he sighs, "Therefore, I will weep for you, Moab" and looking back towards the tall man he says in a louder voice, "Even for all Moab I will cry out."

Then the tonsured man cries with a loud voice, "I thirst" and closes his eyes shut. *The next picture is shot in soft focus and the colors are depicted more brightly.* Suddenly, the little girl in the scarlet tunic is beside him with a cup in her hand. "You can have this drink," she offers, "but you might not like it; it's too bitter for me." The tonsured man takes it from her and drinks. *The picture returns to normal focus and color saturation. The girl is gone and the tonsured man remains with his eyes shut.* Suddenly he opens them and looks around, apparently startled. Then his gaze transfers to the distance and he watches the little girl in the scarlet tunic far away. "I will weep for you, Moab," he repeats in a low voice, nodding.

There are very quick scene changes showing various cities in turn. The tonsured man is no longer in view, but his voice continues. "I will moan for the men of Kir-heres," he intones as a group of men can be seen wailing. "For the fruitful vine of Sibmah," he cries as a mixed crowd of people lift up their voices and all but drown out his voice, "How your fruits, your grapes, your harvest have been destroyed." *There is a momentary flashback that shows (in color) the same crowd of people identically positioned, but differently clothed and, instead of wasteland, choice vines and orchards surround them. They are still crying out, but their cries are the joyful shouts of harvest.*

The inhabitants of another city are wailing and the sound merges with the weeping of the tonsured man until the two are indistinguishable. In yet another town, the inhabitants are dressed in sackcloth and ashes, crying to Chemosh, holding their wounded offspring, kneeling over a dying spouse, screaming in pain. The tonsured man's voice can just about be heard, reeling off names in memorial of the cities that had once existed: Sibmah, Jazer, Heshbon, Elealeh, Jahaz, Zoar, Horonaim, Eglath-shelishiyah, Nimrin, Kir-heres.

The wailing fades as the camera once more changes to an increasingly wider lens. Finally, the only sound is that of the choking sobs of the tonsured man and his disjointed speech as he tries to express a heart that cannot be translated into words. "Moab . . . Moab . . . Moab. My heart aches for you. Oh Moab. Kir-heres . . ." He dissolves into desolate sobbing once more. "I have broken Moab like a pot that no one wants" he repeats again and again, a broken man himself.

[vv. 39–47] The pace slows down and the familiar scene, portrayed in black and white, is that of a destroyed city. For the first time Moab's destroyer can be seen, for guards surround the city and some are beginning to rebuild a few of the fortified booths on the higher places. One of the guards is beating the tall man, whilst his comrades idly watch, half amused, half bored. When the man collapses, the guard kicks him outside the city. The little girl in the scarlet tunic joins him without a word and they sit together, shaking slightly. The tonsured man appears behind them and, unseen by them, looks for a long time. Then he states, before turning quickly away, "The hearts of the mighty men of Moab in that day will be like the heart of a woman in labor. Moab will be destroyed from being a people because he has become arrogant towards Adonai."

It is the same city (still black and white), but now the conquering guards are rounding up Moabite survivors. A number of refugees are hiding in terrified silence in nearby caves, but one by one, with a triumphant shout, the guards find them. Most come meekly out to be tied up and deported as slaves. Others try to flee, but are overtaken by bloodthirsty soldiers on horses who then round them up, in the process trampling some underfoot. Still others, many severely wounded, make their way to the desert, but they are not juniper trees or doves and most are obviously perishing from lack of water and the heat. In a brief interlude in the action, the tonsured man's voice can be heard. "Terror, pit and snare are coming upon you, O inhabitant of Moab. The one who flees from the terror will fall into the pit and the one who climbs up out of the pit will be caught in the snare."

The tonsured man now comes into view, walking silently and purposefully. In the background the slow singing of a taunt song against Moab can be heard. The tonsured man walks along surveying the destruction, to the accompaniment of a song, "A fire from Heshbon has devoured Moab. The people of Chemosh have been taken captive." If it was once a taunt song, the effect now is somewhat lost; instead it has an ironic sadness about it.

Violins continue playing the tune. The tonsured man stops. On the ground in front of him is a small, scarlet tunic. Horses' hooves can be seen imprinted in the ground around. He drops to his knees, with a long, heart-rending moan and clutches the tunic to his chest. "Father, forgive them, for they know not what they do" he murmurs holding the tunic tightly to him and then burying his face into it. He remains there for a few seconds before jumping to his feet abruptly, still holding the scarlet fabric. Swinging around to face the ruined nation of Moab he promises in a resolute tone, "Yet I will restore the fortunes of Moab in the latter days." The earth shakes, rocks split in two and he drops the scarlet tunic into a split rock.

As the camera pans out for this final shot, the little girl is seen standing a few feet in front of the tonsured man and they look at each other. She is dressed in brilliant white and her long hair is blowing out behind her. Then there is darkness.

Conclusion

HAVING STUDIED JER 48, IT APPEARS THAT ITS PURPOSE WAS PRIMARily for Judah and not for Moab. These purposes include being a warning not to trust another foreign nation, a demonstration that YHWH is involved in worldwide events and that history is not "just" history. The distinct characters of individual OANs show that when it comes to the OANs, "one size does not fit all." First, the OANs do not lend themselves to a move that equates the nations with Israel/Judah, except in terms of the language used for YHWH's punishment. Secondly, one foreign nation is not the same as the next and YHWH's attitude and approach is specific to each. Jer 48 exemplifies this with its unique portrayal of YHWH's lament over a foreign nation. At the same time, it is clear from Jer 48 and the other OANs that YHWH is sovereign over the entire world.

There is no obvious reason why the long oracle concerning Moab occurs in the middle of Jeremiah's OANs, although it is understandable why Egypt should be first and Babylon last (and Elam last of the collection if one excludes Babylon). Nevertheless, it might be precisely because Moab is a "standard" foreign nation that she receives the attention she is given. That is, she is not a huge empire, nor a tiny, nomadic people, but a country similar to Israel in terms of size and military strength and therefore perhaps typifies a non-Israelite nation so that the oracle concerning her acts as a model example OAN.

In chapter 1 it became clear that the OANs have, by and large, not attracted much scholarly attention, although in recent years Babylon has become a more popular topic of discussion. The studies that have taken place have tended to have been predominantly concerned with authorship, form, and *Sitz im Leben*. The OANs are often regarded as stemming from the war oracle genre.

Chapter 2 revealed that LXX and MT have distinct nuances (partly governed by the different placing and order of the OAN collections within the book), though their theologies are substantially the same.

MT gives a more vivid, intense portrayal of Moab's calamity, for example, by emphasizing slightly more the aspect of lament and including both the taunt song, which concludes the judgment speech, as well as the final promise of restoration. The length of the oracle in both LXX and MT suggests that the oracle is important and its position at the end of the list of Jeremiah's OANs in LXX reinforces this idea.

The comparison with Isa 15–16 in chapter 3 demonstrated that despite the significant overlap between them, the two texts have been individually shaped in a way that stresses different elements. For instance, Isa 15–16 has a narrower scope, namely lament, whereas Jer 48 has a wider interest (e.g., Moab's sins and hope of restoration), though the tone of lament is at times more intense than in Isa 15–16. It may be that the main purpose behind Jer 48 is to portray the overall picture of Moab's judgment, whereas Isa 15–16 has a different purpose (to elicit Judah's sympathy, perhaps).

Chapters 4 and 5 revealed how various U.S. and UK Christian scholars have read Jer 48 as Christian Scripture. The U.S. scholars (more than the UK ones) tend to draw out from the chapter elements that are conducive to their wider interests. For instance, Fretheim concentrates on the tone of lament, Miller on divine sovereignty and YHWH's opposition to Chemosh, and Brueggemann on Moab's pride and the plays for power in the text. Both UK scholars also bring out the ideas of lament and divine sovereignty, Clements stressing the former and Jones the latter. In addition, Jones argues that the OANs belong to the feast of Tabernacles.

Chapter 6 dealt explicitly with the curse of 48:10 and proposed that it was inserted by a scribe who, seeing that Moab prospered, called for those around to bring to fruition what the oracle threatened, by cutting Moab down with the sword. This may have been in keeping with the sentiments of Ps 149:6b–9 with its reference to the godly wielding swords and Judg 3 where Ehud kills the Moabite king with a sword. Whilst a "plain reading" of 48:10 might be inappropriate within a Christian context, a more figural reading in which the sword is understood as the Word of God might enable this verse to continue to speak to the contemporary community of faith. As well, the right response to it may be the same that its author took with regard to some parts of Jer 48: whilst not liking all he read, he did not delete it.

The substantial final chapter of this monograph attempted to give a Christian reading of Jer 48. This reading was guided by the results of the research in previous chapters and built upon the insights of the interpreters examined. For instance, the comparison with Isa 15–16 showed that the reasons for Moab's judgment have been woven into the fabric of Jer 48 whereas they are not a concern in Isa 15–16. This suggested that they are an integral and significant characteristic of Jer 48 and therefore my reading made special reference to them as well as the tone of lament. In the rhetoric that accompanies the reasons given, it becomes apparent that Moab's offences have led to unforeseen consequences in terms of the charge with which she is judged (for example, arrogance against YHWH) and the intensity of the punishment meted out on her. At the same time there are occasions when one would expect punishment to fall, yet YHWH's tears fall instead, even though punishment does then ensue. Jer 48 is more comprehensive than most in itemizing the wrongdoings of the nation under judgment and it is evident that Moab has committed many of the sins of all the other nations combined.

The similarities between Jer 48 and Isa 15–16 were also helpful when trying to show that Jer 48 was not intended as a taunt in the way that Isa 14:3–21 is over Babylon. For since both belong to the same book, and therefore there is less distance between them, Isa 15–16 acts a better contrasting comparison to Isa 14:3–21 than Jer 48, yet the points made are easily transferable to Jer 48 in this case.

LXX Jer 31 highlighted the greater rhetorical slant of MT Jer 48, another element to which my reading paid attention. For instance, the taunt song from Num 21:28–29 seems to act as a rhetorical tool in MT Jer 48 to infer the cyclical nature of Moab's predicament. The comparison between LXX and MT also led me to abandon the idea of finding a "best witness" since the emphases of the two texts are sometimes sufficiently intricately incorporated to make such a quest unfeasible. Specifically, LXX is less amenable to a concluding promise partly because of the position of the OANs within the book of Jeremiah and also because the oracle concerning Moab is placed last in the collection. Instead, similarly to the reasons for punishment that were absent in Isa 15–16, the absence of the final verse of restoration in LXX highlighted the significance of its presence in MT's oracle, a significance to which my reading attempted to do justice.

I expanded on Miller's and Jones' emphasis on YHWH's sovereignty not by pointing out (as Jones does)[1] that his sovereignty is manifest in grace as well as in his role as divine warrior but in discussing more fully the unfathomable quality behind his tears, the level of punishment and the promise of restoration. The memory of Ruth or Moses' resting place may make the importance of Moab less surprising, and the oracle against Moab may act as a "typical" OAN within Jeremiah. Nevertheless, it seems that ultimately there is no way of knowing with much certainty why Moab assumes such prominence within the book in terms of the length of the oracle against her, or why she is subject to YHWH's mourning. The section arguing that idolatry is not the right terminology to use with regard to the nations builds on Miller's idea that the conflict between YHWH and Chemosh is implicit.

However, most influential to my reading were Brueggemann and Fretheim: Brueggemann with regard to the importance of Moab's pride and also because he draws attention to the rhetorical nature of the text, and Fretheim because of the emphasis he gives to the tone of lament and the kaleidoscopic format of the oracle. Though Brueggemann points out the various occasions where there is an accumulation of vocabulary in the texts, he does not draw attention either to the rhetorical nature of the swapping of audiences, or to the rhetorical effect of the various metaphors (although he talks about individual metaphors). Nor does he note the way that the oracle ends with many of the same themes with which it begins. Similarly, while he elucidates Moab's pride, he does not say much about some of Moab's other sins. Thus, in these ways my reading tries to continue what Brueggemann starts.

Likewise, Fretheim argues that the tone of lament in Jer 48 is not ironic, but space precludes him from addressing the subject properly. My reading attempts to provide the kind of rationale that Fretheim might have made had space allowed it. In addition, I have extrapolated Fretheim's comments about YHWH's mourning by including Luke's account of Jesus' weeping over Jerusalem and suggested that a Christian response to another's judgment might also be one of weeping.

Most of the interpreters surveyed have attempted to give Christian readings of Jer 48 to some extent, but the genre of commentaries does not lend itself as easily as a monograph to such appropriation. Therefore, I have attempted to further the Christianized readings of the interpret-

---

1. Jones, *Jeremiah*, 507.

ers. This has included extending Fretheim's and Jones' visual descriptions of the oracle as, respectively, a "collage" or "mosaic" by means of Codas 1 and 2, which are literary storyboards for imaginary films of Jer 48. Ultimately, like Brueggemann, I suggest that Jer 48 be read from one's own viewpoint but whereas Brueggemann reads it as an American, I suggest that it be read as a critique of the Church.

Bibliography

Allen, Leslie C. *Ezekiel 20–48*. WBC 29. Nashville: Nelson, 1990.
———. *Jeremiah: A Commentary*. OTL. Louisville: Westminster Knox, 2008.
———. *Psalms 101–150: Revised*. WBC 21. Dallas: Word, 2002.
Alter, Robert. *The Art of Biblical Narrative*. New York: Basic, 1981.
Althann, R. "Jeremiah IV 11–12: Stichometry, Parallelism, and Translation." *VT* 28 (1978) 385–91.
American Revision Committee. *The Holy Bible, American Standard Version*. New York: Nelson, 1901.
Amesz, J. G. "A God of Vengeance? Comparing YHWH's Dealings with Judah and Babylon in the Book of Jeremiah." In *Reading the Book of Jeremiah: A Search for Coherence*, edited by Martin Kessler, 99–116. Winona Lake, IN: Eisenbrauns, 2004.
Anderson, Francis I., and David Noel Freedman. *Amos*. AB 24A. London: Doubleday, 1989.
———. *Micah: A New Translation with Introduction and Commentary*. AB 21A. London: Doubleday, 2000.
Andersen, Francis I. *Habakkuk: A New Translation with Introduction and Commentary*. AB 25. London: Doubleday, 2001.
Arnold, Bill T., and John H. Choi. *A Guide to Biblical Hebrew Syntax*. Cambridge: Cambridge University Press, 2003.
Ashley, Timothy R. *The Book of Numbers*. New International Commentary on the Old Testament. Grand Rapids: Eerdmans, 1993.
Augustine. *Exposition on Psalm 149*, edited by Kevin Knight. New Advent, 2008. Online: http://www.newadvent.org/fathers/1801149.htm.
Bailey, Kenneth E. *Jesus through Middle Eastern Eyes: Cultural Studies in the Gospels*. London: SPCK, 2008.
Baltzer, Klaus. *Deutero-Isaiah: A Commentary on Isaiah 40–55*. Translated by Margaret Kohl. Hermeneia. Minneapolis: Fortress, 2001.
Bardtke, Hans. "Jeremia der Fremdvölkerprophet." *ZAW* 53 (1935) 209–39.
———. "Jeremia der Fremdvölkerprophet." *ZAW* 54 (1936) 258–59.
Barker, Kenneth L., and Waylon Bailey. *Micah, Nahum, Habakkuk & Zephaniah*. The New American Commentary 20. Nashville: Broadman & Holman, 1999.
Barstad, Hans M. "Prophecy in the Book of Jeremiah and the Historical Prophet." In *Sense and Sensibility: Essays on Reading the Bible in Memory of Robert Carroll*, edited by Alastair G. Hunter and Philip R. Davies, 87–100. JSOTSup 348. Sheffield: Sheffield Academic, 2002.
Bartlett, J. R. "Edom (Place)." In *ABD* 2:287–95.
———. "The Moabites and Edomites." In *Peoples of Old Testament Times*, edited by D. J. Wiseman, 229–58. Oxford: Clarendon, 1973.

Barton, John. "'The Work of Human Hands' (Ps 115:4): Idolatry in the Old Testament." *Ex Auditu* 15 (1999) 63–72.

Becking, Bob. "Jeremiah's Book of Consolation: A Textual Comparison Notes on the Masoretic Text and the Old Greek Version of Jeremiah XXX–XXXI." *VT* 44 (1994) 145–69.

Begg, C. T. "Babylon in the Book of Isaiah." In *The Book of Isaiah*, edited by Jacques Vermeylen, 121–125. BETL 81. Leuven: Leuven University Press, 1989.

Bellis, Alice Ogden. "Poetic Structure and Intertextual Logic in Jeremiah 50." In *Troubling Jeremiah*, edited by A. R. Pete Diamond, et al., 179–99. JSOTSup 260. Sheffield: Sheffield Academic, 1999.

Bendavid, Abba. *Parallels in the Bible*. 188, 201, 206. Jerusalem: Carta, 1972.

Bentzen, A. "The Ritual Background of Amos i 2–ii 16." In *Oudtestamentische Studiën*, edited by P. A. H. de Boer. Lieden: Brill, 1950.

Berlin, Adele. "Zephaniah's Oracle against the Nations and an Israelite Cultural Myth." In *Fortunate the Eyes that See: Essays in Honor of David Noel Freedman in Celebration of His Seventieth Birthday*, edited by Astrid B. Beck et al., 175–84. Grand Rapids: Eerdmans, 1995.

Berlin, Adele, and Marc Zvi Brettler, editors. *The Jewish Study Bible*. Oxford: Oxford University Press, 2004.

Berman, Joshua. "The 'Sword of Mouths' (Judg III 16; Ps. CXLIX 6; Prov. V 4): A Metaphor and Its Ancient Near Eastern Context." *VT* 52 (2002) 291–303.

The Bible Societies. *The Bible: Authorized Version*. Oxford: Oxford University Press, 1973.

Biblical Studies Foundation. *New English Translation Bible*. Biblical Studies Foundation, 2005. Online: http://bible.org/netbible/index.htm.

Bimson, John J., et al., editors. *New Bible Atlas*. Leicester: InterVarsity, 1985.

Blass, F., and A. Debrunner. *A Greek Grammar of the New Testament and Other Early Christian Literature*. Translated and edited by Robert W. Funk. Cambridge: Cambridge University Press, 1961.

Blenkinsopp, Joseph. *Isaiah 1–39: A New Translation with Introduction and Commentary*. AB 19. London: Doubleday, 2000.

———. *Isaiah 40–55: A New Translation with Introduction and Commentary*. AB 19A. London: Doubleday, 2002.

———. *Isaiah 56–66: A New Translation with Introduction and Commentary*. AB 19B. London: Doubleday, 2003.

Block, Daniel. "Nations." In *NIDOTTE* 4:966–972.

Boadt, Lawrence. *Ezekiel's Oracles against Egypt: A Literary and Philological Study of Ezekiel 29–32*. Biblica et Orientalia 37. Rome: Pontifical Biblical Institute, 1980.

Bodner, Keith. "Go Figure: Narrative Strategies for a New Generation." In *Go Figure! Figuration in Biblical Interpretation*, edited by Stanley D. Walters, 9–24. PTMS 81. Eugene, OR: Pickwick, 2008.

Bons. "שָׁקַט." Translated by David E. Green. In *TDOT* 15:452–57.

Brenton, Lancelot C. L. *The Septuagint with Apocrypha: Greek and English*. Peabody, MA: Hendrickson, 1851.

Briggs, Charles Augustus, and Emilie Grace Briggs. *A Critical and Exegetical Commentary on The Book of the Psalms*. ICC. Edinburgh: T. & T. Clark, 1907.

Briggs, Richard S. Review of *Go Figure! Figuration in Biblical Interpretation*, by Stanley D. Walters. *Review of Biblical Literature* (2009). Online: http://www.bookreviews.org/pdf/6390_6878.pdf.

Bright, John. *Jeremiah*. AB 20. New York: Doubleday, 1965.

Brown, Francis, et al. *Hebrew and English Lexicon of the Old Testament*. Oxford: Clarendon, 1907.

Brownlee, William H., editor and commentator. *The Midrash Pesher of Habakkuk*. SBL Monograph Series 24. Missoula MT: Scholars, 1979.

Broyles, Craig C. *Psalms*. New International Bible Commentary, Old Testament Series. Peabody, MA: Hendrickson, 1999.

Bruce, F. F. "Babylon." In *New Bible Dictionary*, edited by I. H. Marshall et al., 110–12. 3rd ed. Leicester, UK: InterVarsity, 1996.

Brueggemann, Walter. *1 and 2 Kings*. Smyth & Helwys Bible Commentary. Macon, GA: Smyth & Helwys, 2000.

———. "At the Mercy of Babylon: A Subversive Rereading of the Empire." *JBL* 110 (1991) 3–22.

———. "At the Mercy of Babylon: A Subversive Rereading of the Empire." In *Reading the Book of Jeremiah: A Search for Coherence*, edited by Martin Kessler, 99–116. Winona Lake, IN: Eisenbrauns, 2004. (First published in *JBL* in 1991—see above.)

———. *The Bible and Postmodern Imagination: Texts under Negotiation*. Edited by Charles L. Campbell. London: SCM, 1993.

———. *The Book that Breathes New Life: Scriptural Authority and Biblical Theology*. Edited by Patrick D. Miller. Minneapolis: Fortress, 2005.

———. *Cadences of Home: Preaching among Exiles*. Louisville: Westminster/John Knox, 1997.

———. *A Commentary on Jeremiah: Exile and Homecoming*. Cambridge: Eerdmans, 1998.

———. *The Covenanted Self: Explorations in Law and Covenant*. Edited by Patrick D. Miller. Minneapolis: Fortress, 1999.

———. *The Creative Word: Canon as a Model for Biblical Education*. Philadelphia: Fortress, 1982.

———. *Deep Memory, Exuberant Hope: Contested Truth in a Post-Christian World*. Edited by Patrick Miller. Minneapolis: Fortress, 2000.

———. *Hope within History: Prophetic Voices in Exile*. Atlanta: John Knox, 1987.

———. *Hopeful Imagination: Prophetic Voices in Exile*. London: SCM, 1986.

———. *Ichabod Toward Home: The Journey of God's Glory*. Grand Rapids: Eerdmans, 2002.

———. *An Introduction to the Old Testament: The Canon and Christian Imagination*. Louisville: Westminster/John Knox, 2003.

———. *Isaiah 1–39*. Westminster Bible Companion. Louisville: Westminster/John Knox, 1998.

———. *Isaiah 40–66*. Westminster Bible Companion. Louisville: Westminster/John Knox, 1998.

———. *Israel's Praise: Doxology against Idolatry and Ideology*. Philadelphia: Fortress, 1988.

———. *The Land: Place as Gift, Promise, and Challenge in Biblical Faith*. Overtures to Biblical Theology. London: SPCK, 1978.

———. *Like Fire in the Bones: Listening for the Prophetic Word in Jeremiah.* Minneapolis: Fortress, 2006.

———. "Next Steps in Jeremiah Studies?" In *Troubling Jeremiah*, edited by A. R. Pete Diamond et al., 404-22. JSOTSup 260. Sheffield: Sheffield Academic, 1999.

———. *Old Testament Theology: Essays on Structure, Theme, and Text.* Edited by Patrick D. Miller. Minneapolis: Fortress, 1992.

———. *The Prophetic Imagination.* 2nd ed. Minneapolis: Fortress, 2001.

———. *The Psalms and the Life of Faith.* Edited by Patrick D. Miller. Minneapolis: Fortress, 1995.

———. *Solomon: Israel's Ironic Icon of Human Achievement.* Columbia: University of South Carolina Press, 2005.

———. *Testimony to Otherwise: The Witness of Elijah and Elisha.* St Louis: Chalice, 2001.

———. *Texts that Linger, Words that Explode: Listening to Prophetic Voices.* Edited by Patrick D. Miller. Minneapolis: Fortress, 2000.

———. *Theology of the Old Testament: Testimony, Dispute, Advocacy.* Minneapolis: Fortress, 1997.

———. *The Threat of Life: Sermons on Pain, Power and Weakness.* Edited by Charles L. Campbell. Minneapolis: Fortress, 1996.

———. "The Travail of Pardon: Reflections on *slh*." In *A God So Near: Essays on Old Testament Theology in Honor of Patrick D. Miller,* edited by Brent A. Strawn and Nancy R. Bowen, 283-97. Winona Lake, IN: Eisenbrauns, 2003.

———. *The Word that Redescribes the World: The Bible and Discipleship.* Edited by Patrick D. Miller. Minneapolis: Fortress, 2006.

Brueggemann, Walter, and Hans Walter Wolff. *The Vitality of Old Testament Traditions.* 2nd ed. London: John Knox, 1982.

Budd, Philip J. *Numbers.* WBC 5. Waco, TX: Word, 1984.

Budde, K. "Ueber die Kapitel 50 und 51 des Buches Jeremia." *Jahrbücher für Deutsche Theologie* 23 (1878) 428-70, 529-62.

Butterworth, Mike. "נחם." In *NIDOTTE* 3:81-83.

Buttrick, George Arthur. *Psalms, Proverbs.* Interpreter's Bible 4. Nashville: Abingdon, 1955.

Calvin, John. *Commentary on a Harmony of the Evangelists, Matthew, Mark, and Luke,* vol. XVI. Translated by John Owen. Edinburgh: Calvin Translation Society, 1855.

———. *Commentaries on the Book of Psalms,* vol. VI. Translated by John Owen. Edinburgh: Calvin Translation Society, 1855.

———. *Commentaries on the Prophet Isaiah 1-32,* vol. VII. Translated by William Pringle. Grand Rapids: Baker, 1855.

———. *Commentaries on the Prophet Jeremiah and The Lamentations,* vol. V. Translated by John Owen. Edinburgh: Calvin Translation Society, 1855.

Caragounis, Chrys C. "בַּת." In *NIDOTTE* 1:779-81.

Carroll, Robert P. "Halfway through a Dark Wood: Reflections on Jeremiah 25." In *Troubling Jeremiah*, edited by A. R. Pete Diamond et al., 73-86. JSOTSup 260. Sheffield: Sheffield Academic, 1999.

———. *Jeremiah: A Commentary.* OTL. London: SCM, 1986.

Carter, Craig. "Karl Barth on the *Imago Dei*: Typology and the *Sensus literalis* of Holy Scripture." In *Go Figure! Figuration in Biblical Interpretation*, edited by Stanley D. Walters, 121–36. PTMS 81. Eugene, OR: Pickwick, 2008.
Cauvin, Jacques. "Syria (Place) (Prehistoric)." In *ABD* 6:271–74.
Childs, Brevard S. *Introduction to the Old Testament as Scripture*. London: SCM, 1979.
———. *Isaiah*. OTL. Louisville: Westminster/John Knox, 2001.
Christensen, Duane L. *Transformations of the War Oracle in Old Testament Prophecy: Studies in the Oracles against the Nations*. Harvard Dissertations in Religion. Missoula, MT: Scholars, 1975.
Clements, R. E. "גוֹי." In *TDOT* 2:426–33.
———. *Abraham and David: Genesis XV and Its Meaning for Israelite Tradition*. London: SCM, 1967.
———. *The Book of Deuteronomy: A Preacher's Commentary*. Epworth Commentaries. Peterborough: Epworth, 2001.
———. *A Century of Old Testament Study*. London: Lutterworth, 1976.
———. *Deuteronomy*. Old Testament Guides. Sheffield: JSOT Press, 1989.
———. *Exodus*. The Cambridge Bible Commentary. Cambridge: Cambridge University Press, 1972.
———. *Ezekiel*. Westminster Bible Companion. Louisville: Westminster/ John Knox, 1996.
———. *God's Chosen People: A Theological Interpretation of the Book of Deuteronomy*. London: SCM, 1968.
———. *Isaiah 1–39*. The New Century Bible Commentary. London: Marshall, Morgan & Scott, 1980.
———. "Isaiah 14, 22–27: A Central Passage Reconsidered." In *The Book of Isaiah*, edited by Jacques Vermeylen, 93–120. BETL 81. Leuven: Leuven University Press, 1989.
———. *Isaiah and the Deliverance of Jerusalem: A Study of the Interpretation of Prophecy in the Old Testament*. JSOTSup 13. Sheffield: JSOT, 1980.
———. "Israel in Its Historical and Cultural Setting." In *The World of Ancient Israel: Sociological, Anthropological and Political Perspectives*, edited by R. E. Clements, 3–16. Cambridge: Cambridge University Press, 1989.
———. *Jeremiah*. Interpretation: A Bible Commentary for Teaching and Preaching. Atlanta: John Knox, 1988.
———. "The Meaning of Ritual Acts in Israelite Religion." In *Eucharistic Theology Then and Now*, edited by R. E. Clements, 1–14. London: SPCK, 1968.
———. *Old Testament Theology: A Fresh Approach*. London: Marshall, Morgan & Scott, 1985.
———. *The Prayers of the Bible*. London: SCM, 1985.
———. *Prophecy and Covenant*. Oxford: SCM, 1965.
———. *Prophecy and Tradition*. Oxford: Blackwell, 1975.
———. *Wisdom for a Changing World: Wisdom in Old Testament Theology*. Berkeley: BIBAL, 1990.
———. *Wisdom in Theology*. Carlisle, UK: Paternoster, 1992.
Clines, J. A., editor. "גוֹי." In *The Dictionary of Classical Hebrew*, vol. III, 329–34. Sheffield: Sheffield Academic, 1996.

———. "לְאֹם." In *The Dictionary of Classical Hebrew*, vol. IV, 496–97. Sheffield: Sheffield Academic, 1998.

———. "מִשְׁפָּט." In *The Dictionary of Classical Hebrew*, vol. V, 556–64. Sheffield: Sheffield Academic, 2001.

Cohn-Sherbok, Dan. *Judaism*. Religions of the World. Upper Saddle River, NJ: Prentice Hall, 1999.

Committee on Bible Translation. *The Holy Bible: New International Version*. London: Hodder & Stoughton, 1986.

Confraternity of Christian Doctrine. *The New American Bible with Revised New Testament and Revised Psalms, and with Roman Catholic Deutero-Canon*. Washington, DC: Catholic World, 1991.

Conybeare, F. C., and St. George Stock. *A Grammar of Septuagint Greek*. Grand Rapids: Zondervan, 1980.

Cooke, G. A. *A Critical and Exegetical Commentary on Ezekiel*. ICC. Edinburgh: T. & T. Clark, 1936.

Craigie, Peter C., et al. *Jeremiah 1–25*. WBC 27. Dallas: Word, 1991.

Cripps, Richard S. *A Critical and Exegetical Commentary on the Book of Amos: The Text of the Revised Version Edited with Introduction, Notes and Excurses*. London: SPCK, 1929.

Dahood, Mitchell. *Psalms 101–150*. AB 17A. London: Doubleday, 1970.

Danker, Frederick William. *A Greek–English Lexicon of the New Testament and other Early Christian Literature*. 3rd ed. London: University of Chicago Press, 2000.

Darr, Katheryn Pfisterer. "Ezekiel." In *The New Interpreter's Bible: A Commentary in Twelve Volumes*, vol. 6, *Isaiah—Ezekiel*, 1073–1607. Nashville: Abingdon, 2001.

Davies, G. I. "The Destiny of the Nations in Isaiah." In *The Book of Isaiah*, edited by Jacques Vermeylen, 93–120. BETL 81. Leuven: Leuven University Press, 1989.

Davis, Ellen F. "An Abundance of Meaning." In *Wondrous Depth: Preaching the Old Testament*, 63–84. Louisville: Westminster/ John Knox, 2005.

Diamond, A. R. Pete. "Introduction." In *Troubling Jeremiah*, edited by A. R. Pete Diamond et al., 15–32. JSOTSup 260. Sheffield: Sheffield Academic, 1999.

Dillmann, August. *Der Prophet Jesaia*. Kurzgefasstes exegetisches Handbuch zum Alten Testament. 5th ed. Leipzig: Hirzel, 1890.

Division of Christian Education of the National Council of Churches of Christ in the United States of America. *The Holy Bible, Revised Standard Version*. New York: Nelson, 1952.

———. *The Holy Bible Containing the Old and New Testaments with the Apocryphal / DeuteroCanonical Books: New Revised Standard Version*. Anglicized Ed. Oxford: Oxford University Press, 1995.

Dobbs-Allsopp, Leslie. "'Teach me your way, O Lord': Pat Miller's Legacy as Teacher and Scholar." *inSpire* (Summer/Fall 2005) 26–27. Online: http://www.ptsem.edu/uploadedFiles/Publications/inspire/inSpire_summer-fall_205/millersmall.pdf.

Dornemann, Rudolph H. "Syria (Place) (Bronze-Iron Age)." In *ABD* 6:274–81.

Douglas, J. D., and K. A. Kitchen. "Kedar." In *New Bible Dictionary*, edited by I. H. Marshall et al., 3rd ed., 642. Leicester, UK: InterVarsity, 1996.

Driver, Samuel Rolles, and George Buchanan Gray. *A Critical and Exegetical Commentary on the Book of Job*. ICC. Edinburgh: T. & T. Clark, 1921.

Duhm, Bernhard. *Das Buch Jeremia*. Tübingen: Mohr/Siebeck, 1901.

———. "Die Psalmen." In *Psalmen Sprüche, Hiob, Die Fünf Megillot, Daniel, Esra und Nehemia, Chronik*. Kurzer Hand-Commentar zum Alten Testament 5. Tübingen: Mohr/Siebeck, 1899.

Dunn, James D. G. *Romans 1–8*. WBC 38A. Nashville: Nelson, 1988.

Eaton, John H. *Psalms*. London: SCM, 1967.

———. *The Psalms: A Historical and Spiritual Commentary with an Introduction and New Translation*. New York: T. & T. Clark, 2003.

Eichhorn, J. G. *Die hebräischen Propheten*, vol. 3, 243–85. Göttingen: Vandenhoeck & Ruprecht, 1819.

Eichrodt, Walther. *Ezekiel*. Translated by Cosslett Quin. OTL. London: SCM, 1970.

Eisemann, Moshe. יחזקאל *Yechezkel Ezekiel: A New Translation with a Commentary Anthologized from Talmudic, Midrashic and Rabbinic Sources*, vol. 2. ArtScroll Tanach Series: A Traditional Commentary on the Books of the Bible. New York: Mesorah, 1969.

Eissfeldt, Otto. *The Old Testament: An Introduction (including the Apocrypha and Pseudepigrapha, and also the Works of Similar Type from Qumran): The History of the Formation of the Old Testament*. Translated by Peter R. Ackroyd. Oxford: Blackwell, 1966.

Elliger, K., and W. Rudolph, editors. *Biblia Hebraica Stuttgartensia*. Stuttgart: Deutsche Bibelgesellschaft, 1967–1977.

Enns, Peter. "מִשְׁפָּט." In *NIDOTTE* 2:1142–1144.

Fange, Erich A., von. "Budde Hypothesis." In *ABD* 1:783–84.

Faught, Brad. "From Keble to Gore: A Study of the Use of Scripture in the Oxford Movement and by the Lux Mundi Group." In *Go Figure! Figuration in Biblical Interpretation*, edited by Stanley D. Walters, 137–47. PTMS 81. Eugene, OR: Pickwick, 2008.

Feinberg, Charles L. *Jeremiah: A Commentary*. Grand Rapids: Zondervan, 1982.

Ferch, Arthur J. "Nimrim, The Waters of." In *ABD* 4:1116.

Fitzgerald, Aloysius. "*BTWLT* and *BT* as Titles for Capital Cities." *CBQ* 37 (1975) 167–83.

———. "The Mythological Background for the Presentation of Jerusalem as a Queen and False Worship as Adultery in the OT." *CBQ* 34 (1972) 403–16.

Foster, Marshall, editor. *1599 Geneva Bible*. Tolle Lege Press, America's 400th Anniversary Edition, 2007.

Freedman, David Noel, and Erich A. von Fange. "Metrics in Hebrew Poetry: The Book of Lamentations Revisited." *Concordia Theological Quarterly* 60 (1996) 279–305.

Freedman, H. *Jeremiah: Hebrew Text and English Translation with an Introduction and Commentary*. Soncino Books of the Bible. London: Soncino, 1949.

Fretheim, Terence E. "The Color of God: Israel's God-Talk and Life Experience." *Word & World* 6 (1986) 256–65.

———. "Divine Dependence upon the Human: An Old Testament Perspective." *Ex Auditu* 13 (1997) 1–13.

———. *God and World in the Old Testament: A Relational Theology of Creation*. Nashville: Abingdon, 2005.

———. "The God Who Acts: An Old Testament Perspective." *Theology Today* 54 (1997–1998) 6–18.

———. "'I was only a little angry': Divine Violence in the Prophets." *Interpretation* 58 (2004) 365–75.
———. "Is Anything Too Hard for God? (Jeremiah 32:27)." *CBQ* 66 (2004) 231–36.
———. *Jeremiah*. Smyth & Helwys Bible Commentary. Macon, GA: Smyth & Helwys, 2002.
———. "Law in the Service of Life: A Dynamic Understanding of Law in Deuteronomy." In *A God So Near: Essays on Old Testament Theology in Honor of Patrick D. Miller*, edited by Brent A. Strawn and Nancy R. Bowen, 183–200. Winona Lake, IN: Eisenbrauns, 2003.
———. "The Old Testament and Homosexuality: What Is God Doing?" *The Lutheran*, May 2001. Online: http://www.thelutheran.org/article/article_buy.cfm?article_id=858.
———. "The Old Testament in Christian Proclamation." *Word & World* 3 (1983) 223–30.
———. "The Plagues as Ecological Signs of Historical Disaster." *JBL* 110 (1991) 385–96.
———. "The Priestly Document: Anti-Temple?" *VT* 18 (1968) 313–29.
———. "Psalm 132: A Form-Critical Study." *JBL* 86 (1967) 289–300.
———. "Response to McConville (The Judgment of God in the Old Testament)." *Ex Auditu* 20 (2004) 43–46.
———. Review of *Contours of Old Testament Theology*, by Bernhard W. Anderson. *Theology Today* 57 (2000–2001) 136–38.
———. Review of *Word Without End: The Old Testament as Abiding Theological Witness*, by Christopher R. Seitz. *Theology Today* 55 (1998–1999) 478–82.
———. "Some Reflections on Brueggemann's God." In *God in the Fray*, edited by Tod Linafelt and Timothy K. Beal, 24–37. Minneapolis: Fortress, 1998.
———. *The Suffering of God: An Old Testament Perspective*. Overtures to Biblical Theology. Philadelphia: Fortress, 1984.
———. "To Say Something—About God, Evil, and Suffering." *Word & World* 19 (1999) 339–50.
Fretheim, Terence E., and Karlfried Froehlich. *The Bible as the Word of God: In a Postmodern Age*. Minneapolis: Fortress, 1998.
Fritz, Volkmar. *1 and 2 Kings: A Continental Commentary*. Translated by Anselm Hagedorn. Minneapolis: Fortress, 2003.
Geyer, John B. "Another Look at the Oracles about the Nations in the Hebrew Bible. A Response to A. C. Hagedorn." *VT* 59 (2009) 80–87.
———. "Blood and the Nations in Ritual and Myth." *VT* 57 (2007) 1–20.
———. "Desolation and Cosmos." *VT* 49 (1999) 49–64.
———. "Mythology and Culture in the Oracles against the Nations." *VT* 36 (1986) 129–45.
———. *Mythology and Lament: Studies in the Oracles about the Nations*. Society for Old Testament Study Monographs. Aldershot, UK: Ashgate, 2004.
Ginzberg, Louis. "The Exile." In *The Legends of the Jews*, vol. 4, *Bible Times and Characters From Joshua to Esther*, 289–340. Philadelphia: Jewish Publication Society of America, 1913.
Goldingay, John. *Isaiah*. New International Biblical Commentary: Old Testament Series. Peabody, MA: Hendrickson, 2001.

———. *Old Testament Theology*. Vol. 1, *Israel's Gospel*. Downers Grove, IL: InterVarsity, 2003.
Gordon, Robert, translator and commentator. "Habakkuk." In *The Targum of the Minor Prophets: Translated, with a Critical Introduction, Apparatus, and Notes*. The Aramaic Bible 14. Edinburgh: T. & T. Clark, 1989.
Gosse, Bernard. "The Masoretic Redaction of Jeremiah: an Explanation." *JSOT* 77 (1998) 75–80.
Gottwald, Norman K. *All the Kingdoms of the Earth*. London: Harper & Row, 1964.
———. "Holy War." In *IDBSup* 942–44.
Goulder, Michael D. *The Psalms of the Return (Book V, Psalms 107–150)*, Studies in the Psalter IV. JSOTSup 258. Sheffield: Sheffield Academic, 1998.
Gray, George Buchanan. *A Critical and Exegetical Commentary on Book of Isaiah*. Vol. 1, *I–XXVII*. ICC. Edinburgh: T. & T. Clark, 1912.
———. *A Critical and Exegetical Commentary on Numbers*. ICC. Edinburgh: T. & T. Clark, 1903.
Gray, John. *1 and 2 Kings: A Commentary*. 2nd ed. OTL. London: SCM, 1970.
Greenberg, Moshe. *Ezekiel 21–37*. AB 22A. New York: Doubleday, 1997.
Gregory VII, Pope (Hildebrand). *The Correspondence of Pope Gregory VII: Selected Letters from the Registrum*. Translated by Ephraim Emerton. New York: Columbia University Press, 1932.
Gunkel, Hermann. *Introduction to the Psalms: The Genres of the Religious Lyrics of Israel*. Completed by Joachim Begreich. Translated by James D. Nogalski. Macon, GA: Mercer University Press, 1998.
———. "Psalm 149: An Interpretation." *Biblical World* 22 (1903) 363–66.
Haag, H. "בַּת." Translated by John T. Willis. In *TDOT* 2:332–38.
Haak, Robert D. *Habakkuk*. VTSup 44. Leiden: Brill, 1992.
———. "The Philistines in the Prophetic Texts." In *Hesed ve-Emet: Studies in Honor of Ernest S. Frerichs*, edited by Jodi Magness and Symour Gitin Brown, 37–51. Judaic Studies 320. Atlanta: Scholars, 1998.
Hagedorn, Anselm C. "Looking at Foreigners in Biblical and Greek Prophecy." *VT* 57 (2007) 432–48.
Hamborg, G. R. "Reasons for Judgement in the Oracles against the Nations of the Prophet Isaiah." *VT* 31 (1981) 145–59.
Hamilton, Jeffries M. "Hazor (Place)." In *ABD* 3:87–88.
Haran, Menahem. "The Place of the Prophecies against the Nations in the Book of Jeremiah." In *Emanuel: Studies in Hebrew Bible Septuagint and Dead Sea Scrolls in Honor of Emanuel Tov*, edited by Shalom M. Paul, 699–706. Boston: Brill, 2003.
Hart Weed, Jennifer. "*De Genesi ad litteram* and the Galileo Case." In *Go Figure! Figuration in Biblical Interpretation*, edited by Stanley D. Walters, 148–160. PTMS 81. Eugene, OR: Pickwick, 2008.
Hayes, John H. "The Usage of Oracles against Foreign Nations in Ancient Israel." *JBL* 87 (1968) 81–92.
Hayes, John H., and Stuart A. Irvine. *Isaiah: The Eighth-Century Prophet—His Times and His Preaching*. Nashville: Abingdon, 1987.
Hays, Richard B. *Echoes of Scripture in the Letters of Paul*. New Haven: Yale University Press, 1989.

Hayward, Robert. *The Targum of Jeremiah: Translated, with a Critical Introduction, Apparatus, and Notes.* The Aramaic Bible 12. Edinburgh: T. & T. Clark, 1987.
Hess, Richard S. "Elam (Person)." In *ABD* 2:423–24.
Hill, John. "The Construction of Time in Jeremiah 25 (MT)." In *Troubling Jeremiah*, edited by A. R. Pete Diamond et al., 146–60. JSOTSup 260. Sheffield: Sheffield Academic, 1999.
Hillers, Delbert R. *Micah.* Hermeneia. Minneapolis: Fortress, 1984.
———. *Treaty Curses and the Old Testament Prophets.* Biblica et Orientalia 16. Rome: Pontifical Biblical Institute, 1964.
Hobbs, T. R. *2 Kings.* WBC 21. Waco, TX: Word, 1986.
Holladay, William L. "Indications of Jeremiah's Psalter." *JBL* 121 (2002) 245–61.
———. *Jeremiah: A Commentary on the Book of the Prophet Jeremiah.* Vol. 1, *Chapters 1–25.* Hermeneia. Minneapolis: Fortress, 1986.
———. *Jeremiah: A Commentary on the Book of the Prophet Jeremiah.* Vol. 2, *Chapters 26–52.* Hermeneia. Minneapolis: Fortress, 1989.
———. "Style, Irony, and Authenticity in Jeremiah." *JBL* 81 (1962) 44–54.
Holt, Elsie. "The Meaning of an Inclusio: A Theological Interpretation of the Book of Jeremiah." *Scandinavian Journal of the Old Testament* 17.2 (2003) 183–205.
Hossfeld, Frank-Lothar, and Erich Zenger. *Psalms 2: A Commentary on Psalms 51–100.* Translated by Linda M. Maloney. Hermeneia. Minneapolis: Fortress, 2005.
The International Organization for Septuagint and Cognate Studies (IOSCS). "Critical Editions of Septuagint/Old Greek Texts." *IOSCS*, 2005. Online: http://ccat.sas.upenn.edu/ioscs/editions.html.
———. *New English Translation of the Septuagint* (2007). Online: http://ccat.sas.upenn.edu/nets/edition/.
Jenkins, A. K. "The Development of the Isaiah Tradition in Is 13–23." In *The Book of Isaiah*, edited by Jacques Vermeylen, 237–51. BETL 81. Leuven: Leuven University Press, 1989.
Jewish Publication Society. *JPS Holy Scriptures.* Philadephia: JPS, 1917.
Johns, Alger F. *A Short Grammar of Biblical Aramaic.* Rev. ed. Berrien Springs, MI: Andrews University Press, 1972.
Johnson, B. "מִשְׁפָּט." Translated by David E. Green. In *TDOT* 9:86–98.
Joint Committee. *The New English Bible with the Apocrypha.* Oxford/Cambridge: University Presses of Oxford and Cambridge, 1989.
———. *The Revised English Bible: The Old Testament.* Oxford/Cambridge: University Presses of Oxford and Cambridge, 1970.
Jones, Brian C. *Howling over Moab: Irony and Rhetoric in Isaiah 15–16.* SBL Dissertation Series 157. Atlanta: Scholars, 1996.
Jones, Douglas Rawlinson. *Haggai, Zechariah and Malachi: Introduction and Commentary.* Torch Bible Commentaries. London: SCM, 1962.
———. *Instrument of Peace: Biblical Principles of Christian Unity.* London: Hodder & Stoughton, 1965.
———. *Isaiah 56–66 and Joel.* Torch Bible Commentaries. London: SCM, 1964.
———. *Jeremiah.* New Century Bible Commentary. Grand Rapids: Eerdmans, 1992.
———. "The Tradition of the Oracles of Isaiah of Jerusalem." *ZAW* 67 (1955) 226–46.

Joüon, Paul S. J., and T. Muraoka. *A Grammar of Biblical Hebrew, Part One: Orthography and Phonetics*. Subsidia Biblica 14/I. Rome: Editrice Pontificio Istituto Biblico, 1993.

———. *A Grammar of Biblical Hebrew, Part Two: Morphology*. Subsidia Biblica 14/1. Rome: Editrice Pontificio Istituto Biblico, 1993.

———. *A Grammar of Biblical Hebrew, Part Three: Syntax—Paradigms and Indices*. Subsidia Biblica 14/2. Rome: Editrice Pontificio Istituto Biblico, 1993.

Kaiser, Otto. *Isaiah 13–39*. OTL. London: SCM, 1974.

Kaminsky, Joel S. "The Concept of Election and Second Isaiah: Recent Literature." *Biblical Theology Bulletin* 31 (2001) 135–44.

Katzenstein, H. J. "Philistines (History)." In *ABD* 5:326–28.

Keown, Gerald L., et al. *Jeremiah 26–52*. WBC 27. Dallas: Word, 1995.

Kessler, Martin. *Battle of the Gods: The God of Israel versus Marduk of Babylon: A Literary/Theological Interpretation of Jeremiah 50–51*. Assen: Royal van Gorcum, 2003.

———. "The Function of Chapters 25 and 50–51 in the Book of Jeremiah." In *Troubling Jeremiah*, edited by A. R. Pete Diamond et al., 64–72. JSOTSup 260. Sheffield: Sheffield Academic, 1999.

Kidner, Derek. "Isaiah." In *New Bible Commentary: 21st Century Edition*, edited by D. A. Carson et al., 629–70. Downers Grove, IL: InterVarsity, 1994.

———. *The Message of Jeremiah: Against Wind and Tide*. The Bible Speaks Today. Leicester, UK: InterVarsity, 1987.

Kissane, Edward J. *The Book of Isaiah 1–39: Translated from a Critically Revised Hebrew Text with Commentary*. Dublin: Brown & Nolan, 1941.

———. *The Book of Isaiah 40–66: Translated from a Critically Revised Hebrew Text with Commentary*. Dublin: Browne & Nolan, 1943.

Kitchen, K. A. "Aram, Arameans." In *New Bible Dictionary*, edited by I. H. Marshall et al., 65–68, 3rd ed. Leicester, UK: InterVarsity, 1996.

———. "Egypt." In *New Bible Dictionary*, edited by I. H. Marshall, 3rd ed., 293–302. Leicester, UK: InterVarsity, 1996.

———. "Egypt, History of (Chronology)." In *ABD* 2:321–31.

———. "Syria, Syrians." In *New Bible Dictionary*, edited by I. H. Marshall et al., 1143–44, 3rd ed. Leicester, UK: InterVarsity, 1996.

Knauf, Ernest Axel. "Kedar (Person)." In *ABD* 4:9–10.

Koehler, Ludwig, and Walter Baumgartner. "שׁאָ." In *The Hebrew and Aramaic Lexicon of the Old Testament*, edited and translated by M. E. J. Richardson, vol IV, 1374–75. 3rd ed. Revised by Walter Baumgartner and Johann Jakob Stamm. Leiden: Brill, 1999.

———. "שָׁאֲנָן." In *The Hebrew and Aramaic Lexicon of the Old Testament*, edited and translated by M. E. J. Richardson, vol IV, 1375. 3rd ed. Revised by Walter Baumgartner and Johann Jakob Stamm. Leiden: Brill, 1999.

———. "שׁקט." In *The Hebrew and Aramaic Lexicon of the Old Testament*, edited and translated by M. E. J. Richardson, vol IV, 1641–42. 3rd ed. Revised by Walter Baumgartner and Johann Jakob Stamm. Leiden: Brill, 1999.

Kraus, Hans-Joachim. *Psalms 60–150: A Commentary*. Translated by Hilton C. Oswald. Continental Commentaries. Minneapolis: Augsburg, 1989.

Kreuzer, Siegfried. "From 'Old Greek' to the Recensions." In *Septuagint Research: Issues and Challenges in the study of the Greek Jewish Scriptures*, edited by Wolfgang Kraus and Glenn Wooden, 225–37. Septuagint Research 53. Atlanta: SBL, 2006.

Kugel, James L. *The Idea of Biblical Poetry: Parallelism and Its History*. New Haven: Yale University Press, 1981.

Leslie, Elmer A. *Jeremiah: Chronologically Arranged, Translated & Interpreted*. Oxford: Abingdon, 1954.

———. *The Psalms: Translation and Interpretation in the Light of Hebrew Life and Worship*. Nashville: Abingdon, 1949.

Levenson, Jon D. *The Death and Resurrection of the Beloved Son: The Transformation of Child Sacrifice in Judaism and Christianity*. New Haven: Yale University Press, 1993.

———. *The Hebrew Bible, The Old Testament, and Historical Criticism: Jews and Christians in Biblical Studies*. Louisville: Westminster/ John Knox, 1993.

Levine, Baruch A. *Numbers 21–36*. AB 4A. London: Doubleday, 2000.

Limburg, James. *Psalms*. Westminster Bible Companion. Louisville: John Knox, 2000.

———. "Psalms (Book Of)." In *ABD* 5:522–536.

Lindblom, J. *Prophecy in Ancient Israel*. Oxford: Blackwell, 1962.

Lipiński, E., and W. von Soden. "עַם." Translated by David E. Green. In *TDOT* 11:163–77.

Lockman Foundation. *The Holy Bible: New American Standard: Ultra Thin Reference Edition*. Nashville: Broadman & Holman, 1983.

Lohr, Joel N. "Chosen and Unchosen: Conceptions of Election in the Pentateuch and Jewish-Christian Interpretation." PhD diss., Durham University, 2007.

Louth, Andrew. *Discerning the Mystery: An Essay on the Nature of Theology*. Oxford: Clarendon, 1983.

Lundbom, Jack R. *Jeremiah 1–20: A New Translation with Introduction and Commentary*. AB 21A. London: Doubleday, 1999.

———. *Jeremiah 21–36: A New Translation with Introduction and Commentary*. AB 21B. London: Doubleday, 2004.

———. *Jeremiah 37–52: A New Translation with Introduction and Commentary*. AB 21C. London: Doubleday, 2004.

———. "Jeremiah, Book of." In *ABD* 3:706–721.

———. *Jeremiah: A Study in Ancient Hebrew Rhetoric*. 2nd ed. Winona Lake, IN: Eisenbrauns, 1997.

Lust, J., et al. *A Greek-English Lexicon of the Septuagint: Part II—κ-ω*. Rev. ed. Stuttgart: Deutsche Bibelgesellschaf, 2003.

Lutheran Seminary. "Terence E. Fretheim." In the Profiles for Faculty Members section of Lutheran Seminary, St Paul, Minnesota website, 2009. Online: http://www.luthersem.edu/faculty/fac_profile.asp?contact_id=tfrethei.

MacDonald, Nathan. "'Gone Astray': Dealing with the *Sotah* (Num 5:11–31)." In *Go Figure! Figuration in Biblical Interpretation*, edited by Stanley D. Walters, 48–64. PTMS 81. Eugene, OR: Pickwick, 2008.

Mandelkern, Solomon. *Concordance on the Bible*, vols. 1 & 2. Revised ed. New York: Shulsinger Brothers, 1955.

Margueron, Jean-Claude. "Babylon (Place)." In *ABD* 1:563–65.

May, Herbert G., and E. L. Allen. "Ezekiel." In *Lamentations, Ezekiel, Daniel, Twelve Prophets*, edited by George Arthur Buttrick, 39–338. Interpreter's Bible 6. Nashville: Abingdon, 1956.

Mays, James Luther. *Amos: A Commentary*. OTL. London: SCM, 1969.

———. *Micah: A Commentary*. OTL. London: SCM, 1976.

McConville, J. Gordon. "Divine Speech and the Book of Jeremiah." In *The Trustworthiness of God: Perspectives on the Nature of Scripture*, edited by Paul Helm and Carl Trueman, 18–38. Leicester, UK: Apollos, 2002.

———. "Jeremiah." In *New Bible Commentary: 21st Century Edition*, edited by D. A. Carson et al., 671–708. Downers Grove, IL: InterVarsity, 1994.

———. *Judgment and Promise: An Interpretation of the Book of Jeremiah*. Leicester, UK: Apollos, 1993.

———. "The Judgment of God in the Old Testament." *Ex Auditu* 20 (2004) 25–42.

McKane, William. *The Book of Micah: Introduction and Commentary*. Edinburgh: T. & T. Clark, 1998.

———. *A Critical and Exegetical Commentary on Jeremiah*, vol. 1, I–XXV. ICC. Edinburgh: T. & T. Clark, 1986.

———. *A Critical and Exegetical Commentary on Jeremiah*, vol. 2, XXVI–LII. ICC. Edinburgh: T. & T. Clark, 1996.

McKeating, Henry. *The Book of Jeremiah*. Epworth Commentaries. Peterborough, UK: Epworth, 1999.

McKenzie, John L. *Second Isaiah: Introduction, Translation and Notes*. AB. London: Doubleday, 1968.

McKinion, Steven A. *Isaiah 1–39*. Ancient Christian Commentary on Scripture: Old Testament. Downers Grove, IL: InterVarsity, 2004.

McRay, John. "Damascus (Place)." In *ABD* 2:5–8.

Meek, Theophile James. "The Poetry of Jeremiah." *Jewish Quarterly Review* 14 (1924) 281–91.

———. "The Structure of Hebrew Poetry." *Journal of Religion* 9 (1929) 523–50.

Meyers, Carol L., and Eric M. Meyers. *Zechariah 1–8: A New Translation with Introduction and Commentary*. AB 25B. New York: Doubleday, 1987.

Milgrom, Jacob. *Numbers*. JPS Torah Commentary. Philadephia: Jewish Publication Society, 1990.

Millard, A. R. "Elam, Elamites." In *New Bible Dictionary*, edited by I. H. Marshall et al., 304–5, 3rd ed. Leicester, UK: InterVarsity, 1996.

Miller, J. Maxwell. "Moab (Place)." In *ABD* 4:882–93.

Miller, Patrick D. "Dietrich Bonhoeffer and the Psalms." In *Israelite Religion and Biblical Theology: Collected Essays*, 345–54. JSOTSup 267. Sheffield: Sheffield Academic, 2000.

———. "The Divine Council and the Prophetic Call to War." *VT* 18 (1968) 100–107.

———. *The Divine Warrior in Early Israel*. Harvard Semitic Monographs 5. Cambridge: Harvard University Press, 1973.

———. "El, The Creator of Earth." *Bulletin of the American Schools of Oriental Research* 239 (1980) 43–46.

———. "El the Warrior." *Harvard Theological Review* 60 (1967) 411–31.

———. "Fire in the Mythology of Canaan and Israel." *CBQ* 27 (1965) 256–57.

———. "God the Warrior." *Interpretation* 19 (1965) 39–46.

———. "God's Other Stories: On the Margins of Deuteronomistic Theology." In *Israelite Religion and Biblical Theology: Collected Essays*, 593–602. JSOTSup 267. Sheffield: Sheffield Academic, 2000.

———. *The God You Have: Politics, Religion, and the First Commandment*. Minneapolis: Fortress, 2004.

———. "January's Child (Editorial)." *Theology Today* 59 (2002–2003) 525–28.

———. "Jeremiah." In *The New Interpreter's Bible: A Commentary in Twelve Volumes*, vol. 6, *Isaiah—Ezekiel*, 553–926. Nashville: Abingdon, 2001.

———. "Prayer and Divine Action." In *God in the Fray*, edited by Tod Linafelt and Timothy K. Beal, 211–32. Minneapolis: Fortress, 1998.

———. *The Religion of Ancient Israel*. Library of Ancient Israel. London: SPCK, 2000.

———. "Sin and Judgment in Jeremiah 34:17–19." *JBL* 103 (1984) 611–13.

———. *Sin and Judgment in the Prophets: A Stylistic and Theological Analysis*. SBL Monograph Series 27. Chico, CA: Scholars, 1982.

———. "The Sovereignty of God." In *The Hermeneutical Quest: Essays in Honor of James Luther Mays on his Sixty-Fifth Birthday*, edited by Donald G. Miller, PTMS, 29–144. Allison Park, PA: Pickwick, 1986.

———. "Studies in Hebrew Word Patterns." *Harvard Theological Review* 73 (1980) 79–89.

———. "Terror All Around (Editorial)." *Theology Today* 58 (2001–2002) 497–593.

———. "Work and Faith (Editorial)." *Theology Today* 59 (2002–2003) 349–53.

———. "The World and Message of the Prophets: Old Testament Interpretation Past, Present and Future." In *Essays in Honor of Gene M. Tucker*, edited by James Luther Mays et al., 97–112. Nashville: Abingdon, 1995.

Mitchell, Hinckley G., et al. *A Critical and Exegetical Commentary on Haggai, Zechariah, Malachi, Jonah*. ICC. Edinburgh: T. & T. Clark, 1912.

Mitchell, T. C. "Hazor." In *New Bible Dictionary*, edited by I. H. Marshall et al., 447–48, 3rd ed. Leicester, UK: InterVarsity, 1996.

———. "Philistines, Philistia." In *New Bible Dictionary*, edited by I. H. Marshall et al., 3rd ed., 921–23. Leicester, UK: InterVarsity, 1996.

Moberly, R. W. L. *The Bible, Theology and Faith: A Study of Abraham and Jesus*. Cambridge: Cambridge University Press, 2000.

———. *Prophecy and Discernment*. Cambridge Studies in Christian Doctrine. Cambridge: Cambridge University Press, 2006.

Montgomery, James A. *A Critical and Exegetical Commentary on Kings*. ICC. Edinburgh: T. & T. Clark, 1951.

Moulton, James Hope. *A Grammar of New Testament Greek*, vol. 3, *Syntax*. Edited by Nigel Turner. Edinburgh: T. & T. Clark, 1963.

Mowinckel, Sigmund. *Psalmen-Studien II: Das Thronbesteigungsfest Jahwes und der Ursprung der Eschatologie*. Kristiania: Dybwad, 1922.

Nel, Philip J. "שקט." In *NIDOTTE* 4:234–35.

Nicholson, Ernest W. *The Book of the Prophet Jeremiah 1–25*. Cambridge Bible Commentary. Cambridge: Cambridge University Press, 1973.

———. *The Book of the Prophet Jeremiah 26–52*. Cambridge Bible Commentary. Cambridge: Cambridge University Press, 1975.

Niehr, B. "שָׁפַט; שֶׁפֶט." Translated by David E. Green. In *TDOT* 15:411–31.

North, Frank. "The Oracle against the Ammonites in Jeremiah 49:1–6." *JBL* 65 (1946) 37–43.
Obermann, Julian. "Yahweh's Victory over the Babylonian Pantheon: The Archetype of Is. 21:1–10." *JBL* 48 (1929) 307–28.
O'Brien, Julia Myers. *Nahum*. Readings: A New Biblical Commentary. London: Sheffield Academic, 2002.
Oestereich, Thomas. "Pope St Gregory VII (Hildebrand)." In *The Catholic Encyclopaedia*, vol. 6, transcribed by Janet van Heyst. New York: Robert Appleton Company, 1909. Online: http://www.newadvent.org/cathen/06791c.htm.
Oesterley, W. O. E. *The Psalms 2: Translation with Text-Critical and Exegetical Notes*. London: SPCK, 1939.
Oliver, Anthony. "אבל." In *NIDOTTE* 1:243–48.
Oswalt, John N. "שאן." In *NIDOTTE* 4:10–11.
———. *The Book of Isaiah Chapters 1–39*. The New International Commentary on the Old Testament. Grand Rapids: Eerdmans, 1986.
Packer, J. I., general editor. *English Standard Version*. Wheaton, IL: Crossway, 2001.
Pannenberg, Wolfhart. "The Origin of the Doctrine of the Trinity and the Problem of the Logos Christology." In *Jesus, God and Man*, translated by Lewis L. Wilkins and Duane A. Priebe, 2nd ed., 158–87. Westminster: John Knox, 1983.
Paul, Shalom M. "Amos 1:3–2:3: A Concatenous Literary Pattern." *JBL* 90 (1971) 397–403.
Peels, H. G. L. "נקם." In *NIDOTTE* 3:154–56.
Perdue, Leo G. "The Book of Jeremiah in Old Testament Theology." In *Troubling Jeremiah*, edited by A. R. Pete Diamond et al., 320–38. JSOTSup 260. Sheffield: Sheffield Academic, 1999.
———. "Jeremiah in Modern Research: Approaches and Issues." In *A Prophet to the Nations: Essays in Jeremiah Studies*, edited by Leo G. Perdue and Brian W. Kovacs, 1–32. Winona Lake, IN: Eisenbrauns, 1984.
Peters, Melvin K. H. "Septuagint." In *ABD* 5:1093–1104.
Pitard, Wayne T. "Aram (Person)." In *ABD* 1:338.
———. "Aram (Place)." In *ABD* 1:338–341.
Pope, Marvin H. *Job: Introduction, Translation and Notes*. 3rd ed. AB 15. London: Doubleday, 1965.
Preuss, H. D. "לאם." In *TDOT* 7:397–398.
Price, Ira M. "The School of the Sons of the Prophets." *The Old Testament Student* 8.7 (1889) 244–49.
Procksch, D. Otto. *Jesaia I: übersetzt und erklärt*. Kommentar zum Alten Testament. Leipzig: Diechert, 1930.
Provan, Iain. "To Highlight All Our Idols: Worshipping God in Nietzshe's World." *Ex Auditu* 15 (1999) 19–38.
Raabe, Paul R. "Why Prophetic Oracles against the Nations?" In *Fortunate the Eyes that See: Essays in Honor of David Noel Freedman in Celebration of His Seventieth Birthday*, Astrid B. Beck et al., 236–257. Grand Rapids: Eerdmans, 1995.
Rad, Gerhard, von. *Holy War in Ancient Israel*. Translated by John H. Yoder and Marva J. Dawn. Grand Rapids: Eerdmans, 1996.
———. *Old Testament Theology*. Vol. 2, *The Theology of Israel's Prophetic Traditions*. London: SCM, 1975.

Radner, Ephraim. "Leviticus as Christian Scripture." In *Go Figure! Figuration in Biblical Interpretation*, edited by Stanley D. Walters, 107–20. PTMS 81. Eugene, OR: Pickwick, 2008.

———. "The Truth that Casts Out Fear: A Sermon on Leviticus 12 and Luke 2:21–40." In *Go Figure! Figuration in Biblical Interpretation*, edited by Stanley D. Walters, 25–30. PTMS 81. Eugene, OR: Pickwick, 2008.

Rahlfs, Alfred, editor. *Septuaginta id est Vetus Testamentum Graece iuxta LXX Interpretes*. Stuttgart: Württembergische Bibelanstalt, 1935.

Rashi. *The Judaica Press Complete Tanach with Rashi*. Online: http://www.chabad.org/library/bible_cdo/aid/16045.

Reimer, David J. *The Oracles against Babylon in Jeremiah 50–51: A Horror among the Nations*. San Francisco: Mellen Research University Press, 1993.

Rendtorff, Rolf. "How to Read the Book of the Twelve as a Theological Unit." In *Reading and Hearing the Book of the Twelve*, edited by James D. Nogalski and Marvin A. Sweeney, 75–87. SBL Symposium Series 15. Atlanta: SBL, 2000.

Reventlow, Henning Graf. *Das Amt des Propheten bei Amos*. Forschungen zur Religion und Literatur des Alten und Neuen Testaments 80. Göttingen: Vandenhoeck & Ruprecht, 1962.

Rogerson, J. W. "The Rev Professor Douglas Jones: Old Testament Scholar and Churchman." *The Independent*. December 3, 2005. Online: http://www.independent.co.uk/news/obituaries/the-rev-professor-douglas-jones-517952.html.

Rösel, Martin. "Towards a 'Theology of the LXX.'" In *Septuagint Research: Issues and Challenges in the study of the Greek Jewish Scriptures*, edited by Wolfgang Kraus and Glenn Wooden, 238–52. Septuagint Research 53. Atlanta: SBL, 2006.

Rosenthal, Franz. *A Grammar of Biblical Aramaic*. Porta Linguarum Orientalium 5. 6th ed. Wiesbaden: Harrassowitz, 1995.

Rudolph, Wilhelm. *Jeremiah*. Handbuch zum Alten Testament 12. Tübingen: Mohr/Siebeck, 1968.

Sacks, Jonathan. "Credo: Do Remember the Past, but Do not Be Held Captive by It." Chief Rabbi's website. Published in *The Times*, 2004. Online: http://www.chiefrabbi.org/ReadArtical.aspx?id=1143.

———. "Values We Share." In *Celebrating Life: Finding Happiness in Unexpected Places*, 115–118. London: Continuum, 2000.

Schoville, Keith N. "A Note on the Oracles of Amos against Gaza, Tyre, and Edom." In *Studies on Prophecy: A Collection of Twelve Papers*, edited by G. W. Anderson et al., 55–63. VTSup 26. Leiden: Brill, 1974.

Schultz, Richard. "שפט." In *NIDOTTE* 4:213–20.

———. "Response to Provan." *Ex Auditu* 15 (1999) 39–42.

Seitz, Christopher R. *Figured Out: Typology and Providence in Christian Scripture*. Louisville: Westminster/ John Knox, 2001.

———. "History, Figural History, and Providence in the Dual Witness of Prophet and Apostle." In *Go Figure! Figuration in Biblical Interpretation*, edited by Stanley D. Walters, 1–6. PTMS 81. Eugene, OR: Pickwick, 2008.

———. *Isaiah 1–39*. Interpretation: A Bible Commentary for Teaching and Preaching. Louisville: Westminster/ John Knox, 1993.

Severus, Sulpicius. "Letter 2: A Letter of Sulpitius Severus to His Sister Claudia Concerning Virginity." In *Dubious Letters: The Doubtful Letters of Sulpicius*

Severus, edited by Kevin Knight, chapter 19. New Advent, 2008. Online: http://www.newadvent.org/fathers/3504.htm.

Sharp, Carolyn J. "'Take Another Scroll and Write': A Study of the LXX and the MT of Jeremiah's Oracles against Egypt and Babylon." *VT* 47 (1997) 487–516.

Skinner, J. *The Book of the Prophet Isaiah Chapters 1–34 with Introduction and Notes.* Cambridge: Cambridge University Press, 1900.

Smelik, Klaas A. D. "An Approach to the Book of Jeremiah." In *Reading the Book of Jeremiah: A Search for Coherence*, edited by Martin Kessler, 1–11. Winona Lake, IN: Eisenbrauns, 2004.

Smith, George Adam. *The Book of Isaiah Chapters 1–32.* London: Hodder & Stoughton, 1927.

Smith, Ralph L. *Micah–Malachi.* WBC 32. Waco, TX: Word, 1984.

Sommer, Benjamin D. "Isaiah." In *The Jewish Study Bible*, edited by Adele Berlin and Marc Zvi Brettler, 780–916. Oxford: Oxford University Press, 2004.

———. *A Prophet Reads Scripture: Allusion in Isaiah 40–66.* Stanford: Stanford University Press, 1998.

Spalinger, Anthony. "Egypt, History of (Dyn. 21–26)." In *ABD* 2:353–64.

Sperber, Alexander. *The Bible in Aramaic.* Vol. 3, *The Latter Prophets According to Targum Jonathan.* Leiden: Brill, 1992.

Spina, Frank Anthony. "Moses and Joshua: Servants of the Lord as Purveyors of the Word." In *Go Figure! Figuration in Biblical Interpretation*, edited by Stanley D. Walters, 65–92. PTMS 81. Eugene, OR: Pickwick, 2008.

Stacey, David. *Isaiah Chapters 1–39.* London: Epworth, 1993.

Steinmann, Andrew E. "The Order of Amos's Oracles against the Nations: 1:3—2:16." *JBL* 111 (1992) 683–89.

Stenning, J. F., editor and translator. *The Targum of Isaiah.* Oxford: Clarendon, 1949.

Stuart, Douglas. *Hosea–Jonah.* WBC 31. Waco, TX: Word, 1987.

Stulman, Louis. *Jeremiah.* Abingdon Old Testament Commentaries. Nashville: Abingdon, 2005.

Sweeney, Marvin A. "Ezekiel." In *The Jewish Study Bible*, edited by Adele Berlin and Marc Zvi Brettler, 1042–1138. Oxford: Oxford University Press, 2004.

———. "Habakkuk." In *The Twelve Prophets.* Vol. 2, *Micah, Nahum, Habakkuk, Zephaniah, Haggai, Zechariah, and Malachi*, 451–90. Berit Olam. Collegeville, MN: Liturgical, 2000.

———. "Habakkuk, Book of." In *ABD* 3:1–6.

———. "Jeremiah." In *The Jewish Study Bible*, edited by Adele Berlin and Marc Zvi Brettler, 917–20. Oxford: Oxford University Press, 2004.

Tarragon, Jean-Michel, de. "Ammon (Person)." In *ABD* 1:194–96.

Taylor, Cameron Boyd. "In a Mirror Dimly." In *Septuagint Research: Issues and Challenges in the Study of the Greek Jewish Scriptures*, edited by Wolfgang Kraus and Glenn Wooden, 15–31. Septuagint Research 53. Atlanta: SBL, 2006.

Terrien, Samuel. *The Psalms: Strophic Structure and Theological Commentary.* Eerdmans Critical Commentary. Grand Rapids: Eerdmans, 2003.

Thackeray, Henry St John. *Grammar of the Old Testament in Greek according to the Septuagint.* Vol. 1, *Introduction, Orthography and Accidence.* Cambridge: Cambridge University Press, 1909.

Thiel. "שָׁאַן ;שׁאא." Translated by Douglas W. Stott. In *TDOT* 14:265–67.

Thomas, D. Winton, and Theodore Cuyler Speers. "Zechariah." In *Lamentations, Ezekiel, Daniel, Twelve Prophets*, edited by George Arthur Buttrick, 1051–114. Interpreter's Bible 6. Nashville: Abingdon, 1956.

Thompson, J. A. "Ammon, Ammonites." In *New Bible Dictionary*, edited by I. H. Marshall et al., 29–30, 3rd ed. Leicester, UK: InterVarsity, 1996.

———. *The Book of Jeremiah*. The New International Commentary on the Old Testament. Grand Rapids: Eerdmans, 1980.

———. "Edom, Edomites." In *New Bible Dictionary*, edited by I. H. Marshall et al., 3rd ed., 290–92. Leicester, UK: InterVarsity, 1996.

———. "Moab, Moabites." In *New Bible Dictionary*, edited by I. H. Marshall et al., 3rd ed., 775–77. Leicester, UK: InterVarsity, 1996.

Torrey, Charles Cutler. *The Second Isaiah: A New Interpretation*. Edinburgh: T. & T. Clark, 1928.

Tov, Emanuel. *The Septuagint Translation of Jeremiah and Baruch: A Discussion of an Early Revision of the LXX of Jeremiah 29–52 and Baruch 1:1–3:8*. Missoula, MT: Scholars, 1976.

Toy, Crawford H. "The Judgment of Foreign Peoples in Amos i.3–ii.3." *JBL* 25 (1906) 25–28.

Tsevat, Matitiahu. "בְּתוּלָה; בְּתוּלִים." In *TDOT* 2:338–43.

Tucker, Gene M. "Isaiah." In *The New Interpreter's Bible: A Commentary in Twelve Volumes*, vol. 6, *Isaiah—Ezekiel*, 25–552. Nashville: Abingdon, 2001.

Tyndale House Bible Translation Committee. *Holy Bible: New Living Translation: Gift and Award Edition*. Wheaton, IL: Tyndale, 1997.

United Bible Societies. *Good News Bible: Today's English Version*. The Bible Societies, 1976.

Vallat, François. "Elam (Place)." In *ABD* 2:424–29.

Van Dijk, H. J. *Ezekiel's Prophecy on Tyre (Ez. 26,1–28,19): A New Approach*. Biblica et Orientalia 20. Rome: Pontifical Biblical Institute, 1968.

Van Hecke, Pierre J. P. "Metaphorical Shifts in the Oracle against Babylon (Jeremiah 50–51)." *Scandinavian Journal of the Old Testament* 17 (2003) 68–88.

Van Zyl, A. H. *The Moabites*. Pretoria Oriental Series 3. Leiden: Brill, 1960.

Volz, D. Paul. *Der Prophet Jeremia*. Kommentar zum Alten Testament 10. Leipzig: Deichert, 1928.

———. *Studien zum Text des Jeremia*. Beiträge zur Wissenschaft vom Alten Testament 25. Leipzig: Hinrichs, 1920.

Waard, Jan, de. *A Handbook on Jeremiah: Textual Criticism and the Translator*. Vol. 2. Winona Lake, IN: Eisenbrauns, 2003.

Wagner, J. Ross. "The Septuagint and the 'Search for the Christian Bible.'" In *Scripture's Doctrine and Theology's Bible: How the New Testament Shapes Christian Dogmatics*, edited by Markus Bockmuehl and Alan J. Torrance, 17–28. Grand Rapids: Baker Academic, 2008.

Walters, Stanley D. "Death Binds, Death Births." In *Go Figure! Figuration in Biblical Interpretation*, edited by Stanley D. Walters, 93–104. PTMS 81. Eugene, OR: Pickwick, 2008.

———. "Finding Christ in the Psalms." In *Go Figure! Figuration in Biblical Interpretation*, edited by Stanley D. Walters, 31–47. PTMS 81. Eugene OR: Pickwick, 2008.

Waltke, Bruce K., and M. O'Connor. *An Introduction to Biblical Hebrew Syntax*. Winona Lake, IN: Eisenbrauns, 1990.
Wansbrough, Henry, editor. *The New Jerusalem Bible, with Deutero-Canon*. London: Doubleday, 1985.
Ward, William A. "Egyptian Relations with Canaan." In *ABD* 2:399–408.
Ward, W. Hayes. "Habakkuk." In *A Critical and Exegetical Commentary on Micah, Zephaniah, Nahum, Habakkuk, Obadiah, and Joel*, by John Merlin Powis Smith et al., 1–72 (second part of book). ICC. Edinburgh: T. & T. Clark, 1912.
Watts, James W. "Text and Redaction in Jeremiah's Oracles against the Nations." *CBQ* 54 (1992) 432–47.
Watts, John D. W. "Habakkuk." In *The Books of Joel, Obadiah, Jonah, Nahum, Habakkuk, and Zephaniah*, 121–52. London: Cambridge University Press, 1975.
———. *Isaiah 1–33*. WBC 24. Dallas: Word, 1985.
———. *Isaiah 34–66 Revised*. WBC 25. Nashville: Nelson, 2005.
Weber, N. A. "Sulpicius Severus." In *The Catholic Encyclopaedia*, vol. 14, transcribed by Douglas J. Potter. New York: Robert Appleton Company, 1912. Online: http://www.newadvent.org/cathen/14332a.htm.
Weis, Richard. "The Textual Situation in the Book of Jeremiah." In *Sôfēr Mahîr: Essays in Honour of Adrian Schenker Offered by Editors of* Biblia Hebraica Quinta, edited by Yohanan A. P. Goldman et al., 269–93. Supplements to *VT* 110. Leiden: Brill, 2006.
Weiser, Artur. *Der Prophet Jeremia: Kap. 25'15–52'34*. Das Alte Testament Deutsch 21. Göttingen: Vandenhoeck & Ruprecht, 1955.
———. *The Psalms: A Commentary*. Translated by Herbert Hartwell. 5th rev. ed. OTL. London: SCM, 1959.
Wendorf, Fred, and Angela E. Close. "Egypt, History of (Prehistory)." In *ABD* 2:331–36.
Wevers, John W. *Ezekiel*. Century Bible. London: Nelson, 1969.
Whybray, R. N. *The Second Isaiah*. Old Testament Guides. Sheffield: JSOT Press, 1983.
Widyapranawa, S. H. *The Lord Is Saviour: Faith in National Crisis—A Commentary on the Book of Isaiah 1–39*. Grand Rapids: Handsel, 1990.
Wigram, George V. *The Englishman's Hebrew Concordance of the Old Testament*. Strong's Numbering Added. Peabody, MA: Hendrickson, 1874.
Wildberger, Hans. *Isaiah 1–12: A Commentary*. Translated by Thomas H. Trapp. Continental Commentaries. Minneapolis: Fortress, 1991.
———. *Isaiah 13–27: A Commentary*. Translated by Thomas H. Trapp. Continental Commentaries. Minneapolis: Fortress, 1997.
Wilken, Robert Louis, editor and translator. *Isaiah: Interpreted by Early Christian and Medieval Commentators*. The Church's Bible. Grand Rapids: Eerdmans, 2007.
Williamson, H. G. M. *The Book Called Isaiah: Deutero-Isaiah's Role in Composition and Redaction*. Oxford: Clarendon, 1994.
Wiseman, D. J. "Babylonia." In *New Bible Dictionary*, edited by I. H. Marshall et al., 112–17, 3rd ed. Leicester: InterVarsity, 1996.
———. "Damascus." In *New Bible Dictionary*, edited by I. H. Marshall et al., 3rd ed., 251–53. Leicester: InterVarsity, 1996.

Wolff, Hans Walter. *Joel and Amos: A Commentary on the Books of the Prophets of Joel and Amos*. Translated by Waldemar Janzen et al. Hermeneia. Philadelphia: Fortress, 1977.

Würthwein, Ernst. "Der Ursprung der prophetischen Gerichtsrede." In *Wort und Existenz: Studien zum Alten Testament*, 111–26. Göttingen: Vandenhoeck & Ruprecht, 1970.

Young, Edward J. *The Book of Isaiah: The English Text, with Introduction, Exposition, and Notes*. Grand Rapids: Eerdmans, 1965.

Younker, Randall W. "Rabbah." In *ABD* 5:598–600.

Ziegler, Joseph, editor. *Septuaginta Vetus Testamentum Graecum*. Vol. XV. Göttingen: Vandenhoeck & Ruprecht, 1957.

Zimmerli, Walther. *Ezekiel 2:25–48*. Translated by James D. Martin. Hermeneia. Minneapolis: Fortress, 1983.

Zobel, H. "הוֹ." In *TDOT* 3:3–343.

Zvi, Ehud ben. "Zechariah." In *The Jewish Study Bible*, edited by Adele Berlin and Marc Zvi Brettler, 1249–67. Oxford: Oxford University Press, 2004.

Scripture Index

Genesis

	197, 268
4:10	229
12:1	279
19	260
26:24	116

Exodus

	122, 123, 140, 267, 272
2:23–25	264
7:3	272
7:5	264, 272
7:17	264
8:10	264
8:22	264
9:14	264
9:29	264
14:4	264, 272
14:18	264, 272
15:8	174
20:3	263
20:4–6	263
10:1	272
11:9	272
14:18	272

Numbers

	53, 81
21	49, 50, 268
21:27	51
21:28–29	48, **49–52**, 82, 221, 222, 246, 271, 299
21:28	73
21:29	74
22:6	197
22:11	197
22:12	197
22:17	197
23:7	197
23:8	197
23:11	197
23:13	197
23:21	174
23:27	197
24:10	197
24:15–24	231
24:17	73, 82
25:2	59

Deuteronomy

	81, 197
4:20	169
5:7	263
5:8–10	263
7:1	203
7:2	228
7:6	169
7:7	253
7:16	210
10:22	253
14:2	169
20:13	203
23:4	240
26:18–19	169
28:49	72, 72
28:52	72, 73
32:41–43	203

Deuteronomy (cont.)

33:1—34:1	267
33:5	174
34:5–6	268
34:10	268

Joshua

	197, 228, 268
3	268

Judges

	197
2:16–19	210
3	189, 202, **209–10**, 298
3:12–30	210
5:23	210

Ruth

	260, 267
2:11–12	261
3	260
3:10	261
4	263
4:15	261
4:14	263
4:18–22	261

1 Samuel

	197
3:13	205
22	261
22:1–4	261

2 Samuel

	197
1:17–27	258
1:19–27	231
3:32–35	258
7:27	225
8:2	246, 261
16:7	197
16:10	197
16:11	197
16:12	197
16:13	197
19:21	197

1 Kings

	197
1:1	246
2:8	197
3:4–5	246

2 Kings

	197
18:17–37	155
19:21–28	231, 264
24–25	38
24:2	194

1 Chronicles

	197

2 Chronicles

	197

Psalms

	97, 197, 199, 199, 200, 201, 211, 214, 221
1	199
2	174, 199
6	199, 262
7	199
9–10	199
18	174
22	199, 262
22:29	174
24:7–10	174
35	199
38	199, 262
39	262
41	262
42–43	262
44	262
46	174
47	174

Psalms (cont.)

48	174
55	262
59	262
59:5	225
59:8	129
60	262
64	199, 262
68	174
69	262
70	262
72	174
74	262
75:11 (10)	70
76	174
77	262
78	199
79	199, 262
80	262
83	199, 262
83:6	243
84	199
85	262
86	262
88	262
93	174
93:1	174
96	200, 201
96:1	200
96:2	201
96:3	201
96:10	134, 200
96:13	201
97	174
98	174, 200, 201
98:1	200
98:2–3	201
98:6	200
98:9	201
102	262
109	262
122	199
123:4	246, 247, 248
137	262
137:7–9	198
137:8	198, 199
139	199
140	262
142	262
143	262
149	198, 198, 199, 200, 201, 202, 204, 206, 207, 209, 210, 211, 214, 215
149:1	200
149:4	201
149:5	201
149:6–9	189, **198–207**, 210, 214, 215, 298
149:6–7	198
149:6	201, 202
149:9	199, 201, 203, 205, 206, 210, 214, 215

Proverbs

11:28	233
16:18	250

Isaiah

	1, 5, 16, 79, 80, 81, 82, 83, 84, 85, 86, 87, 88, 91, 92, 92, 93, 93, 94, 95, 95, 96, 130, 131, 152, 155, 157, 159, 168, 179, 180, 197, 201, 204, 214, 236, 237, 238, 239, 240, 241, 242, 260, 267
1:2	118
1:21	161
5:9	68, 84
6:11	68
9	90, 91
9:7	206
10:12	236
10:13–14	236
10:15	236
10:33	236
11	90, 91

Isaiah (cont.)

11:4	214
13–23	7, 19, 241
13	5
13:8	73
13:11	236, 241
13:19	236, 241
14:2	240, 241
14:3–21	257, 258, 299
14:4	258
14:5–6	237, 241
14:20	239, 241
15–16	xv, 7, 54, 66, **67–98**, 130, 161, 179, 218, 227, 257, 259, 262, 298, 299
15	80
15:1	67, 80
15:2–7	77, 79, 81
15:2	70, 72, 71, 77, 78
15:3	72, 78, 79
15:4	71, 73, 77, 78, 79, 83
15:5	67, 68, 70, 71, 72, 77, 78, 79, 80, 84, 93, 161
15:6	71, 78
15:7	72, 78
15:8	67, 70, 77, 80, 83
15:9—16:6	91
15:9—16:5	81
15:9	68, 87
16	91
16:1–5	76, 83, 89, 91
16:1–4	89
16:1	68
16:2–3	90
16:2	70
16:3	73, 77, 81
16:4	68, 80, 84, 89, 90
16:5	68, 88, 90, 90, 91, 97
16:6–12	77, 79, 81
16:6	70, 77, 90, 94, 131, 235, 236, 243
16:7–9	83
16:7	70, 74, 77, 84, 94, 256
16:8	32, 71, 78
16:9	71, 71, 78, 84
16:10	71, 78, 84
16:11	72, 78, 81, 83, 84, 261
16:12	71, 71, 78, 79
16:13–14	91, **92**
16:13	74, 84
16:14	74
19	135, 267
19:11	237
19:13	237
19:23–25	114
19:16–25	165
19:21	272
19:21–25	267
19:24–25	124
19:25	178
20	83
20:5	236
20:6	236
21:3	73, 266
21:10	225
22	234
22:4	267
22:8	236
23:9	236
23:12	117
23:17–18	48, 178
24	76
24:5	239
24:16	237
24:17–18	76, 82, 88, **95–96**,
24:17	73
24:18	73
24:21–22	203
25:10–12	261
25:11	75
25:11–12	243
30:6	231
32	258
33:6	91
33:11	91
33:15–16	91
34:5	204
37:16	225

Isaiah (cont.)

40–66	201
41:15–16	203
44:6	174
45–55	265
45:14	203
45:23	165
47:1	69, 117
47:6	240, 241
47:7	236, 241
47:8	236, 241
47:10	236, 241
47:12–13	239
49:7	203
49:23	203
56–66	152, 165, 181
56:3	114
56:6–7	114
56:7	123
60	203
60:12	201
60:14	130, 201
60:22	181
61:5–6	130
66	203
66:15–16	205

Jeremiah

	ix, xv, xvi, 1, 85, 197
LXX 1–32	46
LXX 1–28	46
1:1—25:12	208
1:1–3	106
1:5–10	47
1:5	3
2:26	253, 254, 280
2:34	253, 254, 280
4–5	122
4:7	68
7:16	277
9	258
9:1	267
10:15	264
11:3	197
12:14–17	178, 272
12:14–15	111
13:17	267
14:1	267
14:7–9	275
14:7	276
14:19–22	275
15:1	277
16:21	132
17:5	197
18:3	189
18:7–8	20
19:11	72, 79
19:25	48
20:7	129
20:14	197
20:15	197
22:28	72, 79, 124
23:12	73
23:17–18	48
25	44, 47, 65, 193, 207, 244, 248, 250, 272
25:1–14	40
25:1–13	65
25:1	40
25:2	40
25:3	40, 241
25:4	41
25:5	41
25:6	41
25:7	42
25:8	42, 241
25:9	42
25:10	43
25:11	43, 207, 208, 241
25:12	43, 207, 208, 241
25:13	43, 189, **207–9**
25:14	44, 237, 241
25:15	241
25:17	59, 241
25:18–26	44
25:27	250
25:31	132, 204
25:2	241

Jeremiah (cont.)

26:9	68
28:2	59
28:60	59
28:64	59
LXX 29–52	46
29:14	117
30–31	46, 47, 135
30:6	45, 73
39:12–17	124
30:26	46
31	272
31:27–28	272
LXX 31–32	49
LXX 31	22, 24, 25, 50, 274, 299
LXX 31:1	25, 60, 61
LXX 31:2	25, 61, 64
LXX 31:3	25
LXX 31:4	25, 54, 55
LXX 31:5	26, 55, 64
LXX 31:6	26
LXX 31:7	26, 59, 60
LXX 31:8	26, 60, 61
LXX 31:9	27, 61, 62, 64
LXX 31:10	27, 64, 189
LXX 31:11	27, 59
LXX 31:12	28, 61
LXX 31:13	28
LXX 31:14	28
LXX 31:15	28, 64
LXX 31:16	29, 59
LXX 31:17	29
LXX 31:18	29, 58
LXX 31:19	29
LXX 31:20	30
LXX 31:21	30
LXX 31:22	30
LXX 31:23	30
LXX 31:24	30, 62
LXX 31:25	30
LXX 31:26	31, 61
LXX 31:27	31, 60, 64
LXX 31:28	31, 64
LXX 31:29–30	59
LXX 31:29	31, 57, 58
LXX 31:30	32, 59, 60
LXX 31:31	32, 55, 56, 57
LXX 31:32	32, 56, 61
LXX 31:33	32, 56, 57
LXX 31:34	33, 56, 61, 61
LXX 31:35	33, 59, 60
LXX 31:36	33, 62
LXX 31:37	34, 54, 56
LXX 31:38	34, 54
LXX 31:39	34
LXX 31:40–41	52
LXX 31:40	34, 52
LXX 31:41	35, 52
LXX 31:42	35
LXX 31:43	35
LXX 31:44	35, 48
32	46
32:16–25	178, 183
32:27	132
LXX 32	46
LXX 32:1	207
33	91, 272
33:6	91
33:11	91
33:15–16	91
34:22	68
36	47, 208
LXX 37–38	46, 49
43:12–13	264
44:22	68
45:5	132
46–51	7, 44, 44, 47, 105, 106, 107, 120, 125, 134, 142, 157, 167, 170, 200, 204, 207, 209, 225, 243, 272
46–49	44, 134, 137, 241, 242
46	124, 178, 179, 226
46:1	219
46:10	197, 235,
46:11	117
46:18	69, 132, 157
46:19	68, 117
46:21	235

Jeremiah (cont.)

46:24	117
46:25	235, 264, 267
46:26	74, 165
47	226
47:6–7	197
48	7, 12, 18, 19, 22, 23, 24, 25, 49, 49 50, 51, 52, 53, 54, 66, 67, 74, 75, 76, 80, 81, 82, 82, 83, 84, 85, 86, 87, 88, 89, 91, 92, 93, 94, 95, 96, 97, 98, 99, 100, 102, 105, 106, 107, 108, 109, 110, 111, 112, 113, 114, 116, 117, 120, 121, 122, 126, 127, 128, 130, 134, 136, 139, 142, 144, 145, 146, 147, 148, 150, 157, 158, 160, 161, 162, 163, 164, 169, 170, 171, 173, 174, 176, 177, 178, 179, 180, 181, 183, 184, 185, 186, 187, 189, 192, 195, 198, 199, 200, 203, 204, 205, 206, 207, 210, 211, 213, 215, 216, 218, 219, 222, 223, 224, 226, 227, 228, 231, 233, 234, 241, 242, 243, 244, 245, 250, 257, 258, 259, 260, 262, 263, 264, 266, 267, 268, 269, 270, 271, 273, 274, 275, 276, 277, 278, 280, 281, 297, 298, 299, 300, 301
48:1–13	218
48:1–10	161, 217, 218, 222, 223, **225–44**, **271**
48:1–9	128, 218, 282, 289
48:1–6	225
48:1–5	222, 226, **228–29**, 272, 280
48:1	25, 60, 61, 67, 80, 85, 87, 88, 110, 113, 129, 161, 171, 195, **225–27**, 228, 229, 247, 248, 249, 265, 271
48:2	25, 61, 64, 67, 171, 195, 196, 229, 230, 271
48:3–5	195, 229
48:3	25, 67, 80, 228, 229
48:4–5	225
48:4	25, 54, 58, 67, 206, 223, 228, 229
48:5	26, 55, 64, 68, 77, 79, 80, 83, 93, 158, 161, 223, 229
48:6–27	81
48:6–9	222, 231
48:6–7	195
48:6	26, 62, 63, 68, 129, 230, 271
48:7–8	86
48:7	26, 59, 60, 68, 86, 112, 115, 122, 144, 171, 225, 229, **232–34**, 236, 243, 245, 248, 252, 264, 271, 280, 281
48:8–9	225
48:8	26, 60, 61, 68, 85, 171, 192, 195, 225, 227, 228, 229, 271
48:9	27, 61, 62, 63, 64, 68, 91, 129, 193, 195, 216, 228, 230, 231, 242, 271
48:10–13	218
48:10	27, 64, 68, 88, 92, 97, 129, 131, 161, 162, 173, 177, 181, 187, **188–216**, 219, 222, 225, 229, 231, **242**, 269, 272, 283, 291, 298
48:11–28	223
48:11–20	218
48:11–17	218
48:11–16	284, 292
48:11–13	196, 217, 218, 222, 229, 232, **243–48**
48:11–12	86, 88

Jeremiah (cont.)

48:11   27, 59, 69, 86, 122, 130, 131, 230, 231, 235, 244, **245–47**, 248, 280
48:12–13   131, 244
48:12   28, 61, 69, 84, 87, 94, 144, 171, 196, 209, 228, 244, 245, 256
48:13   28, 69, 82, 86, 88, 161, 164, 171, 228, 235, 236, 244, 245, **247–48**, 249, 253, 264, 281
48:14–28   161, 171, 217, 218, 222, 223, 230, 232, **249–54**
48:14–24   250
48:14–20   109, 129, 218, 222
48:14–15   250, 281
48:14   28, 69, 128, 161, 196, 245, 249, 250, 268
48:15–16   196
48:15   28, 52, 64, 69, 84, 87, 94, 120, 123, 157, 171, 175, 228, 232, 248, 249
48:16   29, 59, 69, 228, 249, 254
48:17–28   284, 292
48:17–20   249
48:17   29, 55, 69, 128, 158, 161, 196, 223, 228, 230, 231, 232, 249, 254, 259
48:18–28   218
48:18–19   249
48:18   29, 58, 69, 18, 118, 118, 124, 129, 171, 228, 229, 249, 279
48:19   29, 69, 249
48:20–21   86
48:20   30, 69, 88, 112, 161, 171, 196, 223, 228, 250, 259
48:21–28   218
48:21–25   196, 222
48:21–24   62, 83, 250
48:21   30, 69, 88, 199, 204, 205, 206, 228, 235, 254, 267

48:22   30, 69
48:23   30, 70
48:24   30, 62, 70
48:25   30, 52, 70, 84, 128, 228, 232, 250, 281
48:26–30   241
48:26–28   222
48:26–27   121, 136, 177, 252, 254, 280, 281
48:26   31, 46, 61, 70, 86, 88, 129, 193, 196, 228, 231, 232, 235, 237, 244, 249, 250, **250–52**, 254, 261, 280
48:27–28   196, 249
48:27   31, 59, 64, 70, 86, 129, 169, 171, 240, 247, 248, 249, 251, **252**, 280
48:28   31, 64, 70, 232, 250
48:29–47   218
48:29–39   217, 218, 222, 230, 232, **255–70**
48:29–38   76, 77, 79, 81, 94, 196, 256, 286, 294
48:29–33   109, 218
48:29–32   223
48:29–31   196, 218
48:29–30   59, 86, 86–87, 171, 222, **255–57**, 263, 280
48:29   31, 57, 58, 70, 77, 94, 114, 161, 236, 255
48:30–33   110
48:30   32, 52, 59, 70, 77, 84, 235, 236, 255, 265
48:31–38   56
48:31–36   226, **257**, 262, **265–69**, 281
48:31–33   111
48:31–32   83, 83, 84, 110, 161, 168, 222, 257, 259, 260
48:31   32, 55, 56, 57, 70, 74, 77, 84, 94, 158, 223, 255, 256, 265, 280
48:32–39   218

Jeremiah (cont.)

48:32–34	161
48:32–33	86, 244
48:32–36	256
48:32	32, 56, 61, 71, 71, 77, 119, 161, 196, 223, 228, 229, 232, 256, 257, 261
48:33–38	196
48:33–35	222
48:33–34	223
48:33	32, 56, 57, 71, 77, 87, 162, 228, 256, 257
48:34–39	113, 218
48:34	33, 56, 61, 71, 77, 34, 80, 83, 228
48:35–36	223
48:35	33, 71, 71, 77, 79, 84, 86, 87, 112, 161, 228, 233, 235, 238, 256, 257, **262–65**, 264, 265, 270, 281
48:36–37	80
48:36	33, 62, 72, 77, 81, 83, 83, 84, 110, 168, 222, 228, 232, 256, 257, 265
48:37–38	265, 266, **269**
48:37–39	222, 223
48:37	34, 54, 56, 72, 77, 158, 265, 266
48:38–39	88
48:38	34, 54, 58, 72, 77, 84, 86, 87, 123, 124, 165, 228, 232, 256, 257, 269
48:39–47	287, 295
48:39–46	81
48:39	34, 72, 88, 171, 196, 228, 232, 258, 269
48:40–47	140, 217, 218, 222, 223, 230, 232, **270–76**
48:40–46	162, 218
48:40–44	161
48:40–42	222
48:40–41	**52–53**, 62, 66
48:40	34, 52, 72, 72, 85, 196, 230, 231, 232, 270, 271
48:41–42	196
48:41	35, 52, 72, 73, 77, 80, 81, 128, 129, 228, 271
48:42–44	50
48:42	35, 73, 86, 165, 171, 228, 235, 237, **250–52**, 271
48:43–46	82
48:43–44	76, 82, 88, 95, 130, 161, 222, 227, 232, 271
48:43	35, 52, 73, 84, 196
48:44–45	196
48:44	35, 50, 52, 73, 82, 84, 86, 87, 165, 235, 256, 270, 271
48:45–47	161
48:45–46	48, **49–52**, 62, 82, 161, 163, 221, 222, 245, 271, 272
48:45	36, 73, 77, 81, 82, 128, 232, 271, 281
48:46	36, 51, 74, 122, 144, 196, 228, 271
48:47	36, 48, 50, 52, 53, 74, 84, 88, 91, 94, 122, 125, 164, 165, 178, 196, 199, 204, 205, 206, 216, 217, 218, 222, 224, 228, 235, 271, **272–76**
49	167
49:1–6	226
49:1–2	177, 235, 240
49:3	68, 264
49:4	117, 118, 235, 235, 236
49:6	74, 165
49:7–22	226
49:7	235, 237
49:12	204, 228, 250
49:16	70, 235, 236
49:19	236
49:22	52, 72, 72, 73

Jeremiah (cont.)

49:25	258
49:23–27	226
49:28–33	226
49:31	235, 236
49:34–39	226
49:39	74, 165
50–51	2, 3, 4, 8, 11, 12, 14, 15, 44, 132, 134, 208, 226, 259
50	8
50:2	264
50:4	278
50:7	235, 240
50:8	259, 260
50:11	266
50:14	235, 237
50:15	198, 199, 235, 237
50:17	235, 240
50:20–23	228
50:20	124, 125
50:21	228
50:23	258
50:24	235, 237
50:25	189, 210, 213
50:27	69
50:29	235, 236, 237
50:31	235, 236
50:32	235, 236
50:33	235, 240
50:38	235, 237, 264
50:42	117
50:44	235, 236
50:49	235
51:6	68
51:7	237
51:9	204, 228
51:13	235, 238
51:18	264
51:24	235, 240
51:29	68
51:37	68
51:39	250
51:41	258
51:44	264
51:47	264
51:49	237
51:50	260
51:51	238, 241
51:52	264
51:57	69, 132, 250
51:58	265
51:60	208, 259
52	46

Lamentations

	81
1	258
1:1	161
1:7	129
2	258
2:1	161
4	258
4:1	161
3:47	73

Ezekiel

	5, 81, 157, 159, 197, 204, 241, 242, 267
5:10	205
5:15	205, 206
11:9–11	205
16:41	205
16:49	247, 248
20	137
21:35 (30)	205
25–32	7, 241
25	6
25:3	238, 240
25:6	240
25:8	240, 243
25:11	74, 75, 204, 205
25:12	240
25:15	240
26:2	240, 241
26:17	239, 241, 258
27	258
27:3	236, 241

Ezekiel (cont.)

27:30–32	258
28	258
28:2	236, 241
28:5	236, 241
28:6	236, 241
28:15	236
28:16	237, 241
28:17	236, 237, 241
28:22	204, 205
28:24	240
28:26	205, 240
29:3	236, 241
29:6–7	240, 241
29:9	236, 241
29:14–15	178, 267
29:14	48, 74
29:16	241
30:6	236, 241
30:14	204, 205
30:18	236, 241
30:19	204, 205
31:10	236, 241
31:14	236, 241
32:2	236, 241
32:12	236, 241
35:5	240, 241
35:6	237, 241
35:10	236
35:11	204, 205, 237, 241
35:13	237, 241
35:15	240, 241
38	203
38:22	204
39	203
39:21	204

Daniel

4:25	264
4:30	264
5:34–36	264

Hosea

7:14	203
8:14	203

Joel

	152, 181, 204, 236, 237, 238, 239, 240
4(3):2	204
4(3):12	204
4 (3):9–16	203
4(3):19–21	203

Amos

	6, 8, 16, 18, 19, 81, 163, 166, 171, 241
1–2	6, 241
1:3	236, 240
1:6	236, 237, 240
1:9	236, 240
1:11	236, 237, 240
1:13	236, 240
1:15	68
2:1	131, 236, 237
2:2	75
2:3	75
5	258
9:7–15	279
9:7	114, 123, 279
9:12	279
9:15	279

Obadiah

	19, 241
1:5	258
1:6	258
3	236
10	240
11	240
12–13	240
13–14	240
21	174

Jonah

	19, 114, 125, 266
3:3	240
3:5–6	266
3:5	240, 266
3:6	240
3:7	266
3:8	266
3:10	125
3:19	237, 240
4:2	125
4:10–11	111
4:11	266

Micah

	201
2:4	258
4:9	73
4:10	73
4:13	203

Nahum

	241
1:11	237
1:15	236, 238
2:12	237
3:1	237
3:4	237
3:16	238
3:19	236

Habakkuk

1:11	246
1:12	205, 206, 246

Zephaniah

	81
1:17	237
2:5	68
2:8–10	252
2:8	75, 236, 240, 243
2:9	225
2:10	70, 75, 238, 240, 243, 253
2:15	236, 258
2:35	225
3:6	68

Haggai

	151, 160

Zechariah

	151, 160, 165, 166, 236, 237, 238, 239, 240, 247
1:14–15	247
1:15	246, 247, 248
2:11	165
6:8	181
9:3	238
9:6	236
9:7	165, 237
9:8	240
11:2–3	236
14	203
14:5	176
14:6	164
14:9	174
14:12	240
14:17–18	239

Malachi

	151, 160

Matthew

5:44	277
7:24–27	234
23:37–39	268
26	216
26:38	224
26:51–52	215
26:75	224
27:3–5	224

Mark

14:34	224
15:1	224

Luke

6:47–49	234
12	233, 281
12:13–21	233, 233
12:20	233
12:33	233
13	269
13:26–27	268
13:30	268
13:31–35	268
13:34–35	268
13:34	268
14:7–11	268
16:19–31	168
16:29	234
22:45	224
22:62	224
23:27	224
23:48	224

John

14–16	116
20:11–15	224

Romans

2:9–12	229, 280
11:25	269

1 Corinthians

10:12	250, 281

Ephesians

6:17	214

Philippians

1:3	v

1 Timothy

6:10	233

Hebrews

4:12	214

James

1:11	233, 243
2:13	272

1 Peter

4:7	277

1 John

4:20	129, 130

Revelation

6:10	216
14	250

General Index

Abraham(ic), 253, 268, 279
Ahab, 246
allegorical / allegory. *See* figural(ly) (reading / interpretation, allegorical)
Allen, Leslie, 10n44, 11n45, 18, 18n74, 19, 19n75, 38n21, 50n38, 61n55, 63n59, 82n12, 93n36, 96n50, 189n4, 200, 200n56, 201n57, 201n61, 202n65, 202n67, 202n71, 203n75, 203n76, 203n77, 204n80, 205n85, 226n19, 227n20, 231n33, 233n37, 244n46, 251n70, 255n79, 259n88, 259n90
Amesz, J., 8, 8n34, 11
Ammon(ites), 2, 39, 45, 48, 118, 125, 128, 149n151, 165, 226, 234, 235, 236, 237, 238, 239, 240, 243, 252, 291
Ancient Near East. *See* ANE
ANE, 4, 8, 12, 47, 113, 120, 264n107
anger. *See* wrath (anger, angry)
apocalpytic, 6, 113
Aramaic, 190
Arameans, 279
arrogance / arrogant. *See* pride / proud (arrogant, haughty, hubris, self-satisfaction)
ashamed / ashamedly / humbled / humbly / humiliate(d) / humiliation / shame(d / ful), 25, 28, 30, 34, 60, 61, 82n12,
88, 103, 106, 107, 108, 110, 113, 114, 126, 128, 129, 139, 142, 148, 149, 171, 181, 222, 223, 225, 228, **247–48**, 249, 250, 252, 254, 264, 268, **269**, 270, 280, 281, 284, 286, 292, 294
Assyria(n), 16, 144, 166, 168, 178, 234, 235, 236, 237, 238, 239, 246, 264, 266, 267n114, 278, 285, 293
audience(s) (of Jeremiah and OANs), 19, 20, 103, 106, 132, 133, 138, 144, 145, 148, 173, 194, 195, 223, **230–31**, 243, 261, 300
Augustine, 214, 214n121, 215
authentic / authenticity / inauthentic, 1, 2, 3, 4, 5, 13, 14, 154, 180, 199, 219
author(s / ship), 2, 3, **4–5**, 9, 11, 21, 44n24, 53, 75, 76, 80, 81, 84, 85, 91, 92, 92n34, 93, 93n37, 96, 97, 100, 101, 126, 138, 145, 148, 157, 161, 162, 177, 194, 199, 203, 204, 205, 209, 231n31, 258, 297, 298

Baal, 113
Babylon(ian / ians), xv, 4, 5, 6, 7, 10, **11–12**, 15, 16, 17, 18, 39, 40, 42, 43, 44, 45, 47, 47n31, 65, 83, 118, 127, 130, 134, 144, 157, 159, 163, 164, 167, 168,

Babylon(ian / ians) (*cont.*)
176, 179, 188, 193, 194, 195, 198, 198n53, 204, 207, 208, 209, 211, 225, 226, 228, 234, 235, 236, 237, 238, 239, 240, 241, 242, 243, 250, 257, 259, 264, 276, 278, 297, 299

Balaam, 197n46, 231, 231n31

Bardtke, Hans, 2, 3, 3n9, 92n35

Barton, John, 263, 263n103

Baruch, 11, 208

Bellis, Alice, 2, 2n7, 8, 8n35, 14

Bendavid, Abba, 71n4, 75, 75n7

Bentzen, Aage, 156, 156n32, 162, 162n64, 174, 174n135, 175, 175n136

Berlin, Adele, 18, 18n69

Berman, Joshua, 202, 202n68, 202n69, 202n70, 210

Bethel / El-Bethel, 28, 82n12, 164, 245, **247–48**, 284, 292

BHS, 26n4, 32n14, 207, 207n93, 262n192

biblical criticism. *See* critic(al / ism / s) (biblical, form, historical, literary, redaction)

blood(y) / bloodshed / bloodthirst(y), ix, 2, 27, 88, 115, 146, 147, 162, 170, 188, 191, 193, 196, 206, 211, 212, 215, 219, 222, 242, 284, 287, 291, 292, 296

Boadt, Lawrence, 8

Boaz, 260, 261, 267

Book of the Twelve, 219

Bright, John, 3, 189n4, 192, 194n31

Broyles, Craig, 200n55, 201n63, 202, 202n66, 202n67, 203

Brueggemann, Walter, xvi, 3, 7, 7n29, 11, 11n50, 12, 14, 14n58, 14n59, 14n60, 16, 20, 21, 21n77, 22, 44n24, 61n55, 64n63, 82n12, 84n18, 87, 87n22, 90n26, 90n27, 90n29, 91n30, 93n36, 93n37, 95n49, 97, 97n51, 97n52, 98, 98n53, 98n54, **99–149**, 150, 159, 171, 186, 189, 189n4, 191n19, 192n20, 193n25, 208, 209n105, 217, 218, 222, 225, 225n18, 227n22, 227n24, 229n25, 230n29, 231n30, 231n33, 232, 232n34, 232n35, 244n46, 245n50, 246n54, 249n61, 251, 251n68, 251n70, 252, 259n88, 259n90, 264n107, 271n119, 273, 273n123, 277, 277n127, 278, 280, 298, 300, 301

Budde, Karl, 4, 5n15

Calvin, John, 61n55, 63n59, 82n12, 83n14, 84, 84n18, 90n25, 90n29, 93n36, 93n37, 114n54, 153, 192n20, 193, 193n28, 211, 212, 212n110, 213, 214, 214n119, 215, 219, 227n22, 227n24, 231n33, 232n36, 233, 233n38, 233n40, 246n53, 249n61, 251n70, 253n75, 255n79, 255n80, 259n88, 264n107, 278, 278n128, 281

Canaan(ite / ites), 8, 113, 162, 203, 228, 246

canon(ical), 13, 14, 16, 18, 21, 75, 102, 103, 104, 139, 147, 154, 155, 197n46, 198, 209, 213, 252, 265, 267, 272, 274, 276

position (of oracle against Moab in MT and LXX), 23, **38–48**, 65

Carroll, Robert, 3, 7, 7n31, 10n44, 11n45, 14, 21, 23n1, 38n21, 44n24, 47, 48n34, 61n55, 82n12, 93n36, 96n50, 188n1, 191, 191n16, 192n20, 194,

Carroll, Robert (*cont.*)
    194n31, 194n33, 194n36,
    195n38, 207, 207n92,
    208n99, 208n103, 209,
    210n108, 218, 227n20,
    227n22, 231n33, 244n46,
    245n49, 246, 246n57, 249,
    250n66, 250n67, 251n70,
    252, 252n72, 253n75,
    255n79, 259n88, 259n90,
    273n121
Carter, Craig, 220, 220n5, 220n6,
    220n9, 221n14
catchwords / catch phrases, 17
Chemosh, 26, 28, 36, 51, 82n12, 86,
    87, 97, 107, 108, 112, 113,
    115, 123, 125, 146, 158, 160,
    161, 163, 164, 172, 232, 233,
    235, 243, 245, **247–48**, 264,
    265, 271, 284, 285, 287, 288,
    292, 293, 295, 296, 298, 300
Childs, Brevard, 16, 84n18, 89,
    89n23, 90n26, 90n27, 90n29,
    91n30, 92n34, 103, 104, 131,
    154, 155, 274
chosen. *See* elect(ed) / election
    (chosen)
Christ / christological(ly), 181, 214,
    220, 220n2, 221, 221n14,
    221n15, 223, 224, 234, 244,
    268
Christensen, Duane, 1, 1n1, 2, 2n6,
    5, 5n19, 6, 6n22, 6n23, 6n24,
    6n25
Christian(s), ix, xv, xvi, 2, 16, 20,
    21, 22, 100, 101, 103, 111,
    119, 124, 129, 135, 136, 139,
    140, 141, 145, 151, 153, 155,
    160, 166, 173, 177, 180, 181,
    182, 183, 185, 210, **211–16**,
    217–81, **289–96**, 298, 299,
    300
Christian Scripture. *See* Scripture,
    Christian / Israel's

Church Fathers. *See* Fathers,
    Church
Clements, Ronald, xv, xvn2, xvi,
    10n44, 11n45, 22, 38n21,
    44n24, 50n40, 64n63,
    83n14, 84n18, 90n26, 90n27,
    91n30, 93n36, 93n37,
    95n48, **150–87**, 190, 190n6,
    190n7, 192n20, 193n25, 195,
    195n39, 198n50, 204n80,
    217, 227n20, 227n22, 230,
    230n29, 233n37, 244n46,
    245n50, 259n88, 259n90, 298
compassion(ate), 111, 121, 125,
    262, 266, 269, 277, 279, 280,
    281, 283, 290
conflict, 107, 112, 113, 194, 265, 300
contemporary (context), ix, 16, 21,
    22, 99, 100, 101, 124, 129,
    139, 141, 142, 143, 145, 147,
    148, 150, 152n9, 153, 181,
    183, 184, 233, 234, 264n107,
    298
correspondence (between sin and
    judgment), 107, 127, 128,
    139, 148
corruption, textual. *See* textual
    corruption
cosm(ic / os), 7, 9, 117, 149, 167,
    169
covenant(al), 6, 117, 123, 166, 186,
    239
    new, 46, 65
creation(al), 105, 112, 115, 116, 119,
    120, 125, 131, 132, 136, 139,
    146, 147, 169, 186, 189n3,
    272
creator, 117, 120, 132
cries / cry(ing). *See* lament(ation
    / ed / ing / s) (crying, dirge,
    funeral, funereal, grief,
    mourning, sadness, sorrow,
    tears, wailing, weeping)

critic(al / ism / s) (biblical, form, historical, literary, redaction), 1, 2, 3, 4, 6, 12, 13, 14, 15, 17, 17n68, 21, 24, 94, 103, 143, 151, 152n9, 153, 154, 155, 157, 171, 180, 185, 197, 219
Cross, the, 141, 183, 185, 215, **223–24**, 276, 280
cult(ic), 6, 153, 157, 158, 167, 175, 175n136, 186
cup of wrath. *See* wrath (anger, angry), cup of
curse(s / d), xvi, 6, 8, 64, 88, 97, 161, 162, 173, **188–216**, 219, 222, 223, 231, 242, 243, 284, 291, 298
cycle (sin–punishment–restoration) / cyclical, 50, 51, 223, 270, 271, 276, 299
Cyrus, 157

Dagon, 119, 123
Dahood, Mitchell, 201n60, 202n71, 203n76, 204, 204n78
Damascus, 39, 45, 83, 226, 234, 235, 236, 237, 238, 239, 240
daughter(s), 51, 117, 118, 124, 261, 267, 267n112, 279
    Dibon, 29, 36, 58, 118n72, 124, 285, 292
David(ic), King, 76, 88, 90, 90n28, 91, 197n46, 231n32, 246, 261, 267, 270, 285, 293
Davies, G., 1, 1n2
Davis, Ellen, 220, 220n6, 220n10, 221, 221n11, 221n12, 221n13, 221n14, 224
Day of Atonement, 9
de Waard, Jan, 63, 63n59, 63n60, 93n36
dead / death, 106, 115, 126, 138, 144, 150, 166, 221, 223, 224, 227, 257, 258, 271, 283, 290
Dead Sea Scrolls. *See* Qumran

desolation. *See* destroy(ed) / destruct(ion / ive) (desolation, devastation)
destroy(ed) / destruct(ion / ive) (desolation, devastation), 25, 26, 27, 28n10, 29, 32, 33, 35, 36, 42, 50, 51, 53, 56, 60, 61, 62, 63, 64, 66, 75, 80, 82, 83, 88, 89, 92, 94n42, 96, 97, 102, 105, 106, 107, 108, 109, 110, 112, 115, 119, 122, 126, 129, 134, 135, 136, 140, 141, 149, 161, 165, 171, 172, 178, 180, 182, 184, 188, 193, 194, 195, 196, 201, 203, 213, 214, 222, 223, **225–44**, 249, 250, **255–70**, **270–76**, 278, 279, 280, 281, 282, 284, 285, 286, 287, 288, 289, 292, 293, 295, 296
destroyer, 26, 28, 29, 32, 53, 56, 60, 61, 66, 98, 121, 161, 171, 196, 222, 223, 229, 230, 231, 270, 285, 287, 292, 295
destruction. *See* destroy(ed) / destruct(ion / ive) (desolation, devastation)
Deuteronomic, 15
Deuteronomist(ic), 261
devastat(e / ion / or). *See* destroy(ed) / destruct(ion / ive) (desolation, devastation)
diachronic, 14, 21, 103, 219
Diamond, A. R. Pete, 7, 7n31, 10, 10n42
Dibon, 29, 30, 58, 82, 82n12, 118, 118n72, 124, 227, 285, 292, 293
    daughter. *See* daughter(s), Dibon
Diman-Haran, M., 5
dirge. *See* lament(ation / ed / ing / s) (crying, dirge, funeral, funereal, grief, mourning, sadness, sorrow, tears, wailing, weeping)

disciple(ship), 216, 224
Dives, 233
Divine involvement, 14, 48, 51, 52, **57–58**, 66, 87, 89, 99, 100, 109, **116–26**, 133, **163–70**, 184, 187, 229, 257, 279
Divine sovereignty. *See* sovereign(ty), Divine (reign, rule)
Divine warrior. *See* warrior, Divine
Drinkard, Joel, 208, 208n98, 208n104
drunkard / drunk(enness), 31, 45, 65, 88, 193, 222, 228, 230, 232, 250, 260, 286, 294
Duhm, Bernhard, 5, 10n44, 14, 44, 44n27, 50n38, 53n43, 61n55, 63n59, 64n63, 82n12, 93n36, 96n50, 188, 188n1, 189n2, 192, 194, 194n30, 197, 197n47, 201n60, 201n64, 208, 208n95, 208n98, 208n101, 227n20, 231, 231n33, 232n35, 245n50, 246n54, 255n79, 259n88, 264n107

eagle, 34, **52–53**, 66, 222, 230, 232, 270
Easter (Sunday), 102, 217, 224, 275, 281
Eaton, John, 202n71, 202n72, 203n75, 203n77, 214, 214n120, 215
Edom, 39, 45, 167, 198n53, 204, 226, 234, 235, 236, 237, 238, 239, 240, 242, 243, 250
Eglon (King), 202, 210
Egypt(ian / ians), 39, 44, 45, 48, 48n35, 83, 118, 122, 123, 124, 130, 137, 138, 165, 174, 178, 179, 204, 225, 226, 234, 235, 236, 237, 238, 239, 240, 241, 242, 264, 267, 272, 297

Ehud, 202, 210, 261, 298
Eichhorn, Johann, 4, 4n13
Eissfeldt, Otto, 1, 2n4, 258, 258n84, 258n85, 258n87
El, 113
Elam, 39, 44, 45, 48, 48n35, 66, 132, 165, 226, 235, 297
elect(ed) / election (chosen), 107, 112, 117, 118, 133, 135, 140, 142, 147, 166, 167, 169, 169n99, 177, 182, 187, 253, 279
Elimelech, 260, 267
emotion(al / s), 106, 110, 160, 162, 163, 177, 229
enemy from the North, 7, 15, 42, 47, 49, 170, 194
enlightenment, 17, 152n9, 165
eschatolog(ical / y), 19, 107, 113, 132, 136, 200, 200n56, 201, 202n67, 203, 211
exile / exilic, 2, 5, 6, 26, 27, 51, 98, 106, 108, 112, 115, 122, 128, 144, 174, 176, 200, 201, 233, 243, 245, 246, 247, 248, 249, 260n90, 280, 285, 293
exodus, 267, 272, 279

faith, ix, 13, 20, 22, 100, 101, 102, 113, 135, 140, 142, 146, 151, 153, 155, 179, 181, 182, 185, 212, 213, 220, 274, 298
faithful(ness), 91, 185
faithless, 118
Fathers, Church, 212, 219
feast / festival(s), 6, 156, 173, 175, 180, 202, 239
  of Tabernacles, 156, 157, 162, 164, 174, 175, 176, 186, 202, 298
Feinberg, Charles, 11n45, 61n55, 63n59, 82n12, 83n14, 93n36, 96n50, 114n54, 190, 190n6, 192n20, 213n117, 226n19,

Feinberg, Charles (*cont.*)
227n20, 227n24, 231n33, 232n36, 244n46, 246n54, 255n79, 255n80, 259n88, 259n90, 264n107, 265n108, 273, 273n122
festival(s). *See* feast, festival(s)
figural(ly) (reading / interpretation, allegorical), xvi, 214, 215, 217, **219–22**, 224, 250, 277, 281, 298
film(s / ic), xvi, 217, 243, **282–88, 289–96**, 301
final form (of text), 16, 17, 18, 19, 39, 51, 103, 155, 252
fire, 36, 75, 202, 221, 222, 230, 265, 281, 288, 296
first person (speech), 56, 57, 66, 84, 87, 88, 195, 196, 223, 230, 245, 255, 256, 257, 260, 265
foe from the North. *See* enemy from the North
fool(ish), 233, 234, 237, 243, 268, 290
foreign / foreigner(s) / foreignness (non-Israelite), xv, 1, 2, 5, 7, 7n31, 9, 9n38, 16, 20, 41, 59, 111, 112, 115, 118, 119, 120, 130, 133, 138, 144, 156, 158, 159, 162, 168, 171, 174, 176, 177, 179, 184, 198, 201, 205, 225, 228, 233, 234, 235, 257, 258, 260, 266, 267, 268, 272, 281, 297
forgive(ness) / pardon, 124, 125, 125n98, 126, 146, 147, 177, 177n148, 296
form criticism. *See* critic(al / ism / s) (biblical, form, historical, literary, redaction)
Fretheim, Terence, xvi, 10n44, 11n45, 14, 22, 38n21, 44n24, 47n30, 50, 50n39, 63n59, 82n12, 83n14, 83n15, 86n20, 92n34, 95n49, 98, **99–149**, 150, 157, 159, 166, 169, 171, 174, 180, 186, 188n1, 190n4, 191n19, 192n20, 193, 193n26, 193n27, 195n38, 196, 197n42, 207, 207n91, 208n98, 217, 218, 225, 225n17, 226n19, 227n20, 227n22, 227n24, 231n33, 232n35, 245n50, 246n54, 248, 251n70, 255n79, 255n80, 257, 257n82, 259n88, 260n90, 264n107, 265n108, 272, 272n120, 273n121, 281, 298, 300, 301
funeral / funereal. *See* lament(ation / ed / ing / s) (crying, dirge, funeral, funereal, grief, mourning, sadness, sorrow, tears, wailing, weeping)

genre, xv, 2, 3, 157, 159, 181, 297, 300
Gentile(s), 171, 269, 270
Germany, 277
Gethsemane, 215, 224
Geyer, John, 1n2, 5, 5n20, 5n21, 6, 7, 7n26, 7n27, 9, 9n39, 17
glory / glorification, 27, 29, 49, 59, 92, 137, 138, 201, 203, 273, 276, 283, 284, 291, 292
gloss(ed / es) / glossator, 2, 27n7, 62, 63, 92, 101, 189, 192, 193, 194, **195–98**, 211, 214
God, 7, 20, 25, 60, 87, 101, 102, 105, 106, 107, 109n36, 110, 111, 112, 113, 114, 115, 116, 117, 118, 119, 120, 121, 122, 123, 124, 124n94, 129, 132, 133, 134, 138, 139, 140, 141, 142, 144, 146, 147, 152, 157, 159, 162, 164, 165, 166, 167, 168, 169, 170, 171, 174, 175, 176, 177, 178, 179, 180, 181, 182, 183, 184, 186, 187, 202, 211, 212, 213, 214, 224, 225, 233,

God (cont.)
	234, 242, 247, 248, 249, 257, 266, 267n111, 267n112, 268, 269, 270, 272, 273, 274, 275, 276, 277, 278, 280, 281, 283, 291, 298
	See also YHWH
god(s), 9, 20, 33, 34, 41, 49n36, 59, 82n12, 98, 107, 108, 112, 113, 115, 119, 120, 123, 125, 137, 142, 146, 147, 162, 164, 233, 243, 262, 263, 264, 265, 266, 278, 280, 285, 293
	See also idol(s) / idolatry
godly, 198, 203, 210, 214, 215, 283, 284, 291, 298
	ungodly, 278
Goldingay, John, 84n17, 90n25, 90n26, 90n27, 91n30, 93n37, 95n49, 98n55, 206, 206n88, 206n90, 256n81, 310
Good Friday, 102, 224, 281
Gospel(s), 221, 234, 275
Gottwald, Norman, 4, 5, 5n16, 5n17, 6
grace, 101, 212, **275–76**, 281, 300
Gray, George, 49n36, 75, 75n7, 81n11, 84n18, 87n21, 89n24, 90n25, 90n26, 90n27, 90n29, 91n30, 91n31, 92n34, 94, 94n39, 95n49, 231n31, 256n81, 308, 311
Greek, ix, 9, 55, 57, 64, 82n12, 233n39, 274
	See also LXX
Gregory VII (Pope, Hildebrand), 213, 213n114, 213n115, 213n116, 215
Gressmann, Hugo, 2
grief. See lament(ation / ed / ing / s) (crying, dirge, funeral, funereal, grief, mourning, sadness, sorrow, tears, wailing, weeping)

Hades, 268
Hagedorn, Anselm, 5, 9, 9n38, 17
hapax legomenon, 62
haughty. See pride / proud (arrogant, haughty, hubris, self-satisfaction)
Hayes, John, 7, 7n30, 8, 8n36, 84n18, 90n26, 90n27, 90n29, 91n30, 93n37
Hazor, 39n22, 226, 234, 235, 236, 237, 238, 239, 243
Hebrew, ix, 5, 11, 58, 63, 100, 191, 197, 206, 219, 235n44, 245, 274
	Hebrew Bible / HB, 2, 168, 260
	See also OT
	Hebrews, 152
	See also MT
Hecke, Pierre, 11, 18, 18n70
hermeneutic(s / al / ally), ix, 16, 99, **100–104**, 126, 145, 146, **150–56**, 165, 185, 187, 217, **218–22**
Heshbon, 25, 33, 36, 49, 50, 82, 82n12, 83, 222, 226, 229, 246, 261, 271, 287, 288, 295, 296
Hezekiah, 230, 231n30, 264
Hildebrand. See Gregory VII (Pope, Hildebrand)
Hill, John, 8, 8n33
historical criticism. See critic(al / ism / s) (biblical, form, historical, literary, redaction)
history, ix, **2–3**, 8, 15, 20, 50, 66, 103, 106, 113, 122, 137, 138, 141, 142, 153, 154, 158, 161, 166, 167, 173, 177, 178, 180, 181, 183, 185, 200, 211, 213, 246n52, 248, 267, 269, 280, 297
Holladay, William, 1, 1n3, 3, 10n44, 11n45, 14, 38n21, 44, 44n24, 44n26, 44n28, 53n43, 61n55, 63n59, 64, 82, 93, 95, 188,

Holladay, William *(cont.)*
189, 190, 191, 192, 196, 197, 198, 199, 208, 227, 231, 244, 245, 251, 253, 255, 259, 260, 264, 265, 273, 312

Holt, Elsie, 7, 7n32, 11, 12, 12n51, 40n23, 47, 47n32, 47n33

holy war. *See* war, holy

hope, 49, 66, 86, 88, 90, 90n27, 91, 97, 107, 115, 119, 132, 133, 135, 148, 149, 170, 178, 179, 183, 184, 224, 267n114, 275, 276, 277, 281, 298

Horonaim, 25, 26, 33, 55, 79, 80, 82n13, 226, 287, 295

hubris. *See* pride / proud (arrogant, haughty, hubris, self-satisfaction)

humble. *See* ashamed / ashamedly / humbled / humbly / humiliate(d) / humiliation / shame(d / ful)

humiliation. *See* ashamed / ashamedly / humbled / humbly / humiliate(d) / humiliation / shame(d / ful)

hymn, 200, 200n56

ideolog(ical / ies / y), 7, 12, 14, 21, 22, 104, 108, 129, 140, 141, 144, 158, 159, 164

idol(s) / idolatry, 18, 59, 105, 112, 115, 233n37, 235, 238, 243, **262–65**, 270, 278, 281, 300

implied reader, 142, 144, 145, 148

insolence / insolent, 31, 32, 38, 57, 58, 59, 107

intercede / intercession / intercessory, 121, 126, 147, 148, 277

interpret(ation / ative / ed / er / ers) / reading, ix, xvi, 8, 11, 12, 13, 14, 16, 18, 20, 21, 22, 23, 24, 26n6, 32n14, 39, 60, 63, 76, 89, **99–149**, **150–87**, 192, 198, 199, 203n74, 209, 210, **211–16**, **217–81**, 298, 299, 300

intertextual, 47, 139, 189, **198–210**, 248

ipsissima verba, 1, 21

ironic / irony, 50, 63, 110, 146, 163, 171, 174, 186, 199, 215, 225, 231, 250, **257–62**, 263, 288, 296, 300

Israel / Israelite(s), ix,2, 5, 7, 8, 18, 19, 20, 25, 28, 31, 45, 47, 48, 49, 49n36, 50, 51, 52, 60, 75, 82n12, 87, 90n28, 92, 98, 99, 103, 104, 105, 107, 108, 111, 112, 113, 114, 117, 118, 118n71, 119, 120, 121, 123, 124, 125, 128, 130, 132, 133, 135, 137, 138, 140, 141, 142, 144, 148, 153, 154, 155, 157, 158, 159, 163, 164, 166, 167, 168, 168n98, 169, 171, 173, 174, 175, 176, 177, 178, 179, 180, 181, 182, 184, 186n175, 197n46, 200, 201, 203, 204n80, 206, 208, 210, 213, 225, 228, 234, 235, 236, 237, 240, 241, 242, 243, 246, 247, 248, 249, 250, 251, 251n69, 252, 253, 254, 255, 258, 260, 261, 262, 263, 267, 267n112, 267n114, 272, 277, **278–80**, 284, 285, 292, 293, 297

Israeli. *See* Jew / Jewish

Israel's Scripture. *See* Scripture, Christian / Israel's

Jacob, 279

Jazer, 32, 32n15, 56, 82, 82n12, 119, 232, 287, 295

Jeremianic, 6, 15, 197, 199, 225

Jerusalem, 40, 47n31, 106, 123, 157, 164, 167, 234n43, 236, 237, 238, 239, 247, 253n76, **268–69**, 270, 281, 300

Jesus, 181, 212, 215, 216, 220, 221, 223, 224, **268–69**, 270, 277, 281, 300
Jew / Jewish, ix, 2, 5, 17, 17n68, 18, 21, 140, 145, 173, 180, 187, 204n80, 214, 231n31, 234, 244n46
Johnson, B., 205, 205n81, 205n82, 205n84, 205n86, 206, 206n88
Jones, Brian, **259–62**, 267
Jones, Douglas, xvi, xvin3, 10n44, 11n45, 22, 44n24, 61n55, 63n59, 75, 75n7, 82n12, 93n36, 95, 95n45, 96n50, **150–87**, 190, 190n6, 190n8, 190n9, 192n20, 193n25, 194, 194n29, 194n31, 195, 195n39, 207, 207n91, 208, 208n97, 208n99, 208n103, 209n105, 213, 213n118, 215, 217, 218, 227n20, 227n24, 231n33, 245n50, 246n53, 247n59, 255n79, 259n88, 260n90, 265n108, 270n117, 273n123, 298, 300, 300n1, 301
Jubilee, 9
Judah / Judahite(s), 7, 8, 12, 18, 20, 40, 44, 46, 47, 49, 65, 66, 76, 90, 90n28, 91, 92, 94, 97, 107, 108, 109, 112, 114, 115, 118, 119, 122, 123, 124, 125, 126, 130, 132, 133, 135, 136, 141, 142, 144, 145, 147, 148, 159, 163, 164, 173, 174, 175, 176, 177, 179, 181, 183, 187, 193, 194, 195, 198, 202, 203, 207, 208, 209, 210, 211, 225, 228, 234, 235, 236, 237, 240, 241, 243, 247, 248, 249, 251, 252, 259, 260, 264, 267, 267n112, 269, 270, 272, 273, 275, 276, 283, 285, 286, 291, 293, 294, 297, 298

Judas, 224
judge(d / s) / judging / judgment(s), xvi, 6, 7, 8, 13, 16, 18, 19, 20, 30, 36, 44, 45, 46, 47, 48, 50, 58, 61, 83, 88, 90, 98, 101, 102, 104, 105, 106, 106n27, 107, 111, 119, 121, 122, 123, 125, 126, 127, 132, 133, 137, 140, 141, 142, 143, 147, 148, 156, 161, 162, 163, 165, 171, 172, 176, 181, 189, 192, 193, 195, 199, 200, 201, 202, 203, 204, 204n80, 205, 205n85, 206, 207, 208, 210, 212, 213, 217, 218, 220, 221, 222, **223–24**, 227, 228, 229, 230, 232, 233, 234, 235, 241, 242, 243, 244, 250, 254, 257, 259n88, 264, 272, 273, 277, 278, 280, 281, 284, 291, 298, 299, 300
just(ice), 8, 88, 90, 91, 121, 122, 126, 168, 184, 204, 206, 228, 268, 281, 299

Kaminsky, Joel, 278, 279n129
Kaufmann, Yehezkel, 5
Kedar, 39, 39n33, 45, 226, 234, 235, 236, 237, 238, 239, 243
Kessler, Martin, 2, 3, 3n9, 3n10, 3n11, 4, 4n12, 4n14, 11, 12, 12n52, 13, 13n53, 13n54, 13n55, 14, 15n62, 18, 18n71, 18n72, 18n73, 208n98
ketib, 24, 30n12, 229n27, 249n63, 250n64, 250n65
Kidner, Derek, 93n36, 93n37, 183n25, 192, 192n20, 195, 195n39, 200n56, 245n50, 255n80, 259n88, 273, 273n123
king, 28, 40, 42, 43, 51, 76, 90n28, 94, 107, 108, 116, 120, 121, 122, 123, 125, 132, 134, 149,

king *(cont.)*
157, 164, 167, 168, 174, 175, 186, 197n46, 200, 201, 202, 210, **249–55**, 257, 261, 266, 284, 285, 292, 293, 298
Kiriathaim, 25, 30, 60, 61, 80, 82n12, 285, 293
Kraus, Hans-Joachim, 200n55, 201, 201n58, 201n61, 201n63, 201n64, 202n71
Kugel, James, 191, 191n14, 191n18, 244, 244n47

laboring woman / women, 35, 52, 53, 66, 81, 287, 295
lament(ation / ed / ing / s) (crying, dirge, funeral, funereal, grief, mourning, sadness, sorrow, tears, wailing, weeping), xv, xvi, 7, 9, 18, 25, 25n3, 26, 29, 30, 32, 32n14, 33, 34, 34n16, 38, 50n40, **54–57**, 58, 64, 66, 75, 76, 79, 80, 81, 83, 83n15, **84–85**, 86, 87, 89, 91, 92, 93, 94, 96, 97, 98, 99, 105, 106, 107, 109, 110, 111, 112, 113, 114, 115, 119, 125, 126, 127, 129, 130, 131, 138, 141, 144, 145, 146, 147, 148, 149, 158, 160, 161, 162, 163, 168, 170, 172, 174, 176, 177, 180, 185, 186, 193, 206, 211, 215, 216, 218, 222, **223–24**, **225–44**, 249, 250, **255–70**, 272, 277, 280, 281, 282, 283, 284, 285, 286, 287, 288, 289, 290, 291, 292, 293, 294, 295, 297, 298, 299, 300
See also woe
land(s), 30, 32, 37, 41, 42, 43, 47, 51, 52, 56, 57, 62, 63, 127, 207, 208, 228, 242, 260, 264, 267, 268, 272, 278, 279, 284, 285, 292, 293

laughingstock. *See* mock(ed / er / ery / ing) (laughingstock, taunting)
law(s), 126, 127, 127n100, 139, 166, 169, 171, 172, 234, 239, 248
Lazarus, 243, 268
Lebanon, 234, 235, 236, 237, 238, 239
length (of Jeremiah's Moab oracle) / long, xv, 12, 45, 46, 65, 75, 76, **83**, 85, 96, 130, 131, 148, 225, 273, 297, 298, 300
Levine, Baruch, 49n36, 227, 227n21, 231n31
literary
criticism. *See* critic(al / ism / s) (biblical, form, historical, literary, redaction)
form / style, **12–17**, 18, 20, 21, 45, 46, 46n29, 49, **64**, 65, 66, 84, 85, 89, 93, 152, **189–98**, 243
storyboard. *See* film(s / ic)
theory, 39, 103, 104, 108, 148, 219, 272
liturg(ical / y), 6, 7, 9, 142, 156, 162, 173, 262
Lohr, Joel, 267, 267n113
Lot, 261
Lundbom, Jack, 10n44, 11, 11n45, 11n49, 14, 38n21, 44n24, 49, 50n38, 50n39, 61n55, 63n59, 64n63, 82n12, 93n36, 95n48, 114n54, 188n1, 190, 190n6, 190n10, 192n20, 192n21, 192n22, 193n28, 194, 194n34, 194n35, 197n47, 209, 209n107, 227n20, 227n24, 231n33, 234, 234n42, 244n46, 245n50, 246, 246n54, 249n61, 250n67, 251n69, 251n70, 253, 254, 254n77, 254n78, 255n79, 255n80, 259n88, 260n90, 271n118, 273n121

LXX, xv, 9, **10–11**, 15, 22, **23–66**, 82n12, 157, 161, 165, 165n79, 189, 190, 191, 207, 209, 233, 233n39, 257, 271, **273–75**, 276, 277, 297, 298, 299
Maccabean / Maccabees, 201, 202, 203, 211
Madmen (place), 25, 37, 82n12, 242
Marduk, 18
Mary, 224
McKane, William, 3, 4, 9, 9n40, 10, 10n41, 10n44, 11, 11n45, 14, 21, 23, 34n16, 37n17, 38n18, 38n19, 38n20, 38n21, 44, 44n28, 50n38, 53n43, 53n44, 55n47, 56n48, 56n49, 58n50, 58n53, 59n54, 61n55, 63n59, 64n63, 82n12, 83n14, 92, 93n36, 95n49, 188n1, 190, 190n6, 191, 191n15, 192, 192n20, 192n21, 192n22, 192n23, 192n24, 194, 194n30, 195n38, 196, 197, 197n42, 197n49, 198n50, 208n98, 209n106, 226n19, 227n20, 227n24, 244n46, 245n49, 246n53, 250n67, 253n76, 255, 255n79, 255n80, 259n88, 260n90, 262n101, 265n108, 273n121
  rolling corpus, 3, 4, 9, 10, 21
mercy, 7, 121, 123, 133, 140, 141, 143, 146, 176, 210, 273
metaphor(s), 18, 24, 53, 66, 88, 97, 108, 116, 117, 118, 119, 120, 121, 122, 123, 128, 130, 132, 147, 153, 200, 202, 202n67, 203, 210, 212, 215, 219, 223, 230, **231–32**, 243, 244, 248, 250, 253, 254, 266, 270, 271, 300
  metaphorical (reading), 148, 203, 210, 212, 213, 214, 215, 219

midrashic, 17
military, 6, 7, 106, 113, 144, 162, 172, 203, 213, 234, 297
Miller, Maxwell, 246n52, 268, 268n115
Miller, Patrick, xvi, 10n44, 11n45, 14, 22, 38n21, 44n24, 61n55, 82n12, 87, 87n22, 92n34, 98, **99–149**, 150, 159, 171, 180, 186, 192n20, 196, 196n41, 208n103, 217, 218, 225, 225n17, 227n22, 227n24, 244n46, 245n50, 246, 246n52, 246n55, 247n58, 249n61, 252, 252n70, 252n73, 259n88, 260n90, 265n108, 268, 268n115, 273, 273n123, 298, 300
Mishnah, 202
Moab / Moabite(s), xv, xvi, 6, 7, 12, 22, 23, 24, 25, 27, 28, 28n10, 29, 30, 31, 32, 33, 34, 35, 36, 37, 39, 45, 46, 48, 49, 49n36, 49n37, 50, 51, 52, 53, 54, 55, 56, 57, 58, 59, 60, 61, 61n55, 62, 63, 65, 66, 75, 76, 77, 79, 80, 82, 82n12, 83, 84, 85, 86, 87, 87n21, 88, 89, 90, 91, 92, 94, 95, 96, 97, 98, 99, 105, 106, 106n27, 107, 108, 109, 110, 111, 112, 113, 114, 115, 117, 118, 120, 121, 122, 123, 124, 124n94, 125, 126, 127, 128, 129, 130, 131, 132, 134, 135, 136, 138, 139, 140, 141, 142, 143, 144, 145, 146, 147, 148, 149, 149n151, 157, 158, 159, 160, 161, 162, 163, 164, 165, 165n79, 168, 169, 170, 171, 172, 173, 176, 177, 178, 179, 180, 183, 184, 185, 186, 187, 188, 193, 194, 195, 196, 197n46, 198, 199, 204, 205, 206, 209, 210, 211, 213, 215,

Moab / Moabite(s) (*cont.*) 216, 217, 218, 219, 221, 222, 223, 224, 225, 226, 227, 228, 229, 230, 231, 232, 233, 234, 235, 235n44, 236, 237, 238, 239, 240, 241, 242, 243, 244, 245, 246, 246n52, 247, 248, 249, 250, 251, 252, 253, 254, 255, 256, 257, 258, 259n88, 260, 261, 262, 263, 264, 264n107, 265, 266, 267, 268, 268n115, 269, 270, 271, 272, 273, 274, 275, 276, 277, 279, 280, 281, 283, 284, 285, 286, 287, 288, 289, 290, 291, 292, 293, 294, 295, 296, 297, 298, 299, 300, 301

Moberly, Walter, iii, xi, 198n51, 263, 263n104, 275, 275n126

mock(ed / er / ery / ing) (laughingstock, taunting), 31, 34, 50n40, 54n45, 58, 60, 63, 64, 75, 108, 126, 127, 128, 142, 143, 144, 161, 164, 181, 222, 230, 235, 243, 248, 250, 251, 251n69, 252, 253, 257, 258, 259, 259n88, 269, 277, 278, 280, 284, 285, 292, 293

    taunt song (of Num 21:28–29), **49–52**, 53, 66, 221, 222, 271, 273, 288, 296, 298, 299

modernism, 218

Moltmann, Jürgen, 102

monotheism 2, 159

mood. *See* tone (mood)

Moses, 166, 171, 233, 267, 268, 270, 300

mourning. *See* lament(ation / ed / ing / s) (crying, dirge, funeral, funereal, grief, mourning, sadness, sorrow, tears, wailing, weeping)

movie. *See* film(s / ic)

Mowinckel, Sigmund, 156, 156n31, 174, 174n135, 202, 202n71

MT, xv, 9, 10, 10n44, 11, 15, 16, 18, 22, **23–66**, 82n12, 87n21, 89, 90, 118, 132, 157, 189, 190, 191, 207, 209, 225, 233n39, 245n48, 257, **273–75**, 276, 297, 298, 299

Muilenburg, James, 104

Naomi, 263, 267

narrative, 5, 46, 47, 119, 148, 224, 260, 268

nation(s) / national(ism / istic), ix, xv, xvi, **1–22**, 23, 25, 34, 38, **39–46**, 47, 48, 49, 49n36, 50, 65, 66, 99, 105, 107, 108, 109, 111, 112, 114, 115, 118, 119, 120, 121, 123, 124, 125, 126, 127, 129, 132, 133, 134, 135, 137, 138, 140, 141, 142, 143, 144, 145, 146, 147, 148, 149, 150, 156, 157, 158, 159, 162, 163, 164, 165, 166, 167, 168, 169, 170, 172, 173, 174, 175, 176, 177, 178, 179, 180, 181, 184, 187, 193, 194, 197n46, 198, 201, 202, 203, 204, 205, 206, 207, 208, 210, 225, 226, 228, 230, 233n37, 234, 235, 236, 240, 241, 243, 244, 246, 247, 248, 250, 251, 252, 253, 257, 258, 260, 261, 263, 264, 265, 266, 268, 270, 271, 272, 273, 275, 276, 277, 278, 279, 280, 281, 283, 291, 296, 297, 299, 300

natural law, 126, 139, 169, 171

natural world, 120, 125, 145

Nebuchadnezzar / Nebuchadrezzar, 40, 42, 123, 194, 264

Negev, 231

New Testament. *See* NT

Niehr, B., 205, 205n81

Nineveh / Ninevites, 125, 266
non-Israelite. *See* foreign / foreigner(s) / foreignness (non-Israelite)
North, Frank, 2, 2n5
NT, xi, 116, 129, 182, 184, 185, 216, 223, 233, 234, 243, 254, 269, 274, 277, 278, 281

OAN(s), ix, xiii, xv, **1–22**, 23, 38, **39**, 45, 46, 47, 48, 49, 65, 66, 83, 94, 99, 100, 104, 105, 106, 107, 108, 109, 110, 111, 112, 115, 117, 123, 124, 127, 127n100, 129, 130, 132, 133, 134, 135, 136, 137, 138, 139, 140, 141, 142, 144, 145, 147, 149, 156, 157, 158, 159, 160, 162, 163, 164, 167, 169, 170, 171, 172, 173, 174, 175, 176, 179, 180, 181, 182, 184, 186, 187, 196, 197n46, 199, 204, 206, 207, 208, 209, 213, 219, 225, **226**, 228, 234, 234n43, 235, **236**, **240**, 241, 242, **243**, 258, 259, 263, 264, 264n107, 265, 272, 273, 274, 275, 278, 280, 297, 298, 299, 300
   purpose(s) (of), ix, xv, 19, 20, 21, 65, 89, **96–98**, 99, 108, 109, 117, **126–39**, 148, 156, 158, 159, 163, 167, 168, **170–80**, 187, 193, 231, 232, 234, 269, 270, 272, 273, 276, 297, 298
Oesterley, William, 200, 200n55, 201, 201n59, 201n60, 201n64, 203n75, 203n77
offences / sin(s / ful) / wrongdoing, 18, 50, 51, 52, **58–60**, 66, 75, 76, **86–87**, 88, 97, 98, 105, 106, 107, 115, 126, 127, 128, 129, 130, 133, 139, 142, 159, 168, 206, 215, 223, 224, 229, **232–34**, **234–42**, 235, 236, 237, 241, 242, 243, 248, 251, 252, 253, 263, 271, 276, 277, 278, 280, 281, 298, 299, 300
Old Testament. *See* OT
oracles against the nations. *See* OAN(s)
order (of nations within oracle), 10, 17, 23, 38, **39–46**, 297
OT, ix, x, xi, xv, 1, 5, 8, 9, 13, 16, 48, 67, 81, 100, 101, 102, 104, 113, 118, 120, 121, 127, 128, 130, 135, 136, 150, 152, 153, 154, 182, 183, 184, 185, 197, 197n46, 198, 199, 206, 206n88, 207, 213, 216, 221, 225, 230, 230n28, 233, 234, 241, 242, 243, 246, 263, 263n106, 269, 274, 278, 279

parallelism / parallelistic, 82n12, 191, 191n18, 205, 206n87, 248
pardon. *See* forgive(ness) / pardon
Passion (narratives), 224
pathos, 64, 105, 107, 110, 114, 115, 180, 265
Paul (Apostle) / Pauline, 171
Paul, Shalom, 17, 17n67, 18, 19, 171
Perdue, Leo, 13, 13n56, 14n57, 15, 15n63, 15n64, 15n65
Perez, 267
perish(ed / ing), 25, 26, 28, 29, 30, 33, 36, 51, 60, 62, 156, 215, 228, 265, 288, 291, 296
Persia(n / ns), 4, 55, 101, 157, 202
Peter, 215, 224
Pharaoh, 264, 267, 272
Philistia / Philistines, 39, 45, 119, 167, 226, 234, 235, 236, 237, 238, 239, 279
Pietersma, Albert, 24, 34n16
pit, 35, 37, 88, 130, 222, 227, 230, 232, 270, 271, 276, 288, 296

place names (proliferation of), 24, 75, 76, **82–83**, 85, 96, 160, 170, 172, 215, 222, **226–27**, 229, 232, 242, 250

plain sense (of Scripture), 212, 213, 214

poem(s) / poetic(al /ally) / poetry, 4, 5, 8, 12, 46, 46n29, 49, 53, 64, 65, 66, 93, 105, 108, 109, 114, 130, 131, 134, 136, 160, 161, 163, 171, 172, 177, 188, **189–92**, 196, 211, 228, 230, 230n28, 244, 244n46, 251, 257, 261, 270

politic(al /s), 6, 7, 12, 21, 103, 108, 120, 123, 125, 128, 129, 134, 136, 138, 139, 140, 144, 145, 146, 147, 157, 159, 164, 167, 168, 175, 177, 183, 263, 278

Pope Gregory VII. *See* Gregory VII (Pope, Hildebrand)

position (of Jeremiah's Moab oracle), xv, 11, 18, 23, **38–48**, 65, 66, 274, 298, 299

post-modern(ism), 218

power(ful / less / s), 7, 8, 12, 14, 16, 21, 45, 85, 97, 101, 107, 108, 109, 121, 122, 128, 129, 134, 136, 137, 138, 139, 143, 145, 146, 147, 149, 159, 160, 164, 167, 168, 176, 177, 181, 182, 195, 202, 203, 215, 218, 232, 234, 249, 250, 251, 264, 265, 277, 278, 298

pride / proud (arrogant, haughty, hubris, self-satisfaction), 18, 31, 57, 58, 59, 75, 86, 87, 97, 105, 106, 107, 108, 109, 114, 126, 127, 128, 129, 134, 135, 136, 138, 139, 142, 143, 148, 149, 162, 168, 171, 172, 178, 180, 218, 222, 223, 232, 234, 235, 236, 237, 241, 243, 245, 246, 247n60, 248, 250, 252, 254, **255–70**, 271, 278, 280, 281, 286, 287, 294, 295, 298, 299, 300

promise(d / s), 7n31, 19, 46, **48–49**, 65, 66, 86, 88, 89, 91, 97, 105, 107, 109, 112, 114, 126, 128, 135, 141, 144, 146, 164, 165n79, 177, 184, 214, 216, 222, 224, 253, 267n114, **270–76**, 277, 281, 288, 296, 298, 299, 300

prophet to the nations, 105, 121

prose, 4, 5, 12, 46n29, 65, 92, 131, 188, **189–92**, 196, 197, 211, 244, 244n46

Protestant, 17, 218

Provan, Iain, 263, 263n105, 263n106

punish(ed / ment), xvi, 8, 10, 12, 35, 43, 44, 45, 46, 47, 48, 49, 50, 51, 52, 58, **60–64**, 65, 75, 76, 84, 86, **87–88**, 89, 97, 107, 108, 126, 128, 159, 167, 168, 177, 198, 202, 204, 205, 206, 207, 211, 212, 215, 223, **229–30**, 231, 232, 233, 234, 235, 241, 243, 247, 252, 255, 256, 259, 263, 264, 270, 272, 275, 280, 283, 291, 297, 299, 300

qere, 24, 58, 66, 79n9, 206n89, 229n27, 249n249, 250n64, 250n65, 250n66, 252n71, 254

Qumran, 10

Raabe, Paul, **19–20**, 230

Radner, Ephraim, 220, 220n7, 220n8, 220n14, 221

Rashi, 34n16, 63, 63n61

reading. *See* interpret(ation / ative / ed / er / ers) / reading

reason(s) (for punishment), xvi, 19, 76, 84, 86, 89, 98, 115, 142, 215, 222, 223, 225, 234, 235,

General Index 351

reason(s) (for punishment) *(cont.)* 241, 242, 243, 245, 271, 280, 299
redaction. *See* critic(al / ism / s) (biblical, form, historical, literary, redaction)
Reformation, 17, 219
Reimer, David, 2, 3, 3n8
relational, 116, 117, 118, 119, 121, 122, 124, 125, 147
relationship, 19, 92, 107, 116, 117, 118, 123, 131, 135, 140, 164, 167, 169, 170, 185, 192n20, 199n53, 200, 224, 251, 263, 275, 279
Rendtorff, Rolf, 219, 219n1
repent(ance / s), 19, 20, 102, 124, 125, 214, 266, 270, 275, 276
restoration / restorative / restore(s), 19, 36, 46, 47, **48–49**, 50, 51, 53, 65, 76, 86, **88–89**, 91, 97, 98, 105, 107, 109, 112, 114, 117, 122, 124, 125, 126, 128, 130, 132, 135, 136, 137, 139, 140, 141, 144, 146, 147, 149, 165, 165n79, 170, 172, 177, 178, 184, 216, 222, 223, 224, 267, 267n114, 270, 271, **272–76**, 277, 279, 280, 281, 288, 296, 298, 299, 300
resurrection, 215, 221
retribution / retributive, 127, 169, 177
revenge. *See* vengeance (avenge, avenger, revenge, vengeful)
Reventlow, Henning, 156, 174, 174n135, 175, 175n136
rhetoric(al), 7, 11, 13, 14, 19, 21, 22, 64, 97, 102, 104, 105, 108, 113, 114, 129, 134, 158, 193, 223, **229–32**, 242, 246, 249, 251, 251n69, 252, 253, 253n74, 255, 257, 265, 271, 279, 281, 299, 300

rich(es / ness), 33, 62, 233, 243, 265, 268, 292
Rietzschel, Claus, 44, 208n99
ritual(s), 6, 7, 54, 156, 173
rolling corpus. *See* McKane, William, rolling corpus
Rösel, Martin, 59
royal, 6, 106, 129, 156, 158, 174
Rudolph, Wilhelm, 3, 3n10, 10n44, 14, 32n14, 44, 44n25, 44n28, 49n37, 50n38, 53n43, 63n59, 82n12, 93n36, 96n50, 188n1, 189, 190n4, 190n5, 191n19, 192, 192n20, 192n21, 193n28, 194, 194n30, 194n32, 197, 197n44, 197n48, 207, 207n93, 208, 208n94, 208n100, 213, 213n117, 218, 226, 226n19, 227n20, 227n22, 227n24, 231n33, 232n35, 244n46, 245n50, 246n54, 252n70, 255n79, 255n80, 259n88, 262n102

sacrifice(s) / sacrificing, 33, 112, 142, 214, 235, 262, 265, 266
sadness. *See* lament(ation / ed / ing / s) (crying, dirge, funeral, funereal, grief, mourning, sadness, sorrow, tears, wailing, weeping)
salt, 27, 27n7, 27n8, **62–64**, 193
salvation / salvific / save(d) / saving, 7, 7n31, 9, 18, 26, 60, 88, 98, 101, 109, 124, 133, 135, 164, 165, 170, 175, 177, 187, 201, 231, 267, 276, 283, 290, 291
Saul (King), 197n46, 231n32, 261
Schultz, Richard, 205n81, 263, 263n106
Schwally, Friedrich, 2, 93n36

scribe(s), 51, 85, 92, 198, 198n52, 199, 200, 203, 206, 210, 211, 216, 283, 291, 298
    scribal addition / scribal gloss, 11, 193, 214, 216
Scripture, Christian / Israel's, ix, xv, xvi, 16, **20–21**, 22, 95, 99, 100, 101, 107, 109, 116, 119, 129, 132, 133, **139–45**, 147, 151, 153, 176, 179, **180–85**, 189, 212, 213, 216, 219, 221, 273, 279, 281, 298
Seeligman, Leo, 5
Seitz, Christopher, 84, 84n18, 90n26, 90n27, 90n29, 91n30, 92n34, 94n39, 220, 220n3, 220n4, 221n14
self-satisfaction. *See* pride / proud (arrogant, haughty, hubris, self-satisfaction)
Sennacherib, 168, 231, 231n30, 264
Septuagint. *See* LXX
Seraiah, 11, 208
Severus, Sulpitius, 212, 212n112, 212n113
shame. *See* ashamed / ashamedly / humbled / humbly / humiliate(d) / humiliation / shame(d / ful)
Sharp, Carolyn, 11, 11n45, 11n48
Sibmah, 32, 56, 82n12, 119, 232, 286, 287, 294, 295
Sidon, 48n35, 204, 235, 236, 237, 238, 239
signs, 27, 27n7, 27n8, **62–64**, 131, 157, 159, 272
Sihon, 36, 50, 51, 52, 82n12
sin. *See* offences / sin(s / ful) / wrongdoing
Sitz im Leben, 4, **6–8**, 21, 277, 297
Smelik, Klaas, 7, 7n28, 11
Smothers, Thomas, 10n44, 61n55, 63, 63n59, 64n63, 71n5, 72n6, 75, 75n7, 82n12,
93n36, 96n50, 188n1, 190n4, 191n19, 192n20, 192n21, 194, 194n37, 195n38, 210, 210n109, 227n20, 231n33, 232n35, 244n46, 245n50, 246n54, 252n70, 255n79, 259n88, 260n90
Sodom, 247, 278
Solomon, 164
sorrow. *See* lament(ation / ed / ing / s) (crying, dirge, funeral, funereal, grief, mourning, sadness, sorrow, tears, wailing, weeping)
sovereign(ty), Divine (reign, rule), 8, 87, 107, 108, 109, 112, 113, 120, 121, 122, 123, 132, 134, 136, 139, 143, 144, 145, 146, 147, 149, 156, 157, 159, 160, 164, 165, 167, 168, 170, 174, 175, 176, 180, 182, 184, 186, 218, 223, 248, 249, 267, 273, 275, 276, 297, 298, 300
    universal, 107, 120, 132, 133, 168, 182, 184, 186, 273, **278–80**, 297
Steinmann, Andrew, 17, 17n66
Stulman, Louis, 11n45, 18, 61n55, 63n59, 93n36, 96n50, 192n20, 192n21, 215n123, 227n24, 231n33, 232n35, 245n50, 246n53, 249, 249n62, 259n88, 260n90
suffer(ed / ers / ing), 59, 106, 110, 111, 114, 115, 119, 127, 141, 163, 172, 176, 177, 178, 180, 183, 194, 206, 218, 228, 233
supernatural, 120
Sweden, 278
sword(s / sman / bearer / wielder), ix, 18, 25, 27, 88, 107, 161, 162, 171, 188, 189, 190, 191, 191n13, 192n20, **193–95**, 196, 197, 198, 200, 201, 202,

sword(s / sman / bearer / wielder) *(cont.)*
    203, 205, 205n85, 209, 210, 212, 214, 215, 216, 222, 229, 240, **242**, 282, 283, 284, 289, 291, 298
    two-edged, 198, 200, 202, 210, 214, 283, 291
synchronic, **12–17**, 20, 21, 103, 219

Targum (Jonathan), 90, 190, 191, 252, 257
taunt song (of Num 21:28–29). *See* mock(ed / er / ery / ing) (laughingstock, taunting), taunt song (of Num 21:28–29)
tears. *See* lament(ation / ed / ing / s) (crying, dirge, funeral, funereal, grief, mourning, sadness, sorrow, tears, wailing, weeping)
temple, 113, 176, 233, 238
Terrien, Samuel, 200n55, 200n56, 202, 202n65, 202n67, 203n77
terror, 35, 37, 88, 130, 141, 222, 228, 230, 232, 270, 276, 288, 296
textual corruption(s), 2, 38, 161
theologian(s) / theological / theologies / theology, xvi, 1, 3, 18, 21, 23, 24, **65–67**, 101, 103, 104, 107, 108, 113, 117, 118, 122, 123, 130, 131, 136, 138, 142, 146, 150, 151, 152, 153, 154, 159, 162, 172, 176, 182, 183, 185, 221, 273, 274, 297
Thompson, John, 11n45, 38n21, 53n43, 61n55, 63n59, 82n12, 92n34, 95, 95n47, 114n54, 188n1, 191, 191n16, 191n17, 192n20, 194n31, 195n38, 208n102, 218, 227n20, 232n35, 233n38, 244n46, 245n50, 246n54, 255n79, 255n80, 259n88, 260n90
tone (mood), xvi, 50, 66, 75, 76, 84, 85, 86, 91, 93, 94, 98, 99, 100, 107, 109, **110–16**, 135, 145, 146, 158, **160–63**, 168, 171, 174, 176, 177, 180, 186, 188, **192–93**, 195, 200, 223, 242, 254, 256, 257, 261, 277, 281, 284, 285, 286, 290, 293, 294, 296, 298, 299, 300
Torah, 234
tradition, 2, 5, 10, 101, 103, 115, 131, 140, 151, 153, 154, 155, 157, 158, 159, 163, 186, 221, 230n28, 246, 246n52, 273, 274
trap, 35, 37, 88, 130, 222, 271, 276
treat(ies / y) (language, curses), 6, 7
Trible, Phyllis, 16
Trinity, 220
trust(ed / ing / s), 26, 27, 59, 60, 86, 102, 104, 108, 232, 233, 234, 235, 236, 243, 248, 249, 271, 278, 280, 281, 283, 290, 297
Tucker, 84n18, 90n26, 90n29, 91n30, 92, 92n33, 93n37, 95n49, 257, 257n83, 258, 258n85
typological / typology. *See* figural(ly) (reading / interpretation, allegorical)
Tyre, 8, 48n35, 83, 178, 234, 236, 237, 238, 239, 241, 242

Ugarit(ic), 8, 9, 27n7, 62, 63, 113
United Kingdom. *See* West / Western (world), UK
United States of America. *See* West / Western (world), U.S. / United States
universal sovereignty. *See* sovereign(ty), Divine (reign, rule), universal

valley of vision, 234, 237
van Dijk, H., 8, 8n37
van Hecke, Pierre, 11, 18, 18n70
vengeance (avenge, avenger, revenge, vengeful), 8, 107, 121, 136, 160, 192, 194, 198, 202, 212, 214, 215, 216, 234, 241, 249, 276, 278, 283, 291
vine, vineyards. See wine (vine, vineyards, vintage)
vintage. See wine (vine, vineyards, vintage)
violence / violent, 60, 88, 115, 117, 122, 169, 219, 228, 237
voice(d / s), 21, 25, 33, 43, 102, 104, 113, 116, 122, 128, 136, 144, 212, 215, 216, 219, 223, 254, 259n88, 274, 285, 286, 287, 288, 293, 294, 295, 296
Volz, D. Paul, 2, 10n44, 14, 44n24, 44n28, 53n43, 61n55, 63n59, 82n12, 93n36, 95n48, 188n1, 192, 193n25, 197n48, 213n117, 225n17, 226n19, 227n20, 231, 231n32, 231n33, 232n36, 244n46, 245n50, 249, 250n66, 255n79, 255n80, 259n88, 265n108
vomit(ing / s), 31, 46, 61, 61n55, 88, 193, 232, 250, 286, 294
von Rad, Gerhard, 5, 5n18, 6
Vorlage(n), 9, 10, 11, 37, 38, 58, 59

Wagner, J. Ross, 274, 274n124, 274n125
wail(ing / s). See lament(ation / ed / ing / s) (crying, dirge, funeral, funereal, grief, mourning, sadness, sorrow, tears, wailing, weeping)
Walters, Stanley, 220n2, 221, 221n14, 221n15, 221n16
war, xv, 1, 5, 6, 9, 28, 35, 52, 106, 112, 113, 115, 119, 120, 121, 137, 158, 159, 163, 164, 174, 175, 186, 194, 201, 203, 211, 213, 215, 245, 284, 291, 292, 297, 300
holy, xv, 106, 113, 115, 158, 159, 164, 174, 175, 186, 194, 201
war oracle(s), 5, 6, 297
warrior, Divine, 6, 107, 113, 115, 119, 120, 121, 146, 149, 300
Watts, John, 11, 11n45, 11n46, 11n47, 40n23, 84n18, 90n26, 90n27, 91n30, 93n36, 95n49, 234n43
weep(ing / s) / wept. See lament(ation / ed / ing / s) (crying, dirge, funeral, funereal, grief, mourning, sadness, sorrow, tears, wailing, weeping)
Weiser, Artur, 4, 14, 44, 44n25, 50n38, 53n43, 82n12, 93n36, 96n50, 188n1, 192, 192n20, 192n21, 201n61, 202n71, 203n76, 215, 215n122, 227n20, 230, 230n28, 231n33, 232n36, 244n46, 245n50, 246n54, 252n70, 255n79, 255n80, 259n88
Wellhausen, Julius, 4
West / Western (world), 16, 143, 144, 218
U.S. / United States, xvi, 16, 17, 98, 99, 143, 144, 150, 160, 185, 186, 187, 217, 277, 278, 298
UK, xvi, 16, 150, 160, 186, 187, 298
wicked(ness), 16, 29, 41, 59, 127, 206, 214, 215, 247, 266, 276
Wildberger, Hans, 71n5, 75, 75n7, 80, 80n10, 82n12, 83n14, 84n18, 89, 89n23, 89n24, 90n26, 90n27, 90n29, 91n30, 92n33, 92n34, 92n35, 93n36,

Wildberger, Hans *(cont.)*
    94, 94n40, 94n43, 95, 95n44,
    95n48, 256n81, 258n85
wine (vine, vineyards, vintage), 32,
    56, 61, 161, 232, 286, 294
wing(s), 27n7, 27n8, 34, 52, **62–64**,
    193, 231, 283, 290, 291
wisdom, 127n100, 152, 169, 186,
    212, 235
woe, 19, 25, 36, 51, 60, 110, 113,
    227, 271
woman in labor. *See* laboring
    woman / women
worship, 41, 79, 106, 119, 120, 146,
    163, 164, 172, 200, 233, 263,
    263n106, 264, 265, 285, 293
wrath (anger, angry), 237, 292
    cup of, 44, 46, 244, 250, 254
    Divine, 41, 42, 110, 115, 116,
        119, 140, 147, 163, 172, 205,
        246, 247, 248
wrongdoing. *See* offences / sin(s /
    ful) / wrongdoing
Würthwein, Ernst, 156, 174,
    174n135, 175, 175n136

YHWH, xv, xvn1, 6, 7, 7n31, 8, 10,
    12, 14, 18, 19, 20, 38, 44, 45,
    47, 48, 50, 51, 52, 56, 57, 58,
    59, 60, 62, 65, 66, 75, 76, 84,
    85, 86, 87, 87n21, 88, 89,
    91, 94, 96, 97, 98, 99, 102,
    103, 104, 105, 106, 107, 108,
    109, 109n36, 110, 111, 112,
    113, 114, 115, 116, 117, 118,
    119, 120, 121, 122, 123, 124,
    125, 126, 127, 129, 130, 131,
    133, 134, 135, 136, 137, 138,
    139, 140, 141, 143, 144, 145,
    146, 147, 149, 156, 159, 160,
    162, 163, 164, 165, 166, 167,
    168, 169, 170, 172, 174, 175,
    176, 177, 178, 181, 182, 184,
    185, 186, 188, 189, 189n3,
    190, 191, 191n13, 193, 196,
    197, 200, 201, 202, 203, 204,
    205, 206, 207, 208, 209, 210,
    211, 218, 222, 223, 224, 225,
    227, 228, 229, 230, 231n30,
    232, 235, 237, 241, 242, 243,
    244, 245, 247, 248, 249,
    250, **251–52**, 253, 254, 255,
    256, 257, 259, 262, 263, 264,
    265–69, 270, 271, 272, 275,
    276, 277, 279, 280, 281, 297,
    298, 299, 300

Ziegler, Joseph, 24, 38, 58
Zion, 6, 82n12, 174, 175, 181, 247
Zobel, H., 227, 227n23
Zogora, 25, 33, 58, 229

www.ingramcontent.com/pod-product-compliance
Lightning Source LLC
Chambersburg PA
CBHW071148300426
44113CB00009B/1130